Sam Storms has written an accessible, faithful, and pastorally applicable commentary on Revelation. Unfortunately too many works on Revelation, especially in more popular form, are lacking in exegetical rigor. Storms has written a commentary that educated readers can understand, and at the same time it is informed by careful scholarship. We need to hear the message of Revelation in our churches, and Storms's commentary aids us in that task.

THOMAS R. SCHREINER
James Buchanan Harrison Professor of New Testament Interpretation,
The Southern Baptist Theological Seminary, Louisville, Kentucky

Sam Storms presents the book of Revelation as edifying, enjoyable, and immensely relevant for the church today. This commentary uniquely blends exegetical insight, theological depth, pastoral application, and passionate worship. Storms is a trustworthy guide to John's apocalyptic visions, which stir our minds and hearts to live for Christ while longing for the beauty and blessings of the age to come.

BRIAN J. TABB
President, Bethlehem College and Seminary, Minneapolis, Minnesota;
author, *All Things New: Revelation as Canonical Capstone*

Our God Reigns!

An Amillennial Commentary of Revelation

Sam Storms

𝕄ENTOR

Sam was formerly the Lead Pastor for Preaching and Vision at Bridgeway Church in Oklahoma City, Oklahoma. He currently serves as the President of Enjoying God Ministries (www.samstorms.org) and is Executive Director of the Convergence Church Network (www.convergencechurchnetwork.com). He has authored or edited 35 books and has published numerous journal articles and book reviews. He is a graduate of The University of Oklahoma (B.A.), Dallas Theological Seminary (Th.M.), and The University of Texas at Dallas (Ph.D.). He and his wife Ann have been married for over 52 years and are the parents of two grown daughters and have four grandchildren.

Unless otherwise noted, Scripture quotations are from the ESV® Bible (The Holy Bible, English Standard Version®), copyright © 2001 by Crossway, a publishing ministry of Good News Publishers. Used by permission. All rights reserved.

hardback ISBN 978-1-5271-1173-8
ebook ISBN 978-1-5271-1237-7

Copyright © Sam Storms 2024

First published in 2024
in the
Mentor Imprint
of
Christian Focus Publications Ltd.,
Geanies House, Fearn,
Ross-shire, IV20 1TW, Scotland, UK

www.christianfocus.com

Cover design by Jesse Owens
Printed by Bell & Bain, Glasgow

All rights reserved. No part of this publication may be reproduced, stored in a retrieval system, or transmitted in any form or by any means, electronic, mechanical, photocopying, recording or otherwise, without the prior permission of the publisher or a license permitting restricted copying. In the U.K. such licenses are issued by the Copyright Licensing Agency, 4 Battlebridge Lane, London, SE1 2HX www.cla.co.uk.

Contents

Introductory Issues

~ 11 ~

CHAPTER ONE

The Revelation of Jesus Christ, the Ruler of Kings on Earth (1:1-8)

~ 29 ~

CHAPTER TWO

Behold the Glory of the Lord (1:9-20)

~ 43 ~

CHAPTER THREE

What Jesus Says When He Speaks to the Church (2:1-7)

~ 57 ~

CHAPTER FOUR

Seeing the "So That" in Suffering (2:8-11)

~ 71 ~

CHAPTER FIVE

God's People in Satan's City (2:12-17)

~ 85 ~

CHAPTER SIX

What is the "Jezebel Spirit"? (2:18-29)

~ 99 ~

CHAPTER SEVEN

Jesus says: "I Know Your Kidneys!" (2:18-29)

~ 111 ~

Contents cont.

CHAPTER EIGHT

A Tragic Embodiment of Nominal Christianity (3:1-6)

~ 125 ~

CHAPTER NINE

Written Down in the Lamb's Book of Life: The Real Reason to Rejoice (3:1-6)

~ 137 ~

CHAPTER TEN

The Church of "Little Power" (3:7-13)

~ 149 ~

CHAPTER ELEVEN

Who am I? Who are You? The Power of Identity (3:7-13)

~ 163 ~

CHAPTER TWELVE

The Church that makes Jesus Sick (3:14-22)

~ 173 ~

CHAPTER THIRTEEN

Enthroned! Encircled! Extolled! (4:1-11)

~ 187 ~

CHAPTER FOURTEEN

"Weep No More!" (5:1-14)

~ 201 ~

CHAPTER FIFTEEN

The Four Horsemen of the Apocalypse (6:1-8)

~ 213 ~

Contents cont.

CHAPTER SIXTEEN
The Voice of the Martyrs (6:9-11)
~ 227 ~

CHAPTER SEVENTEEN
The Second Coming of Christ: Blessed Hope or Dreaded Nightmare? (6:12-17; 8:1-5)
~ 237 ~

CHAPTER EIGHTEEN
The Servants of God: Sealed and Safe (7:1-17; 14:1-5)
~ 251 ~

CHAPTER NINETEEN
When We've Been There Ten thousand Years! (7:9-17)
~ 265 ~

CHAPTER TWENTY
The Trumpet Blasts of Divine Judgment (8:6-13; 9:1-12)
~ 277 ~

CHAPTER TWENTY-ONE
He Shall Reign Forever and Ever! (9:13-21; 11:14-19)
~ 291 ~

CHAPTER TWENTY-TWO
Knowing Who's in Charge Makes all the Difference in the World (10:1-11)
~ 305 ~

CHAPTER TWENTY-THREE
The Church: Prophesying and Persecuted (11:1-13)
~ 319 ~

Contents cont.

CHAPTER TWENTY-FOUR

War in Heaven and on Earth: How the Church Conquers the Devil (12:1-17)

~ 335 ~

CHAPTER TWENTY-FIVE

The "Beast" of Revelation: Who, What, Why? (13:1-10)

~ 349 ~

CHAPTER TWENTY-SIX

666 (13:11-18)

~ 363 ~

CHAPTER TWENTY-SEVEN

Must We Speak of Hell? (14:6-13)

~ 377 ~

CHAPTER TWENTY-EIGHT

Great and Amazing are the Deeds of God! (14:14-20; 15:1-8)

~ 391 ~

CHAPTER TWENTY-NINE

Armageddon! The War to End All Wars (16:1-21)

~ 405 ~

CHAPTER THIRTY

The Great Prostitute, the Scarlet Beast, and the Conquering Lamb! (17:1-18)

~ 419 ~

CHAPTER THIRTY-ONE

The Fall of Babylon (18:1-24)

~ 433 ~

Contents cont.

CHAPTER THIRTY-TWO

You're Invited to the Marriage Supper of the Lamb (RSVP Required) (19:1-10)

~ 445 ~

CHAPTER THIRTY-THREE

Our Blessed Hope! (19:11-21)

~ 459 ~

CHAPTER THIRTY-FOUR

The Millennium, the Final Battle, and the Final Judgment (20:1-15)

~ 469 ~

CHAPTER THIRTY-FIVE

The New Heaven and New Earth (21:1-8)

~ 485 ~

CHAPTER THIRTY-SIX

The Holy City: New Jerusalem (21:9-27; Isaiah 60:1-5,11)

~ 499 ~

CHAPTER THIRTY-SEVEN

Enjoying God Eternally: Eight Blessings of Life in the New Earth (22:1-5, 8-9)

~ 511 ~

CHAPTER THIRTY-EIGHT

The Spirit and the Bride say, "Come!" (22:6-21)

~ 525 ~

Introductory Issues

"Blessed is the one who reads aloud the words of this prophecy, and blessed are those who hear and who keep what is written in it, for the time is near" (Rev. 1:3)

It is crucial for every student of the book of Revelation to read and meditate upon this statement in 1:3. Revelation was written in such a way that it should be not only intelligible to any Christian who reads and/or hears its words, but also a blessing to the person who obeys and believes what it says. Simply put, contrary to popular opinion, and notwithstanding the often bizarre and mysterious images it conveys, God intends for Revelation to be *understandable, edifying, and enjoyable!*

Many do not enjoy wading through the issues related to the authorship, date, and literary composition of a New Testament book. If that is you, feel free to go directly to the first chapter of this commentary. Although, I must say that there is considerable biblical meat to be ingested by thinking deeply about such matters, especially when it comes to how the book of Revelation should be interpreted. If you do choose to skip this Introduction, at least take the time to read my explanation of the ways in which this commentary differs from most others.

Authorship

As Greg Beale notes, "there are three possibilities concerning the author of the book: John the apostle, another John (sometimes referred to as John the Elder), and someone else using 'John' as a pseudonym."[1]

The author of the Revelation identifies himself as "John" (1:1, 4, 9; 22:8). He calls himself a "servant" (1:1), their "brother and fellow-partaker in tribulation" (1:9) and a "prophet" (22:9). He never speaks of himself as an apostle, most likely because his identity as an apostle is so well-known, his authority so self-evident, and his relationship with the people of the churches in Asia Minor so intimate that it was unnecessary for him to use the term.

The earliest tradition within the church ascribes the Revelation to the apostle John: e.g., Justin Martyr (A.D. 135–140), Irenaeus (c. A.D. 200), Clement of Alexandria (c. A.D. 200), and Tertullian (c. A.D. 200). Others often cited as supporting apostolic authorship are Papias, Melito of Sardis, Origen, and Hippolytus. It was not until Dionysius of Alexandria in the third century (c. 250) that any major dissent from apostolic authorship was heard.

Arguments against apostolic authorship are primarily based on supposed grammatical, stylistic and terminological differences between the Revelation and the Fourth Gospel. Some contend that the language of the Gospel is smooth, fluent, and written in relatively simple and accurate Greek, whereas that of the Revelation is harsh, with many grammatical and syntactical irregularities. Stephen Smalley disagrees, reminding us that the uniqueness of the Revelation is due in part to the fact that John was thinking in Hebrew while writing in Greek. Thus "it has a grammar of its own; but this is at least clear and consistent, and it is not *un*grammatical. The style of Revelation is the one which the writer chose to adopt for his own special purposes; and to my mind it is just as majestic, and poetic indeed, as that of the Fourth Gospel."[2]

Others contend that the theology of the two books is so divergent as to preclude identity of authorship: e.g., the *love* of

---

1. G. K. Beale, *Revelation* (Grand Rapids: Eerdmans, 1999), 34.

2. Stephen S. Smalley, *Thunder and Love: John's Revelation and John's Community* (Milton Keynes: Word Publishing, 1994), 65.

God is primary in the Gospel, *wrath* in the Revelation (but this is a difficulty only for those who find these attributes mutually exclusive; they are in truth complementary). The fact is, what differences do appear are traceable to the circumstances under which each document was composed, the nature and genre of each document (gospel vs. prophetic apocalypse), and the purpose for which each was written.

Robert Mounce rightfully concludes that "Since internal evidence is not entirely unfavorable to apostolic authorship and since external evidence is unanimous in its support, the wisest course of action is either to leave the question open or to accept in a tentative way that the Apocalypse was written by John the apostle, son of Zebedee and the disciple of Jesus."[3]

Date

Most commentators date the book either in the late 60s, during the reign of Nero, or in the early to mid-90s, during the reign of Domitian.

Arguments for an Early Date for Revelation

The argument is made that the temple in Jerusalem is described in Revelation 11 as still standing (the temple was destroyed in A.D. 70). In 17:9 "seven mountains" are mentioned, which most agree is an allusion to Rome and its seven hills. These mountains are said to represent seven kings, five of which have fallen, one which "is", and the other yet to come. The sixth king is the one in power as John writes. Advocates of an early date for the book insist that the first of these kings is Augustus, the first official Roman emperor. The sixth is Galba, who reigned briefly after Nero's death (68–69). Some argue that Julius Caesar is the first king, thereby making Nero the sixth and Galba the seventh. In any case, this listing of the seven kings dates the book's composition to the late 60s of the first century. The meaning of the seven mountains and

---

3. Robert Mounce, *The Book of Revelation* (Grand Rapids: Eerdmans, 1977), 15.

seven kings will be addressed in the exposition of Chapter 17. Let it be said here, however, that I tend to agree with Beale that "the seven kings are not to be identified with any specific historical rulers but represent rather the oppressive power of world government throughout the ages, which arrogates to itself divine prerogatives and persecutes God's people."[4] Even should we conclude that seven specific Roman emperors are in view, they may serve simply to symbolize all evil kingdoms through history.

Stephen Smalley makes a case for Vespasian as the sixth king who "is", with Titus being the seventh who "is to come" but who will reign only for a short time (two years, in fact). The eighth, who will eventually be destroyed, is Domitian. Smalley opts for composition sometime during the Jewish war of 66–74, most likely just before the fall of Jerusalem to Titus, Vespasian's son, in the year 70.[5]

Arguments for a Late Date for Revelation

The Revelation portrays Christians as being required to participate in some form of emperor worship under threat of persecution. This fits better with what we know of conditions during Domitian's reign than that of Nero's. After surveying the historical evidence, Beale concludes:

> "Therefore, a date during the time of Nero is possible for Revelation, but the later setting under Domitian is more probable in the light of the evidence in the book for an expected escalation of emperor worship in the near future and especially the widespread, programmatic legal persecution portrayed as imminent or already occurring in Revelation 13, though the letters reveal only spasmodic persecution."[6]

Having said that, it must be noted that "it is by no means easy to plot the growth of the imperial cult, in relation to Christianity, either in

---

4. Beale, *Revelation*, 23-24.
5. Smalley, *Thunder and Love*, 65.
6. Beale, *Revelation*, 9.

Rome or in Asia. The first secure testimony that Christians were required to pay homage to Caesar is provided during the reign of Trajan (A.D. 98–117)."[7] Emperor worship had flourished in Asia Minor since Augustus, and Nero himself was certainly pleased when, in A.D. 55, the Roman Senate set up a large statue of him in the Temple of Mars. As Smalley notes, "all this was well before the time of Domitian; and, even if that ruler asked that he should be called 'Lord and God', there is no evidence that all Christians were required to do so, or that this demand, in itself, provoked a clash between the Roman state and the Christian church." His conclusion is that "the reference to the imperial cultus in the Apocalypse does not rule out a Domitianic timing ... but neither does it establish such a date beyond doubt."[8]

Smalley also reminds us that:

> "the persecution of Roman Christians initiated by Nero was just as fierce as anything that took place under Domitian;... On the other hand, when Eusebius describes Domitian as the successor to Nero in his enmity and hostility towards God, he also records that the later Emperor was as much concerned to attack the Roman aristocracy as the church; and Eusebius does not mention the death of any Christians during Domitian's persecution."[9]

Some point to the condition of the churches in Asia Minor (Rev. 2–3) as indicating a late date. The spiritual lethargy in Ephesus (2:4-5), Sardis (3:1), and Laodicea (3:15-17), so the argument goes, would have taken a significant period of time to develop:

> "For example, that Ephesus had left its 'first love' could mean that the church had done so within only a few years of its establishment, but the language may fit better a longer development, perhaps so that the church was in its second generation of existence. The Laodicean church is called 'wealthy', but the city experienced a devastating earthquake in A.D. 60–61. Therefore, the natural

---

7. Smalley, *Thunder and Love*, 44.
8. Ibid.
9. Ibid., 43.

assumption is that the city took longer than merely three or four years to recover economically. And... the very existence of the church at Smyrna suggests a later date, since it is possible that the church was not even established until A.D. 60–64."[10]

In addition to this, "the hitherto unknown party of the Nicolaitans has by now become firmly established, both at Ephesus (2:6) and Pergamum (2:15)."[11] On the other hand, 1 and 2 Thessalonians, which are among the earliest of the New Testament documents, bear ample witness to the problems in both belief and behavior that can emerge quickly. Also, the Galatians were rebuked by Paul for "so quickly" turning away to "another gospel" (Gal. 1:6).

It is believed by many commentators that Revelation alludes to the so-called *Nero redivivus* or the "revival of Nero" myth (see 13:3-4; 17:8, 11), according to which Nero would revive or resurrect from the dead and lead a Parthian army against the Roman empire. But "if these texts reflect the myth, then Revelation is better dated later than earlier, since presumably it took time for the myth to arise, develop, and circulate after Nero's death in A.D. 68."[12] Smalley again counters by pointing out that "rumours of Nero's 'reappearance', after his suicidal death in A.D. 68, were extant the very next year, 69, during the time of Vespasian."[13]

John's use of the word "Babylon" may point to a late date, insofar as "Babylon" consistently refers to Rome in Jewish literature only *after* A.D. 70. "Jewish commentators called Rome 'Babylon' because the Roman armies destroyed Jerusalem and its temple in A.D. 70, just as Babylon had done in the sixth century B.C."[14]

The earliest patristic witness is to a late date. The most decisive testimony comes from Irenaeus who, in discussing the identity of the Antichrist, writes: "We will not, however, incur the risk of pronouncing positively as to the name of Antichrist; for if it

---

10. Beale, *Revelation*, 16-17.
11. Smalley, *Thunder and Love*, 41.
12. Beale, *Revelation*, 17.
13. Smalley, *Thunder and Love*, 44.
14. Beale, *Revelation*, 19.

were necessary that his name should be distinctly revealed in this present time, it would have been announced by *him who beheld the Apocalypse. For it was seen not very long ago, but almost in our day, toward the end of Domitian's reign.*"[15] Proponents of the early date counter that the words "it was seen" should be rendered "*he* [i.e., John] was seen," so that the phrase means only that John the apostle was seen during Domitian's time but not necessarily that Revelation was written at that time. In other words, what Irenaeus had in mind was to comment on *how long* the author of the Revelation had lived, not on *when* he had written the Revelation. An important, and unanswered, question is "whether Irenaeus made this statement based on some firm tradition" or "was expressing his own opinion."[16] If the latter, how much weight should we give to his statement in deciding on the date of composition?

Some point to Revelation 6:6 and connect it to an edict issued by Domitian in A.D. 92. "This edict," notes Aune, "ordered half the vineyards in the provinces to be destroyed and prohibited the planting of new vineyards in Italy. The opposition to this edict in Roman Asia was so violent that the edict was rescinded before its provisions could be enacted."[17] However, the content of Domitian's edict is different from that of 6:6.

After surveying the evidence, dogmatism on the date of Revelation is inadvisable. My own working conclusion is that the reign of Domitian, during the early 90s, remains the more probable time for its composition.

Literary Form of the Book

In Revelation 1:1 John describes the book as a "revelation", literally *apokalupsis*, from which we get our English term "apocalypse" or "apocalyptic". In 1:3 he calls the book a "prophecy" and in 1:4 he

---

15. *Adv. haer.* 5.30.3; Eusebius, *Ecclesiastical History*, 3.18.3; 5.30.3. Italics mine.
16. Aune, *Revelation,* 1:lix.
17. Ibid., 1:lxiii.

proceeds as if he were writing an "epistle" or "letter" (cf. Rev. 2–3). The fact is, Revelation gives evidence of being all three.

The Revelation as an Epistle – That John was instructed to write a letter to seven churches which contained the substance of his visions is evident (1:4, 11; 2:1, 8, 12, 18; 3:1, 7, 14). In this sense the Revelation corresponds to the other New Testament epistles (see also 22:6-22).

The Revelation as an Apocalypse – The term "apocalyptic" is taken from the Greek word, found in Revelation 1:1, which means a "revelation," an "unveiling" or "uncovering." It is currently used to classify a group of writings prominent in the biblical world between 200 B.C. and A.D. 100 (the term "apocalyptic" was never used in this way by the authors of the literature itself). But there are several important ways in which Revelation differs from standard apocalyptic literature.

- Apocalyptic is usually distinguished from prophecy, yet John calls his book a prophecy (1:3; 22:7, 10, 18, 19).

- The Revelation contains numerous moral imperatives and calls to repentance, an element not frequently found in apocalyptic material.

- The apocalypses are generally pseudonymous and are written in the name of some illustrious predecessor. The writer of the Revelation gives his own name (1:4).

- The pessimism of the apocalyptists is not dominant in Revelation. Although reference is made to an outbreak of Satanic activity and persecution, the general tenor is optimistic for the people of God.

- The apocalyptist retraces history and puts it in the guise of prophecy. From the perspective of some figure in the distant past they forecast what will happen up to their own day. John, on the other hand, takes his stand in the present and forecasts the future.

- In apocalyptic literature the interpretive mediation of an angelic being is almost always dominant, to the degree that at times the entire apocalypse is dependent for its meaning on the heavenly guide. In Revelation we occasionally see angelic interpretation of a symbol (17:7ff.), but the general practice is for the vision to be left to the reader to analyze.

- In apocalyptic literature there is generally a looking forward for the intervention of God. In Revelation the decisive action of God to bring about the new order has already occurred in the past: in the redemptive work of Christ (cf. Rev. 4–5).

The Revelation as Prophecy – That John's writing is prophetic in character will be developed in the exposition of the book. One might note at this point 1:3; 10:11; 19:10; 22:6, 7, 9, 10, 18, 19. John claims, in effect, that what he writes is an authoritative revelation given through the medium of visions. He writes in the present, of the future, and under his own name.

Schools or Methods of Interpretation

The Preterist View

The word "preterist" comes from the Latin word *praeteritus* which means "gone by" or "past". Proponents of this view thus contend that "the closer we get to the year 2000, the farther we get from the events of Revelation."[18] The major prophecies of the book, so they argue, were fulfilled either in the fall of Jerusalem in A.D. 70 (which would, of course, necessitate the earlier date of composition) or in the fall of Rome in 476. In his short commentary, Jay Adams writes:

> "The view of the Apocalypse which this book asserts to be true is that all of the prophecy in the first nineteen chapters, and part of that in the twentieth, has been fulfilled. Furthermore, their

---

18. Kenneth L. Gentry Jr., "A Preterist View of Revelation," in *Four Views on the Book of* Revelation, General Editor, C. Marvin Pate (Grand Rapids: Zondervan, 1998), 37.

fulfillment took place in the lifetime of those to whom John wrote (or shortly thereafter), and not throughout the entire church age."[19]

Gentry contends that Revelation has two fundamental purposes relative to its original audience:

> "In the first place, it was designed to steel the first century Church against the gathering storm of persecution, which was reaching an unnerving crescendo of theretofore unknown proportions and intensity. A new and major feature of that persecution was the entrance of imperial Rome onto the scene. The first historical persecution of the Church by imperial Rome was by Nero Caesar from A.D. 64 to A.D. 68. In the second place, it was to brace the Church for a major and fundamental re-orientation in the course of redemptive history, a re-orientation necessitating the destruction of Jerusalem (the center not only of Old Covenant Israel, but of Apostolic Christianity [cp. Ac. 1:8; 2:1ff.; 15:2] and the Temple" [cp. Mt. 24:1-34 with Rev. 11]).[20]

Preterists appeal to four primary arguments in defense of their belief that Revelation was written before the fall of Jerusalem in A.D. 70. First, they point to John's repeated declaration that the time of the fulfillment of Revelation's prophecies is *near*. "Near", "shortly", and "soon", they contend, mean precisely that; not 1,900 years later.

> " ... to show to his servants the things which must *soon* take place" (Rev. 1:1).

> "Blessed is the one who reads aloud the words of this prophecy, and blessed are those who hear, and who keep what is written in it, for *the time is near*" (Rev. 1:3).

> " ... to show to his servants what must *soon* take place" (Rev. 22:6).

---

19. Jay E. Adams, *The Time is at Hand* (Phillipsburg: Presbyterian and Reformed Publishing Company, 1974), 46.

20. Kenneth L. Gentry, Jr., *Before Jerusalem Fell: Dating the Book of Revelation* (Atlanta: American Vision, 1998), 15-16.

"And he said to me, 'Do not seal up the words of the prophecy of this book, *for the time is near*'" (Rev. 22:10).

Second, there are allusions throughout Revelation to Nero as the current Roman emperor (see 6:2; 13:1-18; 17:1-13). Third, preterists argue that the conditions in the seven churches (Rev. 2–3) best correlate with what we know to have been true of pre-A.D. 70 Jewish Christianity. Fourth, they argue that Revelation 11 portrays the Temple as still standing, thereby demanding a pre-A.D. 70 date.

The Historical View

This view is almost non-existent today, although an array of historical luminaries from the past embraced it in one form or another: e.g., John Wycliffe, John Knox, William Tyndale, Martin Luther, John Calvin, Ulrich Zwingli, Philip Melancthon, John Wesley, Jonathan Edwards, George Whitefield, Charles Finney, and C. H. Spurgeon, just to mention a few. This view understands the Revelation as a symbolic prophecy of the entire history of the church from John's day to the return of Christ and the end of the age. The symbols of the book, especially the seal, trumpet, and bowl judgments, are intended to portray the various historical movements, men and events in the western world. For example, E. B. Elliott contends that the trumpets (8:6–9:21) cover the period from 395 to 1453, beginning with the attacks on the western Roman empire by the Goths and concluding with the fall of the eastern empire to the Turks.

Generally speaking, the interpretation of the book depends on the time and place in history of the commentator. That is to say, *each assumes that the events predicted in the Apocalypse were reaching a climax in his own time.* Joachim of Fiore (1135–1202) believed the fifth head of the Beast was the emperor Henry IV (1050–1106) and the sixth was Saladin (1137–93), the Muslim leader who recaptured Jerusalem from the crusaders. A common feature among advocates of the historical school is identification of the Beast of Revelation 13 with the papacy of Rome. The

Waldensian sect insisted that papal Rome was the whole of Babylon whereas Jacopone da Todi (1230–1306) associated the papacy with the dragon of Revelation 12. The Anglican bishop John Bale (1495–1563) believed that one of the beast's heads was wounded at the Reformation but was healed when Queen Bloody Mary restored Catholicism in England.

One of the principal problems with the historicist view is that it fails to take into consideration events and developments of the church on a global scale. Virtually all of its alleged prophetic references and fulfillments occur within the period of the Middle Ages and the Protestant Reformation. This complete disregard for the life of God's people beyond the boundaries of Europe is a fatal flaw in this view.

The Futurist View

Generally speaking, those who hold this view understand the Revelation as a prophecy of yet future events, concentrated in a short period of time (perhaps seven years), which lead up to and accompany the second coming of Christ. The futurist believes that all of the visions from Revelation 4:1 to the end of the book are yet to be fulfilled in the period immediately preceding and following the second coming of Christ. Within this school of thought are two somewhat variant positions.

The first is *Classical Pre-tribulational Dispensational Premillennialism*. According to this widely popular view, not only is the whole of 4:1–22:21 seen as yet future, even the seven letters of Chapters 2 and 3 are understood to portray seven successive eras of church history. In a sense, then, this school does to Chapters 2–3 what the historicist school does to the entire book. The basic traits of each church depict the chief characteristics of the seven periods of church history, the last of which will be a time of apostasy (Laodicea).[21]

---

21. For a detailed exposition of this view, see J. Dwight Pentecost, *Things to Come: A Study in Biblical Eschatology* (Grand Rapids: Zondervan, 1965), 149-55.

There is also the view known as *Progressive Dispensational Premillennialism*. This view is held both by pre- and post-tribulationists. They reject the identification of the seven letters with seven successive periods of history and find in Revelation 4:1 no reference to the rapture of the church (as do many of the former school). While agreeing with the former view that the purpose of the book is to describe the consummation of God's redemptive plan and the end of the age, this view makes a concerted effort to find within these prophecies of the end time points of application for first-century Christians.

An interesting historical factor is that the futurist view became extremely popular in one form or another among Roman Catholic interpreters in the late Middle Ages and into the time of the Reformation. It provided them with an answer to their critics and the Protestant Reformers who identified the Beast and/or the Whore of Revelation with the papacy. If the prophecies of Revelation were yet future, then no one could legitimately charge the pope (at least not the one then in power) with being the oppressor of the true church.

The Idealist View

This view contends that Revelation is not concerned with any specific period, event, or series of events in church history. Rather, its primary purpose is to describe symbolically the conflict of good and evil throughout history and the principles on which God acts at all times. It is a *timeless* portrayal, therefore, of this ethical struggle. The idealist does not look in Revelation for specific events in history but for a display of the theological and ethical principles that govern the history of both the world and the church.

My view of the book is a mixture of these various schools and is best represented in the commentary by Beale:

> Accordingly, no specific prophesied historical events are discerned in the book, except for the final coming of Christ to deliver and judge and to establish the final form of the kingdom in a consummated new creation – though there are a few exceptions to

this rule. The Apocalypse symbolically portrays events throughout history, which is understood to be under the sovereignty of the Lamb as a result of his death and resurrection.... [Thus] the majority of the symbols in the book are transtemporal in the sense that they are applicable to events throughout the 'church age.'[22]

How Does this Commentary Differ from all the Others?

I've been studying this *apocalypse* for over a half a century. I'm sure others have been reading and writing about it longer than that. In any case, I've encountered countless interpretive methods and styles in an effort to make sense of what many believe is an incomprehensible mystery. Most commentaries on the Revelation display one or more of the following features.

There are many that are deeply academic and require a working knowledge of Greek to enjoy and understand. For those who have a facility in Greek, I highly recommend my good friend, Greg Beale's, commentary. In the same general category is the work of another close friend of mine, Tom Schreiner, whose recent contribution from Baker Publishing is equally superb. What these commentaries provide in terms of exegetical detail they lack in readability and practical application.

A second group of commentaries are more plentiful. These are the treatments that are written for English readers at a level that any adult, educated Christian can grasp. They are heavy on the implications for Christian living but in doing so they all too often gloss over exegetical difficulties and challenging theological issues. Among the better of these are the books by Alan Johnson, George Ladd, Craig S. Keener, Robert Mounce, William Hendrickson, and Michael Wilcock. Three more theologically substantive treatments from a Reformed perspective are by Joel R. Beeke, Richard D. Phillips, and Dennis Johnson. I should add that I do highly recommend all these mentioned in this paragraph.

I should also mention at this point the works that are written from a dispensational, pretribulational, premillennial perspective.

---

22. Beale, *Revelation,* 48.

I hesitate to recommend them for the simple reason that I believe the eschatological framework within which they interpret the book is seriously flawed. I must concede, however, that these are among the more popular treatments among the general Christian public. The late John Walvoord, my former professor and President of Dallas Theological Seminary, has written one of the more accessible of these commentaries. More recently, another professor of Dallas Seminary, Buist Fanning, has written an even better treatment from the dispensational point of view. His book is helpful for the English reader, as he restricts most comments on the Greek text to the many footnotes. Two more technical commentaries, written for those who can read Greek, are by Grant Osborne and Robert Thomas.

So, what then is the distinct style and substance of this treatment of Revelation? Let me mention three features. First, I have written for those who do not have a working knowledge of Greek, but without ignoring the numerous important technical and exegetical details that appear all through Revelation. The same may be said for the many complex and often controversial theological topics that arise. I have tried to provide insight into both the nuances of the Greek text and the deep doctrinal issues in Revelation without writing in such a way that the average Christian adult loses sight of the forest for the multitude of its trees. I do not avoid difficult texts or controversial topics but address them in such a way that virtually all Christian men and women can grasp their significance.

I have also written with the daily, practical life-challenges of the average Christian in view. Revelation is profoundly relevant to the issues we face in our society today and I have kept this much in the forefront of my thinking as I work through the book. Numerous applications for daily living and growth in one's personal relationship with God are found throughout this commentary.

I have written in what I would call an *educated but conversational* style. I refuse to "dumb down" anything in Revelation while simultaneously keeping my interpretations intelligible and, I hope, insightful.

Finally, it's important for you to know up front that my eschatology (i.e., my view of the end times) is decidedly amillennial. If you are not familiar with that term, feel free to skip over to my treatment of Revelation 20 where I unpack its significance (or read in advance, Chapter Seven). The amillennial view is not the most popular among evangelicals today, but I have written hoping that this commentary may contribute to a change in how many understand the book and the truths concerning the return of Christ and the consummation of his kingdom purposes.

As I have only listed the names of authors thus far, here, in alphabetical order by author, is a more complete bibliography of the works cited above, together with a few additional books on various themes in Revelation.

Brief Bibliography

David Aune, *Revelation,* three volumes (Word Biblical Commentary) (Nashville, TN: Word Books / Thomas Nelson, 1997/1998).

Richard Bauckham, *The Climax of Prophecy: Studies on the Book of Revelation* (Cambridge: T & T Clark, 1993), and *The Theology of the Book of Revelation* (Cambridge: Cambridge University Press, 1993).

G. K. Beale, *The Book of Revelation: A Commentary on the Greek Text, in The New International Greek Testament Commentary* (Grand Rapids: Eerdmans, 1999).

G. R. Beasley-Murray, *The Book of Revelation* (Greenwood, SC: The Attic Press, 1974).

Joel R. Beeke, *Revelation* (Grand Rapids: Reformation Heritage Books, 2016).

David Chilton, *The Days of Vengeance: An Exposition of the Book of Revelation* (Ft. Worth: Dominion Press, 1987).

Buist M. Fanning, *Revelation* (Zondervan Exegetical Commentary on the New Testament) (Grand Rapids: Zondervan Academic, 2020).

Kenneth Gentry, *Before Jerusalem Fell: Dating the Book of Revelation* (Atlanta: American Vision, 1998 [revised edition]), and *The Beast of Revelation* (Tyler, TX: Institute for Christian Economics, 1989).

Steve Gregg, *Revelation: Four Views, A Parallel Commentary* (Nashville: Thomas Nelson, 1997).

James Hamilton, *Revelation: The Spirit Speaks to the Churches* (Wheaton: Crossway, 2012).

Colin J. Hemer, *The Letters to the Seven Churches of Asia in their Local Setting* (Sheffield: JSOT Press, 1986).

William Hendriksen, *More Than Conquerors: An Interpretation of the Book of Revelation* (Grand Rapids: Baker, 1939 [the 22nd printing was released in 1977]).

Alan F. Johnson, *Revelation* (The Expositor's Bible Commentary) (Grand Rapids: Zondervan, 1996).

Dennis E. Johnson, *Triumph of the Lamb: A Commentary on Revelation* (Phillipsburg: P & R Publishing, 2001).

Craig S. Keener, *Revelation* (The NIV Application Commentary) (Grand Rapids: Zondervan, 2000).

Craig R. Koester, *Revelation*, The Anchor Yale Bible (New Haven: Yale University Press, 2014).

George E. Ladd, *A Commentary on the Revelation of John* (Grand Rapids: Eerdmans, 1972).

Robert H. Mounce, *The Book of Revelation* (New International Commentary on the New Testament) (Grand Rapids: Eerdmans, 1998).

Grant R. Osborne, *Revelation* (Baker Exegetical Commentary on the New Testament) (Grand Rapids: Baker, 2002).

C. Marvin Pate, Editor, *Four Views on the Book of Revelation* (Grand Rapids: Zondervan, 1998).

Richard D. Phillips, *Revelation* (Phillipsburg: P & R Publishing, 2017).

Vern S. Poythress, *The Returning King: A Guide to the Book of Revelation* (Phillipsburg: P & R Publishing, 2000).

Thomas R. Schreiner, *Revelation* (Grand Rapids: Baker Academic, 2023); and *The Joy of Hearing: A Theology of the Book of Revelation* (Wheaton: Crossway, 2021).

Stephen S. Smalley, *The Revelation to John: A Commentary on the Greek Text of the Apocalypse* (Downers Grove: IVP, 2005).

_____. *Thunder and Love: John's Revelation and John's Community* (Milton Keynes: Word Publishing, 1994).

Sam Storms, *To the One Who Conquers: 50 Daily Meditations on the Seven Letters of Revelation 2–3* (Wheaton: Crossway, 2008).

Brian J. Tabb, *All Things New: Revelation as canonical capstone* (Downers Grove: IVP, 2019).

Robert L. Thomas, *Revelation 1–7: An Exegetical Commentary* (Chicago: Moody Press, 1992), and *Revelation 8–22: An Exegetical Commentary* (Chicago: Moody Press, 1995).

John F. Walvoord, *The Revelation of Jesus Christ* (Chicago: Moody Press, 1971 [1966]).

Michael Wilcock, *The Message of Revelation*, originally published under the title, *I Saw Heaven Opened* (Downers Grove: IVP, 1975).

Ben Witherington, *Revelation* (Cambridge: Cambridge University Press, 2003).

Chapter One

The Revelation of Jesus Christ, the Ruler of Kings on Earth

(Revelation 1:1-8)

The book of Revelation has one primary and profoundly simple theme or big idea: *God wins!* This remarkable and challenging book explains to us how God rescues and redeems his people, defeats Satan, routs evil, transforms creation, and eventually and eternally dwells among us forever.

I can't conceive of another book of Holy Scripture more relevant to our day. But that isn't because it provides us with a blueprint for events at the end of history. If you think Revelation was given to answer all of your speculative questions about current events and when Jesus might return, you will be sorely disappointed by this commentary. Revelation is in our Bibles to reassure suffering Christians of all ages that God wins. *Its focus is the unimpeachable and irresistible sovereignty of our great Triune God in his determination to bring his people into everlasting joy in the new heavens and new earth.* To the degree that you have been led to think otherwise is indicative of how far removed the church today is from the teaching of Revelation.

The word translated "revelation" is the Greek term *apokalypsis* that means something revealed or disclosed or uncovered or made known or unveiled. The English words "apocalypse" and "apocalyptic" are surely familiar to you all. And by the way, the title to the book is Revelation (singular), not Revelations (plural).

The author of the book identifies himself four times as John (1:1, 4, 9; 22:8). I personally believe this is the same John who was one of the twelve original apostles and wrote not only the Gospel account that bears his name but also the three shorter epistles we know as First, Second, and Third John.

There have been extensive debates about when the book was written, but most believe that it was composed either in the decade of the 60s in the first century or more likely at the close of that century, during the reign of the Emperor Domitian, in approximately the year 95. I am inclined to embrace the latter view.

How Should We Interpret Revelation

The battle over the book of Revelation typically begins with differences over the way in which it should be interpreted. I'll only briefly mention here the more popular views and take up this matter in more detail when we arrive at the beginning of Chapter 6. Or you can turn to the Introductory Issues where I explain these alternative positions in greater depth.

So, simply stated, some Christians advocate what is called the *Preterist* view of the book. The word "preterist" comes from the Latin word *praeteritus* which means "gone by" or "past". Proponents of this view contend that the book was written in the decade of the 60s in the first century, prior to the destruction of Jerusalem and its temple in A.D. 70. Therefore, the major prophecies of Revelation describe events leading up to and including the fall of Jerusalem.

By far and away the most popular view of Revelation is the *Futurist* perspective. According to this interpretation, virtually everything from Revelation 6:1 through to the end of Revelation 19 is concerned almost exclusively with what will happen in a seven-year period at the end of history known as the Great Tribulation. In other words, the judgments of God that come in the form of seven seals, trumpets, and bowls describe events that have not yet happened but remain future to all of us.

The so-called *Idealist* view of Revelation contends that the prophecies in this book are not concerned with any specific period, event, or series of events in church history. Rather, its primary purpose is to describe symbolically the conflict of good and evil throughout history and the principles on which God acts at all times. It is a timeless portrayal, therefore, of this ethical struggle.

My view of the book most resembles the idealist view but also includes a mixture of the other perspectives. It doesn't go by any particular name but argues that there are parts of the book that describe events that have already happened in history and are thus in the past, as well as events that are going to happen at some time in the future, in particular the Second Coming of Jesus Christ.

But more central to this view is the belief that *Revelation portrays through vivid and often bizarre symbolism the entire course of events throughout the history of the church from the ascension of Jesus Christ all the way to his Second Coming.* In other words, as we will see when we come to Chapter 6 and following, the seal, trumpet, and bowl judgments are trans-temporal in that they describe the on-going, increasingly intensified conflict between the kingdom of Christ and the kingdom of Satan at any and all times. These judgments are not reserved for the end of history, immediately preceding the Second Coming. They do, indeed, describe that period of time, but they also portray what has happened in centuries past as well as what is happening today.

How the Heavenly Vision was Communicated

I'll only say a few things about the opening three verses of Chapter 1. The first thing we see is how the visions in this book were communicated to John. Note that it begins with God the Father, who in turn "gave" (v. 1) it to Jesus, God the Son. Jesus then sent "his angel" (v. 1b) to make it "known" to John, who in turn communicated everything to the people of God, in particular the seven churches in Asia Minor (v. 4).

(from) God the Father
↓

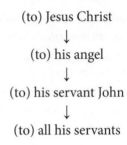

Now, just a brief comment on four things in these opening verses.

First, that to which John bore witness was "the testimony of Jesus" (v. 3). This may be understood in one of two ways: either Jesus is the *object* of the testimony, i.e., it is testimony *about* or *concerning* Jesus, or Jesus is the *subject* of the testimony, i.e., he is its source or origin; he is the one who actually testifies or bears witness. The latter is more likely (cf. 6:9; 11:7; 12:11; 20:4). That to which Jesus testifies or that to which he bears witness is "all" that John "saw," i.e., the actual contents of the book.

Second, the content of this "testimony" concerns what "must soon take place" (v. 1). Notice at the end of verse 3 we read that "the time is near" (v. 3b). In Revelation 22:7, Jesus says, "*I am coming soon.*" In 22:10, the angel declares that "*the time is near,*" and again in 22:12 Jesus says, "*I am coming soon.*" What do these statements mean?

These statements have become the principal basis for the preterist interpretation of the book. Preterists insist that we should interpret these time indicators literally. Thus, John is saying that the vast majority of events in Revelation are all to transpire within the first century (primarily in the events associated with the destruction of Jerusalem and its temple in A.D. 70).

Some say that the words "near", "shortly," and "soon" mean that once the appointed time arrives the events will unfold suddenly or will occur rapidly. In other words, the emphasis is on the speedy *manner* of fulfillment. Still others contend that all that is meant is that the events are *certain* to occur.

Some point to 2 Peter 3:8 ("With the Lord a day is like a thousand years") and argue that John is writing from the divine perspective. What may seem like incessant delay to us is "soon" and "near" for the Lord who views time from a heavenly perspective.

Yet another view is that behind these words is the prophetic principle of *imminence*: i.e., John's point is that the events could transpire *at any time*, even soon (although there is no way for anyone to know that with certainty; therefore, we must always be ready).

I personally agree with G. K. Beale who contends that John's words "quickly" (or "soon") and "near" are a substitute for Daniel's phrase "in the latter days" (e.g., Dan. 2:28). In other words, Daniel, in the sixth century B.C., referred to events that would occur in some distant future, in a time that he called "the latter days." John, in the book of Revelation, understands Daniel's words as applying to his own time. "What Daniel expected to occur in the distant 'latter days' – the defeat of cosmic evil and the ushering in of the divine kingdom – John expects to begin 'quickly,' in his own generation, if it has not already begun to happen."[1] John is declaring that prophetic fulfillment has already been inaugurated in his own lifetime, in the first century. But the consummation, however, is yet to come.

We know from numerous texts in the New Testament that the "last days" began with the resurrection and exaltation of Jesus Christ to the right hand of the Father and will extend all the way until the Second Coming of Christ at the close of history. That is why John substitutes the words "soon" and "near" for "the last days" as found in Daniel. His point is that what was future to Daniel is now being fulfilled in John's day and will continue to unfold and occur until the time of Christ's return.

It seems as if John's intent is to bring events which were once in the distant future into the immediate present. In *that* sense, then, "the time is near." Thus we may translate this phrase, "things which must soon begin to happen." Again, "as soon as his letter reaches its

---

1. Beale, *Revelation*, 153.

destination in the churches of Asia, they will be able to say, 'These things are happening *now*.'"[2]

Third, we have here in verse 3 the first of seven "beatitudes" or "blessings" in Revelation (1:3; 14:13; 16:15; 19:9; 20:6; 22:7, 14). Why is a blessing pronounced on the person who "reads aloud" the words of the book? Because in the first century only a minority of people were literate and there were no individual or separate copies of Revelation that everyone could personally own. But the important thing to note is the blessing is also pronounced on "those who hear" and "who keep" what is written in it. Owning a copy of Revelation isn't enough. Merely reading it or even interpreting it correctly isn't enough. The blessing of God rests upon those who "keep" the things written in it. We "keep" this book when we cherish its every word as God's word. We "keep" it when we respond appropriately to its teaching, whether that be by believing or by repenting or by worshiping or by obeying its commands.

Contrary to what many have said, although Revelation is difficult, God intends for his people to understand it and to obey it. Revelation was never intended to remain a mystery or to tantalize the intellect or to fuel sensational apocalyptic end-time speculations. It was given to instruct Christians how they should behave in light of the marvelous work of redemption in Christ and God's ultimate victory over all evil.

Fourth, you will note that in verse 1 we read that God "made it known" what will soon take place. The verb here literally means "to communicate by means of symbols or signs or pictures." In other words, we are told right from the start that Revelation is a book that contains signs and symbols and figurative language and must be interpreted accordingly. Although everything in Revelation is true, it is rarely literal. It is most often truth communicated through vivid images and pictorial symbols.

---

2. Michael Wilcock, *The Message of Revelation* (Downers Grove: IVP, 1975), 33. This volume was originally published under the title, *I Saw Heaven Opened*.

The Greeting from the Trinity

The book of Revelation is clearly addressed to "the seven churches that are in Asia" (v. 4a). Asia was a common designation for what is today western Turkey. These seven churches are probably to be viewed as *representative of all the churches* then active on the earth and, by extension, the church universal. We deduce this not only from the use of the number "seven" but also from the fact "that the letters addressed to particular churches in chapters 2–3 are also said at the conclusion of each letter to be addressed to all 'the churches.'"[3]

The greeting is unlike anything you or I have ever received from someone writing us a letter. It comes from the Triune God, beginning with the Father. He is described as the one "who is and who was and who is to come" (based on Exodus 3:14 where God is portrayed as "I am who I am"). Some have found in this title a reference to past, present, and future existence. However, the third term is not the future tense of the verb "to be" but the present participle of the verb "to come", lit., "the one who is coming." John's aim is not so much to tell us that God will always exist, although, of course, he will. Rather his point is to remind us that our God is the one who is coming into the world in the person of Jesus Christ at the close of history to bring everything to its proper consummation.

The greeting also comes from the Holy Spirit: "the seven spirits who are before his throne." Four times we read of the "seven Spirits" (1:4; 3:1; 4:5; 5:6). No, there are not seven Holy Spirits! The number seven in Revelation almost always points to perfection or fullness. So the "seven spirits who are before" the throne is simply a vivid way of saying that the fullness or totality or perfected completeness of the Holy Spirit is at work in our world in conjunction with the other two persons of the Triune Godhead, the Father and the Son.

Finally, the greeting comes from Jesus Christ, the Son: "from Jesus Christ, the faithful witness, the firstborn of the dead, and the ruler of kings on earth." Let's consider each of these three descriptive titles of Jesus.

---

3. Beale, *Revelation*, 187.

First, he is "the faithful witness." This is a reference to the faithfulness with which Jesus bore witness to his Father. He spoke truthfully of who God is and why he came into this world. That is why we can trust fully in his promises to us. Second, he is "the first-born of the dead." This phrase is what makes Easter Sunday so directly and personally relevant for all of us. Jesus was the first to be raised from the dead but not the last. The fact that he was raised is God's assurance to us that we who are in Christ by faith will also one day receive our resurrected and glorified bodies! The idea in the word "first-born" is that of a high, privileged position with great prestige similar to the principle of primogeniture in the Old Testament (cf. Ps. 89:27). The first-born son in a family carried a special rank and privilege in inheritance and succession. This position is Christ's by virtue of his resurrection from the dead.

Third, he is "the ruler of the kings of the earth," and that includes Assad of Syria and Kim Jong Un of North Korea, and yes, he is the ruler of every President of the USA as well. Solomon said it with the utmost clarity: "The king's heart is a stream of water in the hand of the LORD; he turns it wherever he will" (Prov. 21:1). When God's purpose was to bring the people of Israel back to Jerusalem from their time of exile in Babylon, how did he do it? He "stirred up the spirit" of the pagan, unbelieving king of Persia, Cyrus, "so that he," Cyrus, "made a proclamation throughout all his kingdom and also put it in writing" (Ezra 1:1).

We will see this incredibly wonderful and reassuring truth all through the Revelation, but especially in Chapter 17. There we read how God will make use of the kings of the earth and even the leaders of the corrupt religious system to accomplish his purpose. We read in Revelation 17:17, "for God has put it into their hearts," that is, into the hearts of the ruling leaders of the pagan kingdoms of the earth, "to carry out his purpose by being of one mind and handing over their royal power to the beast, until the words of God are fulfilled" (Rev. 17:17).

Today we hear and read and see on every hand the movements and decisions and plans of earthly leaders in their efforts to expand their power and gain new territory. And people tremble in fear.

Do not be afraid, Christian! Do not be afraid. Everything they do, down to the most strategic plans formulated in back rooms under the strictest of secrecy, is all in the hands of the risen Lord Jesus Christ. They are unwittingly doing his will.

It often appears that the entire world reels with one blow after another. In Egypt dozens of Christians are killed when ISIS detonates a bomb on Palm Sunday. Bloody civil wars continually erupt all around the globe. Racial strife plagues our own country. Threats against Israel by Iran and other Muslim countries is a daily fixture. And drug cartels continue to supply a seemingly endless flow of illegal narcotics into various countries. The world, by all external appearances, appears horribly unstable and chaotic and out of control.

The churches in Asia Minor, to whom Revelation was first written, were facing their own fair share of persecution and political turmoil. But John speaks words of unimaginable encouragement to them and to us today.

Jesus Christ is alive from the dead and seated at the right hand of the Majesty on high, reigning and ruling and exercising absolute sovereignty over all the kings of the earth, all the events in the Middle East and throughout Central and South America, and even in the lunatic plans of North Korea and China and Russia.

Jesus does not approve of their wicked ways, but he irresistibly overrules the sinful acts of evil rulers and makes their sin and their folly a part of his wise plan for history. I cannot fathom how he does this. In the end, I must fall back on the words of Paul in Romans 11:33, "Oh, the depth of the riches and wisdom and knowledge of God! How unsearchable are his judgments and how inscrutable his ways!"

As "the ruler of the kings on earth" he mysteriously governs and regulates what all earthly kings and presidents do, sometimes restraining them from doing evil, sometimes frustrating their plans, sometimes ordering events so that they might serve his purposes. We can't figure out how he does it, but do it, he does! Thus, Paul declares in 1 Corinthians 15:25 that "he must reign until he has put all his enemies under his feet." So don't just read the newspaper or scour the internet. Read and reflect with the eyes of faith and confidence in the supremacy of Jesus Christ over all things.

A Doxology for the Son

John can't contain himself. No sooner has he said these three things about Jesus than he explodes in praise of him. This is one of those doxological outbursts where a biblical author erupts with exalted worship of God. Again, John mentions three things.

First, to him who "loves us" be "glory and dominion forever and ever" (v. 5b). This the only place in the New Testament where Christ's love for us is in the present tense. John wants you to know that no matter what you endure, no matter how sorely you may be persecuted, no matter how badly circumstances may turn out for you and me, Jesus always has, does now, and always will love us. No matter what we face, he always has our best interests in view. His heart beats with passion for his people at all times. And how do we know he loves us? What has he done to demonstrate that love? The last phrase in verse 5 tells us.

Second, "he has freed us from our sins by his blood." Here we see two motifs joined: the *love* (motive) of Jesus for his people and his voluntary expression of that love by *freeing* (action) us from our sins. This is an echo of what Paul said in Galatians 2:20 – "And the life I now live in the flesh I live by faith in the Son of God, who loved me and gave himself for me." Again we read in Ephesians 5:2 – "And walk in love, as Christ loved us and gave himself up for us, a fragrant offering and sacrifice to God."

If your life is a shambles, if nothing has turned out as you hoped it would, if you are alone and financially destitute and your body suffers from chronic pain or a terminal disease, and all this stirs in your heart the question: "Does he really love me?" ... hear the declaration of John: Yes! He loves you, and you can know this by turning your heart to the concrete, historical, tangible reality of Jesus on a cross for you, shedding his blood for you, and setting you free from death and condemnation.

One more thing to consider here. To say that he has "freed us from our sins by his blood" means that the guilt of our sin that exposes us to divine justice and wrath has been finally and forever removed. We are free from that guilt that puts our souls in eternal jeopardy. And please take note of how this happened. It isn't because we are physically impressive or because of our good intentions or because of our eloquence, intelligence, or the many promises we have kept. And it certainly isn't because we are sincere. We are liberated from guilt and divine judgment because our guilt was imputed to Jesus, our judgment fell upon him. His "blood" shed on the cross is what cleanses us from the stain of sin.

Third, Jesus didn't shed his blood and deliver us from condemnation as an end in itself. He did more than simply save us "from" eternal damnation. His substitutionary death in our place was in order that he might make us "a kingdom, priests to his God and Father." The language in verse 6a is an unmistakable allusion to Exodus 19:6. There God declares of Israel, "you shall be to me a kingdom of priests and a holy nation." This high calling and privilege is applied specifically to the church in 1 Peter 2:9 and here again in Revelation 1:6. Note also that what in Exodus was a future announcement ("you *shall* be") is in Revelation the proclamation of an accomplished fact ("he *has made*").

It is "to him" that we ascribe "glory and dominion forever and ever."

His Coming

Make no mistake: although Revelation is primarily about the way in which God proceeds to secure the ultimate victory for himself and us, his people, it is also most assuredly about the blessed hope, the Second Coming of Jesus Christ. We see this in verse 7.

Here we see the combination of Daniel 7:13 with Zechariah 12:10 which also appears in the Olivet Discourse in Matthew 24 and Mark 13. In the latter texts it refers to the coming of Christ in judgment against Israel in A.D. 70 and his consequent vindication. Here, in a text written subsequent to A.D. 70, it is universalized ("every eye") and applied to his final coming at the end of history, the Parousia (see 14:14).

This should not surprise us once we recognize that the pattern of events that transpired in the period A.D. 33–70, leading up to and including the destruction of Jerusalem and its temple, functions as a local, microcosmic foreshadowing of the global, macrocosmic events associated with the Parousia and the end of history. The period A.D. 33–70 provides in its principles, (though not necessarily in all particularities), a template against which we are to interpret the period 70–Parousia.

One more thing. We can't be certain about the nature of the "wailing" of the peoples of the earth when he returns. That is to say, we don't know if this is the wailing of repentance as they suddenly realize the truth about the one they have rejected, or the wailing of mere pain and anguish as they suffer the penalty of eternal destruction. It may be both.

His Claim

The words "the Alpha and the Omega" are, of course, the first and last words of the Greek alphabet and are taken from Isaiah where it occurs as a self-designation for God (44:6; 48:12). One could hardly find a more explicit claim to exclusive deity than this. As the first and the last, Jesus is not only claiming equality of nature with the Father but is declaring that he both precedes all things as their Creator and will bring all things to their eschatological consummation. He is the origin and goal of all history.

The title "the Lord God, the Almighty" occurs seven times in Revelation (1:8; 4:8; 11:17; 15:3; 16:7; 19:6; 21:22). A shorter form, "God the Almighty" occurs twice (16:14; 19:15). This is probably a translation of the Old Testament title, "the LORD, the God of hosts" (e.g., 2 Sam. 5:10; Jer. 5:14). The word "almighty" points not so much to God's abstract omnipotence as to his actual providential control and oversight of all things. This is designed to reassure Christians in the first century and in every subsequent century up through our own that God and God alone is in absolute control of the affairs of mankind.

Don't be deceived by appearances or boastful claims or threats of mass destruction. The Lord God Almighty has everything completely in hand. You and I may not be able to decipher his ways or understand why he ordains or allows what he does, but rest assured that nothing is outside his control or can ever threaten his ultimate victory. Simply put, with these words Jesus stakes his claim on every millisecond of human history, from the time of creation to the final consummation. He is the Lord over history. He is sovereign over all nations and their armies and over all peoples and their hearts and over all of nature and its multitude of species.

Chapter Two

Behold the Glory of the Lord

(Revelation 1:9-20)

What is it that makes this portrayal of the risen and glorified Christ more than just a fascinating pictorial display? I doubt if there is a more majestic description of our reigning King than what we find here in Revelation 1:12-16. Countless attempts have been made by artists to render an accurate representation of the Lord Jesus Christ. Now that we find ourselves in the age of computers and highly technical tools of graphic design, I'm sure that many will try to supply us with a vivid portrait of Jesus as he is described in this text.

But I would greatly caution against it. After all, what sort of image emerges when you try to paint or draw or sketch a person whose eyes are flames of fire, whose feet are like burnished bronze, and who has a sharp two-edged sword protruding from his mouth? That hardly makes for a flattering portrait! My point is simply that the purpose of this revelation of the risen Christ is not to tell us what he literally looks like in a purely physical sense, but *who he is* spiritually and morally.

Early on in my study of the book of Revelation I came across a statement from G. B. Caird in his commentary. He urged his readers not to become overly obsessed with the particulars of this portrait of Jesus. Whereas each element in this portrait has theological significance, Caird warns us not *"to unweave the rainbow."*[1] In other words,

> "John uses his allusions not as a code in which each symbol requires separate and exact translation, but rather for their evocative and emotive power. This is not photographic art. His aim is to set the echoes of memory and association ringing. The humbling sense of the sublime and the majestic which men experience at the sight of a roaring cataract [waterfall] or the midday sun is the nearest equivalent to the awe evoked by a vision of the divine. John has seen the risen Christ, clothed in all the attributes of deity, and he wishes to call forth from his readers the same response of overwhelming and annihilating wonder which he experienced in his prophetic trance."[2]

That being said, I will attempt to make sense of the various attributes that are mentioned here. Still, we would do well to heed Caird's advice and not attempt to "unweave the rainbow."

So my concern here is not so much with the details of this vision of the risen Christ, although we will in fact examine those details later on. My primary focus will be on asking the question: *Of what practical benefit is it for you and me to behold the glory of Jesus in this vision of John?* What good is it? How does it help us in our struggle with temptation and idolatry?

I'm sure you are aware of this, but there are countless methods and strategies employed by Christians everywhere to accelerate and facilitate change or moral transformation in their lives, most of which leave you with a sour taste in your mouth. Some professing Christians insist that we need to jettison all rules, regulations, and commandments and simply rest in the grace of God that is shown us in Jesus. Others gravitate to the opposite extreme and argue that we need more rules and regulations to help us conform to the image of Jesus, rules and regulations that are nowhere found in the Bible

---

1. G. B. Caird, *A Commentary on the Revelation of St. John the Divine* (New York: Harper & Row, 1966), 25.
2. Ibid., 25-26.

itself. Some contend that abstinence is the key to transformation. If you want to be more like Jesus simply refrain from everything that might remotely have the capacity to bring you joy and happiness. Deprive yourself. Deny yourself. Some insist that the only way to change is to exert one's willpower in saying No to temptation and Yes to God's commands. Then there are those who advocate retreat. Withdraw from the world and close yourself off from its temptations. Perhaps living in a monastery will help. And so the list goes on and on as people try to find the key to successful Christian living.

I mention these misguided approaches to the Christian life in order to throw them into contrast with what I believe is the primary catalyst for growth in Christ and increasing conformity to his image. So, to ask it again, what is the best, most effective way to accelerate and facilitate increasing conformity to Jesus? I believe the answer is found all through the New Testament, but let me direct your attention to what Paul says in 2 Corinthians 3:18:

> "And we all, with unveiled face, beholding the glory of the Lord, are being transformed into the same image from one degree of glory to another. For this comes from the Lord who is the Spirit."

Paul couldn't have been any more precise in making his point. If you and I ever hope to be changed, to be transformed into the image of Jesus himself, *it will only come to the degree that we behold the glory of the Lord and treasure him above all else.* Now, I want you to be patient with me as I try to establish a clear connection between John's vision of the risen Christ here in Revelation 1 and Paul's description of how we are changed to be more and more like Jesus in every way.

In the inner core of every Christian, in the depths of the heart, there is movement, as Paul says, "from one degree of glory to another" (v. 18). If you do not feel an internal impulse and desire to change and be more like Jesus, I doubt very seriously if you are truly born again. I insert that comment as a warning to anyone who can read the portrayal of Jesus in Revelation 1 and feel nothing. If you feel nothing, I urge you to examine your heart and determine if you are truly a child of God. Now, let's move on.

Literally, Paul writes that we are being transformed "*from* glory *unto* glory." Oh, how I love prepositions! The preposition "from" points to *source* and "unto" highlights the ultimate *goal* in view. In other words, God began a work of grace in us at regeneration or the new birth that consisted of the experience of his glory that is building momentum and progressively moving toward the final experience of the fullness of that glory at the return of Jesus Christ (for the latter, see Phil. 3:20-21; Col. 3:4; 1 Thess. 5:23; and 1 John 3:2).

Perhaps the best way to mine this text for all its treasures is to make a series of observations.

First, Paul describes us, all Christians, as those who are "beholding the glory of the Lord" and doing so, unlike the Israelites of old, "with unveiled face." It was the distinct privilege of Moses alone to glimpse the "glory" of God when he saw his "form" (Num. 12:8) and his "back" (Ex. 33:23). But now in the New Covenant all Christian believers without distinction are granted the privilege of seeing or beholding that glory. And unlike the people of Israel, who looked upon the glory as reflected in Moses' veiled face, we see with permanently uncovered faces.

Second, where exactly do we "see" or "behold" that glory? Paul saw the glory of God on the road to Damascus (cf. Acts 22:11; Acts 26:13). In 2 Corinthians 4:3-6 he suggests that God shines the glory of that light "in our hearts" through "the gospel." In other words, whereas Paul literally saw the glory of Christ with his physical eyes in a direct and unmediated vision, we *see* the glory of Christ when we *hear* the gospel. What was for Paul a visual encounter with the glory of Jesus is for us an oral encounter. *We hear what he saw when we read his record of the gospel of Jesus.*

Third, the process that we call sanctification comes only as or because we behold the glory of God. *Apart from beholding there is no becoming.* The more we know him and behold him in the splendor of his glory, the more we are changed into the very image of Jesus himself, in whose face God's glory has shined or is reflected

(2 Cor. 4:4, 6). Sanctification, therefore, is the fruit of seeing and savoring. Ignorance, on the other hand, breeds moral paralysis (if not regression).

Fourth, as much as we all might wish otherwise, sanctification is *progressive*, not instantaneous. As noted earlier, we are gradually moving by the power of the Spirit from one stage or degree of glory (first "seen" in the gospel when we turn to Christ) to another (that of the glorified Jesus, whose glory we will not only see on the day of his return but in which we will also participate).

Fifth, sanctification is by grace (we 'are being transformed'), the agent of which is the Spirit of Christ. We don't transform ourselves by unaided striving. This doesn't eliminate human effort but rather makes it possible. We act because we are acted upon. We work out our salvation with fear and trembling because God, *who is always antecedent*, is at work in us to will and to do for his good pleasure (cf. Phil. 2:12-13)!

Sixth, we see here that "beholding is a way of becoming."[3] That is to say, we always tend to become like or take on the characteristics and qualities of whatever it is we admire and enjoy and cherish most. Fixing the eyes of our faith on Jesus is transformative. Gazing on his glory as seen in the gospel and now preserved for us in Scripture has the power to bump us along, as it were, whether in short spurts of sanctification or great and notable triumphs, toward the fullness that is found in Christ alone but will one day be found in us, by grace, as well!

Can you now see why I am drawing a connection between what Paul said in 2 Corinthians 3:18 about how we are changed and what John saw in his vision of the risen Christ and how he recorded this for us in Revelation 1? This vision that John experienced and then recorded for all Christians to read is intended by God to be a catalyst for change. This is how we are transformed. This is how we find strength and incentive to resist temptation. This is how we resist the seductive appeal of idolatry and greed and lust and

---

3. John Piper, *The Pleasures of God* (Portland: Multnomah, 1991), 17.

pride. It comes as we continue to behold the glory of the Lord Jesus Christ, one example of which is here in Revelation 1.

We've all heard the statement that "Seeing is believing." I suppose that's true. But here in 2 Corinthians 3:18 Paul says that *"Seeing is becoming."* You become like what you behold. Now, pause for a moment and ask yourself: "Why am I not changing more consistently? Why am I not becoming more like Jesus?" Perhaps the answer is found in what you are beholding. If the focus of your sight is the banal trash and mindless sensuality of TV and the Internet and Facebook, is it any wonder that you aren't today substantially different or more like Jesus than you were a week ago, or a year ago? I'll leave it with that and let you meditate on your answer.

Before we go any farther let me make application of this to myself. If what Paul says in 2 Corinthians 3:18 is true, and it is, then my primary responsibility as the author of this commentary is to hold up for your continual gaze the glory and beauty of Jesus Christ. To the degree that I fail to do that consistently and passionately, over time, is the degree to which I have failed you. That is the primary way in which you and I will together become more and more like Jesus.

What this means is that, contrary to what many of you may think, your primary need isn't financial or physical. Your primary need isn't that you lose weight or gain the respect of your peers. Your primary need, my primary need, is spiritual: *we need to be a people who radiate the beauty of Christ that comes from beholding the glory of Christ.*

Now, before we look at this vision of Christ in Revelation 1:12-16, let's take note of the context and how it came about.

John in Exile

Don't miss what John says in verse 9 about the reason for his exile on the island of Patmos. John's presence on Patmos wasn't his choice. This is no vacation. Patmos itself is "a rocky and rugged island about six miles wide and ten miles long, some forty miles southwest of Ephesus in the Aegean Sea."[4] John states that he found himself there "on account of the word of God and the testimony of Jesus." In other words, the prospect of exile on a desolate island did not diminish John's zeal and commitment to Jesus. He was so enchanted with the beauty and majesty of Jesus that the physical comforts of life exerted no influence on his soul.

This vision came to John on "the Lord's day," perhaps while he was engaged in prayer or worship or both. The Greek term *kuriakos* is never used in the New Testament or early church history of "the Day of the Lord" in the eschatological sense but uniformly refers to Sunday, the first day of the week.

What was the nature of John's experience? The phrase "I was in the Spirit" occurs here and again in 4:2. On two other occasions (17:3; 21:10) John says he was carried away "in the Spirit". Was this his way of describing some sort of divine inspiration or does it merely refer to a trance-like experience in which he received visions from God? Probably both. In any case, John was so deeply immersed in the Spirit and subject to his influence that he saw a vision of the risen Christ.

Be it noted that there is nothing to suggest John was seeking or expecting to receive this vision. There are no formulas that might induce such an experience. One should always be postured and prepared to receive whatever God might choose to give, but all semblance of manipulation must be avoided.

Now look closely at what follows in verse 11. Although John alone literally saw the vision it was intended to be communicated and experienced by all Christians. Jesus told John to "write" down what he sees "in a book and send it to the seven churches" in Asia Minor. That means this vision was given to John for you and me as well. It was intended as much for your local church today as it was for the church in Ephesus or Smyrna or Laodicea in the first century. This wasn't some private and altogether personal spiritual experience that one secretly records in his/her journal, never to

---

4. D. A. Carson, Douglas J. Moo, and Leon Morris, *An Introduction to the New Testament* (Grand Rapids: Zondervan Publishing House, 1992), 473.

be shared with others. Jesus appeared to John so that Jesus might appear to us by means of John's written record.

Jesus could have appeared to all of the Christians in the seven churches in the same way he appeared to John. He could appear in the same way to us today. But he doesn't. He appears to us in the inspired words, the written record of what John saw. And this inspired, written portrayal of what John saw is designed to have the same impact on us as it did on John.

People today, on rare occasions, have visions of the risen Christ not unlike what John experienced. I don't see anything in the New Testament that would lead us to believe that such visions are impossible. But they are certainly quite rare. I've never had one. The primary way that we behold the glory of Christ is as he comes to us and shines upon us through the written Word of God. The glory and beauty and majesty of Jesus primarily shine into our hearts through the words of the Bible.

One more brief comment before I go on. Notice in verse 9 John's reference to "the tribulation" that he shares with other Christians. As far as John is concerned, "the tribulation" to which all believers are at some time or other subjected has already begun. More on this as we go deeper into Revelation.

John in the Spirit

So, as John turns to see whose voice was like a trumpet (v. 10), he sees seven golden lampstands and Christ in the midst of them. Verse 20 provides us with an interpretation of the lampstands: "As for the mystery of the seven stars which you saw in my right hand, and the seven golden lampstands, the seven stars are the angels of the seven churches, and the seven lampstands are the seven churches" (Rev. 1:20). So the vision of Jesus that John gets is of our Lord among or in the midst of the churches. Jesus is not merely over the local church as its authoritative King but is actively and truly present in and among the local church as its living Savior, as our friend, as our guide. Jesus is not distant from the church, abiding in some remote galaxy. He is here, right now, as truly and literally as can possibly be imagined. And so he calls on us, he invites us, to look at what John saw.

When John turned, he saw "seven golden lampstands," a clear allusion to Zechariah 4:2, 10. Most believe that the lampstand in Zechariah with its seven lamps stands first for the temple and by extension the faithful within Israel. Here *in Revelation the lampstands represent the church.* The church is to serve as a light to the world. In the middle of these lampstands is the risen Christ. "Part of Christ's priestly role is to tend the lampstands. The Old Testament priest would trim the lamps, remove the wick and old oil, refill the lamps with fresh oil, and relight those that had gone out. Likewise, Christ tends the ecclesial lampstands by commending, correcting, exhorting, and warning ... in order to secure the churches' fitness for service as lightbearers in a dark world."[5]

I now comment briefly on selected parts of this vision:

- *Son of Man* (cf. Dan. 7:13-14) – This description not only points to our Lord's humanity, but even more to his role as *messianic king* through whom God's dominion and power are exercised over all creation. So when John says that he saw "one like a son of man" he means that he saw someone with authority and power and glory and royal dominion over all the nations, kings, and over all the peoples of the world. This is actually very similar to what John meant in verse 5 when he spoke of Jesus as "the ruler of kings on earth."

- The *long robe* and *golden sash* evoke images of the high priest under the Mosaic Covenant (Ex. 28:4; 39:29) and thus point to Christ's function as he who has obtained for us immediate access into God's presence. Jesus, then, is not only the sovereign messianic king ruling the nations, he is also the ultimate high priest who does not offer the blood of bulls and goats but his own precious blood to "free us from our sins" (v. 5).

---

5. Beale, *Revelation*, 208-09.

- The *white hair* reminds us of the Ancient of Days in Daniel 7:9 and thus points again to his deity, his essential oneness with the Father in the eternal Godhead. But the white hair also points to his wisdom and the maturity and dignity that come with age. Sadly, there is a diminishing respect for the elderly in our society. They are viewed as outdated and people to be patronized rather than pursued. But we read in Proverbs 16:31 that "Gray hair is a crown of glory." Jesus isn't literally old, as we measure age on earth. He is unaffected by the passing of time. He is eternally old in the sense that he has always existed and possesses the dignity and knowledge and wisdom of someone who has experienced all of life.

- His *eyes were like a flame of fire* – Seiss writes:

> "Here is intelligence; burning, all-penetrating intelligence. Here is power to read secrets, to bring hidden things to light, to warm and search all hearts at a single glance.... But his sharp look is one of inspiring warmth to the good, as well as discomfiting and consuming terror to the hypocritical and the godless. Will you believe it, my friends, that this is the look which is upon you, and which is to try you in the great day! Well may we pray the prayer of David: 'Search me, O God, and know my heart; try me, and know my thought; and see if there be any evil way in me, and lead me in the way everlasting.'"[6]

  The eyes of our risen Savior do not droop. They are not closed in sleep. They are not sullen or sad. They burn ablaze with power and energy and insight and excitement. He sees everything with all the vitality of youth but thinks with all the wisdom of age.

- *His feet were like burnished bronze, refined in a furnace,* which possibly points to his moral purity and will become the basis on which he exhorts those among whom he walks to reflect this same purity of life (cf. 3:18).

---

6. Joseph A. Seiss, *The Apocalypse* (Grand Rapids: Eerdmans, 1966), 40.

- *His voice was like the roar of many waters* (cf. Ezek. 1:24; 43:2). I have no grid for this or insight on how to interpret it. Needless to say, for John it was utterly overwhelming.

- *In his right hand he held seven stars.* In verse 20 the stars refer symbolically to angels, indicating that Jesus is not only the sovereign ruler of the church on earth but also of the myriads and myriads of angelic beings who exist to worship him and to do his will. Later we will see in Revelation the role angels play in communicating with John and pouring out God's wrath on an unbelieving world. But at all times they are held tightly in Christ's hand, under his complete control.

- The *sword* is not in his hand, but proceeds from his *mouth*, indicating that his *spoken word* is in view. A sword that cuts two ways points to the gospel as that which both brings either life or judgment (cf. Isa. 11:4; 49:2).

- *His face was like the sun shining in full strength* (cf. Judges 5:31). Again, Seiss explains:

"Something of this was seen in the mount of transfiguration, when 'his face did shine as the sun, and his raiment was white as the light.' Something of the same was manifest when he appeared to Saul of Tarsus in 'a light above the brightness of the sun.' And so glorious and pervading is this light which issues from his face, that in the New Jerusalem there will be neither sun, nor moon, nor lamp, nor any other light, and yet rendered so luminous by his presence, that even the nations on the earth walk in the light of it. And so the lightning brilliancy, which is to flash from one end of heaven to the other at the time of his coming, and the glory which is then to invest him and the whole firmament, is simply the uncovering or revelation of that blessed light which streams from his sublime person."[7]

---

7. Ibid., 43.

The Divine Interpretation

How do you explain John's reaction? Why did he fall? Is this a normative phenomenon? It would seem that John's response follows the same four-fold pattern of Daniel 10:5-11 and 10:12-20 – (1) the prophet (Daniel and John) sees a vision, (2) he falls prostrate in fear, (3) is then strengthened by a *touch* (!) from a "heavenly" being, and (4) then receives additional revelation that serves to interpret what he saw. And be it noted that John's response is not one of terrified retreat but of reverential falling at the very feet of his Master.

The words "Fear not" find their basis in the fact that Jesus has conquered both sin and death. The believer need not fear either suffering or martyrdom, for Jesus has endured both and emerged victorious. The "keys of death and Hades" may mean the keys "to death" or the keys "possessed by death." In either case, Jesus has absolute authority and power over this realm. We need never fear death, for it brings us into the immediate presence of this glorified and majestic Lord that John has so vividly described for us.

There have been numerous interpretations of Revelation 1:19. Many try to find in it a clue to the structure of the entire book of Revelation. I'll save my comments on this verse to when we get to Revelation 6 and look more closely at the way this book is put together. Likewise, when it comes to "the angels of the seven churches" in verse 20, I'll have much to say when we come to the letters to the seven churches in Revelation 2–3.

Conclusion

John was overwhelmed by his vision of the risen Lord, *your* risen Lord. It would do us well to meditate on the glorious sufficiency of the glorified Jesus to meet every need. Jonathan Edwards (1703–58) once preached a sermon entitled "The Excellency of Christ"[8] that asks repeatedly the same question: What is it that you need or desire that cannot be found in Jesus? What possible reason

---

8. Jonathan Edwards, *Sermons and Discourses 1734–1738,* edited by M. X. Lesser (New Haven: Yale University Press, 2001), 563-594.

could you have for not casting your life upon him? Allow me to paraphrase how Edwards put it.

"What are you afraid of that hinders you from venturing your soul upon Christ? Are you afraid that he is not strong enough to conquer your enemies or to supply you with what you need? But the risen Christ possesses infinite strength and all things are subject to him, even the demons that threaten to destroy you."

"Are you afraid that even though he is strong enough to take up your cause and defend you he might not be willing to do so? But if he was willing, for your sake, to subject himself to a Roman scourging and ridicule and public humiliation and eventually willing to be crucified naked in order to bear your sin and shame and the wrath you deserved, don't you think he is willing to come to your aid and to help you through every struggle?"

"Are you afraid that if perhaps Jesus might accept and receive you to himself, the Father will not? But could the Father ever consider rejecting his own Son, in whom he delights with infinite delight? And did not Jesus say in John 17 that the Father loves us with the same love that he has for Jesus himself?"

"What spiritual or moral excellencies do you desire in a Savior that cannot be found in Jesus Christ? What is there great or good, adorable or endearing, that cannot be found in Jesus? Do you wish your Savior to be honorable and dignified, strong yet compassionate, powerful yet humble, firm but at the same time gracious, both loving and just? Is that not what Jesus is at all times for us? Is he not both the Lion of Judah who roars with supreme power and at the same time the Lamb led to slaughter in the place of sinners like you and me?"

"Would you have your Savior to be one who is near to the heart of God the Father, whose prayers and intercession for you are readily and joyfully heard by our great God? But who is more near and dear to the heart of the Father than his only-begotten Son, who is, with him and the Holy Spirit, one God, who is beloved of the Father and is never denied anything he asks of him?"

My questions to you could continue without end. And every one of them would be answered in the same way. There is none other than Jesus who can be for you and do for you everything your heart may require. So will you not receive him today as Lord and Savior? Will you who have already received him lift your hearts and voices to declare his greatness and mercy and power and love? Will you now join me to exult in Christ and in so doing exalt him above all others?

Chapter Three

What Jesus Says When He Speaks to the Church

(Revelation 2:1-7)

"*What Christ thinks of the Church.*" That was the title to a short book on Revelation 2 and 3 by British pastor John Stott.[1] I like that. We need to think about what Christ thinks of us, the church. We should care profoundly about what Christ thinks of the church. But I would like to rephrase Stott's title, if I may, and entitle the seven letters of Revelation 2 and 3, *"What Christ SAYS to the Church."* My reason for this is found in the opening verse to each of the seven letters. Seven times over we are told that what we are reading are *"the words"* of the risen Christ to his people.

There's something profoundly personal and urgent in that statement. These words in Revelation 2 and 3 are far more than the words of John the Apostle. They are the very "words" of Jesus himself addressed to his people in seven local churches spread throughout Asia Minor in the first century. But they are no less so the "words" of Christ to your local church today, and to every other local church that professes his name. If nothing else, that should

---

1. Much of my commentary on the seven churches of Revelation 2–3 has been adapted from my book, *To the One Who Conquers: 50 Daily Meditations on the Seven Letters of Revelation 2–3* (Wheaton: Crossway, 2008).

alert us to the importance of listening closely to what our Lord and Savior has to say.

If you've read Revelation 2 and 3 you are aware that each of the seven letters to the seven churches in Asia Minor is addressed to an "angel" (see Rev. 2:1, 8, 12, 18; 3:1, 7, 14). What could Jesus possibly have meant when he instructed John to send this letter "to the angel of the church in Ephesus"? There have been countless theories about the identity of these angels, and I'll only briefly mention them.

(1) When I was still an active member of a Southern Baptist church I heard my pastor (who will remain unnamed) argue that the "angel" in each case was the Senior Pastor of the congregation! There is simply not a syllable in the New Testament that would support that identification.

(2) Another possibility is that the "angel" refers to a prophet or delegated representative of the church. This person may have functioned in an ambassadorial role, or perhaps as something of a secretary who was responsible for maintaining communication with those outside the congregation as well as other tasks that may have been assigned.

(3) Yet a third, more likely option, points to the fact that in Revelation 1:11 (cf. 1:4) the letters are directed to "the churches" (plural). So also at the end of each letter we read: "Let him hear what the Spirit says to the *churches*." Thus the Lord speaks to the *whole church* and not just to an "angel". This leads some to conclude that the angel *is* the church, i.e., a personification of the church. The Greek text would certainly allow (but by no means require) this interpretation, in which case we would translate: "to the angel *which is* the church in Ephesus."

(4) Another theory is that the "angel" of each church is its guardian angel. Angels are described as "ministers" (*leitourgos*), a word that suggests a priestly service (Heb. 1:7, 14; cf. Ps. 103:19-21; Matt. 18:10; Acts 12:15). The most basic and obvious problem with this view is that it doesn't make sense why Jesus would address the letter to the guardian angel of a church rather than directly to the congregation itself.

To be perfectly honest, I don't know what the correct interpretation is, and no one else does either.

Why Ephesus

It was appropriate that the first of the seven letters was sent to Ephesus, for although not the titular capital of Asia (Pergamum held that honor), it was the most important political center. By the time the church received this letter, the city of Ephesus had grown to a population of around 250,000. By their standards, it was huge. It was, in effect, the New York City of the ancient world.

Americans *honor* their President and pray *for* him, and rightly they should (1 Pet. 2:17; 1 Tim. 2:1-2). But in Ephesus, *worship* of the Roman emperor was mandatory. Prayer *to* him was normative. Scattered across the landscape of America are Presidential Libraries, bearing the names and housing the historical artifacts of men such as Harry S. Truman, John F. Kennedy, Ronald Reagan, George W. Bush, and Bill Clinton. Not so in Ephesus. There one would find, not libraries, but *temples* dedicated to the idolatrous veneration of men such as Claudius, Hadrian, Julius Caesar, Augustus, and Severus. Every day Christian men and women in Ephesus passed these imposing structures, going about their daily tasks in an atmosphere filled with pagan praise of mere humans.

Worse still, religion and superstition were hopelessly intertwined and the magical arts were widely prevalent (cf. Acts 19:19). Ephesus was a seething cauldron of countless cults and superstitions. Preeminent among all religious attractions was the Temple of Diana (Artemis), construction of which began in 356 B.C. It was regarded as one of the Seven Wonders of the Ancient World.

Christianity came to Ephesus with Aquila and Priscilla in A.D. 52 when Paul left them there as he traveled from Corinth to Antioch (Acts 18:18-22). On his next missionary journey Paul remained and worked in Ephesus for more than two years (Acts 18:8, 10) and sometime later Timothy ministered there (1 Tim. 1:3).

It's important to remember, therefore, that the first church to receive a letter from Jesus was located in a city that wasn't even remotely Christian. No laws existed to protect their freedom of religious expression. The worship of false deities was institutionalized. The only thing on which the Ephesian believers could rely was God himself and one another. How would you and I fare in such a pagan atmosphere? I ask this because it often appears to me that many Christians believe the church in America can survive only if it is afforded legislative protection, only if certain Christian candidates are elected to national and local office, only if the next appointee to the Supreme Court is pro-life, only if prayer is restored to public schools. Make no mistake. I'm eternally grateful for the laws that safeguard our rights. But have we come to depend so desperately on such political blessings, economic liberties, and the legal protection Christianity enjoys that in their absence we fear the destruction of the church and the silencing of our witness?

The church in Ephesus, as with so many other congregations in the first century, knew nothing of a constitution, a first amendment, or a right to vote. Yet they survived, and thrived, in the midst of what strikes us as unimaginable state-sanctioned idolatry and immorality. Before we panic or lose heart at the state of our country, or the condition of our city, we would do well to remember the promise of Jesus: "I will build my church, and the gates of hell shall not prevail against it" (Matt. 16:18).

Christ's Loving Presence and Power

I want you to notice how Jesus is described. The letter to the church in Ephesus proceeds from him who *"holds"* the seven stars in his right hand and who *"walks"* in the midst of the seven golden lampstands. The meaning of this symbolism is given in the immediately preceding verse (Rev. 1:20).

When John turned, he saw "seven golden lampstands" (see Zech. 4:2, 10) which were symbolic of local churches. What is of special note to us is the *advance* made from the description in 1:13, 16 to that of 2:1. Jesus not only "has" the stars, he "holds" (lit., grasps) them. He not only "stands" in the midst of the lampstands, he "walks" among them! The Lordship of Christ over his people is not passive, distant, or indifferent. It is active, immanent, and intimate. Our Lord patrols the churches with an intense and ever-present awareness of all thoughts, deeds, and activities. Thus it is no surprise that each letter begins with the ominous, "I know your deeds" (2:2, 9, 13, 19; 3:1, 8, 15).

The move from "has" to "holds" and from "stands" to "walks" is designed to highlight both the sovereignty of Christ over the church and his loving presence and unfailing ministry within it. He "holds" or "grasps" the church because it belongs to him. He owns it. He has redeemed it by his blood. At no time does the church slip from his grasp or elude his grip or operate under its own authority. As difficult as church life often becomes, Christ never ceases to be its Sovereign. As disillusioning as human behavior within the church can be, it ever remains "his" body.

But more important still is the fact that he "walks" among the lampstands. He is present in and among his people. He guards and protects and preserves the church. He is never, ever absent! No service is conducted at which he fails to show up. No meal is served for which he does not sit down. No sermon is preached that he does not evaluate. No sin is committed of which he is unaware. No individual enters an auditorium of whom he fails to take notice. No tear is shed that escapes his eye. No pain is felt that his heart does not share. No decision is made that he does not judge. No song is sung that he does not hear.

Christ's Knowledge of Our Works

How does your knowledge of God's knowledge of you change your life? If it doesn't, it should. Consider how David prayed for his son Solomon:

> "And you, Solomon my son, know the God of your father and serve him with a whole heart and with a willing mind, for the LORD searches all hearts and understands every plan and thought" (1 Chron. 28:9a).

Or listen to what the author of Hebrews has to say on this point:

"And no creature is hidden from his sight, but all are naked and exposed to the eyes of him to whom we must give account" (Heb. 4:13).

So, if sin is strengthened by the illusion of secrecy, what better way to destroy its power than by meditating on the exhaustive and gloriously infallible knowledge that God has of us! Here again is the declaration of Jesus: *"I know your works!"* All the works of the Ephesian believers, and ours too, if done in God's grace and for God's glory, will never escape God's gaze. He sees and acknowledges and enjoys our "works" because they testify to his presence in our lives and his power in equipping us to do what is pleasing to him (cf. Heb. 13:20-21).

In a book (Revelation) written to strengthen faith, the emphasis on "works" or "deeds" is important. Works are the criterion of the genuineness of faith. Whoever has true faith, works. Whoever does not, has not. With that understood, note carefully what Jesus says about their works.

His commendation of the church in Ephesus involves three virtues (cf. 1 Thess. 1:3). Under the general category of "works" or "deeds" we find the first two virtues identified as "toil" and "patient endurance." The word translated "toil" looks to something beyond routine effort and focuses on exertion to the point of exhaustion. It refers to a spending of oneself in arduous labor. Apparently Ephesus was a busy, active church. It no doubt had all the "programs" and activities we normally associate with a church that is spiritual and passionate. They were truly diligent and conscientious.

The translation "patient endurance" renders one word in the original text. Jesus is perhaps referring to their diligence in bearing the persecution and hostility of an unbelieving society. Despite the temptations which assaulted them from every quarter, they stood unswerving and firm in their allegiance to Christ. Therefore, to every faithful servant of Christ who has labored in virtual obscurity in the nursery or in children's ministry, I say: "Jesus knows your works!" To every diligent believer who hands out the bulletin or cleans up in the kitchen or picks up trash following the Sunday service, I say: "Jesus knows your works!"

Our Lord is ever mindful of those deeds that are rarely seen and perhaps never acknowledged by other humans. That visit to the nursing home to pray for a lonely widow was for an audience of One. That hot meal prepared for an ailing friend was a fragrant aroma to God. The Lord Jesus may often be the only one who knows, but it is enough that he knows. And I remind you again, he most assuredly knows!

But to each and all of these I also say, "Why do you work? Is it for perks and praise? Is it in hope that your name will be mentioned from the pulpit? Or is your labor and toil and patient endurance pursued for the sake of his name? Is your commitment to the saints and your service for the kingdom motivated by your love for God?" I pray that it is.

Christ's Commendation of Our Orthodoxy

Jesus had already commended the Ephesians for their hard work and perseverance. He now turns his attention to their orthodoxy. Far from being blinded by love, they had 20/20 discernment! They hated evil. Period. No ifs, ands, or buts. Whatever form evil took, whether ethical or theological, they stood resolute in their opposition. No compromise. No cutting of corners. *Their love was revealed in their intolerance.* Unsanctified mercy had no place in the church at Ephesus. We would do well to learn from their example. This virtue (yes, it *is* a virtue) is described in verses 2 and 6. This was their most stellar achievement. No heretical concept could ever raise its ugly head in Ephesus without being decapitated by the swift stroke of biblical truth. The orthodoxy of the Ephesian church manifested itself in three ways:

First, according to verse 2a, they refused to bear with men of evil inclination. They firmly resisted those whose lives were outwardly licentious. We're not talking here about a momentary lapse or an inadvertent sin, but hardened and unrepentant iniquity. And the Ephesians were commendably intolerant of it.

Second, according to verse 2b, they tried and tested those who claimed to be apostles. "Evil men" and false "apostles" is a two-fold reference to the same group of individuals, the former a description of their disposition and the latter of their doctrine. The precise identity of these men is left unstated, but they were probably claiming to be part of the outer circle of apostles, beyond the twelve, which included James, Silas, and Barnabas (see Acts 14:14; 1 Cor. 15:7; Gal. 1:19; 1 Thess. 2:6). But note well: they rejected them only after "testing" them. This was no knee-jerk reaction. Yes, the Ephesians were strict, but they were fair. They listened, they studied, and above all, like the Bereans (cf. Acts 17:11), they tested the teaching of these men and weighed their claims on the scales of Scripture.

Third, according to verse 6, they joined Jesus in hating the deeds of the Nicolaitans (yes, Jesus does *hate* certain things, and so should we). Who were the Nicolaitans? They are mentioned again in 2:15 in the letter to Pergamum and by implication in 2:14 and 2:20-21. The name itself may be derived from two words which mean "victory" (*nikos*) and "people" (*laos*), thus the idea of their consumption or overpowering of the people. They were evidently licentious and antinomian and advocated an unhealthy compromise with pagan society and the idolatrous culture of Ephesus.

The Ephesian believers, however, were not duped. Nor were they so naïve as to believe that Christian charity can tolerate such false teaching. Note also the contrast: they "bear" trials and tribulations for Christ's sake (v. 3) but they cannot "bear" the company of these evil men (vv. 2,6). They endure persecution, but not perversion.

There are many lessons here, but one in particular stands out: *Jesus hates moral and theological compromise.* Any appeal to grace to justify sin is repugnant to our Lord. Any attempt to rationalize immorality by citing the "liberty" we have in Christ is abhorrent to him and must be to us. True Christian love is never expressed by the tolerance of wickedness, whether it be a matter of what one believes or how one behaves.

Much is being said today about the extent of the church's engagement with culture. To what degree should we be involved? How narrowly should we draw the boundary lines for what is permissible, on the one hand, and what is off-limits, on the other? There are no easy answers, but of one thing I'm sure. If "cultural relevancy" threatens in any way or degree to undermine your single-minded, whole-hearted devotion to Christ, end it. To the extent that being "in" the world drains you of the necessary strength to resist its temptations or diminishes the purity of your relationship with Christ, turn and walk away.

Christ's Commendation of Our Suffering

"I know you are enduring patiently," said Jesus, "and bearing up for my name's sake, and you have not grown weary" (Rev. 2:3). Let's be clear about their motivation, the goal in view of which they bore up under oppressive conditions: it was for the sake of Christ's name! That is to say, they endured with a view to making known, especially to their persecutors, that Jesus was a treasure of far greater worth than whatever physical or financial comfort their denial of him might bring.

In the case of the Ephesians, undoubtedly some suffered unto death while others experienced the blessing of deliverance. In both instances it was "for his name's sake." In dying, some declared, "Jesus is more precious than what I'm losing." In living, others declared, "Jesus is more precious than what I'm gaining." In both cases, Jesus is treasured above everything and thus magnified above all.

There's never an excuse for bad theology. We must continually strive to refine our thoughts and bring them into ever increasing conformity to God's Word. *But there comes a time when doctrine isn't enough!*

Stop! Before we go forward with another word, please do not draw unwarranted conclusions from that statement. Don't think for a moment that simply because there is *more* to being a Christian than right thinking that being a Christian is possible with *less* than right thinking. When I say there comes a time when doctrine isn't enough, that in no way justifies theological laxity, compromise, or the embracing of anti-intellectualism, as if the mind did not matter. What I'm saying is that Christianity necessarily entails *both* orthodox belief *and* obedient behavior. It's inconceivable to me that anyone would suggest that it *only* matters *what* we *believe* or, conversely, that it *only* matters *how* we *behave*. The two are inseparably wedded in the purposes of God and each withers in the absence of the other.

Christ's Call to Repentance

Having said that, and it was critically important that I say it, we can now proceed to observe that our Lord's notable commendation of the Ephesians is coupled with an equally incisive complaint: "But I have this against you, that you have abandoned the love you had at first" (Rev. 2:4).

There's no agreement among scholars of Revelation as to what "love" the Ephesians had "abandoned" (ESV) or "left" (NAS). The answer depends in part on how one understands and translates the word "first". Does it mean "first" in terms of time or chronology? That is the view embraced by the ESV, as they render it, "you have abandoned the love you had at first." The idea would be that this is a "love" they experienced immediately after their conversion and during the early days of their Christian life. Although the ESV rendering doesn't require it, the implication would be that the "love" they had abandoned was *brotherly* love, love for other Christians in the church.

Others argue that this love was "first" in the sense that it is the *most important* love that anyone can experience, that is to say, it is that *primary* love for the Lord Jesus Christ that comes before or takes precedence over all other loves in terms of value. This view is suggested by the NAS which translates, "you have left your first love." Surely, if the emphasis is on that "love" which is of preeminent importance, that "love" which must be pursued above all other loves, it is love for Jesus himself.

In his epistle to the Ephesians, written some thirty years earlier, Paul mentioned the fervency of their love for one another (1:15-16) and concluded the letter with a blessing on those "who love our Lord Jesus Christ with love incorruptible" (6:24). But now, these many years later, their zeal and passion had diminished. But which "love" had they now lost: love for one another or love for Jesus or perhaps love for both?

There are two contextual clues that I believe indicate the reference is primarily (but not exclusively) to "brotherly" love. First, how can it be that they've abandoned their love for Christ if in the immediately preceding verse (v. 3) Christ himself commends them for enduring patiently for his name's sake? The latter words imply, if not require, the devotion and affection and love for Jesus that would inspire them to suffer for the sake of promoting and praising his name. If they didn't fervently love Jesus, they wouldn't have endured patiently for his name's sake. And if their endurance wasn't motivated by this affection, Jesus would hardly have commended them for it.

A second clue comes from what follows in verse 5. There, as a repentant antidote, so to speak, to their diminishing love, Jesus commands them to "do the works you did at first" (v. 5). This would more likely suggest that their lost love was love for one another that can be rekindled by deeds of kindness and compassion and self-sacrifice (see Rom. 12:9-13; 1 John 3:11-18 and 4:7-21).

On the other hand, I'm not certain we have to choose between the two. Jesus may well have had both "loves" in view. That decrease in love for Christ issues in a loss of love for our fellow-Christian is self-evident. In other words, I think Jesus could as easily have said to the Ephesians: "How dare you claim to love me at the same time you close your heart to a brother or sister in the body. And when you do love one another, you demonstrate how much you love me [i.e., Jesus]" (see Heb. 6:10).

What we see in the church at Ephesus, therefore, was how their desire for orthodoxy and the exclusion of error had created a climate of suspicion and mistrust in which brotherly love could no longer flourish. Their eager pursuit of truth had to some degree soured their affections one for another. It's one thing not to "bear with those who are evil" (Rev. 2:2), but it's another thing altogether when that intolerance carries over to your relationship with other Christ-loving Christians!

Our Lord does not leave the Ephesians and their problem without a solution. Note the three terse commands of verse 5. Before doing so, however, observe what he does *not* recommend: he does not suggest that they become theologically lax, tolerant of error, or indifferent toward truth! In other words, don't try to cure one problem in a way that will create another.

So, then, here's his counsel. First, *"remember* ... from where you have fallen" (v. 5a). Here their love is pictured as a height from which they had descended. To remember is to reflect and meditate on the peak of brotherly affection they once enjoyed. Recall the former fervor and let the memory of its joys and satisfaction stir you again to mutual devotion. Second, *"repent"* (v. 5b). Simply put, stop ... then start. Stop the cold-hearted disregard for one another (and for Jesus) and start cultivating that affection you formerly had. Third, *"do"*. In particular, do "the works you did at first" (cf. Heb. 6:10).

How important was it that the Ephesians strove by God's grace to cultivate and sustain a passionate affection for both Christ and Christian? I'll let Jesus answer that question. If you don't repent, he solemnly warns, "I will come to you and remove your lampstand from its place" (Rev. 2:5). What this means is that failure to comply will lead to *the imminent termination of their influence or public witness as a body of believers* (cf. 11:3-7, 10; see also Mark 4:21; Luke 8:16). The "coming" of Jesus in verse 5 is not the Second Advent at the end of history but a "coming" in preliminary judgment and discipline of this church (cf. 2:16; the Second Advent, however, is probably in view in 2:25 and 3:11). It may even be that Jesus is threatening the end of this congregation's historical existence. I trust that such is enough to convince us all how important "love" is in the body of Christ!

Christ's Promise for Eternity

We must remember that the tree of life isn't an end in itself. We don't "conquer" or "overcome" (Rev. 2:7) simply to gain access to its fruit. The tree of life is a means to a higher and more exalted end, for it is good only so far as it sustains us to see and savor God. Its purpose is to nourish and support our eternal existence so that we might glorify God by enjoying him forever. The appeal of the tree of life and what its preserving power brings us is cited by Jesus as an incentive to "conquer" or "overcome." Like the conclusion to each of the seven letters, this is an exhortation to heed what has been said. The exhortation assumes a mixed audience, not all of whom will respond positively (cf. Matt. 13:9-17; Mark 4:9,23; Luke 8:8). When confronted with temptation or the pressure to abandon the faith, Jesus says loudly and clearly: "Bring to mind the tree of life! Meditate on its provision! For the one who conquers will eat of its blessed fruit forever!"

But surely something more is in mind than merely plucking fruit from an ordinary tree. There appear to be echoes here of the Garden of Eden, reminding us that paradise future is the redemptive consummation of paradise past.

There is something truly profound in the imagery found in verse 7 that may not be evident at first reading. This is where a knowledge of the cultural setting of the biblical text proves so rewarding. Colin Hemer contends that there was something analogous to the tree of life in the cult of Diana and the Temple in Ephesus dedicated to her that makes this promise especially relevant.[2]

In the first place, the reference to the "tree" (*xulon*) of life may actually be an allusion to the **cross** of Christ. In the book of Acts (5:30; 10:39; 13:29) explicit reference is made to the "tree" (*xulon*) on which Jesus was crucified (likewise in Galatians 3:13 and 1 Peter 2:24). (By the way, the Greek word for "cross" (*stauros*) never occurs in Revelation.)

Hemer also points to the fact that two passages in ancient literature describe the foundation of the Temple of Diana as a *tree shrine*! Inscriptions on coins from that era indicate that the tree, together with the bee and the stag, were distinctively associated

---

2. Colin J. Hemer, *The Letters to the Seven Churches of Asia in Their Local Setting* (Sheffield: JSOT Press, 1986), 41-55.

with Diana of Ephesus. In addition, the Temple was famous as a place of refuge or asylum for fleeing criminals. What makes this significant is that the word used to describe their experience is the same term used throughout the New Testament for our "salvation," (*sōtēria*)!

The contrasts are both stunning and encouraging. For the Ephesian believers, "the cross [the tree of life] was the place of refuge for the repentant sinner in contrast with the tree [in Diana's temple] which marked the asylum for the unrepentant criminal."[3] Diana's so-called "tree" of refuge gave the criminal immunity and license to continue his life of rebellion and crime. Christ's "tree" of refuge, on the other hand, grants the repentant sinner eternal forgiveness and the power of the Spirit to pursue holiness.

The so-called "salvation" of the fleeing criminal actually corrupted the city of Ephesus by granting freedom to the wicked to continue in their perverse behavior. When the Ephesian Christians heard Jesus speak this promise to them in Revelation 2:7, they were able to appreciate in a way that we cannot the concept of an eternal city pervaded and governed by the glory of God. For of *that* city, the New Jerusalem, not this-worldly Ephesus or any other city, it is said that "nothing unclean will ever enter it, nor anyone who does what is detestable or false, but only those who are written in the Lamb's book of life" (Rev. 21:27).

Oh, blessed cross, the only tree that truly brings life!

---

3. Ibid., 55.

Chapter Four

Seeing the "So That" in Suffering

(Revelation 2:8-11)

A straight sail from the island of Patmos of approximately fifty miles brings one to the port of Ephesus at the mouth of the river Cayster. Traveling up coast some thirty-five miles almost due north of Ephesus is the city of Smyrna (population of about 100,000). It is the only one of the seven cities still in existence today (modern Izmir in western Turkey).

Smyrna was a proud and beautiful city and regarded itself as the "pride of Asia." The people of Smyrna were quite sensitive to the rivalry with Ephesus for recognition as the most splendid city of Asia Minor. Of the seven churches, only Smyrna and Philadelphia receive no complaint from the Lord. There is only commendation, encouragement, and a promise of eternal life to the one who overcomes. Perhaps the reason there is no cause for complaint is that *Smyrna was a suffering church*. The letter is devoted almost exclusively to an account of their past and present trials, a warning of yet more persecution to come, and a strengthening word of encouragement from the One who knows all too well the pain of scorn and death. Why did the church in Smyrna suffer? The answer is two-fold.

First, Smyrna was famous for its patriotic loyalty to the empire and its emperor. In A.D. 29 all Asian cities were competing for the coveted favor of erecting a temple in honor of Emperor Tiberius.

Smyrna won! It was a city fervent with emperor worship. The civil authorities didn't care so much that Christians worshiped Jesus, so long as they also worshiped the emperor. So when the believers in Smyrna refused to pay religious homage by sprinkling incense on the fire which burned before the emperor's bust, it no doubt fanned the flames of hostility against them. It was dangerous to be a faithful Christian in Smyrna!

Second, great antagonism existed within the Jewish community toward the church. This no doubt stemmed in part from their conviction that to worship a crucified carpenter from Nazareth was foolishness. Worse still, it was blasphemy (see especially 1 Corinthians 1:18-25). There was also undoubtedly a measure of bitterness at the loss of so many from their ranks to the new faith. The Jews were known to inform the authorities of Christian activities, the latter being perceived as treason. Jewish opposition to the church at Smyrna is the focus of verse 9 where Jesus refers to those "who say that they are Jews and are not, but are a synagogue of Satan." Clearly, in one sense, these people *are* Jews, the physical descendants of Abraham, Isaac, and Jacob, who met regularly in the synagogue to worship. Yet, in another sense, i.e., inwardly, and spiritually, they are *not* Jews, having rejected Jesus and now persecuting and slandering his people.

But if they are false Jews, who, then, are the true Jews? If they are a synagogue of Satan, who, then, constitute the synagogue of God? John does not provide an explicit answer, but the implication seems clear. A "true Jew" is a man or woman, regardless of ethnicity, who has embraced in faith Jesus as Messiah. In Romans 2:28-29 and again in Philippians 3:3, Paul described it this way:

> "For no one is a Jew who is merely one outwardly, nor is circumcision outward and physical. But a Jew is one inwardly, and circumcision is a matter of the heart, by the Spirit, not by the letter" (Rom. 2:28-29).

> "For we are the circumcision, who worship by the Spirit of God and glory in Christ Jesus and put no confidence in the flesh" (Phil. 3:3).

I need to pause here and make a parenthetical comment. There is simply and without qualification no place whatsoever in the Christian faith for any degree of anti-Semitism! Jesus was a Jew. All twelve of the apostles were Jews. The entire Bible, except for the gospel of Luke and the book of Acts, was written by Jews. How much did the Apostle Paul love the Jewish people? "For I could wish that I myself were accursed and cut off from Christ for the sake of my brothers, my kinsman according to the flesh" (Rom. 9:3). He writes in Romans 10:1, "my heart's desire and prayer to God for them is that they may be saved." There is no place in the Christian's heart or in the church of Jesus Christ for Jewish jokes or stereotypes or ridicule.

Sadly, some have appealed to texts like Revelation 2:9-10 to justify anti-Semitism. It is true that some Jews in Smyrna in the first century had been deceived by Satan and were being used by him to oppress and persecute Christians. Many of the Jewish leaders opposed and persecuted Jesus and conspired with Rome to crucify him. But it wasn't true of all Jewish people. And let us never forget that all ethnic groups throughout history have at one time or another been guilty of persecuting Christians. Our attitude toward Jews who reject Jesus as the Messiah must be the same as it is toward anyone of any ethnicity who rejects Jesus: pray for them, love them, and make whatever sacrifice you can to make known to them the love that Jesus has for all sinners.

We live in a day when we Christians will be accused of many things: we are anti-Semitic (because we insist on faith in Jesus as Messiah to be saved), anti-choice (because we oppose abortion), anti-gay (because we won't affirm homosexual intercourse), anti-woman (because we believe in a male only eldership in the local church), and anti-intellectual (because we don't embrace biological evolution). They will accuse us of being unloving, narrow-minded, intolerant bigots because we believe in the reality of something called the "second death" (i.e., hell; verse 11) and that the only way of escape from it is through faith in Jesus Christ. And our response to all such anti-Christian rhetoric is to love them and pray for them and tell them ever more fervently and humbly about eternal life that can be found in Jesus.

The Relationship between Suffering and Sanctification

What is of paramount importance, however, is that we see *the relationship between suffering and sanctity*. No one put it better or more to the point than Peter in his first epistle: "In this you rejoice, though now for a little while, if necessary, you have been grieved by various trials, so that the tested genuineness of your faith – more precious than gold that perishes though it is tested by fire – may be found to result in praise and glory and honor at the revelation of Jesus Christ" (1 Pet. 1:6-7).

This undoubtedly was true of the church at Smyrna. Trials are grievous, says Peter. Let no one pretend they are anything less than painful and distressing. But there is always a divine design in our suffering that, when seen and embraced, energizes the heart to persevere. Observe Peter's *"so that"* in verse 7a above. Praise be to God: there is always a "so that" in our suffering, always a higher spiritual end in view for the sake of which God orchestrates our troubles and trials.

Could this possibly be why the church in Smyrna escaped rebuke and was spared the threat of divine discipline addressed to the Ephesians? Had the "genuineness" of their "faith" been proven in (indeed, because of) the fire of affliction? Had the spurious and surface dimensions of their trust in God been burned away, leaving their faith as pure as gold (at least, as pure as faith can be this side of heaven)? Yes.

Suffering isn't designed by God to destroy our faith but to intensify it. That will never happen, however, if we fail to look beyond the pain to the purpose of our loving heavenly Father. His design is to knock out from underneath us every false prop so that we might rely wholly on him. His aim is to create in us such desperation that we have nowhere else to look but to his promises and abiding presence.

There is, then, an alternative to cratering under the weight of distress. We need not yield either to bitterness, because things haven't gone our way, or to doubt, because we can't figure out God's ways, or to anger, because we feel abandoned. Rather, we can by his grace strive to see the "so that" in his mysterious and providential mercies. And even when we can't see it, trust him anyway!

Suffering comes in many forms and in varying degrees, as the Christians in Smyrna would no doubt testify. But regardless of how it manifests itself, suffering tends to evoke one of two reactions in the soul of the Christian: dependency or disillusionment. One example of the former is found in the Apostle Paul's reaction to a life-threatening incident that brought him to the brink of despair. Rather than yielding to *disillusionment with God* he was driven to *dependency upon him*. The entire scenario, he later said, was "to make us rely not on ourselves but on God who raises the dead" (2 Cor. 1:9). For many, however, disillusionment triumphs over dependency, often leading to a crippling bitterness that threatens both our enjoyment in life and our effectiveness in ministry.

The reason for this, at least in part, is that suffering has a disorienting effect on the soul. What I mean is that pain, whether physical or emotional or both, contributes to a loss of perspective. We can see little else but the problem and its disruptive impact on every sphere of life. We feel lost and directionless, not knowing how to extricate ourselves from the mess we're in. There's no spiritual compass, so to speak, that points us to God and perhaps to some explanation for why we have to endure such unspeakable hurt.

This is why many who suffer experience deep disillusionment with God. "Doesn't he know what is happening? Doesn't he care? And if he does, why doesn't he do something about it? Maybe he's simply too busy or too weak." In any case, they feel lost at sea, adrift and carried hopelessly beyond the safety of the shore by wave after wave of disappointment and pain and shattered dreams and loss of friends and, well, whatever else it is that simply won't go away. To make sense of what is happening we need a point of reference, a "north star", as it were, to guide us back home and restore a measure of hope.

So how did the Smyrnean Christians pull through, given all they were facing? I'll return to the nature and extent of their suffering in a moment, but it surely entailed at least four dimensions. First, they were in the throes of "tribulation" and "poverty" (Rev. 2:9). These are so inextricably linked in the experience of the Christians in Smyrna that I list them as one. Second, they were being slandered (2:9). Third, some of them were about to be imprisoned for their faith (2:10a). Fourth, some even faced martyrdom (2:10b).

My immediate concern is with how the Smyrneans avoided disillusionment, or better still, how Jesus himself proposed that they remain faithful and utterly dependent on God. We know they resisted the temptation to fall into despair or bitterness, but how? Part of the answer is found in the opening words of Jesus in his letter to them. In particular, it's found in how he is identified: "And to the angel of the church in Smyrna write: 'The words of the first and the last, who died and came to life'" (2:8).

This description of Jesus is taken from the portrayal of him in Revelation 1:18. But what possible difference could it make in their lives (or in ours) that Jesus is "the first and the last"? How does knowledge of that truth counteract the discombobulating effects of suffering? At first glance, knowing this about Jesus seems utterly irrelevant in the face of constant pain or financial loss or the breakdown of intimate relationships or, worst of all, the ominous prospect of physical death itself. In fact, however, I suggest that nothing could more readily overcome disillusionment than knowledge of this truth. As I said earlier, suffering tends to bring disorientation to our hearts, a sense of being alone and lost and without a point of reference. Prolonged suffering breeds a feeling of chaos and loss of control. We ask: "Will I ever emerge from this dark tunnel? Is there an end in view? A purpose? Is there anything more ultimate than my own immediate discomfort that might enable me to persevere?"

Yes! In saying that he is the "first and the last" Jesus is affirming his comprehensive control over all of history, over every event that transpires within the parameters established by the terms "first" and "last." As the one who is *first*, he is the source of all things. Nothing preceded him that might account for your suffering or suggest that it is outside the boundaries of his sovereign sway. As the *last* he is the one toward whom all things are moving, the goal for which they exist, and the final explanation for all that is and occurs. They can look at their plight, feel their pain, calculate their losses, and still say: "But our Lord is the One who created it all, and he is the One for whom it is all being sustained and directed. *My condition is not beyond the scope of his authority. He does have jurisdiction!* Furthermore, if he is the 'last', if he is the one who stands as much on the back side of history as he did on the front end, then I know that what I'm enduring for his sake is not without purpose or fruit."

The believers in Smyrna were themselves facing death. Martyrdom was a very real possibility (see Rev. 2:10). They needed to be reassured that physical death was nothing to fear, that it marked not the end but the beginning of true life, and that no matter how severe the suffering they would *never* taste the "second death" (2:11) that awaits those who deny Jesus. In 2:10 he declares, "Do not fear what you are about to suffer." This word of reassurance finds its basis in the fact that Jesus has conquered both sin and death. The believer need not fear either suffering or martyrdom, for Jesus has endured both and emerged victorious, and we are inseparably and eternally "in him"! Suffering is a given, an inescapable fact of life for the Christian. Its effects, on the other hand, are dependent on us. May God graciously energize our souls and enlighten our hearts that we, through the fog of anguish and disappointment, might see the light of *his* sovereignty, the one who is First and Last, who has died and come to life!

The Nature of their Suffering

Jesus singles out four dimensions of the suffering endured by the Smyrneans. Let's look briefly at each, not out of academic curiosity, but in order to ask ourselves: "Is my faith such that it would survive, indeed thrive, under such threats?"

First, reference is made in Revelation 2:9a to their "tribulation" and "poverty". But why were these believers "poor" in a city as prosperous as Smyrna? Perhaps they were from the lower ranks of society, economically speaking. It's possible they had exceeded their means in generous giving to others. But this would not explain why their poverty is part of their tribulation, and the association of the two words here indicates they are linked. In some measure the poverty was due to their voluntary exclusion from the many trade guilds in Smyrna, seedbeds of vice, immorality, and unscrupulous business dealings. In addition, they probably struggled to find employment precisely because they were Christians. Most likely, however, as Hebrews 10:34 indicates, their homes and property had been looted and pillaged. Clearly, it is not always financially lucrative to be a Christian.

Material gain was most assuredly not the ambition of the Smyrneans! I'm confident that, like those believers in Hebrews 10, they "joyfully accepted the plundering" of their "property," knowing that they "had a better possession and an abiding one" (v. 34). In the case of the Christians at Smyrna, they had "riches" their enemies couldn't understand, "wealth" that couldn't be stolen, "possessions" that weren't vulnerable to theft or rust or devaluation or falling stock prices. Indeed, despite their material poverty, Jesus declares that they are "rich" (Rev. 2:9).

Perhaps we should pause quietly and ask ourselves, "How do I measure real wealth? Is the treasure of knowing Jesus Christ of sufficient value that I regard myself as incomparably rich although I own little? If I were to lose everything but him, would I still consider myself blessed?"

Second, they were repeatedly slandered (v. 9a). Jesus doesn't specify the nature of this slander (lit., blasphemy), but I assume it included attacks on their character, mockery of their beliefs ("You put your trust in a crucified carpenter! Ha!"), and most of all hateful indignities heaped on their Lord.

Third, we read that some of them would be thrown into "prison" (v. 10). We must remember that imprisonment in Roman communities like Smyrna wasn't technically considered a punishment. Prisons were used for one of three reasons: (1) to compel and coerce obedience to the order of a magistrate; (2) to keep the accused confined pending the trial date; or (3) to detain the guilty until the time of execution. The words "unto death" (v. 10b) indicate that the third is in view.

There are several options to interpreting the meaning of "ten days" of "tribulation". Some say it means literally ten days and leave it at that. Another view is that it simply refers to a short, limited period of time, while others suggest that it points to extreme or complete tribulation. It's possible that Jesus had Daniel 1:12-15 in mind where the "testing" of Daniel and his three friends is said to be for "ten days".

Fourth, they were facing martyrdom itself. There's simply no escaping the fact that some of them would die. Yet Jesus does nothing to prevent it. He doesn't alleviate their poverty nor publicly vindicate his people in the face of those who hurled their indignant slander. And when Satan moves to incite their imprisonment and eventual execution, *Jesus chooses not to intervene*. There are numerous instances in biblical days and in the history of the church when it was otherwise (see Heb. 11:32-34). But not always (see Heb. 11:35-38).

Perhaps when we encounter such texts our question should be of a different sort. Instead of asking, "Why do Christians suffer persecution?" we ought to inquire, "Why do Christians *not* suffer persecution?" John Stott put it pointedly: "The ugly truth is that we tend to avoid suffering by compromise. Our moral standards are often not noticeably higher than the standards of the world. Our lives do not challenge and rebuke unbelievers by their integrity or purity or love. *The world sees in us nothing to hate*."[1]

Faith Sustained while Suffering

Jesus calls for our faithfulness in such circumstances no less than he called for theirs (v. 10). But it's not automatic. Endurance doesn't "just happen". Faithfulness is the fruit of faith. In other words, there are truths we must embrace if we are to endure. Unbelief leads to bitterness and despair. Although Jesus chose not to intervene and deliver the Smyrneans from suffering, he by no means abandoned

---

1. Stott, *What Christ Thinks of the Church*, 43.

them. Look with me again at his words of counsel, for in them is the power to persevere. There are three things to note.

First, I've already had occasion to mention how his knowledge of our situation is a source of strength ("I know your tribulation and your poverty," v. 9a). Our knowledge of his knowledge of us is a powerful incentive to remain faithful when the world, flesh, and the devil conspire to yell "Quit!" But there's more.

Second, observe closely that there are *divinely imposed limits* on how far Satan can go in his efforts to destroy us. For the Christians at Smyrna, not unlike the situation with Job, the enemy is given a long leash. But he can only go as far as God permits. Satan is unable to act outside the parameters established by the will of his Creator. In this case, he will instigate their incarceration, but only for "ten days" (v. 10). "Wait a minute! How can you say that Satan is limited in what he can do if some of those he throws into prison end up getting killed?" That's a good question. Here's my answer.

Just as there was a divinely imposed limitation on what Satan could perpetrate, there was a divinely ordained purpose for it: to *"test"* them (v. 10). In giving them over to the devil for imprisonment and, for some, death, God had not forsaken his people. This was not a sign of his disdain or rejection, but a means by which to test and try and refine and purify their trust in Christ. I find it incredibly instructive that what Satan intended for their destruction, God designed for their spiritual growth! Satan's intent was to undermine their faith, not to "test" it. Yet God orchestrated the entire scenario as a way of honing and stabilizing and solidifying the faith of the church in Smyrna.

The third encouraging thing for us to note is that *the death Satan inflicts issues in life for the believer*! In verse 10b Jesus encourages the Smyrneans to remain faithful unto (physical) death and he will give them "the crown of life." Jesus reminds them of this because he knows that the power to persevere comes from a vibrant faith in the certainty of God's promised reward. Those who do not love "their lives even unto death" (Rev. 12:11) are granted a "life" that infinitely transcends anything this earthly existence could ever afford. Jesus does not call for faithfulness unto death without reminding us that there awaits us in the future a quality and depth of true and unending life that far outweighs whatever sacrifice is made in the present.

This is precisely the point Paul made in 2 Corinthians 4:16-18. He refused to "lose heart" because he knew that "this slight momentary affliction is preparing for us an eternal weight of glory beyond all comparison, as we look not to the things that are seen but to the things that are unseen. For the things that are seen are transient, but the things that are unseen are eternal." Among the countless "unseen things" on which Paul fixed his faith was undoubtedly the certainty of "the crown of life" given to all who know Jesus. There is power to persevere in the promise of reward. We must intentionally lay hold of the future and impose it on the present.

No Harm from the Second Death

So, I want to briefly address the subject of hell. That's right, hell. Let's pause for a moment and give thanks that those who know and love Jesus "will not be hurt by the second death."

The "second death" is mentioned three other times in Revelation, each of which reinforces the fact that this is Jesus' (and John's) way of referring to *eternal punishment in the lake of fire*. We read in Revelation 20:6, "Blessed and holy is the one who shares in the first resurrection! Over such the second death has no power, but they will be priests of God and of Christ, and they will reign with him for a thousand years." Later in the same chapter (20:14), we are told that "Death and Hades were thrown into the lake of fire. This is the second death, the lake of fire." Finally, in Revelation 21:8 we read, "But as for the cowardly, the faithless, the detestable, as for murderers, the sexually immoral, sorcerers, idolaters, and all liars, their portion will be in the lake that burns with fire and sulfur, which is the second death."

Clearly, then, the "second death" is the lake of fire, the place of eternal torment for those who do not know and love our Lord Jesus Christ. The "first death" would be physical death, the death that Jesus said some in Smyrna would suffer because of their faith in him. The point of his promise, then, is this: no matter how much you may endure physically in the present, you will never suffer spiritually in the future. Therefore, be faithful if you should be called on to die now, for you will never die then! The contrasts couldn't be more vivid. Those who know and love Jesus and remain faithful to him will be granted the "crown of life" (v. 10). They will never, by no means ever (such is the literal force of the double negative in Greek), taste the "second death" (v. 11).

Now, hear me well. There is nothing of which I am more deserving than the second death! There is nothing more fitting, more just, more righteous than that I should suffer forever in the lake of fire. And the only reason why I won't do so is that Jesus has endured in himself the judgment it entails. Jesus has exhausted in his own person the wrath of God that I otherwise would have faced in the lake of fire.

As I reflect on that reality, I can't help but feel complete dismay at those who reject penal substitutionary atonement, or flippantly (and blasphemously) dismiss it as "cosmic child abuse". What hope have we for deliverance from the "second death" if not the suffering of its pains, in our place, by the Son of God? If I receive the "crown of life", which I don't deserve, in place of the "lake of fire", which I do deserve, it can only be for one reason: Jesus Christ, by a marvelous and merciful exchange, has died that I might live, has suffered that I might be set free, has for me faced and felt the wrath of God and absorbed it in himself.

Many today deny that Jesus ever believed in or taught, much less endured in his own person, the reality of hell's torments. What "gospel," then, can they preach? Of what does the "good news" consist if not that Jesus has died, the just for the unjust, having "redeemed us from the curse of the law by becoming a curse for us" (Gal. 3:13)?

As for the Christians in Smyrna, no sweeter words were ever spoken than these. Tribulation was tolerable, knowing that the "second death" died in the death of Jesus. Slander and imprisonment, yes, even martyrdom, were but "slight momentary affliction" when compared with the "eternal weight of glory" (2 Cor. 4:17) that is ours because Jesus died and rose again on our behalf.

Yes, thinking about hell and the "second death" has immense practical benefits! In his famous Resolutions, Jonathan Edwards put it succinctly: "Resolved, when I feel pain, to think of the pains of martyrdom, and of hell."[2]

It is remarkable how tolerable otherwise intolerable things become when we see them in the light of the "second death"! Think often, then, of the pains of hell. Think often of the lake of fire. It puts mere earthly pain in perspective. It puts "tribulation" and "poverty" and "slander" and "imprisonment" and even "death" itself in their proper place. The collective discomfort of all such temporal experience is nothing in comparison with the eternal torment of the "second death" in the "lake of fire."

The one who conquers, said Jesus, "will not be hurt by the second death." Not even when Satan viciously accuses me of sins we all know I've committed. *No, never, by no means ever* will I be hurt by the second death. Not even when others remind me of how sinful I still am, falling short of the very standards I loudly preach and proclaim? *No, never, by no means ever* will I be hurt by the second death. Not even when my own soul screams in contempt at the depravity of my heart. *No, never, by no means ever* will I be hurt by the second death. And that for one reason only: Jesus, in unfathomable mercy and grace, has suffered hurt by it in my place. So, be faithful, Christian man or woman. Rejoice, O child of God. And give thanks that you will *never, by no means ever*, suffer harm from the "second death"!

---

2. Jonathan Edwards, *Resolutions* (no. 10), in *A Jonathan Edwards Reader*, edited by John E. Smith, Harry S. Stout, and Kenneth P. Minkema (New Haven: Yale University Press, 1995), 275.

Chapter Five

God's People in Satan's City

(Revelation 2:12-17)

Ann and I lived in Kansas City, Missouri, known as "The City of Fountains." Before that, we lived near Chicago, "The Windy City". Paris, France, is called "The City of Lights" and New York is often described as "The City that Never Sleeps". We have friends who live in Las Vegas, infamously (but justifiably) referred to as "Sin City", and the list could go on.

So what's the point? Simply this: from what Jesus says in his letter to the church in Pergamum, the Christians there may well be described as living in *"Satan's City"*! "I know where you dwell," said Jesus, "where Satan's throne is" (Rev. 2:13a). Later in the same verse he refers to Pergamum as the place "where Satan dwells" (Rev. 2:13b).

Pergamum was one of the largest cities in the ancient world, with a population of about 190,000. It was the capital city of the Roman province of Asia and retained this honor well into the second century. But it wasn't primarily for either political or economic achievements that Pergamum was famous, but for religion. Pergamum was the center of worship for at least four of the most important pagan cults of the day.

Upon entering the city one couldn't help but notice the gigantic altar of Zeus erected on a huge platform some eight hundred feet above the city, looking down on its inhabitants like a great vulture hovering over its prey. Many have sought to identify "Satan's seat" or "throne" (v. 13) with this altar. Amazingly, a reconstructed form of this altar is on display in the Pergamum Museum in Berlin (which I had the privilege [?] of visiting in 1994)!

Pergamum was also the center for the worship of Athene and Dionysus. However, the most distinctive and celebrated cult of all was dedicated to the worship of Asclepios (or Aesculapius). Often referred to as "Savior" (*sōtēr*) in Greek mythology, Asclepios was the son of Apollo and was thought to have been the very first physician. You may recall that the symbol adopted by the U.S. Department of Health, Education, and Welfare (renamed The Department of Health and Human Services in 1979) is the staff of Asclepios ... with a serpent coiled around it!

But beyond the worship directed at these pagan deities was the fact that Pergamum was the acknowledged center in Asia Minor for the imperial cult of Caesar. In 29 B.C. this city received permission to build and dedicate a temple to Augustus, three years before Smyrna was granted a similar privilege. Perhaps more than any of the other six cities, the people of Pergamum were devoted to the worship of Caesar.

Were it not for the fact that "greater" is he who is in us "than he who is in the world" (1 John 4:4b), it would be frightening to hear that Pergamum is "where Satan dwells" (Rev. 2:13b). Although this may simply be synonymous with "Satan's throne" (v. 13a), it's possible that this is another way of saying that evil was present in Pergamum in a particularly powerful and concentrated way. Could it be that Satan had in some sense made Pergamum the focus of his earthly base of operation?

"I Know Where You Dwell"

To those believers immersed in an explicitly Satanic atmosphere of idolatry and wickedness, Jesus says: "I know where you dwell!" To a people struggling by grace to remain faithful when those around them revel in faithlessness, Jesus says: "I know where you dwell!" To a church that must, at times, have felt abandoned and alone and given over to the enemy, Jesus says: "I know where you dwell!"

We have already seen that our Lord "knows" the churches, for he walks among them (Rev. 2:1). In this letter, however, Jesus declares that his knowledge extends not only to the works that Christians do (as in Ephesus) and to the suffering they endure (as in Smyrna) but to the environment in which they live. "I know where you dwell." Jesus is fully aware of the pagan surroundings and pressures his people face.

The believers at Pergamum would often remind themselves that no matter how hard it was to be a Christian there, no matter how intense the temptation to abandon Christ and serve another "god", Jesus knew where they lived, he knew what they faced on a daily basis, he knew every intimate detail of a life pursued in a city that hated God.

Jesus knows where you dwell! Whether you live in an isolated mid-western town of 5,000 or feel lost in a metropolis of 5,000,000, Jesus knows where you live! He knows the temptations you face, the pressures you feel, the fear that perhaps you've been misplaced or marginalized or lost in the shuffle of life and the countless concerns that our Lord must deal with on a daily basis. Fear not! Jesus knows where you dwell!

You haven't been abandoned, far less ignored. Your life and ministry are as important to Jesus as that of any Christian in any church in any city in any country. You may feel as if our community is a modern Pergamum, devoted to idolatry and immorality and the public ridicule of our glorious Savior. But of this you can rest assured: Jesus has sovereignly and strategically placed us here as his witnesses, to hold forth his name and to display his glory. That is why, contrary to what we read in verse 13, every city is Christ's City!

The letter to the church at Pergamum consists of "the words of him who has the sharp two-edged sword" (Rev. 2:12). When we hear or read of someone who has a "sharp two-edged sword" we typically envision it in his hand, to be wielded either in defense against an on-coming attack or used offensively to slay his enemies. But in the case of Jesus, the sword proceeds from his mouth! Although the "mouth" of our Lord isn't explicitly mentioned in

Revelation 2:12, the description of him here is taken from the vision given to John in Revelation 1:16 where we read, "In his right hand he held seven stars, from his mouth came a sharp two-edged sword, and his face was like the sun shining in full strength" (1:16; cf. 19:15, 21).

This is clearly figurative language, for not even the crassest literalist would argue that there is a literal sword proceeding out of the literal mouth of Jesus. But to say it is figurative is not in any way to diminish the very real point that the "words" of Jesus are an infinitely powerful force not only in the defense and building up of his people but also in the judgment and destruction of his enemies.

The reference to a "sword" in this passage (Rev. 2:12) carried special significance for the Christians in Pergamum, given the fact that the sword was the symbol of the Roman proconsul's total sovereignty "over every area of life, especially to execute enemies of the state (called *ius gladii*),... This tells the church that it is the exalted Christ, not Roman officials, who is the true judge. The ultimate power belongs to God, and nothing the pagans can do will change that."[1]

The church in Pergamum was in desperate need of the power of Christ's words. On the one hand, they were sorely tempted to abandon the faith. Death had already come to one of their number (see 2:13) and others no doubt faced a similar fate. Christ's words were designed to strengthen their resolve and satisfy their souls lest they be drawn to another lover.

Whereas it is true that "the whole world lies in the power of the evil one" (1 John 5:19b), Pergamum was especially vulnerable to Satan's influence. In some sense, as previously noted, this was his city. Pergamum was the center of his authority, the place of his throne, the focal point of his activity and interests. There must have been an almost tangible sense of his presence, a heaviness in the air, an oppressive spiritual atmosphere that was unmistakable and inescapable.

---

1. Grant Osborne, *Revelation,* Baker Exegetical Commentary on the New Testament (Grand Rapids: Baker, 2002), 140.

There have been times and places when I was keenly aware of an extraordinary spiritual darkness, all physical evidence to the contrary. In other words, a city, for example, can be outwardly prosperous, socially vibrant, and culturally sophisticated, yet all the while an underlying demonic energy animates and defiles its life and ethos. We shouldn't be surprised that our enemy might choose to concentrate his efforts in particular geographical areas or at unique and critical moments in history. It's all part of his strategy to undermine Christian faith and promote the kingdom of darkness.

Words of Commendation

Our Lord's commendation of the Christians in Pergamum comes in two forms. He first applauds them for continuing to "hold fast" his "name", i.e., his identity as God incarnate and his redemptive work at Calvary, in spite of the presence of Satan's throne (Rev. 2:13a).

How often do we today, in public, speak in a hushed whisper when the name of Jesus is mentioned? What accounts for this? Could it be shame or embarrassment, or the prospect of "losing face"? I think it more likely that silence is driven by our fear of what might happen should those around us detect that we are Christians. It's remarkable, actually, given the fact that we face no persecution to speak of, no official resistance from our government. Yet, the Christians at Pergamum knew that a vocal public witness to the name of Jesus guaranteed precisely that, and worse.

I say worse because of what we read in the second half of verse 13. Not only were they presently holding forth a public testimony of the name of Jesus, in the past they had refused to deny their faith in spite of the martyrdom of an outspoken Christian named Antipas. Jesus commends them because they "did not deny my faith even in the days of Antipas my faithful witness, who was killed among you, where Satan dwells" (Rev. 2:13b).

An important point to note is that the believers in Pergamum held fast to their faith "even in the days of Antipas". The ESV translates it this way, rightly so in my opinion, to highlight the fact that there were life-threatening circumstances that might have made their silence a matter of prudence. Who could have blamed them, from a worldly perspective, that is, had they chosen to keep their mouths shut, or perhaps even deny Jesus altogether? But no, they didn't let the prospect of their own martyrdom close their mouths or diminish their commitment or mollify their zeal. What they are specifically said not to have denied is "the faith of me." This odd phrase should probably be rendered "faith in me", pointing to their unyielding and sturdy confidence in Jesus and the truth of his gospel.

Words of Complaint

However, as noted earlier, there was something wrong in Pergamum. Notwithstanding their remarkable devotion to the Lord, they had become overly tolerant of others whose immorality threatened to undermine the purity of the church. If the Ephesian church was guilty of elevating truth above love, the church at Pergamum had elevated love above truth. Their commitment to peace and tolerance had apparently degenerated into a weak sentimentality that now posed both a serious ethical and theological threat.

Whereas they had maintained their own theological convictions they were, at the same time, tolerating in their fellowship certain false prophets who advocated licentious behavior, ostensibly in the name of Christian freedom (see vv. 14-15). Although they had not themselves denied the faith, they had become inexplicably lax toward falsehood in the assembly and had endured the presence and teaching of ethical error. For this, Jesus severely rebukes them.

This is a truly remarkable, indeed puzzling, situation. They were devoted to the truth of who Christ is and the essentials of the gospel message. They were even willing to die for it! But they fudged when it came to dealing with those in the church who compromised the ethical implications of that very gospel. It's almost as if they said, "I personally will never back down, even if it means my death. On the other hand, perhaps we need to be less rigid and a bit more tolerant when it comes to those who draw different conclusions about the practical implications of the saving grace of our Lord."

"NO!" said Jesus. This is horribly inconsistent and must be immediately and firmly addressed (v. 16). There's nothing to indicate why they had adopted this posture. It certainly wasn't out of fear. Perhaps they reckoned that such ethical and theological deviations were of little consequence or that they could more easily win over the dissidents by declining to rock the ecclesiological boat. Whatever the case, they were misguided in granting them such a wide berth, and must act swiftly to put things right. The bottom line is this: sometimes peace and love come at too high a price!

Although grace is surely amazing, it is also subject to distortion, especially by those who use it to excuse loose and licentious behavior (see Galatians 5:13; Jude 4). The justification comes in a variety of forms: "If all my sins have been forgiven, they are now of little consequence." "If I can't be saved by works, I need not be concerned with their absence in my life." "If Jesus has set me free, I'm obligated to no law or leader." "Because I'm free in Christ, I can participate in the idolatrous culture of my city without fear of contamination."

According to Revelation 2:6, the Ephesians "hated" the work of the Nicolaitans and refused to tolerate their pernicious behavior. The Pergamemes, on the other hand, had welcomed them into the fellowship of the church and given them freedom to propagate their destructive ways. There's no indication these false teachers had openly denied the "name" to which the others at Pergamum held fast. In other words, I doubt if the error of the Nicolaitans was a denial of the incarnation of Christ, his propitiatory work on the cross, or his bodily resurrection. Rather, as noted above, they were guilty of turning the grace of God into licentiousness.

Jesus describes them as holding to "the teaching of Balaam, who taught Balak to put a stumbling block before the sons of Israel, so that they might eat food sacrificed to idols and practice sexual immorality. So also you have some who hold the teaching of the Nicolaitans" (Rev. 2:14-15).

We read about Balaam in Numbers 22–24. Balak, King of Moab, had solicited Balaam to curse the children of Israel who were preparing to cross over into the promised land. But God intervened. Every time Balaam spoke, words of blessing came forth. Moved by greed for the reward Balak offered him, Balaam advised Balak that Moabite women should seduce the men of Israel by inviting them to partake in their idolatrous feasts (which invariably led to sexual immorality). Balaam knew that this would provoke the judgment of God against his people (which is precisely what happened).

What Balaam was to the children of Israel in the Old Testament, the Nicolaitans were to the church of Jesus Christ in the New. Balaam is a prototype of those who promote compromise with the world in idolatry and immorality (see also Jude 11 and 2 Peter 2:15). The Nicolaitans had dared to insinuate that freedom in Christ granted them a blank check to sin. The fault of the Pergamemes was not so much that they had followed this pernicious teaching but that they had allowed it to be vocalized in the congregation. This matter of indifference to the licentiousness of the Nicolaitans was of grave concern to the risen Lord.

What was the precise nature of their sin? They put a stumbling block in the way of God's people "so that they might eat food sacrificed to idols and practice sexual immorality" (v. 14). The former probably refers to eating food sacrificed to idols in the context of idolatrous worship. Perhaps, then, the Nicolaitans were advocating, in the name of Christian freedom, participation in the worship service both of the local church and the local pagan temple (see 1 Corinthians 10:14-22).

And what of the reference to the practice of "sexual immorality"? Often in the Old Testament spiritual idolatry was described metaphorically in terms of prostitution and sexual immorality (Jer. 3:2; 13:27; Ezek. 16:15-58; 23:1-49; 43:7; Hos. 5:4; 6:10). In Revelation, to "fornicate" (*porneuō*) and its cognates usually are metaphorical for spiritual apostasy and idol worship (14:8; 17:1, 2, 4, 5, 15, 16; 18:3, 9; 19:2). When these words are used literally, they are part of vice lists (9:21; 21:8; 22:15).

However, we can't dismiss the possibility that the Nicolaitans were teaching that forgiveness of sin and their newfound freedom in Christ have now released them from what they regarded as "slavish obedience" to rules and regulations concerning sexual conduct. How tragic that today we still hear such arguments in the defense of both heterosexual and homosexual immorality.

But why not just "live and let live"? Is it really necessary that the faithful in Pergamum confront these libertines? Why rock the boat? Doesn't Christian "love" call for tolerance and "minding our own business"? I'll let the words of Jesus answer those questions: "Therefore repent. If not, I will come to you soon and war against them with the sword of my mouth" (Rev. 2:16).

Two things deserve comment. First, the repentance Jesus calls for entails immediate acknowledgment of the error in their thinking and the lack of courage in their stance regarding the antinomians. "Recognize and confess," says Jesus, "that you are doing no one a favor by overlooking and allowing such sin in your midst! Confronting the Nicolaitans may be uncomfortable for you, even painful, but not nearly as painful as the judgment they will suffer if they remain in their sin!"

Second, notice that Jesus says, "I will come to you" soon, but will "war against them". The faithful at Pergamum aren't off the hook. If they don't repent Jesus will bring discipline against them (in precisely what form we aren't told). But the Nicolaitans will be the focus of judgment. It is against "them" that Jesus will make "war". Such language suggests that their lack of repentance would be evidence of a lack of saving faith. Their persistent licentiousness and morally compromising behavior undermined their claim to know Jesus in a saving way.

Words of Promise

There's no way around the fact that "peace" and "harmony" may suffer when we are committed to living out the ethical implications of the gospel of grace. But it's a price we must be willing to pay. In the immediate present there will be some attendant pain when hard decisions are made and morally compromising behavior is confronted. But look at what Jesus promises in the long run for those who are obedient, i.e., for those who "conquer" (Rev. 2:17) by repenting from such "sloppy agape" and refuse to participate with or permit the teaching of the Nicolaitans. They will receive "some of the hidden manna" (Rev. 2:17), as well as "a white stone, with a new name written on the stone that no one knows except the one who receives it" (Rev. 2:17).

Jewish tradition records that a pot of manna was preserved in the Ark of the Covenant (Ex. 16:32-34; Heb. 9:4). According to 2 Maccabees 2.4-7, when the temple was destroyed in 586 B.C., either Jeremiah or an angel supposedly rescued the ark, together with the manna, both of which would be preserved underground on Mt. Sinai until the messianic age, when the manna would again become the food for God's people. When the Messiah would come, Jeremiah would reappear and deposit both ark and manna in the new temple in Jerusalem.

But the manna, most assuredly, is Jesus himself (John 6:48-51). The promise to those who "conquer" in Revelation 2:17, therefore, is the assurance that they will feast forever on the person of Christ! That's a wonderful thought, a moving metaphor, but what does it mean? It means that Jesus, and only Jesus, will be the sustenance of our body and soul for all eternity. On him alone shall we spiritually feed and draw strength. He is the source of our on-going and eternal life. We are forever dependent on the infusion of his grace and mercy, upheld in existence by the exertion of his marvelous power.

It means we will experience, in relation with him, depths of intimacy utterly inconceivable in our present state of being. Our fallen minds cannot conceive the dimensions of spiritual ecstasy that await us in the ages to come. Our deceitful hearts cannot fathom the spiritual joy we'll feel forever as the magnitude of his affection for us is made known afresh each moment of each passing day.

It means that when it comes to our knowledge of his personality and the glory and wisdom of his ways, words such as "consummation" and "termination" and "completion" will be utterly out of place. The revelation of his character will be eternally incessant. The display of heretofore unknown facets of his beauty will suffer no lack.

It means that we will never grow weary of seeing his splendor or become bored with the disclosure of his grace. Jesus, as the manna of eternal life, will be an infinite supply of refreshment and joy and affirmation and delight. It means that even as eating now brings a physical satisfaction, as hunger pains are silenced and cravings are met, so the "bread of life" will satisfy our souls and enrich our resurrected bodies and fascinate our glorified minds beyond our wildest and most outrageous dreams!

It means that Jesus will be for us an endless, self-replenishing spring of refreshing water, an inexhaustible, infinitely abundant source of excitement and intrigue, an eternal, ever-increasing database of knowledge and insight and discovery that will never diminish in its capacity to enthrall and captivate. It means that because of Jesus, and Jesus alone, we will experience the odd but glorious sensation of never being deficient but always desiring increase, of ever being filled but constantly hungry for more.

Some argue that the "white stone" (2:17) signified acquittal by a jury, as over against a black stone that pointed to the guilt of the defendant. If that is the background to our text, Jesus would be highlighting the reality of our forgiveness. What a blessed image indeed, that God the Father pronounces us not guilty by virtue of the redemptive work of his Son, our Savior.

Others point to the practice of certain pagan religions in which people would carry an amulet or stone with the name of their deity inscribed upon it. It supposedly was used as a source of magical power. If this is the background to our Lord's reference, the name would be that of God or of Christ (see Rev. 3.12; 14.1; 19.12). "To know the name of a deity was to possess a claim upon his help: here the power of Christ to save and protect is exalted over that of his pagan rivals."[2]

White stones were often used as tokens of membership or tickets for admission to public festivals. If this is the background for the

---

2. Hemer, *Letters*, 99.

text, the white stone may be a symbol for the believer's admission to the messianic feast of Revelation 19. It is "white" in order to portray the righteousness of those who are granted entrance. As we read in Revelation 19:8, it was granted to the Bride, i.e., the church, "to clothe herself with fine linen, bright and pure, for the fine linen is the righteous deeds of the saints."

I must confess that I'm even more intrigued by the "new name" written on the stone "that no one knows except the one who receives it" (Rev. 2:17). This is clearly an allusion to the prophecy in Isaiah 62:2 ("The nations shall see your righteousness, and all the kings your glory, and you shall be called by a new name that the mouth of the Lord will give") and 65:15 ("but his [God's] servants he will call by another name"). In both cases these concern Israel's future kingly status and restoration to Yahweh, but are here applied to individuals within the church, she who is the true Israel of God.

Another question is whether this new name given to the overcomer is Christ's or that of the individual. I'm inclined to think the "new name" in verse 17 is one given uniquely to each individual believer and that it points to the fact that in Christ we are a new creation (2 Cor. 5:17). We have a new identity in him. All things about us are made new in Christ and our sinful past is a long-forgotten memory.

This isn't to say that the old or original name, given to us by our parents or the world, is evil or to be casually discarded. Rather, one's name, at least in biblical times, typically signified or pointed to one's character or calling or function. In other words, a person's name was more than simply a label to differentiate them from others. You didn't simply have a name: a person was his name. Name ideally reflected nature.

All this is to say that God will re-name each of us in accordance with the transformation of our nature into the likeness of his Son, to reflect the new and altogether unique identity each has received by grace and the irrevocable destiny we have in Christ. My new name, like yours, will reflect the character of the new creation in which I am a participant, as over against the old or original creation corrupted by sin and death. My new name, like yours, will be suitable to the new heavens and new earth in which I'll dwell, a place devoid of evil and error.

But there is more to this "new name" than merely its newness. It is a name that "no one knows" except for the individual "who receives it." Might this point to the intimate, intensely personal nature of one's life in God? Could it be that Jesus is highlighting the depths of intimacy and acceptance that each of us enjoys (and especially will enjoy) in the secret recesses of our souls? Yes, I think so.

In this regard we must also remember that the "manna" given to us is described as "hidden" (Rev. 2:17a). Some believe this is simply a reference to its having been "hidden" in a jar in the Ark of the Covenant, but I think something more is involved. If Jesus is himself the manna, perhaps the point is that all that awaits us in him is "hidden" in the sense that it is reserved and kept safe and guarded against all possibility of loss so that we might revel in its certainty and the assurance that what God has promised, he will indeed provide.

To sum up, there is an identity you have in God, reflected in your new name, that transcends whatever shame or regret or disappointment is wrapped up in who you are now. There is a very private and personal place of intimacy with him that brings hope and freedom and joy that none can touch or taint or steal away. Paul said it best when he declared that "your life is hidden with Christ in God" (Col. 3:3b). Peter echoed much the same thing in saying that we have "an inheritance that is imperishable, undefiled, and unfading, kept in heaven" for us (1 Pet. 1:4).

Chapter Six

What is the "Jezebel Spirit"?
(Revelation 2:18-29)

Why in the world should we burden ourselves with understanding what is known as "The Jezebel Spirit"? There are two reasons. First, there are people alive and well in the professing evangelical church today who are guilty of the same perverted behavior as was this woman named Jezebel back in the church in Thyatira in the first century. Second, I love the spiritual gift of prophecy. I hold it in extremely high regard. It plays an important role in our corporate and private spiritual experience at my home church. And I am jealous to protect it from abuse and perversion. Paul commanded us in 1 Corinthians 14:1 to earnestly desire spiritual gifts, especially that we might prophesy. Why? Because, as he said two verses later in 1 Corinthians 14:3, prophecy builds up, encourages, and consoles other Christians. So, when someone appears on the scene in church history, like Jezebel did in the first century, we need to take time to identify her sin and equip ourselves to oppose its presence in our midst.

After reading in Revelation 2:19 of the splendid spiritual qualities in Thyatira, it is genuinely tragic to discover that moral compromise was present in the church. "I have this against you," said Jesus, "that you tolerate that woman Jezebel, who calls herself a prophetess and is teaching and seducing my servants to practice sexual immorality and to eat food sacrificed to idols" (Rev. 2:20).

John Stott put it bluntly: "In that fair field a poisonous weed was being allowed to luxuriate. In that healthy body a malignant cancer had begun to form. An enemy was being harboured in the midst of the fellowship."[1]

The similarity between Thyatira and Pergamum and their joint dissimilarity with Ephesus here comes to the fore. The Ephesians could not bear the presence of falsehood and took no uncertain steps in ridding the cancerous error from their assembly. But it was done at the expense of love. Not so with Thyatira. While abounding in love they had lost their sensitivity to error and had compromised the glorious truths of both doctrinal and moral uprightness.

The exact nature of the heresy in Thyatira was wrapped up in the person and practices of this woman called "Jezebel." Several suggestions have been made as to her identity.

Who was Jezebel?

Some have suggested that Jezebel is none other than Lydia herself (Acts 16:14), who, if it were true, had badly fallen from the initial spiritual heights that we read about in Acts 16. Of course, there is nothing at all in the biblical text to suggest this identification.

A few Greek manuscripts include the possessive pronoun "your" (v. 20), on the basis of which it is argued that Jezebel was the wife of the senior pastor in Thyatira! But even if the pronoun is original, it probably refers to the corporate church in Thyatira since the preceding four uses of the singular "your" in verses 19-20 clearly do so.

Jezebel may be a veiled reference to the pagan prophetess Sibyl Sambathe, for whom a shrine had been built just outside the walls of the city. This is doubtful, however, and for two reasons: first, she is spoken of in rather definite terms, implying that a distinct historical personality is in mind and not merely a shrine to a pagan goddess; and second, the text suggests that the individual was actually a member of the church (externally, at any rate) of Thyatira and under the jurisdiction and authority of its leaders.

---

1. Stott, *What Christ Thinks of the Church*, 71.

The most likely interpretation is that, in view of the opportunity granted to her for repentance, Jezebel was a female member of the church who was promoting destructive heresies and leading many into moral compromise. She was a real person, but the name "Jezebel" is probably symbolic. It's hard to imagine anyone deliberately naming their daughter "Jezebel"! Note the parallel in the letter to Pergamum in which the Nicolaitans are subsumed under the name of an Old Testament figure: Balaam. The name "Jezebel" had, in fact, become proverbial for wickedness. Thus, this disreputable, so-called "prophetess" was as wicked and dangerous an influence in Thyatira as Jezebel had been to Israel in the Old Testament.

Note also that she "calls herself a prophetess" (v. 20). I can't imagine Jesus using this language if her prophetic gift was of the Holy Spirit. Some contend she was a born-again believer who had simply gone astray, but I suggest that her behavior and beliefs are an indication that whatever claims she made to being saved and prophetically gifted were spurious. This isn't to say she didn't have a supernatural power, but the latter need not always be from God (Matt. 7:21-23; Acts 16:16-18; 2 Thess. 2:9-10).

According to 1 Kings 16:31, Jezebel was the daughter of Ethbaal, king of the Sidonians, who married Ahab, king of Israel. Largely because of her influence in seeking to combine the worship of Yahweh with the worship of Baal, it is said of her husband that he "did more to provoke the LORD, the God of Israel, to anger than all the kings of Israel that were before him" (1 Kgs. 16:33). Hardly an endearing legacy!

Jezebel was responsible for the killing of Naboth and confiscation of his vineyard for her husband (1 Kgs. 21:1-16). She sought the death of all the prophets of Israel (1 Kgs. 18:4; 2 Kgs. 9) and even came close to killing Elijah (1 Kgs. 19:1-3). Her death came as a result of being thrown from a window where she was then trampled by a horse. When an attempt was made to recover her body for burial, it was discovered that the only thing left was her skull, her feet, and the palms of her hands. According to 2 Kings 9:36-37, dogs had eaten her flesh, in fulfillment of a prophetic word from Elijah:

> When they came back and told him, he said, "This is the word of the LORD, which he spoke by his servant Elijah the Tishbite, 'In the territory of Jezreel the dogs shall eat the flesh of Jezebel, and the corpse of Jezebel shall be as dung on the face of the field in the territory of Jezreel, so that no one can say, This is Jezebel'" (2 Kings 9:36-37).

Although the first Jezebel had been dead for over 1,000 years, her "spirit" had, as it were, found new life in this woman of Thyatira. She may even have been the leader or hostess of a house-church in the city. The complaint of the Lord lies in the unhealthy degree of toleration granted this woman. When it is said, "you tolerate that woman Jezebel," the implication is that the church in general did not accept her teaching nor adopt her lifestyle. But the subsequent mention of her "lovers" and children in verse 22 indicates that a number in the community did so. These would have formed a distinct group within the church, and the church as a whole was content for them to remain.

Whereas it is probable that one individual lady is in view, others have suggested that the reference to "the woman" and "her children" sounds strangely similar to the phrase "the elect lady and her children" in 2 John 1. In 2 John this refers to the church community as a whole and to the individuals who are each a part of it. Perhaps, then, "Jezebel" is not a single person but a collective reference to a group of false prophets and prophetesses in Thyatira. Whether one or many, the presence of such a corrosive and corrupting influence in the church, in any church, simply cannot be allowed.

The Longsuffering Christ

I'm constantly stunned by the gracious and longsuffering character of our Lord Jesus Christ. Listen to his words to the church in Thyatira: "I gave her time to repent, but she refuses to repent of her sexual immorality. Behold, I will throw her onto a sickbed, and those who commit adultery with her I will throw into great tribulation, unless they repent of her works, and I will strike her children dead" (Rev. 2:21-23a).

What a stunning display of kindness and mercy, that this woman who so horribly perverted the grace of God and used it as an excuse for idolatry and licentiousness should receive the extended opportunity to turn from her ways and receive the salvation of God! By all counts she should have been immediately cast into eternal darkness. But then, so should all of us. Praise God for his blessed longsuffering! But our Lord's patience has its limits. He will not indulge sin forever. He is no less holy and just than he is good and gracious.

Jezebel obviously presumed on God's grace and interpreted his longsuffering as approval or endorsement of her sinful ways, or at least his indifference toward her chosen paths. There may have been a definite time in the past when through some means, whether a prophetic word or direct encounter or perhaps through John, he issued this woman a warning, no doubt repeatedly. Whatever the case, the culpability of the false prophetess is evident. She "refuses" to repent. She clearly knew what was at issue and chose voluntarily to remain in her sin.

Was Jezebel a Christian?

This raises an important theological and practical question: Was Jezebel a Christian? My earlier comments would indicate I believe her to be unsaved, and thus some may react in horror that I raise the possibility that she might be born again. At first glance, the nature of her sin and her refusal to repent point to an unregenerate heart. But there are other factors to be considered.

For example, her judgment is said to come in the form of personal sickness, disease, or physical affliction of some sort. Jesus says, "I will throw her onto a sickbed," language that is reminiscent of the discipline imposed on the Christians at Corinthians who had persistently abused the Eucharist (1 Cor. 11:30-32). And before we too quickly conclude that someone born again could not commit such sins as are described in this passage, we should note that she is specifically charged with "teaching and seducing my servants to practice sexual immorality and to eat food sacrificed to idols" (v. 20). Note well: those whom Jesus calls "my servants" are guilty of "sexual immorality" and eating "food sacrificed to idols."

Of those who participated with her in these sins, Jesus says, "I will strike her children dead." The text could literally be translated, "I will kill with death," a proverbial statement that means "to slay utterly". Although this sounds more severe than what we might call "divine discipline" of a wayward believer, is it so different from how God dealt with Ananias and Sapphira in Acts 5?

The fact that they are called her "children" does not mean they are the actual physical progeny of her many sexual infidelities. They are, rather, men and women in Thyatira who had so identified with her sin that they are best described as younger members of her family. In other words, "those who commit adultery with her" (v. 22) and her "children" (v. 23) are the same people.

This also raises, yet again, the question of whether or not the "sexual immorality" in view is literal/physical or a metaphor of spiritual unfaithfulness and idolatry, perhaps especially manifest in unhealthy and illicit compromise with pagan culture. The evidence is mixed. On the one hand, I can't dismiss the possibility that literal sexual promiscuity is involved. After all, it is rare for one to embrace idolatry without yielding to sexual temptation (see Romans 1:18ff.). So it may be a false dichotomy to insist that she be guilty of either sexual immorality or religious idolatry. They seem so often (always?) to go hand in hand.

On the other hand, since there were surely at least some female followers of Jezebel, the "adultery" they are said to have committed "with her" would likely, at least in their case, be metaphorical for spiritual infidelity.

Jesus says they must repent of "her" works, i.e., since they have joined "with her" in this sin, to repent of what she did is to repent of what they, too, did. If they do not, Jesus will "throw" them "into great tribulation." The precise nature of this "tribulation" is not specified, but it would surely involve, at minimum, physical illness that in the absence of repentance would culminate in physical death.

So, was Jezebel a true Christian or not? I think the answer is No, she was not.

First, the fact that she is designated by a name that is linked historically to a woman of almost unimaginable wickedness and perversity suggests that she, too, is utterly unregenerate and devoid of spiritual life.

Second, having said that, I must also say, reluctantly, that Christians can fall into grievous and horrific sin. As noted, Jesus here says that his "servants" have joined with Jezebel in her works. The divine response of our heavenly Father to his backslidden children isn't eternal judgment but firm and loving discipline (see especially Hebrews 12). If that discipline is not met with heartfelt repentance, it may well lead to physical (not spiritual) death. This was certainly the case with Ananias and Sapphira (Acts 5) as well as the believers in Corinth. It would appear also to be the case with some of those in the church at Thyatira.

These are difficult matters that cannot be ignored, treated casually, or dismissed with cavalier dogmatism. Having said that, I am confident of two things. First, our Lord will deal with unrepentant sin. He himself declares in verse 23, "I will give to each of you according to your works." It may not happen immediately (longsuffering as he is), but in the absence of heartfelt conviction and repentance, it will most assuredly happen. Second, although we may not have the discernment to know infallibly who is and is not saved, "the Lord knows those who are his" (2 Tim. 2:19).

The Jezebel Spirit

How is it that this woman called "Jezebel" came to exert such incredible power over the lives of Christians in Thyatira? What accounts for the authority she possessed to convince the followers of Jesus to abandon their commitment to ethical purity and engage in sexual immorality and other forms of compromise with the surrounding culture?

There's no indication that she held an ecclesiastical office. She wasn't an elder or pastor or apostle. But she did claim to possess the gift of prophecy. Jesus said she "calls herself a prophetess" (v. 20).

Some may be tempted to dismiss Jezebel's claim based on their belief that women are not allowed to exercise this spiritual gift. A quick look at several texts from the New Testament will demonstrate that women did indeed prophesy under the influence of the Holy Spirit. That doesn't mean that Jezebel did, but her gender was itself no barrier to the proper exercise of this gift.

In Peter's speech on the day of Pentecost he explicitly said that a characteristic of the present church age is the Spirit's impartation to both men and women of the prophetic gift. Look closely at his citation of Joel's promise: "And in the last days it shall be, God declares, that I will pour out my Spirit on all flesh, and your sons and your daughters will prophesy, and your young men shall see visions, and your old men shall dream dreams; even on my male servants and female servants in those days I will pour out my Spirit, and they shall prophesy" (Acts 2:17-18).

In Acts 21:9 Luke refers to the four daughters of Philip as having the gift of prophecy. And in 1 Corinthians 11:5 Paul gave instructions regarding how women were to pray and prophesy in the church meeting.

Is Jesus suggesting she only claimed to have this gift but in fact did not? Or did she have a genuine spiritual gift but abused it in ways inconsistent with New Testament guidelines on how it was to be exercised? If Jezebel was not a Christian, as I have argued, it is most likely that she exercised a supernatural "prophetic-like" ability that was energized by demonic power rather than the Spirit of God. That this was (and is) distinctly possible is evident from Matthew 7:21-23 and Acts 16:16-18 (and perhaps 2 Thessalonians 2:9-10).

It's not out of the question that the presence of such false prophets and the havoc they wreaked in the early church was the principal reason why some in Thessalonica had grown weary of this phenomenon and had begun to "despise" all prophetic utterances (1 Thess. 5:20), even those that clearly were prompted by the Spirit. Paul's exhortation is that they should not allow the damage perpetrated by the spurious to undermine the benefits that accrue from the genuine.

I want to suggest that it was possibly (probably?) through this alleged "prophetic" ability that Jezebel gained power and authority in the church at Thyatira and adversely influenced a number of Christians there. It's not difficult to see how this could (and does) occur. (By the way, a man can display the characteristics of "Jezebel" no less than a woman. This is one sin that is by no means gender specific.)

A brief word is in order about my use of the phrase, "spirit" of Jezebel or "Jezebel spirit," language that, although not strictly biblical, has been bandied about in charismatic circles for generations, but perhaps is not as familiar to those in mainstream evangelicalism. I've read numerous articles, books, and listened to an equal number of sermons on the so-called "Jezebel spirit". To be honest, I haven't found them very helpful. In most cases they are speculative meanderings that show little concern for the biblical text.

Let me be brief and simply say that the word "spirit" is used here in one of two ways: either (a) of the human spirit, perhaps an attitude, disposition, habit, or set of characteristics displayed by a particular individual, or (b) of those whose supernatural "prophetic" ability is energized by a demonic spirit. In either case, regardless of the animating force, a person with a "Jezebel spirit" is one who displays the insidious, manipulative, and evil tendencies manifest in this woman of Thyatira.

So what kind of person do I have in mind, and what is it that they do? All too often we hear of individuals using their authority or position in the local church as well as their supernatural gifting (whether it be of God or of the enemy), to manipulate others into behavior they would not normally embrace. I'm burdened by the number of instances in which even Christians who are prophetically gifted use their endowment to expand their sphere of influence for personal profit or are afforded unwarranted privileges in the local church.

Virtually everyone is aware of some situation in which a Christian has used a spiritual gift, whether teaching, administration, pastoring, or another of the charismata, to gain illicit control and influence within the wider body of Christ. So it should come as no surprise that someone who legitimately possesses the gift of prophecy might abuse it to enhance their status or broaden their liberties or even seek monetary gain.

The most heinous abuse of a "prophetic" gift is when appeal is made to special "revelatory" insights in order to justify immorality (or, at minimum, to ignore it). Similarly, because of the "wonderful contribution" that a person has made to the kingdom, he/she is virtually untouchable and rarely held accountable to the normal rules of ethical behavior that govern all other Christians. Anyone who "hears" God with such regularity and alleged accuracy, so they contend, is unique, extraordinarily anointed, and therefore so highly favored of God that they needn't worry about the temptations that average Christians face or the tendencies of the flesh against which we typically wage war on a daily basis.

On occasion, a person with a Jezebel spirit will claim to have "revelation" that trumps Scripture (although they would rarely, if ever, put it in such stark terms; a person with this "spirit" is subtle, if nothing). Because such "words" from God are direct and immediate, and can't be explained by appeal to what one knows by natural means, they are falsely perceived as carrying greater authority than the inspired text itself. Or it is "revelation" that allegedly provides a superior and formerly unknown interpretation of Scripture that makes it possible to circumvent (or at least treat with casual disdain) the Bible's doctrinal precepts and ethical commands.

A person with a "Jezebel spirit" is one who appeals to his/her "spirituality" or spiritual gifting to rationalize (or again, at minimum, to overlook) sensuality. Often they don't even believe it to be sinful or illicit, but are so blinded by pride, the praise of men, and sensational supernatural experiences that what may well be inappropriate for mainstream believers is, in their case, permissible. It's just one of the perks.

Religious prestige is thus employed to foster sexual liberty. Under the pretense of anointed "ministry" a person exploits his/her platform and power to gain sexual favors or to lead others into similar behavior. This person is generally unaccountable to the leadership of the church, believing that the pastor and elders are "un-anointed" or insufficiently gifted to appreciate the level of supernatural spirituality at which he/she operates on a daily basis.

Eventually a double standard emerges: one set of strict, biblical guidelines to govern ordinary Christians and the exercise of their gifts within the body, and a lax, minimal, or more flexible list of expectations by which the "Man/Woman of God" is to live. Needless to say, it's a prescription for moral disaster.

Make no mistake, the Jezebel who lived in Thyatira undoubtedly appealed to her prophetic gift (and "anointing") to excuse her sexual immorality. She was using her power to manipulate others into sensuality and idolatry.

You may wonder why anyone would yield to such obvious unbiblical counsel, no matter how "gifted" the individual might be. It's not that difficult to understand. Some of you may be unaware of how mesmerizing and enticing the prospect of supernatural activity can be. When one witnesses what one believes is a genuine supernatural or miraculous event, otherwise normal theological defense mechanisms often fail to operate. Discernment is cast aside, lest it be viewed as a critical spirit or the response of a cynic. No one wants to be perceived as stiff-necked and resistant to the voice of God or the manifestation of his power. So, it is hard for some to resist and challenge the "ministry" of a recognized (or "alleged") prophet in the church.

Conclusion

The "spirit" of "Jezebel" was not unique to the church in Thyatira. It is alive and well in the body of Christ today. One need only read the latest headlines. It is an insidious, yet subtle, spirit. It is destructive, yet enticing. It typically gains momentum among those who are so fearful of quenching the Spirit (1 Thess. 5:19) that they fail to rein in the flesh. The solution is not to repudiate the prophetic altogether, or any other spiritual gift for that matter. Rather, we must become good Bereans, "examining the Scriptures daily" (Acts 17:11) to see if these things are of God or not. In sum, we would do well to heed Paul's counsel: "Do not despise prophecies, but test everything; hold fast what is good. Abstain from every form of evil" (1 Thess. 5:21-22).

Chapter Seven

Jesus says: "I Know Your Kidneys!"

(Revelation 2:18-29)

Let's continue our time in this passage with a test. Don't worry, no one will grade you other than yourself and God. And there is only one question on this exam. Here it is: Where are you today, in terms of Christian growth and zeal and love for Jesus, in comparison with where you were when you first became a Christian?

Let me put this one question in slightly different terms. Think back to the early days of your Christian life, perhaps the first year or so after your conversion. Do you remember the zeal for God and fascination with all things biblical you felt in the wake of saving grace? Think back on your evangelistic zeal and the courage you displayed in sharing your faith with unsaved family members and friends. Think back on the time and energy expended in service and prayer and ministry in the local church. Bring to mind how devoted you were to reading and studying Scripture. Is it all fresh in your mind? Got the picture?

Now, compare it with where you are today. Has your affection for God's people grown cold? Are you filled with doubts and fears rather than faith and confidence? Have you found excuses not to give generously to the local church or lead a small group? Do you find yourself rationalizing your absence from corporate worship or nurturing bitterness toward another believer who harmed you?

Do you spend as much time today reading and memorizing and meditating on Scripture as you did in your early days as a believer?

I'm taking the test myself, and I have to admit that it's painful and convicting to compare where I was with where I am, where I used to be with where I ought to be in my Christian growth. Some who profess faith in Christ aren't in the least unnerved by this challenge. They're content with the spiritual status quo. In fact, the only thing that irritates them is people like me challenging them to press on to greater conformity to Christ and more fervent love for his people. "Christianity is all about getting saved and escaping the horror of hell," so they say. "I'm happy where I am in life. Don't pressure me with a call to greater service. I've done my fair share of religious duties. My timecard has been punched and I'd really like to be left alone to work on my golf game."

If that's an exaggeration of what professing Christians actually say, it's spot on target with how they actually live. They walked the aisle. They signed the card. They prayed the prayer. They wrote the check. What more do you expect? Well, a lot more, actually.

The Christians who lived in ancient Thyatira would never have understood that mentality. In fact, it's the one thing for which Jesus praised them. Having been born again, they refused to coast. Their early diligence in ministry and mercy toward others had only increased with time. Hardship hadn't dimmed their faith. Familiarity with Christ had certainly not bred contempt. Right at the start of this letter Jesus said to them: "your latter works exceed the first" (Rev. 2:19).

Thyatira

Thyatira was the least known, least remarkable, and least important of the seven cities to receive a letter from the Lord (perhaps its only claim to fame was that Lydia had lived there; see Acts 16:11-15). Yet the letter addressed to it is the longest and most difficult to interpret. The obscurity of the letter and the enigmatic character of certain words and phrases are largely due to the fact that background information on the history of Thyatira, specifically the cultural conditions and circumstances in the first century, is almost wholly lacking. Its spiritual condition, on the other hand, is similar to that of Pergamum. Although they are commended for increase in growth and service, there is toleration of falsehood and moral compromise in their midst.

As noted, Thyatira was a comparatively unimportant city. It had no significant military, political, or administrative responsibilities, and if it is to be noted for anything it is its commercial enterprises. It was a center for manufacturing and marketing and its most distinguishing characteristic was the large number of trade guilds (think of the modern "labor union") that flourished there, the existence of which posed a special problem for Christians. One thing is clear: by the close of the first century the church in Thyatira was both prosperous and active.

The description of Jesus as one with "eyes like a flame of fire" and "feet" like "burnished bronze" is probably an allusion to the fiery furnace of Daniel 3 into which Shadrach, Meshach, and Abednego were thrown. The added reference to Jesus as "the Son of God" (only here in Revelation, but forty-six times in the New Testament) confirms this, for the three Jewish men were delivered by "one like a son of the gods" (Dan. 3:25).

The Thyatirans ought to be encouraged by this word of commendation. Among the "deeds" or "works" that Jesus knows are their "love and faith and service and patient endurance." But surely the best thing said of them is that their "latter works exceed the first." In other words, the church in Thyatira was a growing church, not so much numerically but in Christlike qualities. They had learned that the Christian life is one of growth, progress, development, and spiritual increase. Merely maintaining the moral status quo, whether individually or corporately, is inadequate.

Thus whereas Ephesus was backsliding, Thyatira was moving forward. I think we're justified, then, in adding this as another quality of the church that is approved of by Jesus: to the doctrinal orthodoxy of Ephesus, the suffering for righteousness' sake of Smyrna, the love existing in Pergamum, we now add the growth and development of Thyatira.

That's a wonderful legacy, to be known as a church that has faithfully built on the original foundation of love, laboring in God's grace to fan that first flame into a full-blown forest fire of affection and devotion to one another. Not only that, but their faith had increased. Their knowledge of God and his ways and the confidence it breeds had deepened and expanded. But doctrine hadn't gone merely into their heads; it had also energized their hands as they grew in service and sacrifice for one another. And when times became tough, and the temptation to quit grew more alluring, they persevered.

Surprisingly, though, there was something missing. Some in Thyatira (clearly not all, as verse 24 makes clear) had grown tolerant of the "woman Jezebel" (v. 20) and her wicked ways. The fruit of this compromise had grown rotten and threatened the very life of the body as a whole. And Jesus simply would not stand for it.

But there is this to learn from the church in Thyatira: the Christian life is an ever-upward trek toward greater heights of holiness and love and theological understanding. Being born again is only a beginning, not an end; an inauguration, not a consummation. Appealing to one's initial zeal as an excuse for shifting into spiritual cruise control won't set well with our Lord.

So, how did you do on the test? Are there signs of growth in your life? Has your love grown, or simply grown old (and cold)? Do your works of late exceed those first done? Here's my prayer for myself and for my own church: "Lord, shatter our complacency! Disrupt our indifference! Move us off dead center! Overcome our spiritual inertia and lovingly lead us into new heights of knowledge of you and love for your people and commitment to your kingdom and zeal for the presence and power of your Spirit! May we, by your grace, be people of whom it is said, 'your latter works exceed the first.' Amen."

Words of Complaint

How tragic, after reading of the splendid qualities in Thyatira, to discover that moral compromise was present in the church. "I have this against you," said Jesus, "that you tolerate that woman Jezebel, who calls herself a prophetess and is teaching and seducing my servants to practice sexual immorality and to eat food sacrificed to idols" (Rev. 2:20). Of course, we have already spent an entire chapter looking at this woman Jezebel and the nature of her sin. So I won't spend much time repeating myself here.

Our Lord clearly states that the casting of Jezebel on a sickbed and the infliction of her children with great tribulation, to the point of physical death itself, will be an unmistakable sign to all that nothing escapes his gaze or slips in beneath the radar, so to speak. But how does Christ's judgment against the unrepentant reveal to all Christians everywhere that he has exhaustive and altogether accurate knowledge of the hearts and minds of everyone?

Look again at Revelation 2:23. Following his declaration of impending discipline, he says, "and all the churches will know that I am he who searches mind and heart, and I will give to each of you as your works deserve."

Before considering this issue I want to make clear how loudly this passage shouts: "Jesus Christ is God!" We see it in verse 23 in two ways. First, he is omniscient, a recurring theme throughout these letters to the churches. The statement here is an obvious allusion to verse 18 where he is described as the one who "has eyes like a flame of fire." His gaze penetrates all human pretense. His searing vision yields to no barrier. Try as we may to obscure his sight or distract his focus, our Lord sees through and beyond every human façade, every evasive tactic, every clever cover-up. Unlike the comic book hero Superman whose vision could not penetrate lead, the sight and knowledge of Jesus suffer no such hindrance.

But there is a second way in which our Lord's deity is seen. Revelation 2:23 is an unmistakable allusion to Jeremiah 17:10, where we read, "I the LORD search the heart and test the mind [lit., "kidneys" in Hebrew], to give every man according to his ways, according to the fruit of his deeds." The significance of this latter text is that it is Yahweh who is speaking of himself. Yet here in Revelation it is a description of Jesus! Jesus is Yahweh incarnate! He is not only the omniscient Deity; he is also the Judge of all mankind. He sees and knows all and will call all to account for their deeds. Does it have any significant impact on you to think about the fact that Jesus is constantly thinking about precisely what you're thinking about at every single millisecond of your life? It should.

Let's return now to the issue at hand. Jesus declares that his decisive action against unrepentant sinners in Thyatira is a warning to all. It should forever put to rest any lingering doubts about whether he knows what is going on in his churches and whether he is of the inclination to take whatever steps are necessary to rectify matters when they get out of hand.

By observing what befalls those in Thyatira, Christians in other congregations will immediately know that Jesus knows and that he will hold all accountable for their deeds. There's no miscarriage of justice here. No legal sleight of hand. No such thing as inadmissible evidence or testimony being stricken from the record. The judgment of Jesus is based on comprehensive knowledge of every idea in the mind and every impulse of the heart of all mankind.

The word translated "mind" is literally the word for "kidneys" (*nephros*). It was often used to describe the inmost, secretive, solemn movements of the soul. Those deep inner impulses we so naively think are hidden from everyone but ourselves are seen with utmost clarity by the Lord Jesus. Every intent of the heart, every meditation of the mind, every fantasy, fear, emotion, doubt, deliberation, and decision is the focus of his penetrating gaze.

That is why we can rest assured that those who suffer, as did those in Thyatira, are not mistreated. The disciplinary hand of God is guided by the comprehensive scope of his understanding. No one can protest by saying, "But God, that's not what I truly meant," or "But God, I actually intended to do otherwise," for God knows every purpose, plan, and premeditation.

Every affection is seen for what it is, no matter how hard we may strive to conceal it within. Every attitude is known for what it entails, notwithstanding our most diligent efforts to convince ourselves and others that we never entertained such thoughts or conceived such fantasies.

No one expressed it more clearly than the apostle Paul, whose language in 1 Corinthians 4:3-5 veritably echoes that of Jesus in Revelation 2.

> "But with me it is a very small thing that I should be judged by you or by any human court. In fact, I do not even judge myself. I am not aware of anything against myself, but I am not thereby acquitted. It is the Lord who judges me. Therefore do not pronounce judgment before the time, before the Lord comes, who will bring to light the things now hidden in darkness and will disclose the purposes of the heart. Then each one will receive his commendation from God" (1 Cor. 4:3-5).

Spiritual Osteoporosis

Much of the church today is suffering from an advanced case of what I call spiritual osteoporosis. It's not widespread throughout the "body" of Christ but is concentrated along the spine. What I have in mind is the church's loss of its theological backbone!

We see this in any number of ways. For example, many have begun to fudge on the ethical status of homosexuality. Fearful of being labeled "homophobic," they've adopted a "live and let live" approach to the issue. Others, not wanting to appear elitist or exclusivist, no longer insist on personal faith in Christ as essential for salvation. Then there are those who've gone "soft" on the very concept of doctrine itself, believing that theological orthodoxy is both elusive and divisive and should be minimized for the sake of some ethereal and ill-defined unity.

I'm certainly no fan of angry sectarianism or the sort of dogmatic arrogance that judges and separates over secondary issues. At the same time, there are standards of truth to uphold and principles of behavior on which we must insist.

It's good to know that, notwithstanding the problems in ancient Thyatira, there were some in the church who refused to compromise or cut corners. Jesus describes them and delivers a special word of encouragement in Revelation 2:24-25: "But to the rest of you in Thyatira, who do not hold this teaching, who have not learned what some call the deep things of Satan, to you I say, I do not lay on you any other burden. Only hold fast what you have until I come."

There are four things here worthy of our attention. First, they are described as those "who do not hold this teaching," i.e., the teaching of Jezebel. Not only do they not embrace the doctrines she espouses but neither do they practice her wicked ways. In other words, these are folks who refused to take the easy path by looking the other way. They were neither gullible nor easily persuaded by the novel and deceptive concepts circulating in Thyatira. These were people who weren't afraid of calling heresy, heresy! The men and women Jesus addresses here knew that sometimes discrimination can be a virtue. They believed in the existence of absolute truth and unyielding ethical principles and were prepared to identify deviations from it. These were people who refused to embrace theological relativism, as if what one believes is less important than the sincerity and fervency with which one believes it.

Second, they are described as those "who have not learned what some call the deep things of Satan." This intriguing phrase calls for explanation. Some believe it to be a sarcastic reversal of the claims of Jezebel and "her children". They claim to know "deep [spiritual] things" when in fact what they know comes from and concerns the devil himself. In other words, the phrase "of Satan" is a sarcastic addition by Jesus designed to tell the faithful in Thyatira the true nature of those ideas and experiences. Those of Jezebel may actually have used the words "of God" which Jesus deliberately alters to make the point.

Others suggest that the "deep things of Satan" is a reference to their insistence that in order to appreciate fully the depths of grace and of God (cf. 1 Cor. 2:10) one must first plumb the depths of evil and the enemy. They would claim that, because of their spiritual maturity and superiority, they need not fear nothing from the devil.

In any case, it's stunning to realize that people who profess to know Christ and attain to positions of authority and influence in the church can be proponents of Satanic doctrine and practitioners of ethical compromise. What we desperately need today, as they did then, is an increase of (back) bone density, a strengthening of resolve to hold fast the line of orthodoxy and a courageous commitment to that holiness of life that will assuredly evoke disdainful accusations of being narrow-minded and puritanical.

Third, Jesus obviously knew that what he expected of them wasn't easy. It called for sacrifice and diligent attentiveness to belief and behavior, the sort that would expose them to ridicule and perhaps loss of income and influence. Thus he says, "I do not lay on you any other burden." It is enough, says Jesus, that you stand firm. It is enough that you do not lose heart. It is enough that you resist every temptation to cater to popular opinion or adjust your convictions to whatever theological "trend" is emerging in your city.

Fourth, and finally, he encourages them to "hold fast" what they have until he comes. In a word, persevere in what you have already received. Be immovable! Don't yield an inch! Cut not a corner!

All too often, especially in charismatic circles, the penchant for novelty or the hankering after some "fresh" word from God dictates the ministry or mission of a church. The frequency with which a pastor or teacher offers heretofore unknown "insights" into Scripture is made the measure of his "anointing" and favor with God. I'm not saying there is nothing more to learn from the Bible than what we now know. Far from it! But we must be careful lest the allure of "newness" or novelty detract us from focusing on the "old, old story of Jesus and his love" (I fear that few will recall that hymn!).

As for my concern with spiritual osteoporosis in the church today, I have no desire to see it replaced by a hardening of the theological arteries! Speaking the truth in love is never easy. But we must never play off one against the other. Jesus believed both were possible. So must we.

Another Promise to the One who Conquers

Those who "overcome" or "conquer" are the very people who are persecuted, thrown in prison, and even subjected to martyrdom (Rev. 2:3, 9-11, 13). The promise to them is that if they keep Christ's "works until the end" they will be given authority to rule over nations even as Christ has been given authority from his Father to rule (see Psalm 2).

Who or what are these "nations" and when is it that Christians will exercise their rule over them? Some (perhaps most) believe this is a promise to be fulfilled on the millennial earth, the 1,000-year period of human history that Premillennialists believe will follow the second coming of Christ and precede the inauguration of the eternal state.

Bear with me as I make an alternative suggestion. Could it be that the reward noted here is the authority granted to the saints when they enter into co-regency with Christ in heaven, now? A similar promise is made to the faithful in Laodicea: "The one who conquers, I will grant him to sit with me on my throne [namely, the place of rule, government, and authority], as I also conquered and sat down with my Father on his throne" (Rev. 3:21).

My point is that this co-regency with Christ is fulfilled now, in heaven, in the so-called "intermediate state" where the dead in Christ live in conscious, intimate fellowship with the Savior. To put it simply and to the point: The "conquerors"/"overcomers" are not merely those over whom Christ will rule but those with whom Christ now rules.

We often fail to grasp the glory of what awaits those who "die in the Lord" and enter his presence. Although it is an intermediate state, that is to say, it is in between our present earthly existence and our final and glorified experience when we receive the resurrection body, it is nevertheless a wonderful and joyful and meaningful time. It is during this time, simultaneous with the present church age, that those who have died in Christ experience the fulfillment of this promise: they are even now ruling and reigning over the nations of the earth together with and alongside their sovereign Lord.

For those of you not familiar with the debate over biblical eschatology, this is the perspective known as Amillennialism. Contrary to the label which suggests such don't believe in the existence or reality of a millennium (observe how the alpha privative "a" seemingly negates the word "millennial"), they most assuredly do! The "millennium" is concurrent/simultaneous with the church age in which we live.

Again, contrary to the charge of "spiritualizing" the millennial kingdom, the saints truly and literally are enthroned with Christ, they are truly and literally reigning with Christ. This is not a metaphor, but a concrete and living reality. The millennium, therefore, isn't the experience of Christians in the church on earth but that of the saints in heaven. They have been enthroned. They now rule. They share in the exercise of Christ's dominion and sovereignty over the affairs and events and nations of the earth.

The apostle Paul had this in view in 1 Corinthians 15:24-26. There he describes Christ's current sovereign rule over the affairs of both heaven and earth, one in which Jesus says (in Rev. 2:25-29) his people who "conquer" will share. Look at it closely:

> "Then comes the end, when he delivers the kingdom to God the Father after destroying every rule and every authority and power. For he must reign until he has put all his enemies under his feet. The last enemy to be destroyed is death" (1 Cor. 15:24-26).

Practically speaking, this means that the Apostle John and Augustine, as well as Thomas Aquinas, John Calvin and Martin Luther, Jonathan Edwards and John Wesley, together with my earthly father and mother, and Mary Magdalene, Susannah Wesley and the untold millions of others who are absent from the body but present with the Lord (2 Cor. 5:1-10) are now exercising a divinely delegated authority in the providential oversight of the nations of the earth!

This enthronement and rule of the saints in heaven, with Christ, will continue far beyond the "millennial" phase in which it currently exists. There is an eternal expression of this experience that will unfold not only in the New Heavens but also on the New Earth (cf. Rev. 5:10) that will be created at the coming of Christ (Rev. 21-22). The nature of that authority and rule will undoubtedly change, given the fact that all unbelievers will have by then been banished to their eternal punishment in hell, but our co-regency with Christ will never cease.

As I read further in this passage it appears that the promise of co-regency with Christ is reinforced yet again. In verse 28 Jesus declares that the overcomer will receive "the morning star". It's possible that this is a reference to Jesus himself (see Rev. 22:16). But there is another option that relates this statement to what has preceded it in the immediate context. The "morning star" is generally regarded as referring to Venus (although technically a planet), which itself was an ancient symbol for sovereignty. In Roman times, notes Beasley-Murray,

> "it was more specifically the symbol of victory and sovereignty, for which reason Roman generals owned their loyalty to Venus by erecting temples in her honour... and Caesar's legions carried her sign on their standards.... If then the morning star was the sign of conquest and rule over the nations, this element in the promise to the conqueror strengthens the statement that has gone before. It embodies in symbol the prophecy already cited from the psalmist. The conqueror is therefore doubly assured of his participation with Christ in the glory of his kingdom."[1]

I certainly have no illusions about resolving the often acrimonious debate over biblical eschatology. In fact, I suspect my comments will provoke no little response (perhaps most of it negative). But as I read this passage, in conjunction with the whole of Scripture, I see a glorious affirmation of the destiny of the faithful who die in Christ.

To all outward appearances and the judgment of the unbelieving eye, it may seem that Christians have suffered loss. Yet, for the believer, to die is to live! What strikes the world as defeat and humiliation is for the Christian an entrance into life and exaltation! Let us never forget that the saints have "conquered" Satan "by the blood of the Lamb and by the word of their testimony, for

---

1. G. R. Beasley-Murray, *The Book of Revelation* (Greenwood, SC: The Attic Press, 1974), 94-95.

they loved not their lives even unto death" (Rev. 12:11; see also Rev. 15:2; 17:14.).

Conclusion

One final word of exhortation is needed. I hear news, almost on a daily basis, or read an article on the Internet describing a famous Christian or yet another local church that has turned its back on some biblical truth or ethical principle. They often will insist that we Christians are on the wrong side of history and out of touch with the ever-changing beliefs in our culture. "Get on board and adapt," so they say, or be left behind in the wake of a culture that is increasingly hostile to the things of Christ. "Your ancient beliefs, based on the Bible, will only serve to alienate you from the society in which you live."

To this, I would only echo to you and your local church the words of Jesus to the church in Thyatira: "Only hold fast what you have until I come" (Rev. 2:25). Hold fast! Hold fast!

Chapter Eight

A Tragic Embodiment of Nominal Christianity

(Revelation 3:1-6)

One of the more important lessons I've learned through the years, especially when it comes to church life, is that seeing isn't always believing. I don't want to sound cynical or pessimistic, but you shouldn't always trust your eyes. What I'm trying to say is that I'm not as impressed as I used to be when I hear of a church with a surging membership, multi-million-dollar budget, expansive facilities, and a reputation for programs, ministries, and a growing influence in the community. The problem I have in mind isn't restricted to the so-called "mega-church", it's just more conspicuous in their case. Even small congregations can be widely known for countless religious activities yet devoid of authentic commitment to Christ as Lord.

One of my hobbies, if you can call it that, is reading church websites on the internet in an effort to learn more about what other local church communities are doing and what they believe. It can be quite discouraging. Some of the sites look like a promo for the Ringling Brothers, Barnum & Bailey Circus. They've got gimmicks, gadgets, celebrity guest speakers and goodies of all sorts, most of which are designed to sell you an image of being alive and worthy of your attendance (and money, of course).

The church in first-century Sardis was just such a congregation. Let me illustrate. Try to envision the scene at a typical funeral with its sprays of flowers, and bright, vivid colors, all of which is designed (at least in part) to divert one's attention from the dark reality of death. The church at Sardis was like a beautifully adorned corpse in a funeral home, elegantly decked out in the visible splendor and fragrance of the most exquisite floral arrangement, set against the background of exquisite drapery and soft, but uplifting music. Yet beneath the outward façade was death and spiritual putrefaction of the vilest sort. I don't recall who said or wrote it, but here is one pastor's exhortation to his own church to avoid the errors of Sardis:

> "Ecclesiastical corpses lie all about us. The caskets in which they repose are lined with satin and are decorated with solid silver handles and abundant flowers. Like the other caskets, they are just large enough for their occupants with no room for converts. These churches have died of respectability and have been embalmed in self-complacency. If by the grace of God this church is alive, be warned to our opportunity or the feet of them that buried your sister (Sardis) will be at the door to carry you out too."

Sardis was a city trying to live in the wake of its past glory. It had at one time been the capital of the ancient kingdom of Lydia and reached its pinnacle of fame and influence in the sixth century B.C. But it was suffering from serious decline, aggravated by a devastating earthquake in A.D. 17 (described by Pliny, early in the second century, as the greatest disaster in human memory). Despite the generous aid granted by the emperor Tiberius, "no city in Asia presented a more deplorable contrast of past splendour and present unresting decline."[1]

It comes as no great shock, then, when we discover that the letter our Lord addressed to the church in Sardis is one of the most severe of the seven. It is, in point of fact, along with the letter to Laodicea, a church for which the Lord has no words of

---

1. R. H. Charles, *A Critical and Exegetical Commentary on the Revelation of St John* (Edinburgh: T. & T. Clark, 1975: I:78).

commendation. Simply put, Jesus had nothing good to say about the church in Sardis!

This letter stands out in sharp contrast to the four which have preceded. To Ephesus, Smyrna, Pergamum, and Thyatira our Lord sends his greetings followed by a word of encouragement and praise. Their faults, as bad as they were, appear to be exceptions to the general spirit of obedience and growth. But in Sardis there is no word of praise: obedience and growth, at best, are the exception, not the rule. Furthermore, we note that although Sardis is similar to Pergamum and Thyatira in that they all have mixed membership, in the latter two churches the faulty members are in the minority, but in Sardis they predominate. Only a "few names" in Sardis "have not soiled their garments" (v. 4). The majority had incurred defilement, which is to say, they had given themselves over to idolatry and immorality.

We might also ask why both Jews and Romans apparently left this church untouched when they so vigorously persecuted their neighbors. The answer may be its lack of spiritual integrity and whole-souled devotion to Christ. As G. B. Caird notes, "content with mediocrity, lacking both the enthusiasm to entertain a heresy and the depth of conviction which provokes intolerance, it was too innocuous to be worth persecuting."[2] Simply put, Sardis was the classic embodiment of inoffensive Christianity.

The church in Sardis had acquired a reputation (v. 1b) in Asia Minor as a superlative congregation. To all external appearances, as far as what could be seen and heard, Sardis was a progressive church, first among its sister congregations to initiate a new program, full of vitality, overflowing with zeal, no doubt quite large. As you read John Stott's description of the church in Sardis, ask yourself whether it applies today. The answer could be painful.

> "[Sardis] was positively humming with activity. There was no shortage in the church of money or talent or manpower. There was every indication of life and vigor.... But outward appearances are

---

2. Caird, *Revelation,* 48.

notoriously deceptive; and this socially distinguished congregation was a spiritual graveyard. It seemed to be alive, but it was actually dead. It had a name for virility, but it had no right to its name. Its works were beautiful grave clothes which were but a thin disguise for this ecclesiastical corpse. The eyes of Christ saw beyond the clothes to the skeleton. It was dead as mutton. It even stank."[3]

There are numerous mega-churches, mini-churches, and everything in between that are not only outwardly active but also inwardly vibrant, genuine, and Christ-exalting in every way. We should thank God for them. But there are just as many churches in which the relentless swirl of religious activity is designed to divert attention away from the hypocrisy and spiritual sterility that exists within. We simply can't afford to be fooled into concluding all is well based solely on what we see or hear of them. A reputation without a corresponding reality is worthless in the eyes of Jesus Christ. His words of warning are forceful and to the point. We would be well-advised to heed them.

If the surrounding culture declares that we are alive and Jesus says that we are dead (Rev. 3:1), something is seriously wrong with our standard of success. Our discernment is seriously flawed. Worse still is when we ourselves think we're alive but in fact are dead. All too often, the criteria by which we judge success and the criteria employed by God are vastly at odds. What constitutes good, effective, Christ-exalting ministry is one thing to the world, even the church, and another thing altogether to God.

Reputation vs. Reality

This was the case in the church at Sardis, where Jesus declared that they had the "reputation of being alive" but in fact were "dead." By "dead" Jesus didn't mean altogether lifeless or utterly hopeless. Later, in verse 4, he indicates that the church still has "a few ... who have not soiled their garments." And his appeal to the church that it "wake up, and strengthen what remains ... and repent" indicates that all is not lost. There is one final chance for renewal and

---

3. Stott, *What Christ Thinks of the Church,* 85.

life and hope for the future. But the church is in a sorry state: filled with religiosity and hypocrisy, in many respects only nominally Christian.

That a church could be widely known for its activity and influence, yet all the while "dead" in the estimation of Christ, is a frightening, sobering reality. Obviously, what impresses men does not necessarily impress God!

Let's get right to the point. This letter to the church in Sardis ought to alert us to the fact that a church can be confident of its place in the community, increasing in membership, energetic in its religious activities, liquid in its financial assets, fervent in its outreach to the broader culture, and yet be dead!

Some who hear this will respond: "Yes, but that's not us." Such are particularly in jeopardy. It is the unsuspecting church, the unexamined church, the spiritually smug church which simply can't believe that a congregation that appears to have been so richly blessed by God could possibly be the focus of a divine rebuke such as we find in the words to Sardis.

The Indictment

The particular problem that moved our Lord to speak in such forceful terms is found in the phrase: "I have not found your works complete in the sight of my God" (v. 2b). What is Jesus saying? A brief glance at the list of works in 2:19 will help us understand what is intended: love, faith, service, patient endurance. All these were no doubt evident in Sardis, but in a hypocritical, haphazard, half-hearted, or again, "incomplete" way.

Perhaps their motives were wrong. Perhaps they performed the deeds well enough, but did so for selfish, even mercenary reasons. The words "in the sight of my God" indicate that whereas their deeds may gain human approval, God's evaluation was another matter. Their efforts were perfunctory, lacking that zeal informed by knowledge, noted for beginnings that rarely came to anything of lasting worth. They were the works of a church that had become addicted to mediocrity. They were, in a word, wishy-washy!

This is stunning! The world looked at this congregation and said: "Wow! What impressive works you've performed. What a powerful impact you've had. You've done so much for so many." God looked at this congregation and said: "You're dead! I admit, your works are many, but they are motivated by pride, greed, and are driven by a desire that you be known as great rather than that I be known as great."

Sardis may well have been the first church in history to have been filled with what we call today nominal Christians (see Isa. 29:13; Matt. 15:8-9; 23:25-28; 2 Tim. 3:5). Thus far in these letters we have noted the marks of the church of which Jesus approves: doctrinal orthodoxy, suffering for Christ's name's sake, love, growth, and now at Sardis we learn of the importance of reality, genuineness, authenticity, a life-style that matches profession.

The Exhortation

Our Lord's instruction begins with the exhortation, "wake up, and strengthen what remains and is about to die." Such words leave room for hope, for they indicate that, although death is near, the possibility for renewal remains. There is an ember, so to speak, which is quickly cooling off, but may yet be fanned into flames of life if only the appropriate action is taken. There's a slight possibility that "what remains and is about to die" is a reference to individual members of the church, making this a call to the faithful few to minister to those who are languishing in spiritual lethargy.

The exhortation to "wake up" suggests that a church can experience "spiritual slumber," having fallen asleep, and thus inattentive to what matters most. "You're in a dream state," says Jesus. "You're living in an unreal world created by your own false criteria of what is pleasing to God. Shake yourself awake and return to reality." Being asleep, the church is oblivious to its perilous condition, unaware of the threat it faces. This is no time to take a nap.

If one sleeps incessantly, one becomes weak: sluggish, with slow reflexes, incapable of resisting temptation or fighting the onslaught of the enemy. Not everything has altogether died. But much is on life-support, hanging on in spiritual intensive care. Therefore, "strengthen" what remains of what is good. Apply yourself to revitalize your commitment to Christ and your pursuit of all things holy.

There are three ways this can be done. First, remember. Just as Jesus exhorted the Ephesians (2:5), so also those in Sardis. Past history should challenge them (us) to present endeavor. Recall the blessings of divine grace and be strengthened by the assurance that what God once did he can certainly do again.

Second, hold fast ("keep it"; cf. 2:24b-25). You don't need anything new; simply hold firmly to what you've already received. The terms used here ("received and heard") probably refers to the theological truths transmitted to the believers in Sardis when their congregation was founded.

Third, repent. Stop sinning! Start obeying! When was the last time you witnessed (or participated in) a church that repented corporately, confessing its failures without pretense or pride, and committed afresh to the "main and plain" of Holy Scripture?

The Threatened Discipline

The threatened discipline for failure to do so is vivid (see verse 3b). It's unclear whether this refers to an impending "coming" of Christ in judgment and discipline against the church in Sardis or a broader reference to the second "coming" of Christ. In either case, the emphasis is on the unexpected ("like a thief") nature of the coming. It would seem however, since repentance would forestall the need for Christ's "coming," that a historical visitation in the first century is in view, not the second coming at the end of history.

Most churches rarely if ever consider the potential for Jesus himself taking disciplinary action "against" (v. 3) them. We envision ourselves solely as individuals who are accountable to him, but rarely do we think in corporate terms. The church is more than a collection of individuals: it is a community, in which spiritual solidarity of vision and mission must be embraced and nurtured. There were a few faithful folks in Sardis who hadn't yielded to the problems that plagued the congregation as a whole. But they will inevitably suffer from whatever disciplinary action the Lord might take against the public witness and financial stability and very existence of the church as a whole.

So, in what ways is the contemporary church asleep, on the verge of death, facing the sure disciplinary visitation of Christ himself?

It is enough that I point to the abandonment of the centrality and supremacy of Jesus Christ. Most churches would scoff at the suggestion they are anything less than Christ-centered. But how does our professed commitment to being Christocentric express itself in how we worship, in the frequency and fervency with which we celebrate the Eucharist, in what we sing, in how firmly we embrace and how loudly we publicly confess our theological convictions and how faithfully we share the gospel with our friends, neighbors, and co-workers?

How does our alleged Christo-centricity make itself felt in the way we instruct (or merely entertain) our children on Sunday morning, or in the way we evangelize our community, or in how consistently we unpack in our preaching the inspired and authoritative word that Christ himself has given us in Scripture?

If we are as energized and driven by the supremacy of Christ as we allege, would visitors to our Sunday service, or to a small group meeting on Wednesday night, immediately recognize it? When our annual report is published in January, would the centrality of Jesus Christ be seen in how funds were used, in how missionaries were supported, in the sort of literature we make available in the bookstore, in the criteria by which elders are selected to serve?

This letter was then and is now a literal "wake up call" for the church of Jesus Christ. If unheeded, we may well experience a "visitation" from the Lord, but unlike what we hoped for.

The Wrong Response

Yet it would be a mistake to throw in the towel when it comes to the local church or to conclude that it is irredeemable or that its influence is so minimal as to justify the creation of a new model or new expression for being the people of God.

This, it seems, is what George Barna suggested in his book *Revolution*.[4] He documents the exodus from the local church of countless folk he calls "Revolutionaries". Finding the local church to be excessively authoritarian, out of touch with the spiritual needs of its members, devoted primarily to its own preservation and comfort, and without much of a witness or influence in the surrounding society, many are simply walking away and allegedly finding satisfaction for their spiritual needs through other expressions of religious life.

Nowhere in these seven letters in Revelation 2-3 does Jesus even remotely suggest that the local church is dispensable. Notwithstanding his promised disciplinary visitation to those congregations that refuse to repent, there is no indication that he envisioned his people living out their lives together and pursuing the values and goals of the kingdom of God in any other way than through the ministry of the local church.

We see this in his letter to the church at Sardis. As bad as it was, and it was really bad, there were still "a few names in Sardis, people who have not soiled their garments" who are promised that they "will walk" with Jesus "in white, for they are worthy" (v. 4).

In a word, there was in the church at Sardis, as there is (most likely) in all churches, a faithful, believing, godly remnant who have refused to compromise their convictions and whom the Lord is determined to bless and favor with his manifest presence and goodness. This is an important point to remember. Our tendency is to pronounce an irreversible judgment on churches that we believe have abandoned the gospel or have compromised in some way. But Jesus here reminds us that even in the most lifeless churches, churches whose "works" fall far short of what God expects of us, there is often a faithful, godly remnant of true, Christ-exalting, gospel-centered people. It is primarily for them that we should pray.

Our Lord uses an interesting word in verse 4, when declaring that these of the remnant have not "soiled" or "stained" (Gk., *molunō*)

---

4. George Barna, *Revolution* (Wheaton: Tyndale House, 2005).

their garments. G. K. Beale believes this term is evidence that the sin of the majority was either idolatry or a decision to suppress their witness by assuming a low profile in idolatrous contexts of the pagan culture in which they had daily interaction. He points out that "soiled" (*molunō*) is used elsewhere in Revelation for the threat of being polluted by the stain of idolatry (see 14:4, 6-9).[5]

There is another important lesson for us here. I see nothing in this passage or anywhere else in the New Testament that would lead me to believe that the solution to idolatry or immorality or any other pervasive problem is the abandonment of the local church or the decision to "seek God" via some alternative movement. Yes, sometimes it is necessary to leave a particular congregation. But this must always be with a view to planting or joining another one. We are not required to remain in a church or denomination that has abandoned the gospel or has seriously compromised its ethical posture or refuses to acknowledge the supreme authority of Scripture (although I think, at times, Christians are too quick to leave; church hopping is not a sanctioned biblical sport!). What is clear is that we are not free to ignore the New Testament witness concerning the necessity of involvement in a community of Christians whose corporate life is consistent with the principles of a local church as found, for example, in the pastoral epistles of Paul.

As bad as it was in Sardis, Jesus does not counsel the faithful few to depart. As noted earlier, there's a slight possibility that our Lord's exhortation to "strengthen what remains and is about to die" (v. 2) is a reference to individual members of the church, making this a call to the faithful few to minister to those who are languishing in spiritual lethargy. Even if not, Jesus envisions them remaining within the church at Sardis and laboring for its renewal.

---

5. Beale, *Revelation*, 276.

The Promised Reward

The reward promised to those who persevere is four-fold, two of which I'll note briefly here and two of which I'll save for the next chapter.

First, in verse 4, they will "walk" with Jesus "in white, for they are worthy." Some see a reference here to the resurrection body, but this is more likely a promise of victory and irrevocable purity both in the intermediate state and in the messianic kingdom when those who have remained faithful will experience the consummation of fellowship with Jesus. The reference to "white" probably refers to the righteousness imputed to us in the act of justification, although we can't dismiss the possibility that Jesus has in mind the experiential purity of life for which he in verse 4, and elsewhere in these seven letters (cf. 2:2-3; 2:9-10; 2:13; 2:19; 3:8,10), commends them. This is confirmed by what we read in Revelation 19 concerning the Marriage Supper of the Lamb:

> Then I heard what seemed to be the voice of a great multitude, like the roar of many waters and like the sound of mighty peals of thunder, crying out,
>
> "Hallelujah! For the Lord our God the Almighty reigns. Let us rejoice and exult and give him the glory, for the marriage of the Lamb has come, and his Bride has made herself ready; it was granted her to clothe herself with fine linen, bright and pure" – for the fine linen is the righteous deeds of the saints" (Rev. 19:6-8).

What does he mean when he says, "they are worthy" (v. 4b)? He doesn't mean that because of their personal godliness they have become worthy in the sense that they now have earned or merited salvation. They are "worthy" in two senses. First, God has made them worthy by imputing to them the righteousness of Jesus. Their "worth," our "worth," is a gift of God's grace, not a reward for our obedience. Second, at the same time Jesus calls on us to walk in a way that is "worthy" of our calling (cf. Eph. 4:1), which is to say, we are to live in a way that accurately reflects the glory, beauty, holiness, and great privilege of being a child of God. This glorious promise finds its ultimate and consummate fulfillment in the Marriage Supper of the Lamb.

Second, the "overcomer" or "conqueror" will be "clothed in white garments" (v. 5a; cf. 3:18; 6:11; 7:9-14; 19:13). Again, this refers both to the experiential holiness of life now, by virtue of the gracious, sanctifying work of the Spirit (cf. Rev. 19:6-8), as well as the righteousness of Christ himself that is imputed to us by faith.

Conclusion

I'll close this chapter with two important comments. First, the language of the saints being clothed in white garments is consistently used in Revelation for those who have persevered through suffering (see 6:9-11; 7:9, 13-14). In other words, refusing to accommodate or conform to the behavior of the crowd came at a high price. It's rarely easy to be in the minority, especially when it costs you a job, or a promotion, or popularity, or perhaps even your physical safety and freedom. These "few" in Sardis no doubt suffered intensely for their commitment, but the reward made it all worthwhile.

I also believe Jesus wants us to understand and appreciate the emotional, perhaps even psychological, implications of this truth. What I mean is this. All too often those who know Christ and by grace wholeheartedly desire to walk in purity of life fail to fully embrace and enjoy their status as God's forgiven children. They wallow in shame over sins long since confessed and of which they've sincerely repented. Contrary to their status as the adopted and justified children of God, they feel condemned and struggle to walk in the liberty and joy of the elect.

If that is you, remember this: God sees you in his Son! Although your clothing in white will be consummated in the age to come, you are now, and forever will be, a pure, spotless Bride in his sight (cf. 2 Cor. 11:2; Eph. 5:26-27; Rev. 19:7)! This glorious truth is not to be perverted into an excuse to sin, but is an incentive, by God's grace, to live passionately and resolutely in the pursuit of a practical purity that conforms ever more to the standing we already have in him.

Chapter Nine

Written Down in the Lamb's Book of Life: The Real Reason to Rejoice

(Revelation 3:1-6)

In what do you take deepest delight? What is it that brings the greatest and most intense joy and happiness to your heart? If I were to say to you, "Rejoice, because _____," how would you fill in the blank?"

I'm sure that many of us would point to our families, perhaps our children. Others might say that their greatest source of joy is their good health and good friends and a robust bank account. Of course, if Christians give much thought to the question, they will eventually say something like, "My greatest source of joy is in knowing Jesus and being assured that I will spend an eternity in intimate fellowship with him." Others might point to the truth of our adoption as God's children, or our being justified or declared righteous in God's sight through faith in Jesus, and the list of answers could go on almost without end.

There was an event in the lives of the first-century followers of Jesus that brought this question very much into play. It's found in Luke 10. There Jesus sent out seventy-two disciples, not apostles, but average followers like you and me. He told them to heal the sick and proclaim the presence of God's kingdom. When they returned to Jesus to give him a report of what happened, we read this:

> "The seventy-two returned with joy, saying, 'Lord, even the demons are subject to us in your name!' And he said to them, 'I saw Satan fall like lightning from heaven. Behold, I have given you authority to tread on serpents and scorpions, and over all the power of the enemy, and nothing shall hurt you'" (Luke 10:17-19).

I can understand why the disciples of Jesus were so excited and filled with joy. To exercise the authority of Jesus himself in subduing demonic spirits is a wonderful thing. But then Jesus said this:

> "Nevertheless, do not rejoice in this, that the spirits are subject to you, but rejoice that your names are written in heaven" (Luke 10:20).

Jesus isn't saying that it is wrong to rejoice that we have authority over demons. This is a standard way of speaking in biblical times. His point is that compared with having your name written down in heaven exercising authority over demons is next to nothing. So, if this is to be a reason for our great joy, what does it mean to have our names written down in heaven? That glorious reality is one of the four promises given to the faithful few in the church in first-century Sardis. We looked at the first two promised blessings in the previous chapter, and now we turn our attention to the third and fourth of these promises.

The Lamb's Book of Life

The promise to those who conquer continues in Revelation 3:5, a passage that has stirred considerable discussion and controversy. "The one who conquers," said Jesus, "will be clothed thus in white garments, and I will never blot his name out of the book of life. I will confess his name before my Father and before his angels. He who has an ear, let him hear what the Spirit says to the churches."

Some are frightened by this or filled with anxiety that perhaps one day they will fail to conquer and thus have their name blotted out of the book of life. Others read it as a glorious promise of security, a solid rock of assurance, a declaration by Jesus himself that our names will never be deleted from God's eternal register.

Let's begin by trying to identify what the "book" is that Jesus mentions. There are at least five possibilities.

(1) Colin Hemer refers to one particular custom in ancient Athens according to which the names of condemned criminals were erased from civic registers before their execution. The Greek word translated "to erase" (*exaleiphein*), "was the technical term for such degradation."[1] As insightful as this may be, it is more likely that we should look for a biblical background to this imagery.

(2) In the Old Testament God's "book" (or its equivalents) was a register of the citizens of the theocratic community of Israel. To have one's name written in the book implied the privilege of participation in the temporal blessings of the theocracy, while to be erased or blotted out of this book meant exclusion from those blessings. In other words, this book had reference to the rights of citizenship for the Jewish people.

> "So Moses returned to the LORD and said, 'Alas, this people has sinned a great sin. They have made for themselves gods of gold. But now, if you will forgive their sin – but if not, please blot me out of your book that you have written.' But the LORD said to Moses, 'Whoever has sinned against me, I will blot out of my book'" (Ex. 32:31-33; cf. Ps. 69:28; Isa. 4:3).

(3) The concept of a "book" was also used to portray God's all-inclusive decree (Ps. 139:16); i.e., the very days of one's life are ordained and written in God's "book" before one of them occurs: "Your eyes saw my unformed substance; in your book were written, every one of them, the days that were formed for me, when as yet there was none of them."

(4) There is also the notion of "books" of judgment in which are recorded men's deeds. They serve as that by which or from which one shall be judged: "And I saw the dead, great and small, standing before the throne, and books were opened. Then another book was opened, which is the book of life. And the dead were judged by

---

1. Hemer, *Letters*, 148.

what was written in the books, according to what they had done" (Rev. 20:12; cf. Dan. 7:10).

(5) The most vivid usage, however, is the concept of the book as the register of those who have been chosen for salvation from eternity past. It is not temporal or earthly blessings that are in view, but participation in the eternal kingdom of God as recipients of eternal life. It would appear from these texts that not all are written in this book, but only the elect.

> "Behold, I have given you authority to tread on serpents and scorpions, and over all the power of the enemy, and nothing shall hurt you. Nevertheless, do not rejoice in this, that the spirits are subject to you, but rejoice that your names are written in heaven" (Luke 10:19-20).

> "I entreat Euodia and I entreat Syntyche, to agree in the Lord. Yes, I ask you also, true companion, help these women, who have labored side by side with me in the gospel together with Clement and the rest of my fellow workers, whose names are in the book of life" (Phil. 4:2-3).

> "But you have come to Mount Zion and to the city of the living God, the heavenly Jerusalem, and to innumerable angels in festal gathering, and to the assembly of the firstborn who are enrolled in heaven, and to God, the judge of all, and to the spirits of the righteous made perfect" (Heb. 12:22-23).

> "all who dwell on earth will worship it [i.e., the Beast], everyone whose name has not been written before the foundation of the world in the book of life of the Lamb that was slain" (Rev. 13:8).

> "The beast that you saw was, and is not, and is about to rise from the bottomless pit and go to destruction. And the dwellers on earth whose names have not been written in the book of life from the foundation of the world will marvel to see the beast, because it was and is not and is to come" Rev. 17:8).

"But nothing unclean will ever enter it [the New Jerusalem on the New Earth], nor anyone who does what is detestable or false, but only those who are written in the Lamb's book of life" (Rev. 21:27).

If it is this fifth and final view which Jesus had in mind, and I believe it is, there are three possible interpretations.

On the one hand, Jesus may be saying that it is possible for a sinning, unrepentant Christian (such as were many at Sardis) to fail to overcome or conquer and thereby to forfeit their place in the book of life. Their names, already inscribed in the book, will be erased, signifying the loss of their salvation.

Others suggest that to have one's name blotted out refers to something other than salvation. In Revelation 3:1 Jesus referred to the people at Sardis as having a "name" for being alive, i.e., they had a reputation for spiritual vitality. The idea, then, is that such people are saved, but will forfeit any hope of an honorable position in the coming kingdom of God. They are saved but will experience shame on the last day. It is not the loss of life, *per se*, but the loss of a certain quality of life that otherwise could have been theirs. Thus, what one loses by having their name erased from the book of life is eternal rewards in the kingdom.

Several factors lead me to conclude that John does not envision the possibility of a true Christian forfeiting salvation. We should begin by noting that all of the other promises to the "conqueror/overcomer" are coined in positive terms with no threat (implied or explicit) of losing a salvation once gained (see 2:7, 11, 17, 26-27; 3:12, 21). This isn't to suggest that Christians cannot backslide and sin badly. The rebukes in these seven letters indicate otherwise. Nevertheless, the evidence of the reality of true saving faith is perseverance (i.e., "overcoming"; cf. 1 John 2:19).

If it is asked why this promise is couched in negative terms, the answer is obvious: Jesus could not say "I will write his name in the book of life" because the names of the "overcomers" (i.e., the elect) were already written in the book from eternity past (see Rev. 13:8; 17:8). There is no indication in Scripture, least of all in Revelation, of additional names being inscribed in the book as a reward for faithfulness or perseverance. Rather, faithfulness and perseverance are the evidence or fruit of having had one's name written in the book. Those who worship the "beast" do so precisely because their names were not written in the book in eternity past (13:8; 17:8).

We need to look more closely at Revelation 13:8 and 17:8 to understand what our Lord is saying in 3:5.

> "all who dwell on earth will worship it [i.e., the Beast], everyone whose name has not been written before the foundation of the world in the book of life of the Lamb that was slain" (Rev. 13:8).

> "The beast that you saw was, and is not, and is about to rise from the bottomless pit and go to destruction. And the dwellers on earth whose names have not been written in the book of life from the foundation of the world will marvel to see the beast, because it was and is not and is to come" (Rev. 17:8).

Note carefully that there are two and only two groups of people. On the one hand are those whose names have not been written in the book of life from eternity past. They "worship" and "marvel" at the Beast. The second group consists of those whose names have been written in the book of life, which constitutes the reason why they refuse to give their allegiance to the enemy of Christ. Nowhere does it suggest a third group: people whose names had been written in the book in eternity past but, because they worshiped the Beast, they failed to overcome or conquer, and thus have their names blotted out.

In other words, as John Piper explains, "having our name in the book of life from the foundation of the world seems to mean that God will keep you from falling and grant you to persevere in allegiance to God. Being in the book means you *will not* apostatize."[2] Or again, being written in the book means that God is committed to guarding your heart so that you will "conquer" and "overcome" the Beast by not yielding to the temptation to worship his name or receive his mark.

---

2. John Piper, "Can the Regenerate Be Erased from the Book of Life?" 12/22/06 at www.desiringgod.org..

Those who worship the Beast do so because their names were not in the book. Having one's name written in the book from eternity past is what guarantees a life that overcomes, a life that perseveres, a faith that conquers. Piper summarizes:

> "This fits with Revelation 3:5, 'He who overcomes . . . I will not erase his name from the book of life.' The triumph *required* in 3:5 is *guaranteed* in 13:8 and 17:8. This is not a contradiction any more than for Paul to say, 'Work out your salvation ... for God is at work in you to will and to do his good pleasure' (Philippians 2:12-13). It is not nonsense to state the condition: if you conquer, God will not erase your name (3:5); *and* to state the assurance: if your name is written, you will conquer (13:8 and 17:8). God's 'written-down-ones' really *must* conquer, and really *will* conquer. One side highlights our responsibility; the other highlights God's sovereignty."[3]

Therefore, this declaration of Jesus is a promise to the elect that nothing will ever, by any means (he uses a double negative), prevent them from possessing the eternal inheritance to which they have been ordained. In other words, we must take note of what Jesus does not say. He does not say that anyone will be erased from the book of life. Rather, he says the overcomers will not be erased. His words are a promise of security to overcomers, not a threat of insecurity to those who lapse. So again, Jesus nowhere says he will erase names previously inscribed in the book of life.

What joy! What comfort! What incentive to love him and praise him and serve him. Jesus will never blot my name out of the book of life!

One more thing. People often ask: "What must one do to have his/her name written down in the Lamb's book of life? Can someone whose name is not now written in the book do something, such as believe in Jesus, so that his/her name will be written in the book?" The answer to the first question is, nothing. The answer to the second question is, No. Names are inscribed in the book of

---

3. Ibid.

life before the foundation of the world. This is by God's sovereign and altogether gracious choice. You don't believe in Jesus in order that your name will be written in the book. You believe in Jesus because your name has already been written down in the book. To those who do not presently believe in Jesus, we say: "Repent and believe!" If they do, it is because their names were written in the book of life before the foundation of the world.

God has not chosen to reveal to us the names written in the Lamb's book of life. It is none of our business. We are not free to speculate about it. What he has revealed is the responsibility of each individual to repent and believe the gospel. If a person does not believe the gospel, he has no one to blame but himself. If he does believe the gospel, he has no one to praise but God.

None of us deserves to have his/her name written down in God's book. We all deserve eternal damnation. The only explanation for why a hell-deserving sinner had his/her name written down in the Lamb's book of life before the foundation of the world is because God is gracious and merciful and wishes to provide his Son with a Bride that will enjoy his glorious presence and love for eternity. Had God chosen not to inscribe anyone's name in his book, he would have done no one an injustice.

He Knows Your Name!

I'm amazed at how seemingly little things in life can have such a massive impact on other people. Take, for example, when someone remembers your name. Perhaps it's a person you admire greatly, whom you've only met once before, but they instantly smile when they see your face and say, "Hey, Susie, how are you? It's good to see you again." You feel affirmed and honored that someone who is well-known and successful actually knows who you are. Maybe that's because it strokes your ego and awakens personal pride. Whatever the case, no one can deny how good it feels.

Or consider the converse, when you find yourself in the presence of a person who has either forgotten your name or, for whatever reason, has little desire to be seen with you. We've all been in these situations (at least I have!) and they are undeniably painful. You get the distinct impression that you're an embarrassment to them. When someone walks up, they pretend to be occupied with other matters, perhaps even turning their back on you. The discomfort is almost tangible. If pressed about who you are, they quickly divert the focus of the conversation to something less threatening.

It's precisely this sort of relational phenomenon that makes the words of Jesus in Revelation 3:5 so powerful and so glorious. Here we find the fourth and final promise to the faithful in Sardis. He's already assured them they will "walk" with him "in white," that they will "be clothed in white garments," and that he will never, by no means ever, blot their names out of the book of life. To these Jesus adds: "I will confess his name before my Father and before his angels" (Rev. 3:5b).

Revelation 3:5 actually appears to be a combination of two statements found on the lips of Jesus in the gospels. In Matthew 10:32 he declared, "So everyone who acknowledges me before men, I also will acknowledge before my Father who is in heaven." Again, in Luke 12:8, we read, "And I tell you, everyone who acknowledges me before men, the Son of Man also will acknowledge before the angels of God." Let's unpack this remarkable promise with several observations.

First, this is no grudging concession on the part of Jesus, but a joyful and heartfelt proclamation to the Father and the myriads of angelic beings: "He's mine! She belongs to me! They are worthy!" The words "acknowledge" or "confess" often suggest a reluctant admission on the part of the person speaking, less a willing declaration than a concession to the unavoidable.

That's not what Jesus has in mind when he uses these words! These names are on his lips because they are first in his heart. Jesus isn't embarrassed by those whom he confesses before the Father. He doesn't worry what the angels might think – that he would dare speak your name or mine in their presence.

We all know what it's like to feel embarrassed to be in someone's company, fearful they might bring reproach on us or cost us standing in the sight of our peers (I'm not suggesting that's a good thing). Whatever the reasons that make us hesitant to be seen with them, it happens. Not Jesus! He "is not ashamed" (Heb. 2:11) to call us brethren. He rejoices that we are his and he happily speaks each name with delight and satisfaction.

A second thing to note is that Jesus evidently will speak each of our names individually. Yes, we are the body of Christ, the church, the Bride whom he loves with an everlasting love. Our corporate identity as the people of God is an indescribable blessing. But according to Revelation 3:5 Jesus says, "I will confess his name [singular]", not merely "their name" before the Father and the angels. People on earth may forget your name or feel uneasy in your presence or reluctantly concede your accomplishments. But Jesus knows your name and will say to the Father, "This is Steve. He is righteous in me. Father, this is Mary. She is mine!"

How does one put into words the thrill and life-giving power of hearing Jesus speak your name? Mary Magdalene has been much in the news of late, especially with the publication a few years ago of Dan Brown's book and then the movie of the same title, *The Da Vinci Code*. If she were present today, I hardly think she would care that everyone knew her name, and certainly not for that reason. But there was one occasion when it meant more than all the world to her.

Following the resurrection of Jesus, she stood outside the tomb, weeping. Turning around, she "saw Jesus standing, but she did not know that it was Jesus. Jesus said to her, 'Woman, why are you weeping? Whom are you seeking?' Supposing him to be the gardener, she said to him, 'Sir, if you have carried him away, tell me where you have laid him, and I will take him away.' Jesus said to her, 'Mary' (!). She turned and said to him in Aramaic, 'Rabboni!' (which means Teacher)" (John 20:14b-16).

Do you know the difference between being called "Woman" and being called "Mary"? One lady did! This woman, at one time indwelt and tormented by seven demons (Luke 8:2), filled with shame and reproach, hears the sweetest and most comforting word imaginable, her name: "Mary!" But it wasn't the name so much as the man on whose lips it was willfully, happily, and confidently found: Jesus! "He knows my name! He remembers me! I'm not an embarrassment to him. He's not ashamed of me!"

This is what each of us who knows him will experience one day, without reservation or qualification. He will speak your name and my name before his Father and the angels. But this is more than merely hearing your name called as if a teacher is taking roll. This is no perfunctory ritual as Jesus reels off one name after another, to which you respond, "Here," "Yo!" or "Present". This is an open, glad-hearted, public acknowledgment, an owning by Jesus of you and me. "Father, these are the ones you gave me out of all flesh (John 17:2). I declare them to you now. I proclaim their names as those who have come to faith and have rested in what I've done alone, without looking to another lover, another savior, or another god."

Third, could it be that Jesus speaks our names as he reads them from the book of life? In view of the immediately preceding context (Rev. 3:5a), we can't dismiss the possibility that the names he speaks, one after another, were those who had been written down in that glorious volume from before the foundation of the world (cf. Rev. 13:8; 17:8).

But won't Satan be present to object, to bring up every sin and failure and fault, reminding God and the angels of how often we fell short, repented, only then to fall short again? Well, I'm not sure Satan will be present on that day, but if he were, let your fears be put to rest, for "who shall bring any charge against God's elect? It is God who justifies. Who is to condemn? Christ Jesus is the one who died – more than that, who was raised – who is at the right hand of God, who indeed is interceding for us" (Rom. 8:33-34).

Fourth, there may well be a legal or forensic dimension to this declaration by Jesus of the names of those in the book of life. This isn't at all to diminish the personal and relational reality of what will occur, but only to emphasize that this is our final vindication from all charges; it is Christ's declaration that we are righteous through faith in him alone. It is, in a word, our ultimate and eternal "justification"!

Fifth, and finally, given the context of both the two references in the gospels where this statement is found (see above on Matthew 10:32 and Luke 12:8) and the situation envisioned among the churches in Asia Minor, it may be that the emphasis is on "confessing the name" of the Christian who has bravely confessed the name of Christ in the face of persecution. His confessing our name comes only after we, by the grace of God, have confessed his name to an unbelieving world, willing to endure whatever negative consequences that might bring (cf. Matt. 10:33; Luke 12:9).

Envision the scene. You are standing in the blazing presence of the immeasurable and unfathomable God, an all-consuming fire, the God of infinite and unending glory, the God of unsearchable and incomparable righteousness. Small, frail, weak as you are, Jesus takes hold of your hand and leads you "before" his Father and beneath the penetrating gaze of myriads of angels. Then he proudly and happily and joyfully and confidently declares: "Father, Sam is mine! I am his! He is clothed in white! I've paid his debt. I suffered his penalty. He is clean. He is pure. He is in me and I am in him. Sam is righteous!"

He knows my name! And if you know his, he also knows yours!

Chapter Ten

The Church of "Little Power"

(Revelation 3:7-13)

One could make a strong case that the letters to Smyrna and Philadelphia are the most important of the seven, for in neither of them do we find a single word of complaint. They both receive unqualified praise and approval. These, then, are truly churches of which Christ heartily approves.

What makes this all the more remarkable is the statement by Jesus in Revelation 3:8 that the church in Philadelphia has "but little power" (ESV). This isn't a rebuke. It's a commendation! Let me clarify that. Jesus isn't saying that having "little power" is inherently and always good. He's simply saying that having "little power" isn't inherently and always bad.

In spite of your lack of size and influence, says Jesus, you faithfully kept my word and, in the face of persecution and perhaps even martyrdom, refused to deny my name. People threatened you. The culture mocked you. The Jewish community slandered you (cf. verse 9). The temptation to jump ship must have been intense. Yet you stood firm. Your lack of resources, money, and manpower proved no obstacle to your accomplishing great things for the kingdom of God!

It's reassuring to know that size is no measure of success. In other words, there is no sin in being big, but neither is there in being small. There are temptations in both circumstances. Those with "little power" can become bitter and resentful of those who outwardly prosper. Those with "great power" can become arrogant and condescending toward those of less stature. The "mini-church" may be tempted to think they've missed the mark or failed to articulate a vision that is pleasing to God. The "mega-church" may point to their sizable offerings and overflowing crowds as indicative of divine approval. They could both be wrong.

We don't know if the Christians in Philadelphia were despondent or mired in self-doubt. But the fact that Jesus applauds their efforts in spite of their modest dimensions would suggest they needed this word of encouragement. Our Lord's declaration of what he has done and will continue to do on their behalf (see vv. 8-11) is worthy of our close consideration. But first we need to look at his description of himself in verse 7.

Who is this Jesus who Speaks?

Who is the one who speaks such uplifting words to this tiny congregation? He is "the holy one, the true one, who has the key of David, who opens and no one will shut, who shuts and no one opens" (v. 7). I can't be dogmatic on this point, but I strongly suspect that at the heart of their having "kept his word" and having "refused to deny his name" is their holding forth of Jesus as he has described himself to them. In other words, notwithstanding the vile threats and taunts they endured on a daily basis, these believers proclaimed Jesus as the holy one, the true one, the one who has the key of David!

The Philadelphian believers did more than simply not deny the name of Jesus. They loudly and proudly proclaimed him as "the Holy One"! Their boast was not in their property or multiplicity of programs but in the Holy One of Israel. This title is likely derived either from Isaiah 40:25, where Yahweh asks, "To whom then will you compare me, that I should be like him? says the Holy One," or from Isaiah 43:15 where he again proclaims, "I am the LORD, your Holy One, the Creator of Israel, your King" (see also Job 6:10; Ezek. 39:7; Hos. 11:9; Hab. 1:12; 3:3). According to Isaiah 57:15, his very name "is Holy"!

There is none with whom he can be compared or against whom he fails to measure up. He is altogether unique, transcendently other, truly in a class by himself! And note well: this glorious, almost indescribable, attribute of God is here predicated of Jesus! Holiness is that in virtue of which God alone is God alone. Holiness is moral majesty.

Some churches that have "but little power" doubt the legitimacy of their existence. They wonder if their sacrifice is worth the effort. Perhaps the kingdom would be better off without them. If the Philadelphians were inclined to think in this way, I suspect they renewed their strength and re-ignited their passion by reflecting on the beauty of divine holiness. "He, our Lord, is the Holy One! How can we not keep his word and proclaim his name, for he is Holy, he is ours, and we are his!"

Second, he is called "the true one". To the Greek mind this would mean "genuine," or what is real and thus corresponds to reality. To the Hebrew mind it means "faithful" and "trustworthy," deserving of our confidence, dependable, reliable, consistent, and steadfast (see Ps. 146:5-6; Ex. 34:6; Deut. 7:9; 2 Tim. 2:13; Num. 23:19; Lam. 3:22-23). No one ever trusted our God and Savior, the Lord Jesus Christ, in vain!

Third, he is the one "who has the key of David." This is an allusion to Isaiah 22:22 and the role of Eliakim, steward of the household, who was given authority to control who was either admitted to or excluded from the king's presence. This position was quite prominent, perhaps only secondary to the king himself. The point is that Jesus alone has the key to the Davidic or messianic kingdom and that he alone has the undisputed authority to admit or exclude from the New Jerusalem.

Fourth, and finally, he is the one "who opens and no one will shut, who shuts and no one opens." When he opens to his followers the door of the kingdom, no one can shut them out; and when he shuts the door on those who oppose his cause, none can reverse the decision.

Jesus loves the "mini-church"! He says it explicitly in Revelation 3:9. The greatness of a church is not measured by its membership roll or budgetary prowess but by the size of the Savior whom it faithfully honors and passionately praises and confidently trusts. The "big" church is any church that boasts in a big God, attendance and acreage notwithstanding. Were the Philadelphians envied by any? Probably not. Yet they had no lack, at least in what mattered. Keeping Christ's word and not denying his name is easy for those who know him well. When he is small and unknown, he becomes dispensable, deniable, and easily dismissed for the sake of some grand vision of church growth. A "mega-church" without a "mega-Christ" is of little benefit to anyone. A "mini-church" with a "mega-Christ" makes them big in the eyes of him whose opinion is the only one that matters.

Whatever God Promises, He Fulfills

One of my spiritual mentors was often heard to say, "Whatever God requires he provides; whomever God chooses, he changes; and whatever God starts, he finishes." I'd like to add a fourth: "Whatever God promises, he fulfills." That's incredibly reassuring, especially for those who struggle with doubt and uncertainty and the fear that one day, notwithstanding the promises in his Word, God will pull the rug out. Life has taught us, often painfully, that if something appears to be too good to be true, it probably is. Why should it be any different with God? Will he really deliver on what he has declared? Can I trust him?

I think those questions echo ever more loudly in our heads when times are tough. It's a lot easier to believe God when there's money in the bank and our loved ones are healthy and people like us. Maybe that's one reason Jesus spoke so pointedly to the Christians in Philadelphia. Life was anything but easy for the church in that city. The fact that Jesus applauds their perseverance (v. 10a) and faithfulness in keeping his word (v. 8) and commends them for not denying his name (v. 8), more than suggests that they were faced with a relentless temptation to quit. The opposition they faced from the Jewish community only made things worse (v. 9).

They may well have asked themselves, "Could all this mean that Jesus has abandoned us? Are his promises vain and empty?

How can we know he's still on our side?" Jesus speaks directly to such fears with three powerful promises. It is the first one, in Revelation 3:8a, that has caught my attention. Perhaps it's because at first glance it seems so insignificant. I have to confess that for a long time I took no notice of it. Not anymore! "Behold," said Jesus, "I have set before you an open door, which no one is able to shut."

What is the "open door"? Is it a great opportunity for missionary activity (cf. 1 Cor. 16:9; 2 Cor. 2:12; Col. 4:3). That's certainly a possibility. But the preceding verse (3:7) spoke of a messianic kingdom, access to which is under the absolute control of Christ. He is the one who possesses the key and can open and shut at his own will. Here in verse 8 he reminds the Christians at Philadelphia who may have been excommunicated from the local synagogue that he has placed before them an open door into the eternal kingdom, and no one can shut them out.

This is a powerfully encouraging word of assurance to all Christians who face similar threats or assaults from both human and demonic powers. It's short but sweet, simple but profound, and speaks gloriously to the point of one of our greatest needs: to be reassured by our great God and Savior, Jesus Christ, that we are forever his and that no amount of hardship in this life can undermine our salvation, that no depth of pain or deprivation can interrupt, disrupt, or counteract his divine determination to bring us safely into our eternal reward.

Think about what this statement says concerning our Lord's determination concerning you and your relationship with him. His mind is made up. His will is resolute and unchangeable. His goal is clear and the means to its accomplishment are undertaken with an immutable and omnipotent commitment. There is a sense, then, in which we might reverently speak of his holy and righteous stubbornness when it comes to the welfare of his people. He simply won't allow anyone to slam shut the door that he has opened.

Not all the persecution in the world can reverse his decree. Not all the hatred and animosity of the enemy can tempt him to change his mind. Not all the posturing and strutting of a secular and unbelieving culture can induce him to close the door on those to whom he has decided to open it. Not all the threats, slander, resistance, or any other attempt on the part of the people around us to undermine our relationship with Christ will succeed.

"No one is able to shut" this door into eternal relationship and intimacy with Jesus, this entrance into eternal joy and life in his presence. No one. Not your worst enemy. Not even those who mock you for your faith. Not Islamic terrorists or economic collapse or a terminal illness. Nothing. Not the collective power of an entire world, not the combined energy of all demonic beings, neither Satan nor any other created being, can overturn the decree of Christ who says: These are my people and shall remain so forever.

Often we fear that Satan has the power or freedom to counteract Christ's saving work, or that he can orchestrate a scenario that will lead to our ultimate demise. Or perhaps he can put a stumbling block in our path that will ensnare or entangle us in such a way that not even God himself can extricate us or deliver us from his nefarious strategy. Ah, but who is this God? Is he not the one "who is able to keep you from stumbling and to present you blameless before the presence of his glory with great joy" (Jude 24)?

I'm also reminded of what Paul said in Romans 8:31, a precious passage indeed: "If God is for us, who can be against us?" His purpose isn't to deny that we have enemies. Our enemies are numerous and powerful and relentless in their assault against the saints. His point, rather, is that they will always fail! Yes, they will continue to attack and accuse and adopt an adversarial posture. They can inflict injury, bring disappointment, shatter dreams, and disrupt relationships. But they can never close the door that Christ has opened!

Or to use the language of Paul again from Romans 8, they shall never "separate us from the love of Christ" (8:35). Their weapons may include "tribulation," "distress," "persecution," "famine," "nakedness," "danger," and "sword" (8:35). They may even kill us, treating us "as sheep to be slaughtered" (8:36). But in all these things, yes, in all these horrific experiences, "we are more than conquerors through him who loved us" (8:37), through him who opened the door and allows no one to shut it!

This glorious truth of God's sovereignty in our salvation, far from precluding the need for personal holiness, empowers and undergirds it. We must persevere in our commitment to him, and we shall persevere because of his commitment to us. There is in the heart of our Lord, as I said, a holy stubbornness. He will not be deterred. His purpose will come to pass. His promise will be fulfilled. No one can close the door he has opened. Entrance into the bliss of eternal joy is assured to those who know Jesus.

As I said, whatever God promises, God fulfills. This marvelous truth puts legs beneath our Lord's declaration that the door he has opened for us no one can shut (v. 8). But there's yet more in his promise to the faithful in Philadelphia and therefore more in his promise to you and me:

> "Behold, I will make those of the synagogue of Satan who say that they are Jews and are not, but lie – behold, I will make them come and bow down before your feet and they will learn that I have loved you" (Rev. 3:9).

We've already encountered the presence of those who "lie" about being Jewish (see Rev. 2:8-9). What is especially noteworthy here is how our Lord describes his vindication of those who've remained faithful in the face of persecution. Literally, Jesus says he will "give" these false Jews of "the synagogue of Satan" to the church at Philadelphia, i.e., he will cause them to bow down at their feet and to know that Jesus has loved them.

Does this imply that these Jewish opponents will become Christians? Some say Yes and contend that the "open door" of verse 8 pertains specifically to evangelistic opportunity and success among the Jewish population of the city. Appeal is also made to the word translated "bow down" (*proskuneō*), used elsewhere on several occasions in Revelation of voluntary worship. However, if they were to be saved, it would be strange for them to bow down in worship at the feet of fellow-Christians. Here, to "bow down" is simply the traditional (oriental) expression of respect and honor.

It may be that recognition on their part that Jesus loves the church is the occasion (indeed, the stimulus) for their conversion, much in line with Paul's thought in Romans 11 where he describes the Jews being provoked to jealousy upon seeing Gentiles savingly grafted into the olive tree. It must be admitted, however, that "make them to come" is odd language for conversion. Furthermore, the point of their being "made" to prostrate themselves before Christians is so that they might acknowledge the love Jesus has for the church. But if they are no less converted, i.e., no less Christian, than the church, they too would be the objects of Jesus' saving love. But is not his point to demonstrate to the persecutors of the church that God's love is precisely for those seemingly insignificant and weak believers in Philadelphia (irrespective of ethnic identity)?

Perhaps, then, John has in mind either (1) some event (or process) by which these Jews are compelled to acknowledge that the Philadelphian believers are the beloved people of God and that such status is not the result of ethnic heritage or national affiliation but rather faith in Jesus, or (2) the final judgment day at which "every knee shall bow and every tongue confess that Jesus is Lord" (Phil. 2:10-11).

The most intriguing feature of this passage is that it appears to be an allusion to several Old Testament texts in which it is prophesied that Gentiles will come and bow down before Israel in the last days. For example, "The sons of those who afflicted you shall come bending low to you, and all who despised you shall bow down at your feet; they shall call you the City of the Lord, the Zion of the Holy One of Israel" (Isa. 60:14). In Isaiah 45:14 we read how Gentile peoples will "come over to you [Israel] and will be yours; they will walk behind you, they will come over in chains and will bow down to you." Once again, "with their faces to the ground they [the Gentiles] shall bow down to you [Israel], and lick the dust of your feet. Then you will know that I am the Lord; those who wait for me shall not be put to shame" (Isa. 49:23). The irony here is so thick you could cut it with a knife! In all these Old Testament texts it is the Gentiles who grovel before Israel, whereas in Revelation 3:9 it is the Jews who will bow at the feet of this predominantly Gentile Christian church.

The irony intensifies when we note that in Isaiah 60:14 it is the Gentiles who will call the Israelites "the City of the LORD, the Zion of the Holy One of Israel." But now, in 3:12, the tables are turned: it is the CHURCH that is described in such glorious terms. There we read that the overcomers before whom these Jews prostrate themselves are given the name of "the city of my God, the new Jerusalem"!

We should also note that the words they will "know that I have loved you" may be an allusion to Isaiah 43:4 ("Because you [Israel] are precious in my eyes, and honored, and I love you ..."). Again this reinforces the notion that Jesus saw in the church the fulfillment of these Old Testament prophetic promises. In other words, the fulfillment of these prophecies in Isaiah "will be the reverse of what the Philadelphian Jews expect: *they* will have to 'bow down before *your* feet', and acknowledge 'that I have loved *you*'. Let the Christians take heart, for it is on them that the Lord has set his favour."[1]

Beyond the theological (and eschatological) implications of what this says about the church as the true Israel of God is the profoundly encouraging boost it gives to the oppressed heart seeking to stand firm in faith for Jesus. These believers in Philadelphia were no doubt hearing the taunts of their oppressors, similar to what David often lamented in the Psalms: "O LORD, how many are my foes! Many are rising against me; many are saying of my soul, there is no salvation for him in God" (Ps. 3:1-2). Or again, in Psalm 71:11, the psalmist refers to his enemies as declaring, "God has forsaken him; pursue and seize him, for there is none to deliver him."

The pagan world looked with disdain on the church in Philadelphia and concluded that people who suffered in this way must be unloved by their God, if not entirely abandoned by him. Perhaps you've heard similar words: "What kind of God is it who permits his children to endure such pain and oppression? He obviously doesn't love you very much. You matter little to him.

---

1. Wilcock, *The Message of Revelation*, 54.

Otherwise he would heal you. If his love were genuine, he would spare you such distress. Where is he when you need him most? If he cared, he would long ago have delivered you from people like us."

There's no guarantee that vindication will come in this life. We may die with such blasphemous words echoing in our ears. But the affection of our great God will not forever remain hidden from view. Jesus assures us that a day is coming when the world will know, all too painfully, that we are loved with an immutable and infinitely intense passion. All ridicule will be redressed, every scoff will be silenced, each sneer wiped from their faces. Then there will be an indescribable display of divine delight and loud celebration as Jesus will say (shout? sing?), for all to hear, and show, for all to see, that he truly loves his own!

Jesus, the Keeping King

If you've ever wondered whether it mattered much to Jesus that you've kept the faith and maintained your commitment to him, this promise to the church of Philadelphia should put your fears to rest. Such resolute commitment to stay the course, spiritually speaking, may not get your name in the church bulletin or result in an invitation to appear on the 700 Club, but it matters pre-eminently to Jesus! The world may mock you for it, laugh, and consider you a fool to sacrifice so much of a monetary and personal nature simply for the sake of retaining your public and private commitment to Jesus, but this is no small matter.

If you doubt what I'm saying, look closely at our Lord's words in Revelation 3:10-11. "Because you have kept my word about patient endurance," said Jesus to the church in Philadelphia, "I will keep you from the hour of trial that is coming on the whole world, to try those who dwell on the earth. I am coming soon. Hold fast what you have, so that no one may seize your crown" (3:10-11). Patient endurance is no small feat, especially given our proclivity for impatience, self-preservation, and our desire for personal peace and comfort. Add to this the longing to be liked and the love of money, and you can begin to grasp the significance of our Lord's promise to the faithful.

As you probably know, people often appeal to this text in support of the doctrine of the pre-tribulation rapture of the church. Personally, I don't believe Jesus had any such thing in mind. A few observations should make this clear.

First, the notion that any Christian is assured of special protection from trials, tribulations, and persecution is unbiblical. We've seen repeatedly in these seven letters that suffering for the sake of Christ and the gospel is something all believers must embrace (see Rev. 2:2-3; 2:9-10; 2:13; 3:8-10). According to Paul, it is "through many tribulations (*thlipsis*; the same word used in Revelation 1:9; 7:14) we must enter the kingdom of God" (Acts 14:22). Jesus declared that "in the world you will have tribulation (*thlipsis*)" (John 16:33). Again, we are to "rejoice in our sufferings (*thlipsis*)" (Rom. 5:3; see also John 15:19-20; Acts 5:40-41; 1 Cor. 4:11-13; 2 Cor. 4:7-12; 11:24-25; 2 Tim. 3:12).

Second, the trial or tribulation that is coming is designed for the judgment of unbelievers, not Christians. "Those who dwell on the earth" (v. 9) or "earth-dwellers" is a stock phrase in Revelation that always refers to pagan persecutors of the church (6:10; 8:13; 11:10; 12:12; 13:8, 12, 14; 14:6; 17:2, 8). They are the ones who suffer the seal, trumpet, and bowl judgments of Revelation which characterize the entire church age, from the first coming of Christ to his second.

Third, the promise, then, is for spiritual protection in the midst of physical tribulation. Jesus is assuring his people that he will provide sufficient sustenance to preserve them in their faith, no matter what they face. The promise here is similar to what we find in Revelation 7:1-3, 13-14 where the people of God are "sealed" lest they suffer spiritual harm from "the great tribulation (*thlipsis*)" (v. 14; cf. also Rev. 11:1-2; 12:6, 14-17). Clearly, believers endure and emerge from tribulation spiritually secure. As Beale notes, "they are not preserved from trial by removal from it, but their faith is preserved through trial because they have been sealed by God."[2]

Fourth, pre-tribulationists have typically insisted that the only way God's people can be spiritually protected from the outpouring of divine wrath is by being physically removed from the earth. But this is clearly not the case, as John 17:15 makes clear (as also does the presence of the Israelites in Egypt during the time of the ten plagues). In this passage we find the only other place in the New Testament where the precise phrase "kept from" (*tereō ek*) is used. There Jesus prays to the Father: "I do not ask that you take them out of the world, but that you keep them from the evil one."

It's important to note in this text that "keep from" is actually contrasted with the notion of physical removal. Jesus prays not that the Father "take them out of the world" (i.e., physically remove them), but that the Father "keep them from" Satan's effort to destroy their spiritual life. Thus, when we turn to Revelation 3:10 we see that it is from the wrath of God poured out on "earth-dwellers" (unbelievers) that he promises to "keep" them. In the face of certain opposition and oppression from Satan, the Beast, and unbelievers, this is a glorious promise indeed.

Fifth, we must never forget that it is precisely in remaining faithful unto death that our greatest victory is achieved (not in being "raptured" to safety; cf. Rev. 2:10). Believers conquer Satan and the Beast "by the blood of the Lamb and by the word of their testimony, for they loved not their lives even unto death" (Rev. 12:11).

But what, precisely, is "the hour of trial that is coming on the whole world," and when will it occur? Of one thing I'm certain: the promise of protection must be of practical benefit and reassurance for the people of the church in Philadelphia in the first century. Thus, contrary to what is argued by some, this "hour of trial" cannot be restricted to (although it may be inclusive of) a time of tribulation at the end of the present age.

---

2. Beale, *Revelation*, 292.

If you are inclined to insist on a strictly futurist interpretation of the "hour of trial", ask yourself whether it seems odd (dare I say, impossible) that Jesus would promise one church in Asia Minor in the first century that they were to be protected from an event that not one single individual in that church would ever see, indeed, an event that allegedly would not transpire for at least another 1,900 years! How could this "hour of trial" be an event centuries after the Philadelphian Christians lived, especially since their protection from it is the very specific reward to them of their very specific, and historically identifiable, resistance to persecution and steadfast faithfulness in proclaiming the word of God? They are promised protection because they "kept the word" of Christ's perseverance.

I'm persuaded that Jesus is referring to that "tribulation" (*thlipsis*) which has already begun for Christians (including the Philadelphians) and will continue throughout the present age. In writing to the churches, John identifies himself as their "brother and partner in the tribulation [*thlipsis*] and the kingdom and the patient endurance that are in Jesus" (Rev. 1:9). In other words, "the hour of trial" is likely a reference to the entire, inter-advent church age, during which there will always be suffering and tribulation for those who stand firm in their witness for Christ. Thus, we are in the "hour of trial" right now and will continue to be until Jesus returns.

This isn't to deny that there will emerge an especially intensified and horrific period of tribulation in connection with the return of Christ at the end of history (regardless of how long you conceive it to be). But Jesus must have in mind an experience that was impending or already present for the Philadelphian believers in the first century and for all believers in subsequent centuries of the church's existence.

Jesus concludes with both a word of assurance and an exhortation: "I am coming soon. Hold fast what you have, so that no one may seize your crown" (Rev. 3:11). Is this "coming" the Second Advent at the close of history or a first-century disciplinary visitation? Possibly the former, but assuredly not the latter. After all, given the obedience of the Philadelphian church, there was no need for a "coming" of Jesus to judge or chastise (as was the case with Ephesus in 2:5, Pergamum in 2:16, and Sardis in 3:3).

However, there may be another option. The "coming" referred to in verse 11 is the heightened or intensified presence of Christ that will protect these believers when they pass through suffering and tribulation. In other words, this may be a spiritual coming to provide comfort and the power to persevere, a drawing near to their hearts to energize them in their commitment. His "coming" or approach to them is not spatial, but spiritual and sanctifying, in which he intensifies his sustaining influence in their souls. If he can "come" to the churches at Ephesus, Pergamum, and Sardis to discipline, he can certainly "come" to the church at Philadelphia to strengthen and bless.

And if he can "come" to the church at Philadelphia in the first century, he can also "come" to your local church today!

Chapter Eleven

Who am I? Who are You? The Power of Identity

(Revelation 3:7-13)

The Bible has a remarkable capacity to challenge and overcome our misperceptions about who we are. When we are inclined to think of ourselves as orphans, the biblical text declares that we are the adopted children of God. If we are wracked with guilt, the inspired word reminds us that we are forgiven. The feeling of being stained and soiled by sin is overcome with the realization that we are cleansed by the blood of Christ and clothed in his righteousness.

It's much the same when it comes to our place and role in the church. Many are inclined to view themselves as a blight or blemish on the body of Christ, a useless, transient appendage that contributes little to the advancement of God's kingdom. Utility becomes the measure of their worth. If they do little, they are little. Feeling ungifted and unqualified, they linger in the shadows, sitting on the back row, rarely if ever asked for their opinion and even less often willing to step forward and contribute positively to the welfare of the body as a whole.

Here in Revelation 3:12-13, the Word of God again graciously reminds us of God's perspective and reverses the paralyzing impact of false perceptions. Our Lord's words of promise and reassurance to those who persevere in their commitment to Jesus have bolstered and buoyed our faith throughout the course of these seven letters.

Nowhere is this more vividly seen and felt than in his comments to the church in Philadelphia. To the one who conquers, he again promises,

> "I will make him a pillar in the temple of my God. Never shall he go out of it, and I will write on him the name of my God, and the name of the city of my God, the new Jerusalem, which comes down from my God out of heaven, and my own new name. He who has an ear, let him hear what the Spirit says to the churches" (Rev. 3:12-13).

We Are God's Temple

The imagery of the individual Christian and the corporate church as the temple of God is a familiar one in Scripture. For example,

> "Do you not know that you are God's temple and that God's Spirit dwells in you? If anyone destroys God's temple, God will destroy him. For God's temple is holy, and you are that temple" (1 Cor. 3:16).

> "Or do you not know that your body is a temple of the Holy Spirit within you, whom you have from God?" (1 Cor. 6:19).

> "in whom the whole structure, being joined together, grows into a holy temple in the Lord. In him you also are being built together into a dwelling place for God by the Spirit" (Eph. 2:21-22).

> "As you come to him, a living stone rejected by men but in the sight of God chosen and precious, you yourselves like living stones are being built up as a spiritual house, to be a holy priesthood, to offer spiritual sacrifices acceptable to God through Jesus Christ" (1 Peter 2:4-5).

Permit me this momentary aside. The only temple in which God will ever dwell is his Son, Jesus Christ, and the body of Christ, the church. Any suggestion that God will sanction and approve of the rebuilding of a literal, physical temple in Jerusalem is utterly inconsistent with what we read in the New Testament. We are the temple of God. God's people, the church, are his dwelling place.

The metaphor is obviously fluid and thus there is no inconsistency in affirming that we are both the temple and the pillars within it. In declaring that he will make us pillars our Lord is homing in on one (or perhaps several) crucial truth about our relationship with him and our place in his purposes.

There are several Old Testament references that might serve as the possible backdrop for this portrait. We read in 1 Kings 7:13-22 of the two pillars constructed for Solomon's temple, ornate and awesome in their beauty and strength.

The reference to the "pillar" may continue (from Rev. 3:7) the allusion to Isaiah 22:22 where Eliakim's relatives achieve glory by hanging on him as a peg firmly attached to a wall (v. 24). Beale points out that "some Greek Old Testament witnesses even refer to Eliakim as being set up as a 'pillar' in Isa. 22:23." Thus, "in contrast to Eliakim's dependents, who eventually lost their glory and position in the palace when he was finally removed (cf. Isa. 22:23-25), the followers of Jesus will never be removed from their position in the temple/palace because Jesus, the 'true' Messiah, will never lose his regal position in the presence of his Father."[1]

The concept of God's people as a "pillar" is also found in Jeremiah 1:18 where the emphasis is on strength and stability and resistance to attack from the enemy. There is certainly New Testament precedence for describing God's people as "pillars", as seen in 1 Timothy 3:15 where the church itself is called "a pillar and buttress of the truth." In Galatians 2:9, Paul refers to James, Peter, and John as "pillars" of the New Testament church.

So what point is Jesus making in Revelation 3:12? In what sense will he make the overcomer or "the one who conquers" a "pillar in the temple" of his God?

A few have suggested that this is an allusion to the custom in which the provincial priest of the imperial cult, at the close of his tenure in office, erected in the temple area his statue or pillar inscribed with his name (together with the name of his father, his

---

1. Beale, *Revelation*, 295.

home town, and his years in office). However, several have pointed out that little evidence exists for this practice and that Philadelphia didn't even have a temple dedicated to the imperial cult until early in the third century A.D.

Perhaps the language is simply a metaphor of eternal salvation. Special emphasis may be on the security of our position as God's dwelling place in view of the assurance that "never shall he go out of it." This declaration would have carried special significance for those in Philadelphia: although they are expelled from Satan's synagogue (Rev. 3:9) they find a permanent place in God's temple.

Furthermore, as Mounce has noted, "to a city that had experienced devastating earthquakes [a massive quake devastated the city in 17 A.D.] which caused people to flee into the countryside and establish temporary dwellings there, the promise of permanence within the New Jerusalem would have a special meaning."[2] Thus, to a people familiar with uncertainty and weakness (cf. 3:8), it certainly conveys the idea of stability and permanence in the believer's relationship with God.

A friend recently reminded me that the key to this passage may be found in Psalm 144:12: "May our sons in their youth be like plants full grown, our daughters like corner pillars cut for the structure of a palace" (or, "fashioned as for a palace," NASV). From this we see that the purpose of a pillar was more than simply to uphold a palace, more than simply to provide support or serve a load-bearing function. Rather, pillars were designed to adorn a palace. Perhaps, then, it is the beauty of a pillar that is in view and not simply its utility.

This man wrote to me of his many journeys throughout the Middle East and especially his visit to countless mosques. A number of pillars he saw were made of elaborately hand-carved wood, while others were covered with thousands of individually handcrafted ceramic tiles. He noted that "even the adjective 'opulent' seems too restrained for many of these pillars." More important still, "the degree and level of the craftsmanship of a

---

2. Mounce, *Revelation*, 120-21.

mosque is always in direct correlation to the status of the builder, its beauty a visible demonstration of the builder's benevolence to the community." While such pillars may serve practical functions, "their aesthetic beauty deliberately overshadows their usefulness, and for the thoughtful soul this opens a wonderful window into the imagery" of Revelation 3.

"In much of the church world," he astutely notes, "our usefulness is what seems to matter: if we can teach the Bible in a community group, lead an outreach, or organize a committee, then we are 'an asset to the church.' But in his words to the church of Philadelphia, Jesus assures us that our place in God's presence is not based on our utility – he certainly does not need us to uphold his temple!" Rather, we are placed near the King of kings, and adorned with his profound spiritual beauty in order to reflect the majesty and graciousness of the One in whom we "are being built together into a dwelling place for God by the Spirit" (Eph. 2:22).

Whatever struggle may be yours in trying to identify yourself and your place in the kingdom of God, never forget that you are his dwelling place, the heart of his abode, and as a pillar in this temple you will reflect his beauty and splendor forever and ever, never to go out of it, ever!

The Life-Changing Power of Knowing Who You Are

As mentioned earlier, Christians often struggle with a sense of identity. They fail to grasp who they are by virtue not merely of their creation but especially of their regeneration and redemption. A failure to embrace our new identity and the privileges and responsibilities that come with it can be devastating. Virtually every assault and accusation of Satan is grounded in his effort to convince us we are not who God, in fact, declares we are. God says, "This is who you are," and Satan says, "No, you're not." If the enemy can persuade you that you are a spiritual impostor, an interloper, an unwanted and unqualified intruder into the kingdom of God, his victory is virtually assured.

On the other hand, if I'm able to rest securely in who I am in Christ, an identity forged by forgiveness not failure, by his goodness rather than mine, I am enveloped and enclosed in a veritable fortress of strength and protective love. No assault will prevail. No accusation will stand. No insinuation, however subtle, will undermine my confidence or sow seeds of suspicion in my soul. I am who he says I am by virtue of what he has done and will do. It's just that simple.

Three New Names

This is the great practical payoff of a glorious principle based on a God-ordained promise in Revelation 3:12. Look at it again:

> "I will make him a pillar in the temple of my God. Never shall he go out of it, and I will write on him the name of my God, and the name of the city of my God, the new Jerusalem, which comes down from my God out of heaven, and my own new name. He who has an ear, let him hear what the Spirit says to the churches" (Rev. 3:12-13).

If ever you and I needed to "hear what the Spirit says to the churches," it is now. So may God enable us to listen carefully and confidently.

Here is your current identity and ultimate destiny if you know Christ truly. It consists in having inscribed on your heart the name of God, of his city, and of his Son! There is, of course, as is the case with virtually all spiritual realities, a sense in which this is already true of us though not yet consummated. What we are now, we shall be in eternal verity, forever.

First, written on us is "the name of my God," says Jesus. There is a rich background in the Old Testament for this statement. One hardly knows where to begin. But let's start with Exodus 28:36-38, where we read,

> "You shall make a plate of pure gold and engrave on it, like the engraving of a signet, 'Holy to the Lord.' And you shall fasten it on the turban by a cord of blue. It shall be on the front of the turban. It shall be on Aaron's forehead, and Aaron shall bear any guilt from the holy things that the people of Israel consecrate as

their holy gifts. It shall regularly be on his forehead, that they may be accepted before the LORD" (Ex. 28:36-38).

It doesn't stop there. Consider these several instances of God's people receiving his name:

> "... everyone who is called by my name, whom I created for my glory, whom I formed and made" (Isa. 43:7).

> "I will give in my house and within my walls a monument and a name better than sons and daughters; I will give them an everlasting name that shall not be cut off" (Isa. 56:5).

> "The nations shall see your righteousness, and all the kings your glory, and you shall be called by a new name that the mouth of the LORD will give" (Isa. 62:2).

> "You shall leave your name to my chosen for a curse, and the Lord GOD will put you to death, but his servants he will call by another name" (Isa. 65:15).

In the priestly blessing that we often cite today as a benediction, God declares that "they will put my name upon the people of Israel, and I will bless them" (Numbers 6:27; see also Deuteronomy 28:10 and Daniel 9:18-19).

In ancient times, especially in the world of magic, to know someone's name was to gain power over them. As a counterpoint, then, to be called by God's name certainly suggests his sovereign rights over us as his children. It also points to ownership and consecration: our lives should be dominated and determined by our identity as his own, shaped and fashioned in godliness according to his glorious image.

Second, Jesus promises to inscribe on us "the name of the city of my God, the new Jerusalem, which comes down from my God out of heaven." This should come as no surprise, given what the New Testament says about our citizenship in the New Jerusalem (Gal. 4:26; Phil. 3:20). The author of Hebrews makes this clear: "But you have come to Mount Zion and to the city of the living

God, the heavenly Jerusalem, and to innumerable angels in festal gathering" (Heb. 12:22).

Furthermore, in Revelation 21:2-8 the people of God are virtually identified with the New Jerusalem. In other words, to bear the name of the city of God is more than simply a way of identifying its citizens, its rightful inhabitants. There is also a sense in which we are the New Jerusalem (cf. Isa. 56:5; Ezek. 48:35)! At minimum it is a way of stressing our permanent and ever so intimate presence with God and his presence in and for us, forever.

Third, and perhaps most important and precious of all, we shall bear Christ's "own new name." Note the emphatic position of the adjective, literally, "my name, the new." Christ's new name can hardly be any of those with which we are already familiar, such as Lord, Messiah, Savior, Son of God, Son of Man, Word, etc. "New" (*kainos*) means more than simply different or recent, as over against what one formerly was designated. Here it means new in quality, belonging to and characterized by the life and values of the new creation for which we have already been re-born (2 Cor. 5:17).

This "new name" is another way of alerting us to the fact that there awaits us a fuller, indeed infinitely expansive, revelation of the glory and beauty of Christ beyond anything we have seen, heard, or understood in this life. Whatever we know of Christ, however rich the treasures we enjoy of him in the present, whatever knowledge or insight into the unsearchable depths of his wisdom, knowledge, ways, and judgments we are graciously enabled to experience, all is but a sub-microscopic drop in the vast ocean of a spiritually macroscopic revelation yet to come!

Let's also not forget that being given a new name in biblical tradition is most often associated with the idea of receiving a new status, function, or change in character and calling (see Genesis 32:28). I can't even begin to speculate on what this entails for us in the ages to come!

And what, precisely, is this new name? We don't have a clue! In fact, its secrecy or hiddenness is one of its priceless qualities, for an unknown name suggests again that we who are called by it and have it inscribed on our souls are invulnerable to the enemy's attack. What Satan does not know, he cannot destroy. To be called by this "new name" is to be preserved for fellowship and intimacy with our Lord that none can touch or disrupt.

Conclusion

I close this chapter with a vivid illustration of the power of identity in the life of God's people, as seen in a brief clip from the movie *Blood Diamond*. The year is 1999 and the place is Sierra Leone in Africa. The country has been ravaged by political unrest. One particular rebel faction known as the Revolutionary United Front (or RUF) is terrorizing the countryside. They attack villages without mercy, take captive everyone who survives, and then force them to harvest diamonds to fund their war effort.

One man who is forced to search for diamonds by the RUF is a fisherman named Solomon Vandy. One morning he discovers an enormous pink diamond in the riverbank and buries it with the intent of returning later to keep it for himself. When the area is raided by government security forces, Vandy is thrown in jail, where he meets a man named Danny Archer, played by Leonardo DiCaprio. Archer is a Rhodesian gun runner who is trying to smuggle diamonds into Liberia.

Archer finds out about the pink diamond that Vandy discovered and works to have him released from detention. Meanwhile, in one of the attacks launched by the RUF, Vandy's young son, Dia, is captured and forced to serve in the RUF as a child soldier. They seem to have brainwashed Dia and turned this precious young boy into a vicious fighter. Archer joins Solomon Vandy in a search to recover his son Dia with the understanding that Vandy will show him where the pink diamond is buried.

They find Dia among the RUF, but he refuses to acknowledge his father. Mercenaries attack the camp and kill virtually all of the RUF soldiers. Archer and Vandy escape, dig up the diamond, only to be confronted at gunpoint by young Dia.

What I'm asking you to take note of is the transformation that occurs in young Dia as his father awakens him to who he is. A young boy who has been brainwashed by his captors and turned into a vicious child soldier is angry and defiant. You can see it in his eyes as he holds his own father at gunpoint. But when he is confronted with the love of his father, Vandy, when he is reminded of his true identity, everything changes. The transforming power of a renewed awareness of one's identity is unmistakably powerful. I've provided you with a translation of Vandy's comments to young Dia.

> "Dia. What are you doing? Dia. Look at me. What are you doing? You are Dia Vandy, of the proud Mende tribe. You are a good boy who loves soccer and school. Your mother loves you so much. She waits by the fire making plantains and red palm oil stew, with your sister N'yanda. And the new baby. The cows wait for you, and Babu the wild dog who minds no one but you. I know they made you do bad things. But you are not a bad boy. I am your father who loves you. You will come home with me and be my son again."

Those of you who know Jesus Christ as Lord and Savior, do you know who you are? You are a child of the Most High God who loves you, who wants you to come home with him and be his son, his daughter, once again. And how important is it for you to know who you truly are? Simply put, your life will never change for the good until you embrace your true identity in Christ. Identity governs behavior. You will always behave in accordance with who you believe you are. It was true of young Dia, and it is all the more true for you and me.

Chapter Twelve

The Church that makes Jesus Sick

(Revelation 3:14-22)

I've lived in nine cities. I was born in Shawnee, Oklahoma, from which we moved when I was ten to settle in Midland, Texas. I attended high school in Duncan, Oklahoma, and went to college in Norman. My wife and I lived in Dallas, Texas, for twelve years, and then moved back to Oklahoma, this time to Ardmore, in 1985. Since then we've lived in Kansas City, Chicago, once again in Kansas City and now OKC.

I'm grateful for what I experienced in each city. I'm not sure the same could be said for our seventh and final city in Revelation 2–3. Whether the citizens of ancient Laodicea were proud of their hometown or ashamed of its failures is impossible to know. But of one thing we may be sure, the church there had massive spiritual problems and called forth the most stringent and stinging rebuke yet issued by our Lord. The severity of this letter is unmistakable, as is also the absence of a single word of praise or commendation. This church and this letter are the most famous (infamous?) of the seven.

The courier entrusted by the apostle John with the seven letters to the seven churches neared his journey's end. Having embarked from the island of Patmos with the book of Revelation securely tucked away in his messenger's pouch, he would have begun his travel along the circular route by first visiting Ephesus. Moving northward he would pass through the cities of Smyrna and Pergamum, at which point, turning southeast, his journey would lead him to Thyatira, Sardis, and Philadelphia. Finally, having come almost full circle along the well-beaten trade route, he would arrive at his final destination: Laodicea.

A brief introduction to Laodicea will prove beneficial in our study of the letter. Laodicea was perhaps the wealthiest city in Phrygia. It was a city known not simply for its monetary success (it was a banking center), but also for its linen and wool industries (especially black sheep!), as well as its medical school. Probably the most famous medicinal product to come out of Laodicea was an eye ointment made from a powder produced in Phrygia.

We don't know how or when the gospel came to Laodicea. Paul most likely never visited the church, although he did pray for it (Col. 2:1), and he went out of his way to make certain that his epistle to the Colossians was also read to them. As if that weren't enough, Paul even wrote a letter to the Laodiceans! He refers to it in Colossians 4:16 as "the letter from Laodicea," leading some to believe it was a letter written to Paul by the Laodicean church, or perhaps by its leadership, or even one of its members. But it's more likely that Paul had in mind a letter from him, currently in the possession of the Laodiceans, written to them, that he now wanted to be read to the church in Colossae.

We don't know what happened to this letter, but it's possible that it was destroyed in the massive earthquake that hit the region in the year 61. But that's only speculation. You shouldn't be bothered by this, given that Paul likely wrote four (!) letters to the Corinthian church, although only two of them are included in our canon of inspired Scripture (see 1 Corinthians 5:9-11, a reference to a letter written in the year 54, now lost; and 2 Corinthians 2:4, 9, a reference to a letter written in the summer of 55, often called the "severe" or "tearful" letter, also now lost).

We have no idea why God chose not to preserve these and other apostolic writings for the church of subsequent generations. Evidently once they served their divinely designed function for the early church, God sovereignly arranged for their disappearance or destruction. In his infinite and gracious wisdom he determined that the content of those epistles was not essential for the life and faith of the church beyond the first century. Ultimately, we must trust in divine providence and believe that God has preserved for us everything that is necessary for a life of truth and godliness.

Jesus is the Amen!

Of the three things said about Jesus in verse 14, I want to focus on only two. Note well: Jesus doesn't just say "Amen," he is "the Amen"! He himself is the validation, the ratification, the confirmation, the authentication of all that God has said and promised he will do for his children.

"Amen!" was the biblical way of making known, "Yes! I agree! By all means! So be it! Undoubtedly so! Yep! Absolutely!" When the people of God heard the word of God they typically responded with "Amen!" as a way of making it unmistakably clear: "We participate with you in declaring this to be so. There is an echo in our hearts to what you say. This truth reverberates loudly in our souls."

When we come to Revelation 3:14 this glorious declaration of affirmation is elevated even higher, for here it becomes one of the names of Jesus Christ himself (cf. Isa. 65:16)! So much is this a reflection of his character and wholly consistent with his nature that he is properly named "the Amen"!

So, what does this mean to you and me? How does it serve to heighten our confidence and deepen our assurance and drive out the doubts that so often plague us? Look closely with me at Paul's statement in 2 Corinthians 1:20. There we're told that "all the promises of God find their Yes in him. That is why it is through him that we utter our Amen to God for his glory."

Whatever God has promised to us, whether by way of covenant stipulation or stated intent, regardless of the context or time, no matter how unrealistic or far-fetched it may at first appear, will come to pass because of who Christ is and what he has done. He is the "Amen!" to all God has said he will do. This is true not simply because Jesus adds his personal word of confirmation or stamps it with his seal of approval. It is true because he actually secures it and effectually brings it to pass by virtue of his death and resurrection. Whatever obstacles may have stood in the way of God's promises coming true, such as our sin and Satan's power, have been overcome by the blood of the Lamb!

Jesus, the Sovereign Lord over the New Creation

On this point I'll be brief. The title "beginning of the creation of God" does not mean that Jesus is himself a created being, but rather that he is the source, cause, or the one through whom creation occurs. In fact, this phrase likely refers not to Jesus' sovereignty over the first or original creation (although he surely has that!), but points to his resurrection as demonstrating that he is the inauguration or cause of and the sovereign ruler over the new creation that is described in Revelation 21–22.

Lukewarm

Our Lord's diagnosis of the problem in Laodicea is twofold. He first discerns a moral and religious tepidity in the church, a lukewarmness that borders on outright indifference to the things of God and a life of godliness. Second, he traces this to a prideful self-sufficiency (v. 17). To come straight to the point, Christianity at Laodicea was flabby and anemic! Our Lord uses the language of "cold," "hot," and "lukewarm." What does he mean by this description?

People have typically believed that by "hot" Jesus is referring to zealous, lively, passionate, hard-working Christians, and that by "cold" he is referring to lifeless, unregenerate pagans, devoid of any spiritual life whatsoever. Hot, so goes the argument, refers to spiritually active believers whereas cold refers to apathetic unbelievers. But this creates the problem of Jesus appearing to say he would rather they be in utter unbelief than in a backslidden, lukewarm, albeit still saved condition.

The key to making sense of this comes from an understanding of certain features of the topography of the land in which the Laodiceans lived. Laodicea lacked a natural water supply and was dependent on its neighbors for this vital resource. This, I believe, explains the imagery in this remarkable passage. In all likelihood, "hot" and "cold" don't refer to the spiritual "temperature" or religious "mood" or "attitude", as it were, of the believer and the unbeliever, as has traditionally been thought. Rather, the word "hot" refers to the well-known medicinal waters of Hierapolis (six miles north of Laodicea), whose "hot springs" reached 95 degrees. The word "cold", on the other hand, points to the refreshing waters of Colossae (twelve miles to the east).

If this is what Jesus had in mind, the church is not being rebuked for its spiritual temperature but for the barrenness of its works. The church was providing neither refreshment for the spiritually weary (portrayed through the imagery of "cold" water from Colossae), nor healing for the spiritually sick (portrayed through the imagery of "hot" water from Hierapolis). The church was simply ineffective.

If correct, this relieves the problem of why Christ would prefer the church to be "cold" rather than "lukewarm". The church in Laodicea is rebuked, therefore, for the useless and barren nature of its works, indicative of its stagnant spiritual condition. "You've become of no benefit to anyone," says Jesus, "and I will not stomach such behavior."

The topography of the region also sheds light on his use of the word "lukewarm". As the hot, mineral-laden waters from Hierapolis traveled across the plateau towards Laodicea, they gradually became lukewarm before cascading over the edge directly in view of the Laodicean populace. There are archaeological remains in Laodicea of an aqueduct system that would have carried water from Hierapolis. The people in Laodicea would have been keenly aware of the nauseating effect of drinking from that source.

"That is what you are like to me," says Jesus. "When I look upon your lack of zeal, your indifference toward the needs of others, and your blasé response to my beauty, I feel like a man who has drunk tepid, tasteless water." It's difficult to rid one's mind of the picture of Jesus lifting to his lips a cup of what he anticipates being a flavorful and refreshing drink, only to regurgitate it in utter disgust.

Then there is the rather revolting image of Jesus spitting or vomiting the Laodicean church out of his mouth. Notwithstanding the numerous threats of discipline and judgment throughout these seven letters, there's something about Jesus being sickened to the point of vomiting his people out of his mouth that strikes us as uncharacteristically unseemly. Does the "spitting" / "spewing" / "vomiting" of such people from his mouth suggest that all hope is lost for their salvation and enjoyment of eternal fellowship with Christ? Not necessarily. This imagery, at minimum, indicates a serious threat of divine discipline. But there may yet be hope through repentance and obedience.

Their Misguided Self-Awareness

Why was it so important for the Laodiceans to understand their spiritual plight? Why was Jesus so concerned that the blinders of self-deception and self-sufficiency be stripped away, and they see and sense their utter and absolute dependence on him for all they are and have? The answer is simply that God will not tolerate any attitude in us or activity by us that in any way detracts from his glory.

"I am the Lord; that is my name; my glory I give to no other" (Isa. 42:8).

"My glory I will not give to another" (Isa. 48:11b).

The self-sufficient, self-congratulatory, self-aggrandizing, self-promoting pomp and pride of the Laodiceans was not something Jesus would long tolerate. No one, not the Laodiceans, not you or I or the most magnificent mega-church on the earth, will be permitted to detract from God's glory or take credit for what he has accomplished.

Tragically, the Laodiceans had grown religiously plump and proud of themselves, blind to their desperate need for what only Christ can supply. "For you say, I am rich, I have prospered, and I need nothing, not realizing that you are wretched, pitiable, poor, blind, and naked" (Rev. 3:17).

Our Lord's use of terms in this passage points to a deliberate contrast on his part between the church at Smyrna and that of Laodicea. Smyrna suffered from material poverty (*ptōcheia*) but was regarded by Jesus as spiritually wealthy (*plousios*). Laodicea, on the other hand, was materially wealthy (*plousios*) but spiritually poor (*ptōcheia*). Thus, despite their banks, they were beggars! Despite their famous eye-salve, they were blind! Despite their prosperous clothing factories, they were naked!

Part of what it means to be spiritually lukewarm is to be smug, complacent, satisfied with the spiritual status quo, at rest with one's progress in the Christian life, with little or no self-awareness, little or no recognition that all is of God and his Christ. To be lukewarm is to live as if what you presently know and experience of Christ is enough. No need or desire to press on further. No need or desire to seek after God. Little or no longing to pray and fast. Little or no longing to break free of sin. Satisfied with the current depth of delight in the Spirit. Satisfied with the current extent of knowledge of the Father. The Laodiceans were content with life as it was and not in the least ashamed or hesitant to take full credit for what little they had achieved.

They took stock in their spiritual assets and evaluated their religious portfolio and felt rich and prosperous and in need of nothing, not even what God might give. Our Lord's assessment was of another sort. "You're spiritually bankrupt," he said, "and morally wretched and visually impaired and shamefully exposed. You have no grasp of your utter dependence on me for life and forgiveness and hope and joy and understanding and righteousness."

But there's still hope, if only they will listen and learn from "what the Spirit says to the churches". Says Jesus: "I counsel you to buy from me gold refined by fire, so that you may be rich, and white garments so that you may clothe yourself and the shame of your nakedness may not be seen, and salve to anoint your eyes, so that you may see" (Rev. 3:18).

Lukewarm, professing Christians, though poor and bereft of spiritual resources, can still cash in on the only currency that counts, now and in eternity: pure gold, refined by Jesus himself.

Those plagued by moral nakedness and the shame of exposure can yet be adorned in clothing that may not qualify as "fashion" in today's world but is more than adequate to provide covering and a standing before a God who sees through every outward façade. And those blinded by a false sense of self-importance, who fancy themselves enlightened and "on the cutting edge", may yet submit to an ophthalmic physician whose healing salve strips the scales from our darkened vision and brings clarity of sight to behold the beauty of the King.

Continuing to draw on imagery derived from their own commercial activities, Jesus counsels them to make several purchases in those areas where they fancy themselves self-sufficient. He likens himself to a merchant who visits the city to sell his wares and competes with other salesmen. "I advise you," he says, "to forsake your former suppliers and come trade with me."

True spiritual wealth, the sort that cannot rust or be stolen or suffer from a Wall Street crash or plummeting interest rates, is the "gold" that is purified of all dross and rid of every alloy by the refining fires of suffering (cf. Job 23:10; Prov. 27:21; Mal. 3:2-3; 1 Pet. 1:6-9). This is the "gold" of knowing Christ, enjoying Christ, savoring Christ, treasuring Christ, prizing Christ, and finding in him alone the fullness of joy that will never fade or lose its capacity to please.

There is an obvious paradox here, for how can "poor" people purchase a commodity as expensive as gold? You do so with the only currency that counts in God's presence: need. The coin of the realm is desperation. We don't pay him out of our resources but from an acknowledgment of the depths of our abject poverty. The price God requires is that faith in him which humbly concedes that one has nothing with which to bargain, nothing with which to trade, nothing with which to make so much as a meager down-payment.

For people living in first-century Laodicea, the imagery would have evoked an unmistakable contrast in their minds between the famous and profitable "black" wool from the sheep in Laodicea and the "white" woolen garments essential to their spiritual lives.

Finally, they are desperately in need of the restoration of their spiritual vision. The founder of the medical school at Laodicea was a famous ophthalmologist named Demosthenes Philalethes. As helpful as his remedies might be for the physical eye, only Jesus can apply that soothing, healing, restorative salve that enables us to behold and enjoy beauty that never fades or fails.

Revelation 3:19 is nothing short of shocking. Earlier in verse 16 Jesus expressed disgust towards those in Laodicea, declaring that he is on the verge of vomiting them out of his mouth. Yet now, in verse 19, he affirms his love for them! May I boldly suggest that it is precisely because he loves his people that he refuses to tolerate their lukewarm indifference toward spiritual matters? In other words, the harsh words in this letter, the firm discipline evoked by their backslidden behavior, together with the strong counsel (v. 18) that they "be zealous and repent" (v. 19), are all motivated by our Lord's love for his own!

If you're looking for an explanation of our Lord's posture in relation to Laodicea, you need go no farther than Revelation 3:19. He says and does what we read in this letter because of his loving commitment to them! "Those whom I love, I reprove and discipline, so be zealous and repent" (Rev. 3:19). There's no escaping the fact that sometimes love hurts. I don't mean that it hurts because we love someone who fails to love us back (although, of course, that's often true). I'm talking about God's love. Sometimes, because God is love, you will hurt. His discipline is often uncomfortable and painful.

Consider the words of Solomon in Proverbs 3:11-12, the passage to which Jesus obviously alludes in Revelation 3:19 – "My son, do not despise the LORD's discipline or be weary of his reproof, for the LORD reproves him whom he loves, as a father the son in whom he delights."

It was a hard lesson for the Laodiceans to learn. Whether or not they eventually grasped this truth and did what Jesus commanded ("be zealous and repent") remains a mystery. The only remaining and relevant question is whether we will embrace the discipline of our loving Lord and run to him, rather than from him, when we sin.

Jesus at the Door

Next to John 3:16, this is perhaps the most famous evangelistic verse in the New Testament. The question is, Should it be? To this lukewarm and backslidden church, Jesus issues this stunning invitation: "Behold, I stand at the door and knock. If anyone hears my voice and opens the door, I will come in to him and eat with him, and he with me" (Rev. 3:20).

Most people simply assume this is an evangelistic appeal to non-Christians to open the door of their hearts and invite Jesus in to save and forgive them. Let me say first of all that if you came to saving faith in Christ in response to the use of this passage in an evangelistic presentation, praise God! The fact that this text was, in all likelihood, used in a way inconsistent with its original intent in no way invalidates the spiritual life God graciously imparted to you through it.

There's one more thing to note before we proceed. Colin Hemer has pointed out that Jesus has once again drawn on imagery familiar to the people of Laodicea in order to make his point, for the city was situated foursquare on one of the most important road junctions in Asia Minor. Each of the four city gates opened onto a busy trade route. The inhabitants of Laodicea, therefore, "must have been very familiar with the belated traveler who 'stood at the door and knocked' for admission."[1]

The most likely view is that the invitation is addressed to backslidden, unrepentant believers who, in their self-sufficiency, had excluded (indeed, excommunicated) the risen Lord from their congregational and personal lives. But in an expression of indescribable condescension and love Jesus asks permission to enter and re-establish fellowship with his people, a fellowship portrayed in the imagery of a feast in which Christ and Christians share.

One final view to consider is eschatological in nature. One interpretation says that the invitation (v. 20) has future fulfillment. It is addressed to backslidden believers in the church at Laodicea

---

1. Hemer, *Letters,* 204.

and pertains to Christ's second coming. The door at which Jesus stands is a metaphor for the imminence of his return (cf. Jas. 5:9). Those who are prepared and alert to receive their Savior at his coming will enjoy intimate communion with him in the messianic feast of the age to come. This view links verse 20 with verse 21 and the promise of co-regency in the future kingdom.

Thus the appeal of verse 20 is not to unbelievers so that they might be saved. Rather it is an appeal to individuals ("anyone") within the church to repent and forsake their spiritual half-heartedness. As a result, one may experience even now the intimate communion and fellowship of which the feast in the messianic kingdom is the consummation. Present fellowship with Jesus is a foretaste of that eternal felicity which will be consummated in the age to come.

Enthroned with Jesus!

Note once again Revelation 3:21. "The one who conquers, I will grant him to sit with me on my throne, as I also conquered and sat down with my Father on his throne." Perhaps this promise would rest more easily in my heart if it weren't for the fact that Revelation 4 and 5 follow immediately on this concluding letter to the church at Laodicea. You see, when I pause to reflect on what Christ meant when he referred to his "throne", a throne on which his people, together with him, will sit, I can't help but be drawn into the majestic scene that follows in the subsequent two chapters.

What we see and hear and feel in Revelation 4 and 5 is the pinnacle of biblical revelation. There simply is no greater, more majestic, or breathtaking scene than that of the risen Lamb sitting on the throne, surrounded by adoring angels and unusual creatures, with ear-popping peals of thunder and blinding bolts of lightning.

If my earlier discomfort was due to the seeming impropriety of sinners sitting on that throne, nothing is more proper or fitting or apropos than that Jesus should be there. Nothing makes more sense than that he should be the focus of all creation – whether of elders falling down mesmerized by his beauty or of strange animals singing endlessly of his holiness. He belongs on the throne! He is

God! He has died and redeemed men and women from every tribe and tongue and people and nation! By all means, let us sing:

> Crown Him with many crowns, the Lamb upon His throne.
> Hark! How the heavenly anthem drowns all music but its own.
> Awake, my soul, and sing, of Him who died for thee,
> And hail Him as thy matchless King through all eternity.
>
> Crown Him the Lord of Heaven, enthroned in worlds above,
> Crown Him the King to Whom is given the wondrous name of Love.
> Crown Him with many crowns, as thrones before Him fall;
> Crown Him, ye kings, with many crowns, for He is King of all
> (George J. Elvey)

Yes, he is the Lord of Heaven (and earth) and is rightly "enthroned in worlds above." But what, for heaven's sake, are we doing there? More shocking still, what are the Laodiceans doing there? And what, for heaven's sake, will the twenty-four Elders think? What will be the reaction of the four living creatures, not to mention the myriads of angelic beings who surround the throne, pouring forth wave upon wave of endless praise? Will they not be shocked and scandalized to see sinners there? I would be!

We must be very careful and theologically precise on this point. We are not enthroned with Christ because we are Christ, as if salvation entails the merging of our being with his in such a way that he is less than the Creator or that we are more than creatures. Our union with him is vital and glorious but he is always the one and only living Lord and we are redeemed sinners who depend on him not only now but for all eternity.

We are not enthroned with him because we will have been deified, as if we will have left behind our humanity and been transformed into divinity. We are not enthroned because we are God but because he is! Although we will be "made like him" (1 John 3:2; Phil. 3:21), gloriously devoid of all sinful impulses, our presence on his throne is a gift, not a right. We are there not by nature or deed but by grace alone, having been made co-heirs by him who alone is worthy of worship.

Having said all that, I'm still a bit incredulous when it comes to this promise in Revelation 3:21-22 (cf. Rev. 2:26-27). But at least I know why I'm enthroned with him, and why not. I'm there because he died for me and poured out the love of God into my heart through the Spirit who was given to me (Rom. 5:5). I'm there because of mercy, not merit. I'm there to share his rule, not usurp it. I'm there to exercise an authority that is rightfully his and derivatively mine.

I don't expect ever fully to understand what this promise means or entails. Its shape is still uncertain to me. What it will feel like is yet foreign. Its plausibility confronts me like an insurmountable mountain peak. That Christ Jesus should ever make room within his reign for a scurrilous sinner like me is no doubt a theme that will occupy my thoughts and inquiries for all eternity. As for now, I don't know what else to say but, "Thank you, Lord!"

Chapter Thirteen

Enthroned! Encircled! Extolled!

(Revelation 4:1-11)

What is happening in heaven right now? And by "right now" I mean right now! Literally. John was given a vision that answers this question and the portrait it provides is undoubtedly as true today as it was nearly 2,000 years ago.[2]

This passage, together with Revelation 5, is a vision of the majesty of a sovereign God in complete control of his creation. From an earthly perspective, it might seem that the enemies of the kingdom of God are winning. Christians are being persecuted, imprisoned, and martyred. Tragedy and trial and turmoil are rampant and the Great Dragon (Satan), the Beast, and the False Prophet appear to have the upper hand. All hope of light at the end of the tunnel grows dim because the tunnel has no end. The tunnel is all there is. History simply has no purpose. Dreams of finally emerging out the other side are shattered ... there is no other side!

But John's vision reveals that appearances can be deceiving! The course of history isn't determined by political intrigue or military might, but by God. What John discovered is that there are two worlds or two dimensions of reality. One is earthly and visible; the other is heavenly and invisible. And remarkably, it is the latter

---

2. Much of what follows in this and the subsequent chapter has been adapted from my book, *One Thing: Developing a Passion for the Beauty of God* (Christian Focus, 2010), and is used here with permission.

which controls and determines the former. Or better still, it is God who is sovereign over both!

It's as if the Holy Spirit says to John (and to us): "Listen to me. Things are not as they appear. I'm about to show you things as they really are. I'm about to take you into the throne room of God himself. Things aren't running amok. The devil hasn't won. Evil hasn't triumphed. Neither fate nor cruel chance governs the universe. He who was and is and is to come has everything well in hand." Here in Revelation 4–5 we are given a biblical worldview: not a Hollywood worldview, or a worldview shaped by the materialistic values of Wall Street, or a worldview shaped by the power brokers in Washington, D.C. This is the worldview of the Bible, a worldview that comes from seeing God as he truly is.

The voice is that of Jesus Christ (cf. 1:10-11). As John looks, he sees a vision of the Triune God, enthroned, encircled, and extolled. In Exodus 33:18 Moses made a simple request of God: "Please show me your glory." God placed him in the "cleft of a rock" and caused his glory to pass by. Here in Revelation 4–5 we are granted access to the sight of God's glory that Moses only saw in passing, in part.

The first two words in Revelation 4:1, "After this," do not mean that the events of Chapters 4–5 occur after the events of Chapters 1–3, as if this were a description of their chronological sequence. Rather, these words only indicate that the vision of Revelation 4–5 came to John after the vision of Revelation 1–3. In other words, this is the sequence in which John saw the visions but not necessarily the order of their occurrence as historical events. See also 7:1, 9; 15:5; 18:1; 19:1.

Enthroned!

The voice John hears is that of Jesus Christ (cf. 1:10-11). As John looks, he's confronted with a breathtaking, knee-knocking, heart-pounding, eye-popping vision of the Triune God. He sees the Lord enthroned, encircled, and extolled. What follows in Chapters 4 and 5 of the Apocalypse stretches the imagination and tests our capacity to grasp the beauty of God. Resist the temptation to read these verses as you would a newspaper or novel or even the book of

Romans. In fact, it is precisely here that we are confronted with the limitations of human language. Nothing in our vocabulary is fully adequate to explain, account for, or illustrate the ineffable majesty of God.

In Revelation 4:3 we see God in a resplendent blaze of unapproachable light, the jewels refracting the glory and majesty of his luminous beauty. Here is where all worship begins: in the throne room of heaven where God reigns supreme! When we see God as he is, incomparably sublime and incontestably sovereign, we will praise him as we should in unison with the heavenly hosts. This is not a pathetic deity wringing his hands over a world catapulting into oblivion. He does not pace the floor of heaven with furrowed brow, riddled with anxiety over the outcome of human history. God reigns!

If asked to describe God, what terms would you employ? I fear that many Christians are so deficient in their knowledge and experience of God that they portray him as a formless, passionless, gray blob of abstract power. John's vision, on the other hand, is a virtual kaleidoscope of color and sound and sight and smell! John sees all the colors of the rainbow magnified!

The one on the throne has the appearance of jasper, an opaque stone that tends to be red but is also found in yellow, green, and grayish blue. It suggests the qualities of majesty and holiness and is used later in Revelation as an image for the overall appearance of the New Jerusalem, which manifests the glory of God (21:11), and is the material from which its walls are constructed (21:18), as well as the first of its twelve foundations (21:19). The sardius (or carnelian) was a red stone, similar in appearance to a ruby. It evokes the image of both divine jealousy and righteous wrath, both the burning zeal of God for the fame of his name and his just and resolute response to those who would bring reproach upon it.

The rainbow reminds us of the faithfulness of God when he first set this sign in the heavens as a pledge to Noah following the great flood. Also found in Ezekiel 1:28, the rainbow reminds us that God's wrath and judgment, perhaps symbolized by the sardius as well as described in the subsequent visions, are tempered by his mercy and his promise to Noah never again to totally destroy the earth. In Ezekiel the rainbow is explicitly said to portray the radiant appearance of God's glory. Here it emanates like an emerald, reminding us that our God is filled not only with jealous zeal but tender-hearted affection.

Of course, John is not saying that God is a jasper or a sardius, but that his appearance was like such precious stones. This is not photographic reproduction but symbolic imagery. He wants to stir our imaginations and inflame our hearts, not fill our minds with endless facts.

The atmosphere of this scene is bathed in mystery and awash in wonder. Worship without wonder is lifeless and boring. Many have lost their sense of awe and amazement when it comes to God. Having begun with the arrogant presumption of knowing about God all that one can, they reduce him to manageable terms and confine him to a tidy theological box, the dimensions of which conform to their predilections of what a god ought to be and do. That they have lost the capacity to marvel at the majesty of God comes as little surprise. Warren Wiersbe explains:

> "We must recognize the fact that true wonder is not a passing emotion or some kind of shallow excitement. It has depth to it. True wonder reaches right into your heart and mind and shakes you up. It not only has depth, it has value; it enriches your life. Wonder is not cheap amusement that brings a smile to your face. It is an encounter with reality – with God – that brings awe to your heart. You are overwhelmed with an emotion that is a mixture of gratitude, adoration, reverence, fear, – and love. You are not looking for explanations; you are lost in the wonder of God."[3]

Our wonder in God's presence, however, is not borne of ignorance but of knowledge. We know something about the majesty of God and for that reason are lost in wonder, love and praise. We cannot stand in awe of someone of whom we are ignorant. Our wonder deepens with each degree of understanding.

---

3. Warren Wiersbe, *Real Worship* (Nashville: Thomas Nelson, 1990), 44-45.

But is it practical to worship when the world is falling apart? John's life is at risk. Of all the apostles, he alone has survived. Who knows how much longer he has? In such a crisis, why would the Spirit escort John into heaven and point to the adoring and passionate praise of angels and unusual creatures and saints? Because it's the only thing that makes sense! Worship is no flight from reality. Nothing is more real than what John sees and hears and senses around the throne of God.

Some will read Revelation 4–5 and say: "Ah, this is all well and good. But what practical benefit is it to me at work? How does this help me respond to an abusive and overbearing boss? How does it help me fight the temptation to lust after one of my co-workers? How does it help me love my spouse and my kids? How does it strengthen me to endure times of financial strain and physical pain?"

This vision of God enthroned, encircled, and extolled is eminently practical because adoring and affectionate praise is what restores our sense of ultimate value. It exposes the worthless and temporary and tawdry stuff of this world. Worship energizes the heart to seek satisfaction in Jesus alone. In worship we are reminded that this world is fleeting and unworthy of our heart's devotion. Worship connects our souls with the transcendent power of God and awakens in us appreciation for true beauty. It pulls back the veil of deception and exposes the ugliness of sin and Satan. Worship is a joyful rebuke of the world. When our hearts are riveted on Jesus everything else in life becomes so utterly unnecessary and we become far less demanding.

Encircled!

In John's vision the throne of God is, as it should be, at the center of all heavenly activity. The throne is the focus of a series of concentric circles made up first of a rainbow, then a circle of the four living creatures, then a circle of the twenty-four thrones upon which the twenty-four elders sit. According to Revelation 5:11 (and again in 7:11), a great host of angels also encircle the throne. Eventually all creation joins the worshiping throng (see 5:13).

We read in verse 3 that "around the throne" was a "rainbow" and now in verse 4 "around the throne" are twenty-four thrones on which sit twenty-four elders. They wear white garments and golden crowns (4:4), prostrate themselves before God in worship (4:10; 5:14; 11:16; 19:4), and cast before him their golden crowns (4:10). They sing hymns of praise to God (4:11; 5:9-10; 11:17-18), and hold harps and bowls full of incense that are said to represent the prayers of Christians (5:8).

Who are they? What are they? Some see in them an exalted angelic order, like the cherubim and seraphim. There are several things that point to them being a species of angels. In 5:8 they are described as bringing the prayers of the saints to God; in 5:5 and 7:13 they interpret for John the meaning of his visions, a typical angelic function in Scripture; and in 4:9-10; 5:8, 14; 7:11; and 19:4 they join with the four living creatures and the rest of the angels in worshiping God.

On the other hand, nowhere else in Scripture are angels called "elders." And in Revelation it is the people of God who wear crowns and are clothed in white and sit on thrones (2:10; 3:4-5; 3:21; 20:4; 7:13-15; 19:7-8, 14). But this may be due to the possibility that these are angels who symbolize or represent the saints.

Others think they are exalted Old Testament believers. King David organized the temple servants into twenty-four orders of priests (1 Chron. 24:3-19), twenty-four Levitical gatekeepers (26:17-19), and twenty-four orders of Levites commissioned to prophesy, give thanks, praise God, and sing to the accompaniment of harps and lyres and cymbals (25:6-31).

Another possibility is that they are exalted New Testament saints, in particular, individual Christians who have sealed their faith through martyrdom and are now glorified and participating in an exalted heavenly life. Thrones are sometimes used as a metaphor for the heavenly reward of the righteous. But if they are only New Testament saints, why the number twenty-four? Could this be a symbol for their continuous, twenty-four-hour worship, day and night?

I find it difficult not to see in the number "twenty-four" a reference to the twelve tribes of Israel and the twelve apostles of the New Testament church (they are associated again in 21:12-14). If so, the elders may be representatives of the entire community of the redeemed from both Testaments. But are they human or angelic representatives? Probably the latter insofar as they bring the prayers of the saints before God (5:8) and sing of the redeemed in the third person (5:9-10). Also, the fact that these twenty-four elders are distinguished from the redeemed multitude in Revelation 7:9-17 indicates that they are angelic representatives of all the people of God.

Rest assured of one thing. If they are angels, I doubt they look anything like the fat little cherubs with dimpled cheeks that hang playfully suspended above a baby's crib. These are powerful and majestic creatures whose radiance reflects the glory of the One they so adoringly worship and serve. What's important, however, is not who they are but what they are doing. They are mesmerized by the majesty of God, obsessed with his glory, and committed to unending and adoring praise.

The lightning and thunder, undoubtedly quite literal, are also symbolic of God's awesome power and infinite might and remind us of the revelation of God at Mt. Sinai (Ex. 19:16–18; 20:18–20). They may well be emanations of the endless energy of God's own being, pointing to the limitless depths of divine power. The number "seven" in Revelation often symbolizes divine perfection and completeness. Thus the seven spirits are the one Holy Spirit represented under the symbolism of a seven-fold or complete manifestation of his being.

The four living creatures remind us of the seraphim of Isaiah 6 and the cherubim of Ezekiel 1:5-25 and 10:1-22. Could they be symbolic of the created world itself, all of which is responsible to render praise to God? This is suggested by the number "four" which points to the totality of the natural order: the four points of the compass, the four corners of the earth, and the four winds of heaven. Are they angels, or perhaps another "species" of created, supernatural beings?

They are standing upon something that looks like a sea of glass resembling crystal (v. 6). Its surface stretches out before the throne to reflect the flashing light that proceeds from the character of God. They appear to stand in front, behind, and on either side of the throne (they are "in the midst" of and "around" the throne in 4:6, and "before" the throne in 5:8; 19:4). Some suggest they are supporting the throne itself. Their focus is entirely on God, not each other or anything or anyone else in heaven.

The description of them in verse 7 may be designed to suggest qualities in the God they serve: the lion pointing to royal power; the calf/ox, a symbol of strength; the man, an expression of intelligence and spirituality; and the eagle, an embodiment of swiftness of action.

Extolled!

Their worship (v. 8) is unending: "Day and night they never cease to say" (cf. Rev. 14:11). As there is constant and perpetual punishment in hell, so there is constant and perpetual praise in heaven. I know that some of you struggle to remain focused and engaged during the twenty or thirty minutes of praise that happens each Sunday at your own local church. Twenty minutes? Thirty minutes? Really? Are you actually prepared to tell me that this God who is portrayed for us in Revelation 4 and 5 is not worth at least thirty minutes of your undivided attention and adoration? Thirty minutes in a week? Too long? Too much? Really? Have you actually read these two chapters? Are you sincerely prepared to tell me that thirty minutes is excessive when it comes to this God? Really?

The focus is on three of God's attributes: his holiness, his sovereignty, and his eternity. First, is his holiness, an echo of Isaiah 6. When Isaiah saw God for who he is, he saw himself as well. Knowledge of God always awakens a knowledge of oneself. God's holiness always exposes our sinfulness. But the holy God is also the gracious redeemer, for the hot coal applied to Isaiah's lips spoke of forgiveness and cleansing.

The God who captivates them is also sovereign. He is "the Almighty" for he sits on the divine "throne" (mentioned fourteen times in this chapter, a symbol of divine authority and dominion and power).

He is also the eternal God "who was and is and is to come" (cf. Ex. 3:14). Although timeless in his essential being, it must be noted that the phrase "who is to come" points more to the impending return of God in the person of Jesus to consummate his kingdom than to the idea of eternal existence.

The praise that comes from the four living creatures gives way to that of the twenty-four elders (vv. 9-11). The word "worship" means to fall prostrate at someone's feet. What gloriously appropriate repetition: they fall down before him to fall down before him! This is the first occurrence in Revelation of the paired verbs "to fall down" and "to worship" which are used to describe two stages of a single act of adoration and thus appear to be synonymous (they are also paired in 5:14; 7:11; 11:16; 19:10; 22:8; this combination is also found in Matthew 2:11; 4:9; 18:26; Acts 10:25; and 1 Corinthians 14:25).

Why did the elders fall face down? Over and over again, they hit the ground, prostrate in God's presence (4:10; 5:8,14). Did one of the four living creatures shove them? Was it simply mechanical obedience to some heavenly liturgy? What did they see or hear or feel or believe or think that could have induced such an extravagant response? What possessed them to fall over and over and over again?

No sooner do they stand than they fall! It isn't that they fall, come to their senses, and then stand, dusting themselves off, a little embarrassed for having momentarily lost their composure. No! They stand, then come to their senses, and fall! The only reasonable, rational, sensible thing to do is to fall down! They can't bear the thought of standing in the presence of such beauty and glory. Nothing would be more inappropriate or out of order than to remain upright and erect. They don't fall because they are wounded or weak or intimidated or fearful. They fall because they are overwhelmed!

Why do the four living creatures not cease day or night from praising? Is it an expression of mere "duty"? Is their adoration coerced or perhaps the fruit of bribery? Undoubtedly not! Consider every alternative. What else could possibly compare with the joy of unending adoration and delight in the splendor of God? No one put a gun to their head or threatened them with hell should they decline to worship. Why should they cease? For whom should they give up their praise? To do what? To go where? What can compare, what can rival, what can compete in its capacity to fascinate and fulfill and satisfy and entrance? Is there another being more splendid? Is there another 'god' more beautiful?

True worship, such as we see in Revelation 4–5, is not simply unending, it is uninhibited. The atmosphere around the throne is charged with an unashamed exuberance. Physical expressions of delight and fear and joy and awe are a commonplace. Unlike heaven, unfortunately, worship wars continue to rage in churches on every continent on earth. Whereas some enjoy the atmosphere of a religious carnival, Sunday morning in other churches bears a striking resemblance to the local morgue! Your choice these days is often between the frenzy of unbridled chaos or the rigidity of immovable concrete.

Our personal preferences notwithstanding, in heaven affections are ablaze for God. Bodies are prostrate in his presence. Praise is passionate. Enjoyment is extravagant. There is little, if any, fear of feelings.

I am surprised by how unsettling this is to some people. Could it possibly be due to their lack of familiarity with the central figures in Scripture? Consider, for example, David the king of Israel. Do you know why people love the psalms and seem always to return to them in time of need? Look no farther than the passion of their author, a man who virtually breathed holy desperation for God. A man whose heart beat with intense yearning and deep gratitude and a persistent longing for God's presence. A man who panted and thirsted and hungered for God and rejoiced and exulted and reveled in God. A man who was as exuberant in his celebration of righteousness as he was broken when injustice prevailed.

Or consider the apostle Paul. Although you may not think of him as an emotional or passionate person, there is hardly an epistle of his that does not drip with earnest longings of soul and spirit.

His heart was ablaze with love for God and his mind flooded with high and exalted thoughts of his Savior. He happily spurned the comforts of this life, counting all things as refuse, esteeming them dung (Phil. 3:8), that he might experience the unparalleled thrill of knowing Jesus. He was constrained by love, often moved to tears of sympathy, and roused to holy anger by those who would bring harm to the church of Jesus Christ.

Paul's letters are filled with references to his overflowing affection for the people of God (2 Cor. 12:19; Phil. 4:1; 2 Tim. 1:2; and especially 1 Thess. 2:7-8). He speaks of his "bowels of love" (Phil. 1:8; Phile. 12, 20) for them, of his pity and mercy (Phil. 2:1), of his anguish of heart and the tears he shed for their welfare (2 Cor. 2:4), of his continual grief for the lost (Rom. 9:2), and of his enlarged heart (2 Cor. 6:11).

Surely Jesus himself was a passionate man greatly moved in heart and spirit with holy affection. He was not ashamed or hesitant to pray with "loud crying and tears" (Heb. 5:7). The Gospel writers speak of him as experiencing amazement, sorrow, and grief (Mark 3:5), zeal (John 2:17), weeping (Luke 19:41-42), earnest desire (Luke 22:15), pity and compassion (Matt. 15:32; 18:34), anger (John 2:13-19), love (John 15:9), and joy (John 15:11). In Luke 10:21 he is said to have "rejoiced in the Holy Spirit" as he was praying to the Father. He declared in John 15:11 and 17:13 that one of the principal aims in his earthly mission was to perfect the joy of his followers. Thus our joy is the joy of Jesus in us!

I don't believe it's possible to truly understand and appreciate the great things of God without being stirred with passion and zeal and joy and delight and fervor. Only obdurate spiritual blindness prevents the human soul from being greatly impressed and powerfully moved by the revelation of such eternal splendor.

The inhabitants of heaven feel compelled to cast down their crowns to acknowledge that any personal honor or power or authority is ultimately God's. They proclaim the Creator worthy of glory and honor and power because by his will "they existed and were created" (literally, "they were and they were created," 4:11).

But why the apparent illogical order of the verbs? How can the "existence" of everything precede creation? In one sense, all things "first" existed in God's mind and then came into being by God's will. Or perhaps the preservation of all things is mentioned before creation to encourage the persecuted people of God with the assurance that whatever befalls them is encompassed within their Creator's ultimate purpose.

Conclusion

What is the practical takeaway or the practical payoff of our time in Revelation 4? I'm actually a little surprised that anyone would ask such a question, but let me give you one short answer as it relates to our battle with temptation.

Again, the question is this: What does this vision of God in Revelation 4 have to do with my holiness and my struggle with sin? How does meditating and prayerfully reflecting on this majestic description of God affect my battle with temptation? Why spend so much time and energy on the character and beauty of God?

The answer is easy. It is so that you will walk out of this auditorium and through the course of every day spiritually dazed, with a deeper grasp on the grandeur of God and a heart filled with adoration and awe. I want you to leave here with your mouth wide open in wonder and your eyes bulging from your head in stunned incredulity. And here is why.

Spiritually stunned people are not easily seduced by sin. People in awe of God will always find sin less appealing. When you are dazzled by God it is difficult to be duped by sin. When you are enthralled by his beauty it is hard to become enslaved by unrighteousness. People whose attention has been captured by the beauty of Christ find little appeal in the glamor of this world. People whose hearts are enthralled with the revelation of God's greatness turn a deaf ear to the otherwise alluring sounds of sin, the flesh, and the devil. Here is how James Hamilton put it:

> "What will it take to set you free from the world's idolatries – what will it take to keep you from trusting in things that are no gods at

all? What will make you free from the world's immoralities – what will it take to make you untouched by the lust for smut that the world peddles and with which worldlings ruin their lives? What will it take to liberate you from the world's false perspective on the way things are – the perspective that assumes there is no god, there is no revelation of truth in the Bible, and there will be no judgment? I'll tell you what it will take: it will take seeing God as he is. Beholding God will break the chains of idolatry because when you see God, you see what Deity is, and that exposes the idols as worthless and unworthy of [your] trust. Beholding God will purify you from immorality because when you see God you see what beauty and faithfulness are, and that exposes the ugliness of adultery. Beholding God will give you new lenses through which to look at the world because God himself defines reality."[4]

---

4. James M. Hamilton, Jr., *Revelation: The Spirit Speaks to the Churches* (Wheaton: Crossway, 2012), 130.

Chapter Fourteen

"Weep No More!"

(Revelation 5:1-14)

To be perfectly honest, there are times when I feel the same way John did as he stood before the throne of God. Not that I've ever been in the presence of the throne of God, but reading Revelation 5:3-4 resonates with my own fears and anxieties about where human history is going and whether or not we are ever going to emerge from this colossal mess we've created for ourselves.

I don't need to elaborate on how bad things are. You know it painfully even as I do. It was bad in John's day in the late first century. John was himself the last apostle, exiled to the island of Patmos. Five of the seven churches to which Jesus had written letters were struggling. John is keenly aware of the pressure and persecution that has already come upon the people of God. You may recall that back in Revelation 1 he identified himself in verse 9 as "your brother and partner in the tribulation and the kingdom and the patient endurance that are in Jesus."

I'm not in the least surprised that he reacts the way he does now in Revelation 5. He sees "in the right hand of him who was seated on the throne a scroll written within and on the back, sealed with seven seals" (v. 1). This "scroll" in all likelihood has written within it the content of God's purpose in human history. In other words, the scroll contains the content, course, and consummation of history. In it is written how things will end for both Christians and non-Christians. In other words, this scroll will tell John, and us, who wins, and how. The fact that "no one in heaven or on earth or under the earth was able to open the scroll or look into it" (v. 3) understandably stirs John's fears and stokes his anxiety.

Scholars disagree on whether the book was a rolled-up scroll or a codex (the forerunner of the modern book form). Those who believe it was a scroll contend that its contents cannot be revealed until all seven seals are broken. However, others have pointed out that there is evidence that seals on a legal document would have written upon them a brief summary of the contents of the scroll. Thus with the breaking of each seal an element of the more complete contents of the scroll would be revealed. If that is the case, the book's contents would consist of what transpires immediately in Chapter 6 and the remainder of Revelation.

It's quite amazing, is it not, that none of the four living creatures could break the seals on the scroll and discover its content? Nor could any of the twenty-four elders or any among the millions of angels surrounding the throne. "No one," says John, literally no one, "was found worthy" or qualified or powerful enough "to open the scroll or to look into it" (v. 4).

You'll notice that in verse 2 a "mighty angel" is the one who proclaimed that no one in heaven or on earth was able to open the scroll or reveal its contents. This wasn't an ordinary angel, but a "mighty" or "strong" angel. Furthermore, this angel had never sinned. This angel refused to join Satan in his rebellion against God. Yet not even a strong and sinless angel could open the book.

And so all creation in heaven and earth stands motionless and speechless as a search is undertaken for someone worthy to open this book. Is no one capable of bringing history to its ordained end? Call your Congressman! Call your Senator! Write letters of inquiry to the most brilliant of scientists and astrophysicists! If necessary, get in touch with the White House! Surely someone here on earth is worthy enough and strong enough to open the book of human history and tell us its contents and its consummation.

No. John's disappointment evokes a flood of tears as he contemplates the painful postponement of God's redemptive purposes. Is there no one who can take authority over history and make certain that God's enemies will be judged and his people vindicated?

Yes, there is. "Stop crying, John," says one of the elders. *"Weep no more! There is one who is worthy."* But when this person appears, symbolically in the form of an animal, it isn't what John expected. After first seeing a lion (in verse 5), he is amazed to see a lamb (in verse 6)! And what is even more amazing is that the Lion and the Lamb are the same person! The fact that it is a "lamb" points to his atoning sacrifice (Isa. 53:7; perhaps also the Passover Lamb is in view). Yet this lamb is "standing, as though it had been slain," or more literally, "slaughtered", with its throat cut.

So what is it that makes Jesus, the Lion of Judah, worthy to do what a strong and sinless angel couldn't do? Well, for one thing, the Lion of the tribe of Judah created this angel, together with all the other myriads of angelic beings. But that isn't the primary reason he alone is worthy to open the book. He is worthy because he has "conquered" (v. 5b). But how did he conquer, and what did he conquer? Merely dying wouldn't make him worthy. The two thieves crucified on either side of Jesus also died but they are hardly worthy. How then is his death a victory?

The death of Jesus qualifies him to break the seals and reveal the content of the scroll because, as verse 9 makes explicitly clear, by means of his "blood" alone, people from every tribe and language and people and nation were "ransomed" or redeemed or delivered from sin and condemnation. He "conquered" because his death was not the end but was followed by resurrection. And he has made those whom he ransomed into "a kingdom and priests" to God who will "reign on the earth" (v. 10).

The word "between" or "in the midst of" (v. 6) could suggest that the Lamb is actually on the throne, surrounded by the four creatures and the twenty-four elders. But it is more likely that the Lamb is standing near the throne, for in verse 7 he is portrayed as coming up to the throne and taking the book from the one who sits upon it. Thus again we see the consistent New Testament portrait of the Son at the right hand of his Father's throne.

The phrase "the slaughtered Lamb" is also found in 5:12 and 13:8. Here the fact that the word "slain" or "slaughtered" is introduced with the comparative particle "as though" or "like" does not mean that the Lamb only appeared to have been slaughtered but rather that the Lamb had been slaughtered and was now alive, thus combining the two theological motifs of death and resurrection.

But if it is slain, how does it stand? Clearly, having once been slain the Lamb has now been raised. Here we see again the glorious truth of resurrection! The Lamb isn't slumped over in a lifeless heap or limping along as if on its last legs. The Lamb stands as a sign of its resurrected life! This is John's forthright way of saying in no uncertain terms: Jesus Christ is alive!

Up until the time that Jesus Christ returns to this earth in the Second Coming, victory is achieved not by the sword but by a sacrifice. Jesus conquers through the cross! The power to change lives and orchestrate history flows from the love of a crucified carpenter who then literally and physically rose from the dead! Our King, Jesus Christ, does not win converts by killing his enemies, but by dying for them! And then rising again to eternal life. Make no mistake. When he returns it will be to destroy his enemies. At that time mercy will give way to judgment.

Here we see not just the key that unlocks the mystery of why the universe exists. We see the mystery itself. It is Jesus. He is why there is something rather than nothing. God created the universe not only through Jesus but for Jesus. By saying the universe exists for Jesus I mean that everything that exists was brought into being to admire and adore and enjoy and celebrate and relish the beauty and splendor of the Lamb of God in his victory over sin, death, and the devil! And in that admiration and celebration we find our most satisfying joy and delight.

Prayers and Praise

At the sound of such gloriously great news, there is only one appropriate response: singing! But before we note the singing don't miss the reference to praying. The "prayers of the saints" (v. 8b) are more than simple requests or petitions for personal blessing. They are more than likely impassioned pleas of men and women on earth, in the church, for God to reveal his glory and his justice in bringing righteous retribution on his enemies and in vindicating truth and goodness (see 6:9-11; 8:3-4).

The term translated "bowl" or "vial" occurs twelve times in Revelation (5:8; 15:7; 16:1, 2, 3, 4, 8, 10, 12, 17; 17:1; 21:9). The meaning of "bowl" in 5:8, however, appears to be slightly different from the meaning in the other eleven references. Here the "bowls" are filled with incense and are used in a positive, beneficial way, while in the other references they are said to contain the wrath of God and are used to inflict punishments on the earth and its inhabitants.

The four living creatures and the twenty-four elders sing a "new song" (cf. Ps. 98:1-3; Isa. 42:10-13) because the Lamb has defeated the powers of evil and has inaugurated a new creation. And why is the Lamb worthy of praise? Because he has died, and by dying has redeemed men and women from every corner of the earth, and by redeeming them has made them (i.e., you and me!) into a kingdom and into priests.

The best manuscript evidence for verse 10 leads to the translation: "And you have made them a kingdom and priests ..." rather than "made us." If the latter were correct, it would lend support to the idea that the elders are human, but the far better attested "them" would seem to differentiate the elders from "those" who are redeemed by the Lamb and made a kingdom of priests.

There is also the question of the verb tense of "reign" in verse 10. Both the future ("they shall reign on the earth") and the present tense ("they are" or "do reign on the earth") are supported by substantial manuscript evidence. According to Revelation 1:5-6 we are already a kingdom and priests to God, as is also the case here in 5:10. This would lend support to the idea that the redeemed currently reign on the earth. This is an example of the "already / not yet" tension in Scripture. We already reign as a kingdom and priests, but we have not yet entered into the full dimensions of that reign (which will come only with the creation of the "new earth").

God's Love of Ethnic Diversity

God loves ethnic diversity as is clearly evident from the purpose of Christ's sinless life, substitutionary death, and bodily resurrection. God's aim is to have a redeemed bride for his Son from more than one or two or ten ethnic groups, but from all ethnic groups, from "every tribe and language and people and nation" (v. 9b). Ethnic diversity is at the very heart and core of God's saving purposes in Christ. And his purpose is that they will live and worship and serve in Christ-centered harmony. All of them are priests, none more so than others. All rule and reign, none more so than others.

White Christians are not one kingdom of priests and black Christians another. Chinese Christians do not constitute their own kingdom of priests while Arab Christians comprise another. We are all, regardless of ethnicity, regardless of physiological differences, one kingdom of priests. You cannot have a functioning, God-glorifying kingdom of priests if they despise one another because of racial differences or live in suspicion of the worth and value of the other based on racial distinctions.

When you permit feelings in your heart of dislike and suspicion and disdain toward a person of a different skin color, you are blaspheming the majesty of the Creator God. You are denouncing the redemptive work of Jesus Christ. You are despising the shed blood of the cross. You are slandering the power of God in shaping men and women of all ethnicities in his image. You are denigrating and denying the purpose of God in redeeming men and women of all ethnicities and colors and making them a kingdom of priests. Racism is blasphemy.

You cannot worship and glorify the majesty of God or embrace his redemptive purposes in Christ while treating his supreme creation with contempt – whatever color or culture or age that creation might be. Immediately following the outrageous events in Charlottesville, August 11–12, 2017, Al Mohler, President of the Southern Baptist Theological Seminary in Louisville, Kentucky, said this:

> "A claim of white superiority is not merely wrong, and not merely deadly. It is a denial of the glory of God in creating humanity –

every single human being – in his own image. It is a rejection of God's glory in creating a humanity of different skin pigmentation. It is a misconstrual of God's judgment and glory in creating different ethnicities. Most urgently, it is a rejection of the gospel of Christ – the great good news of God's saving purpose in the atonement accomplished by Christ. A claim of racial superiority denies our common humanity, our common sinfulness, our common salvation through faith in Christ, and God's purpose to create a common new humanity in Christ. You cannot preach the gospel of Jesus Christ and hold to any notion of racial superiority. It is impossible."

We come to praise and worship God as kings and priests in his kingdom. It bears repeating: "What kind of God makes kings of his enemies?"

An Avalanche of Praise

Suddenly there is a snowball effect that leads to an avalanche of praise. A holy turbulence engulfs the heavens. As the choir sings of God's majesty the adoration of the Lamb moves out in ever-widening circles (see vv. 11-13), almost a ripple effect as if a huge stone had been cast into the center of an otherwise calm lake.

At first, it was the four living creatures singing their song of praise. They are then joined by the twenty-four elders. In verse 11 myriads and myriads and thousands and thousands of angels follow suit. And if that were not sufficient, we read in verse 13 that "every creature in heaven and on earth and under the earth and in the sea, and all that is in them" begin to praise the risen Lamb. The seven-fold shout of worship in verse 12 rings out like the resounding chimes of a huge bell:

POWER! ... WEALTH! ... WISDOM! ... MIGHT! ... HONOR! ... GLORY! ... BLESSING!

Education – Exultation – Exaltation

If we don't know who God is and how he thinks and what he feels and why he does what he does, we have no grounds for joy, no reason to celebrate, no basis for finding satisfaction in him. That is why our careful and meticulous study of the heavenly vision in Revelation 5 is so crucial to our lives as Christians.

Delight in God cannot occur in an intellectual vacuum. Our joy is the fruit of what we know and believe to be true of God. Emotional heat such as joy, delight, and gladness of heart, apart from intellectual light (i.e., the knowledge of God) is useless. Worse still, it is dangerous, for it inevitably leads to fanaticism and idolatry. The experience of heaven's inhabitants confirms that our knowledge of God (education) is the cause or grounds for our delight in him (exultation), which blossoms in the fruit of his praise and honor and glory (exaltation).

What this tells us is that the ultimate goal of theology isn't knowledge, but worship. If our learning and knowledge of God do not lead to the joyful praise of God, we have failed. We learn only that we might laud, which is to say that theology without doxology is idolatry. The only theology worth studying is a theology that can be sung!

Adoration of the Lion and the Lamb

What is it about Jesus that makes him worthy of your adoration and praise? What is it about Jesus that makes him irresistibly attractive? Why is he alone worthy of your wholehearted allegiance and love?

Consider once again the portrait of Jesus in symbolic language. In Revelation 5:5 he is called "the Lion of the tribe of Judah," but in 5:6 he is also portrayed as the "Lamb" who had been slain, though now standing, because alive. So, which is he? Both! Jesus is both Lion and Lamb. And it is in this glorious juxtaposition of what appear to be two contrasting images that we find the answer to our question. Think about this for a moment:

The Lion in whom we find unimpeachable authority is also the Lamb who embodies humility and meekness in the highest degree.

The Lion who wields power and strength that none can resist is also the Lamb who walked this earth in weakness and suffering, resisting none.

The Lion who rules the world and governs its every move is also the Lamb who was meekly led to slaughter by his enemies.

The Lion who is known for his uncompromising commitment to righteousness is also the Lamb who overflows in love to sinners like you and me.

The Lion whose majestic beauty captivates the human heart is also the Lamb who condescended to take upon himself the likeness of a man and was, in appearance, quite ordinary and unimpressive.

The Lion who commands total obedience from everyone is also the Lamb who in his earthly life submitted himself in obedience to the law of God.

The Lion who is holy and pure beyond our wildest imagination is also the Lamb who is gracious and kind and tender-hearted to all.

The Lion who could silence a raging storm with a single word is also the Lamb who refused to speak or revile against those who nailed him to a cross.

The Lion who is life itself is also the Lamb who willingly dies for his enemies.

The Lion who is exalted high above the heavens, immeasurably beyond all of creation and myriads of angels, before whom the greatest and most powerful kings and commanders on earth are but a speck of dust on the balance, is also the Lamb who stooped low, who condescended to become one of us and suffer the trials and challenges put upon him by weak and sinful men.

The Lion who is in himself infinite holiness and righteousness and purity and power is also the Lamb who welcomes broken sinners into his presence and makes intimate friends of his enemies.

The Lion who in himself needs nothing, being altogether self-sufficient, is also the Lamb who gives and gives and then gives yet again so generously and abundantly.

The Lion who is in himself of such blinding glory and brilliance that adoring angels cover their faces is also the Lamb who humbled himself and identified with his creatures so that they might behold him and enjoy him forever.

The Lion who, as Paul says in Philippians 2, exists from all eternity in perfect equality with the Father and the Spirit, equal in all respects as to his divinity, is also the Lamb who in time and history humbled himself and took on the likeness of sinful men and women.

The Lion who is known for his majesty is also the Lamb who is known for his meekness.

The Lion who drove the robbers and thieves out of the Temple is also the Lamb who only days later allowed those very robbers and thieves to nail him to a cross.

The Lion who commands absolute obedience from his creatures is also the Lamb who in obedience honored every command of his Father.

The Lion who rightly burns with wrath against the rebellious and unbelieving is also the Lamb who in the place of the rebellious and unbelieving endured in his own body and soul that very wrath.

He is at one and the same time a Lion-like-Lamb and a Lamb-like-Lion without any inconsistency or contradiction.

God of Love, God of Wrath

An important point that many would prefer that I skip is that the God who is adored for his beauty and holiness and majesty in Revelation 4–5 is the same God who pours forth wrath and destruction and terror through the series of seal, trumpet, and bowl judgments.

It is the four living creatures who worship God in Revelation 4–5 who also call forth the four horsemen of the first four seal judgments in 6:1ff. The seven trumpets are blown by the seven angels who stand before God in heaven (8:2,6). And the designation of God in 4:9-10 as he "who lives forever and ever" is found in 15:7 in connection with the "bowls full of the wrath of God." As Richard Bauckham observes, "it is the God whose awesome holiness the living creatures sing unceasingly who manifests his glory and power in the final series of judgments."[1]

Even more explicit is the literary link between the seventh of each series of judgments and the statement in 4:5a. In the latter we read of "flashes of lightning and sounds and peals of thunder" issuing from the throne. This formula is then echoed at the opening of the seventh seal judgment (8:5), the sounding of the seventh trumpet (11:19), and the pouring out of the seventh bowl (16:18-21). In other words, the holiness of God described in Revelation 4–5 is most clearly manifested in the judgments on evil in the seals, trumpets, and bowls.

Is it any wonder, then, that when George Frederick Handel read and reflected on the vision of the Lion-like-Lamb and the Lamb-like-Lion, Jesus Christ, he put to music these glorious words:

> Hallelujah! Hallelujah!
> For the Lord God Omnipotent reigneth!
> Hallelujah! Hallelujah!
> The kingdom of this world has become the kingdom of our
> Lord, and of His Christ.
> And He shall reign for ever and ever,
> King of kings, and Lord of lords,
> And He shall reign forever and ever,
> King of kings, forever and ever,
> And Lord of lords,
> Hallelujah! Hallelujah!
> And He shall reign forever and ever,
> King of kings! And Lord of lords!
> And He shall reign forever and ever,
> King of kings! And Lord of lords!
> Hallelujah! Hallelujah! Hallelujah! Hallelujah! Hallelujah!

---

1. Richard Bauckham, *The Theology of the Book of Revelation* (Cambridge: University Press, 1993), 41.

Conclusion

We must resist any inclination to disregard John's vision as irrelevant, as if it were but a distant dream, an ethereal far off heavenly phenomenon of which we on earth can only wonder. This is not virtual reality. This is not a computer-generated facsimile. It is far more real than anything this temporal world can offer.

The glory of the Holy Spirit is that he can take each syllable of this inspired portrait and set it ablaze so that the fire of its truth and life-changing power might forever burn within our hearts. Thus may we be led to join the twenty-four elders and the four living creatures and the chorus of countless millions of angels, together with the redeemed even now in heaven, in the relishing and enjoyment of our great and glorious God!

Why, you ask? Because this is why you exist! This is the reason there is a "you" and a "me". This is the purpose for which Christ died and rose again, this is the goal of all history that is contained in the scroll, namely, that we might glorify and honor and exalt our great Triune God by finding in him and his love and beauty and grace and power the deepest delight that our hearts could ever hope to experience.

Chapter Fifteen

The Four Horsemen of the Apocalypse

(Revelation 6:1-8)

Perhaps the single greatest controversy surrounding Revelation and the most important issue when it comes to interpreting the book, is the question of its structure. Many, perhaps most, evangelicals read Revelation as if it is describing a short period of time that is still in the future. Those who embrace what may be called the futurist view of the book most often will argue that what we have in Revelation 6–19 is a description of events that will take place in the future in a period of seven years they call The Great Tribulation.

And as you probably know, there are many who insist that Jesus will return and rapture his people out of this world prior to the outpouring of divine judgment in the "Great Tribulation." The result is that what we are about to read in Revelation 6–19 has little, if any, immediate practical relevance for a lot of Christians. For them it is fascinating to talk about, but it has little impact on how they live. One often hears: "Praise God that I won't be here for any of this. Jesus will rescue me so that I won't ever have to suffer what others endure."

Although I held this view for many years, I don't any longer. Now, please understand that I do believe that what we read in Revelation 6–19 applies to the end of the age, just before and including the second coming of Jesus. But I think it also applies to and describes what happens throughout the entire course of church history, including our own day and age. In other words, I believe *Revelation 6–19 (actually 6–20) portrays for us the commonplaces of history spanning the period from the first coming of Jesus all the way through to his second coming.*

Think about it this way. You are at a college football game. And you have been given the privilege of recording on camera the entire game from a variety of different vantage points. So, you place one camera on the fifty-yard line, about ten rows up. It is the perfect vantage point from which to view the game. Whether with your I-phone or some other form of video camera you begin recording everything that occurs, from the opening kickoff through to the end of the game.

Now imagine that you are able to record or videotape the same game but from a different place in the stadium. This time your seat is located in the north end zone, about fifty rows up. Instead of viewing the game horizontally, from left to right, or right to left, you record everything vertically, as the action moves away from you, from one end zone near you to the far end zone at the other end of the field. You video tape the same game, the same plays, but the camera in the end zone provides you with a different perspective on how the game unfolds. You see the players spread across the field and can see much more accurately how a play will unfold.

Now imagine that another camera is in the opposite end zone, at the south end of the field. From this vantage point you can see the game moving toward yourself, as your team takes the ball from the far end of the field and gradually moves it toward the end zone directly in front of where you are sitting.

Now, for one more example, suppose another camera is placed in the Goodyear Blimp, hovering overhead, and providing an entirely different perspective of how the game unfolds and develops. You are still watching the same game. But from this vantage point, overhead, you will have a recording of how the teams run and pass and eventually move from one end of the field to the other. From this angle in the blimp you can see both teams equally well.

You can observe movements of players in a way that no one sitting anywhere in the stadium can.

In each of these positions you would be watching and recording and eventually describing how the same game and the same plays and the same events unfold. But your explanation of how the game started and ended would sound somewhat different every time. But it's still the same football game, with the same events unfolding, with the same players on both teams, leading to the same outcome.

This would actually greatly enhance your understanding of what happens in the game. You get to watch it from different perspectives, from different vantage points. Each of the cameras provides its own unique contribution to the same game. One camera focuses almost exclusively on the offense, while another focuses on the defense. Yet another camera homes in on only one player, recording every move he makes. And then there is a camera that sets its sights on the coaches and how they interact on the sidelines with their players.

I want to suggest that this is basically what is happening in the book of Revelation. The technical term for this is *recapitulation*. John the Apostle is, in my opinion, describing the events of this entire present age in which we live. His description covers the expanse of church history from the first coming of Christ in the first century to the second coming of Christ in some later century, perhaps our own. Sometimes he provides a panoramic view of the entire age of church history. At other times he focuses on one major event or a series of developments. On occasion he may concentrate on telling us about one person or movement in the course of history.

However, when John replays for you and me his videos of the game, as it were, he doesn't do it in chronological order, as if from the first play in the first quarter up to the last play in the fourth and final quarter. He jumps around, at one time describing events that occur in the second quarter and then something that happened in the first quarter and then plays what occurred in the fourth quarter. But in each case he concludes his video presentation and his written account by describing the last few minutes of the game when the winning team is known.

I believe John does this multiple times in Revelation. Some believe there are seven progressively parallel sections in which John describes this. Regardless of how many times it happens, the principle of recapitulation is the same. John describes the commonplaces of church history spanning the time between the two comings of Christ. By *commonplaces* I mean the conditions, circumstances, situations, environments in which people find themselves between the two comings of Christ. As he finishes one section, concluding with the second coming of Christ and the end of history, he circles back around to start all over again at the start of the game. Once he concludes yet another journey he circles back around and recapitulates the same period of time from yet another vantage point.

The book of Revelation is built around three series of seven judgments. There are seven seal judgments, followed by seven trumpet judgments, and finally seven bowl judgments. According to the principle of recapitulation, the seven seal judgments, together with the seven trumpet and bowl judgments, are descriptive of events throughout the course of history between the two advents of Jesus. The only difference in the way John portrays what is happening is that at one time he may describe a preliminary, introductory, and somewhat moderate or limited aspect of God's judgment, and then at another time portray that judgment in its more complete and devastating expression.

All three series of seven judgments (seals, trumpets, bowls) portray events and phenomena that occur repeatedly throughout the course of history between the first and second comings of Christ. All three series of seven judgments bring us to the consummation at the close of human history where we see the final judgment of unbelievers, the salvation and vindication of God's people, and the full manifestation of the kingdom of Christ.

The fact that the trumpet judgments are partial and somewhat limited and the bowl judgments are more complete and final simply indicates that what can occur in a limited or partial manner at any point in history between the two advents of Christ can also occur at any point in history between the two advents of Christ in a universal or more thorough-going manner. The effect or impact of these plagues of judgment on the unbelieving world is at one time and in one place restricted, while at another time in another place widespread.

Thus, contrary to the futurist interpretation, Revelation is not concerned merely with events at the close of history, immediately preceding the second coming of Christ. Rather, there are multiple sections in the book, each of which recapitulates the other, that is to say, each of which begins with the first coming of Christ and concludes with the second coming of Christ and the end of history. Each of these sections provides a series of progressively parallel visions that increase in their scope and intensity as they draw nearer to the consummation.

Try to think of it in the analogy of that football game I described a moment ago. Each section of John's book is like each of the many cameras placed throughout the stadium or in the blimp hovering above. In each section John is describing, generally speaking, the same period of time, just as each camera is recording for us the same football game. But each section and each camera provide their own distinctive points of emphasis.

One objection often raised by the futurist to the concept of progressive parallelism or recapitulation is the fact that John repeatedly moves from one vision to the next by using a phrase such as "after this," or "after these things," or "and I saw." The futurist contends that this indicates John is writing down the temporal sequence in which the visions occur in history, which is to say, one right after another. But these phrases need only indicate the sequence in which John saw the visions. In other words, those phrases that serve to connect or link one vision with another are literary in nature, not historical. They tell us that John first saw vision "A" and then saw vision "B" and after that saw vision "C", but not necessarily that the events in vision "A" occur before those in vision "B" or that the events of vision "C" occur after those of vision "B".

Introduction to the Seal Judgments

There is no mistaking the fact that these judgments proceed from Jesus Christ. Each seal is broken, and thus its judgment unleashed on the earth, by the "Lamb" (v. 1). Furthermore, each of the four horsemen is beckoned forth respectively by one of the four living creatures who surround the Lamb on his throne. It's important to remember that angels, such as the four living creatures, always do God's will. This statement in Psalm 103 is only one of many that express this truth:

> "Bless the LORD, O you his angels, you mighty ones who do his word, obeying the voice of his word! Bless the LORD, all his hosts, his ministers, who do his will" (Ps. 103:20-21).

The point is that these phenomena are not an accident of nature, nor did they originate with Satan. They are of divine origin and are designed to call all people everywhere to repentance, to punish unbelievers, and to purify and refine the faith of God's people.

The First Seal

Three Old Testament passages sound remarkably similar to Revelation 6:1-8 and its portrayal of the four horsemen of judgment: Leviticus 26:18-28, Zechariah 6:1-8, and Ezekiel 14:12-23. In each of these texts judgment, similar to that in Revelation 6, is threatened against either Israel or its pagan neighbors.

There is considerable debate as to the identity of the first horseman. Some contend that it is symbolic of the successful power of the gospel gone out into all the earth. Others argue that the horseman is the antichrist while others say it is none other than Jesus himself. Let's look at the arguments in favor of identifying this first horseman as Jesus.

The text may be an allusion to Psalm 45:3-5 where we read of an Israelite king who defeats his enemies with bow and arrows. He is portrayed as riding forth victoriously "for the cause of truth and meekness and righteousness" (Ps. 45:4). According to Hebrews 1:8, this psalm was messianic, pointing to Jesus. In Revelation 19:11-16, Jesus has crowns on his head and rides a white horse in the defeat of his enemies. However, I would point out that there are also dissimilarities. The rider in Revelation 6 carries a "bow" and wears a wreath (*stephanos*) of victory, while the rider in Revelation 19 has a sharp two-edged sword in his mouth and wears many diadems (*diadēmata*), symbols of sovereignty. In Revelation 14:14, Jesus is described as sitting on a white cloud "having a golden crown on his head." Elsewhere in Revelation Jesus is often said to "conquer" (*nikaō*; cf. 3:21; 5:5; 17:14).

Aside from this text, the color "white" is used fourteen times in Revelation and always symbolizes righteousness or is associated with the holiness of God. Advocates of this view also point out that the white horseman, unlike the other three, is not explicitly said to be the means for judgment. "Conquering" could be interpreted positively.

Others contend that the first horseman is a Satanic parody or imitation of Jesus and must be interpreted as evil. Here are their reasons. In Revelation 13 we see that one of Satan's primary tactics is to imitate Christ in appearance and activity. The language of "conquering" is also used in Revelation of the beast oppressing and persecuting the people of God (11:7; 13:7). Beale points out that "the horsemen form a quartet to be distinguished literarily from the remaining three seals, like the first four trumpets and bowls with respect to the remaining trumpets and bowls. Since the first four trumpets and bowls represent parallel judgments, the same parallelism is probably present with the horsemen."[1] Yet there are too many points of identity between the first horsemen and the remaining three to make such a radical distinction between their natures. For example, each horseman is called forth by one of the four creatures, each horseman comes forth in response to that command, the color of each horse and the object carried by each rider point to the kind of woe that he brings, and the same statement of authorization ("was given to him") is used of the first two of the four.

---

1. Beale, *Revelation*, 376.

The "bow" is the symbol of intention to conquer by military might and tyranny. Nowhere in Revelation or in the New Testament does Jesus carry a bow. Rather, he is pictured with a sword. It also seems a bit odd that Christ would be both the one who opens the seal and the content of the seal itself. There is also a possible parallel in Revelation 9:7 where we read of demonic agents of judgment that are like "horses prepared for battle" with "crowns" on their heads. The same clause of authorization ("was given to them"; 9:3, 5) is used.

Although we can't be dogmatic, it would appear that the first horseman is a Satanic parody or imitation of Jesus (19:11-16) sent forth by God ("it was given to him" is a typical way of referring to divine authorization in Revelation [see 6:11; 7:2; 8:2-3; 9:1,3,5; 11:2-3; 12:14; chp. 13; etc.]) to provoke war on the earth. There are also several Old Testament texts in which "bow and arrows" are symbolic of divine chastisement (Deut. 32:42; Isa. 34:6; Hab. 3:9; Lam. 3:12-13; Ps. 7:13-14). Thus, the rider on the white horse symbolizes every form of tyranny and oppression that comes with war.

The Second Seal

If the first rider introduces war into the earth, the remaining three delineate specific consequences of war. The second horseman has power to take peace from the earth so that people kill one another. This may also include persecution of Christians (cf. Matt. 10:34), for the word translated "slay" is literally "slaughter" (*sphazō*) which is used consistently by John to describe the death of Jesus or the martyrdom of his followers (5:6, 9, 12; 6:9; 13:8; 18:24).

The Third Seal

The third horsemen is the agent for famine. In the ancient world "scales" were used to ration food for distribution during times of scarcity (cf. Lev. 26:26; 2 Kgs. 7:1; Ezek. 4:10, 16). A voice (surely that of Christ; note its origin) then issues a command that would indicate a limitation on the severity of the famine. Foods essential for life ("wheat" and "barley") will still be available. A "denarius" was typically a day's wage (cf. Matt. 20:2) in those days. A "quart of wheat" would be enough for one person for one day and "three quarts of barley" would last for three days. The prices mentioned here are anywhere from eight to sixteen times the average for the Roman Empire at that time. That the "oil" and "wine" (metonymy for olive trees and vines) are not affected also indicates a limitation on the intensity of the famine. In other words, the sparing of oil and wine may simply be an indication of God's mercy in the midst of judgment. The overall picture here is of both scarcity and plenty, an economic imbalance in the supply of food and the necessities of life.

The Fourth Seal

Unlike the other horsemen, the fourth is given a name: "Death". "Hades" (the abode of the dead) is said to follow after him. There are two things to note.

First, this horseman is given authority from God to inflict death by four means: sword (war), famine, pestilence (lit. "death", but commonly used with reference to pestilence), and wild beasts. Second, although severe, these judgments are limited in their scope, touching only a quarter of the earth. This preliminary, partial judgment of the earth is designed to prepare us for the final, consummate judgment that will come with the seventh in each of the three series of woes. Wilcock writes: "The wiping out of a quarter of the human race sounds like a disaster of the first magnitude, until one realizes that nothing has been said to indicate that this is a single catastrophic event. After all, every man dies sooner or later, and what is probably meant here is that a sizeable proportion of those deaths are the unnecessary ones caused by war and famine and kindred evils."[2]

Here we see once again God's sovereignty over history. These judgments of the four horsemen are a wake-up call to humanity. They are an appeal to everyone everywhere to repent.

---

2. Wilcock, *The Message of Revelation*, 72.

What should we do? Is it permissible to give our money, time, and labor to overcome or bring a remedy to those who suffer in this way? Yes. Disease is an expression of divine judgment because of human sin, yet Jesus healed the sick. The measure of our commitment to Christ is often seen in our willingness to sacrifice in order to bring relief to the hungry and hurting (Luke 3:11; Jas. 2:14-17). Earthquakes, floods, tornadoes, and the devastation of war can rightly be seen as God's judgment against the rebellion and idolatry of man. But we are still responsible to do everything we can to alleviate suffering wherever it occurs and to call everyone everywhere to repent.

The history of war, famine, and pestilence is an ugly one. Let me give you just a few examples. The reality of tyranny, oppression, and the loss of human life in the twentieth century alone is one with which we are all too familiar. May I remind you that Hitler and Nazi Germany were responsible for the deaths of more than six million Jewish men, women, and children. Mao in China slaughtered tens of millions of his political enemies. Pol Pot ruled over a country, Cambodia, which at the time had some ten million citizens. He slaughtered more than two million of them, one in five. And Joseph Stalin killed more than twenty million of his own citizens (some say the number is closer to thirty million). And all this in the twentieth century alone.

It would be impossible to account for all the wars and civil conflicts since the first century, so let's just begin with the Civil War here in America. More than six hundred and forty thousand died in our Civil War in the nineteenth century. Forty-one million from a variety of countries died in WWI. Over sixty million died in WWII. More than 1.3 million, both civilian and military, died in the Viet Nam War. Globally, there were 3,168 conflicts between 1870 and 2001.

The toll taken on humanity by pestilence and famine is even worse. Approximately 2.8 million people in France, fifteen percent of the population, starved to death between 1692–1694 (a span of only three years). In 1695, famine struck Estonia, killing a fifth of the population. In 1696 nearly a third of the population in Finland died.

The Black Death, also known as the Bubonic Plague, began in the 1330s somewhere in east or central Asia. The culprit was a bacterium known as Yersinia pestis that was carried by fleas. Most likely rats, infested with these fleas, carried the disease to Europe and North Africa. Between seventy-five and two hundred million people died, more than a quarter of the entire population of Europe and Asia combined. In England, four out of ten people died. The city of Florence lost fifty thousand of its one hundred thousand inhabitants. Yes, that's half of the entire population of Florence.

In March of 1520 when the Spanish fleet arrived in Mexico, the population of our southern neighbor was twenty-two million people. Eight months later only fourteen million were still alive. That's right: in eight months eight million people in Mexico died. The culprit was smallpox. Within sixty years of the arrival of Spaniards in Mexico, the population dropped from twenty-two million to less than two million.

The British explorer James Cook arrived in Hawaii in 1778. The Hawaiian Islands were densely populated by half a million people. Cook and his men introduced flu, tuberculosis, and syphilis to Hawaii. Subsequent European visitors brought typhoid and smallpox. Seventy-five years later there were only seventy thousand survivors in Hawaii.

In January of 1918 the so-called "Spanish Flu" struck soldiers in the trenches of northern France. Within a few months about half a billion people were infected with it, nearly a third of the entire population of the earth. Experts differ on the number of people who eventually died, but they range anywhere from a low of fifty million upwards of a hundred million deaths.

And let's not forget, that as of today, more than thirty million have died of AIDS and best estimates are that more than three million died of Covid in 2020.

Conclusion

Finally, it's important for us to remember two things regarding the multiple outpouring of judgments on the earth and the resultant suffering and death.

First, God does not want you to get him off the hook. The judgments of the seven seals, seven trumpets, and seven bows are released by the Lord Jesus Christ himself or by one of many angelic beings who serve God and do his will. However, this does not necessarily mean that God should always be viewed as the direct cause of the suffering and death that falls on the earth.

This leads to my second point, which is that God sustains differing levels of responsibility for the judgments in Revelation. (1) In some cases he directly pours out his wrath and is the immediate cause for the destruction of his enemies. Take, for example, the portrayal of Christ as his second coming: "From his [Christ's] mouth comes a sharp sword with which to strike down the nations, and he will rule them with a rod of iron. He will tread the winepress of the fury of the wrath of God the Almighty" (Rev. 19:15).

(2) In other instances, God lifts the restraining influence of his common grace. Common grace is the ministry of the Holy Spirit by which he restrains or inhibits or curtails the sinful and destructive impulses and actions of unbelievers. Much of the suffering and destruction described in Revelation comes to pass because God chooses to withdraw his preventative influence and allow the wickedness of man against man to manifest itself in its fullness.

(3) There is finally God's release of Satan to inflict famine, pestilence, suffering, and death on the earth. This is very similar to what happened in the case of Job. God did not directly bring destruction on Job's family and property, nor on his body in the way of disease and suffering. But he did give Satan permission to afflict Job. We see this explicitly stated in Revelation 12 where it is said that Satan "was thrown down to the earth, and his angels were thrown down with him" (12:9). Again, "But woe to you, O earth

and sea, for the devil has come down to you in great wrath, because he knows that his time is short!" (Rev. 12:12b).

Thus in each of these three ways God is still sovereign over everything that happens, but his sovereignty is revealed and expressed in different ways. In some cases he directly pours out wrath. In other instances his judgment occurs when he lifts the restraint he would otherwise exercise on the will of wicked people. And finally, in many instances he simply grants Satan free reign to wreak havoc on mankind. But of this we may be certain. God's wrath never falls on his children. The objects of his anger are "those who dwell on the earth," a standard reference in Revelation to non-Christians.

It would be easy, and almost understandable, to give way to despair. When one adds to these countless disasters the utter decay of morality and the rampant idolatry that surrounds us, I once again want to join John and weep loudly. But praise be to God that I am told: "Weep no more! For the Lion of the tribe of Judah, the Lamb who was slain and rose again and redeemed men and women from every tongue and tribe and nation, he is worthy to take hold of the book of history and to open its contents and to orchestrate and providentially direct all things to their righteous consummation. Jesus wins. And because we are his, a kingdom and priests to our God, so do we!"

So let the horror of divine wrath and judgment in Revelation awaken you to two inescapable realities: gratitude and evangelism! First, the fact that you have trusted Jesus to endure in your place the wrath and judgment you otherwise deserved to experience ought to awaken profound thanksgiving for the forgiveness of sins. Second, countless individuals still abide under the wrath of God. If ever there was an incentive to take the gospel to men and women around us, this is it.

Chapter Sixteen

The Voice of the Martyrs

(Revelation 6:9-11)

Often when we speak of those who suffer from persecution and martyrdom, we hear only words and the impact on our hearts is minimal. So I want to begin this chapter by putting a face with a name. His name was Sharoon Masih and he was sixteen years old. I say "was" because on August 27, 2017, during only his fourth day at school, he was savagely beaten to death inside his school by his classmates.

Against tremendous odds, Sharoon earned extremely high grades at his former school. His Christian teachers were so impressed by his academic abilities that they challenged his poverty-stricken parents not to put him to work but to encourage him to pursue higher education. His father Elyab Masih (35) saved some money from the work he does as a laborer on a brick kiln and paid for the admission for Sharoon to enroll in a better school in Pakistan's Punjab Province. Because he was the only Christian in his grade, he was isolated from the very first day and endured endless taunting, even torture on the part of his classmates. They tried to convert Sharoon to Islam, but he resisted.

One Muslim student shouted at him: "You're a Christian; don't dare sit with us if you want to live." While beating him, the attacking students shouted insults, but no teacher or administrator bothered to come to his aid. He died almost immediately. The lead teacher has since been dismissed and the primary suspect in the murder has been arrested. However, few other students feel any remorse for killing a Christian and no one is willing to implicate the other murderers by naming them.

The victim's mother, Riaz Bibi, said her son had been warned by his peers not to mix with Muslims at the school. She said her son was called a "chura," a derogatory term which refers to the people who belong to the lowest caste, according to the hierarchy in some South Asian societies. His mother was quoted as saying:

> "My son was a kind-hearted, hard-working and affable boy. He has always been loved by teachers and pupils alike and shared great sorrow that he was being targeted by students at his new school because of his faith. Sharoon and I cried every night as he described the daily torture he was subjected to.... The evil boys that hated my child are now refusing to reveal who else was involved in his murder. Nevertheless one day God will have His judgement."

What happens when a Christian like Sharoon dies for his faith? Although the Apostle John is here concerned only with those whose deaths were violent, who were martyred because they refused to deny Jesus, their experience is no different from all believers who leave this world and enter the presence of Christ in heaven.

The Souls of the Martyrs in Heaven

Upon reading of Sharoon's brutal beating and death, I will understand if you find it difficult to concentrate while continuing to read this chapter. So let me make it as easy as I can by simply drawing several observations from the passage we are considering.

What can we say about those who have been martyred for their faith? Of course, as I noted, all who have died in faith, whether martyred or by some other means, are included here. John focuses on the martyrs because he wants to encourage and inspire those believers in the seven churches in Asia Minor by reminding them that they need not fear death. They need not worry about what happens should they lose their lives for no other reason than that they love and treasure Jesus as Lord.

(1) The first thing that is obvious from what John says is that those who have died for their faith are *conscious*. They are keenly aware and conscious of the Lord's presence and are able to articulate their request concerning what they hope God will do. That they are very much alive, conscious, able both to think and feel, is seen in the fact that they "cried out with a loud voice." Clearly, they are experiencing deep and intensely passionate emotions as they ask God for justice.

It betrays an ignorance of the nature of apocalyptic language to ask how John could see "souls". Again, the revelatory medium here is symbolic and visionary, not photographic literalism. Nevertheless, they are in a disembodied state ("souls") and do not sleep. They are keenly aware of what happened to them.

This, then, is yet one more New Testament passage that portrays for us what theologians call *the intermediate state*. It is that condition or experience of all Christians who have died and are now in heaven. It is called "intermediate" because it is "in between" our experience now on earth and our experience that is yet to come when Christ returns and gives us our glorified and resurrected bodies (cf. 2 Cor. 5:1, 8-10; Phil. 1:20-23). Those in the intermediate state are not "sleeping" or in a state of unconscious repose. They burn with desire for the purposes of God to be fulfilled on earth and for righteousness and vindication of the truth.

(2) These believing "souls" are "under the altar." The altar in view is probably the golden altar of incense which stood near the holy of holies (cf. 8:3-5; 9:13). The blood from the Day of Atonement was poured upon it and incense was regularly burned there (Ex. 30:1-10; Lev. 4:7; Heb. 9:4). Thus the altar is symbolic of the prayers of all God's people.

Why are they "under" the altar rather than merely near it or beside it or in front of it? Beale contends that in Revelation the "altar" is virtually synonymous with God's throne (cf. 8:3-4; 9:13; 20:4,6). Thus, the point is the protection and security afforded the saints from the sovereign Lord who rules heaven and earth. Portraying the saints under the altar "emphasizes the divine protection that has held sway over their 'soul' despite even their loss of physical life because of persecution."[1]

(3) The reason for their deaths is made explicitly clear: they "had been slain for the word of God," by which John means they had boldly and courageously stood up for Jesus and had borne "witness" to him. These are men and women who refused to back down when asked if they were Christians. They held their ground and knew that the only thing they needed to do to preserve and prolong their earthly lives was to keep their mouths shut. But they didn't. Nothing, not even the threat of horrendous torture and execution could silence them.

You and I typically keep our mouths shut because we are threatened with ... well, with what? Usually nothing. At most we stand to lose a client, a friend, an invitation to a college football game, or perhaps the respect of people that we admire. But no one has yet put a sword to my throat or a gun to my head. I haven't

---

1. Beale, *Revelation*, 392.

been evicted from my house or told that if I don't convert to Islam or merely deny Jesus that I'll lose my job or my home or my car.

Why was young Sharoon brutally and savagely beaten to death in his school classroom? It was because, like these in Revelation 6, he stood courageously for "the word of God" and did not back down from his "witness" concerning how Jesus had saved him.

These men and women, like Sharoon, were faithful unto death, not valuing their own lives above the gospel testimony. I'm reminded of Paul's confession when he spoke to the elders of the church at Ephesus:

> "I did not shrink from declaring to you anything that was profitable, and teaching you in public and from house to house, testifying both to Jews and to Greeks of repentance toward God and of faith in our Lord Jesus Christ. And now, behold, I am going to Jerusalem, constrained by the Spirit, not knowing what will happen to me there, except that the Holy Spirit testifies to me in every city that imprisonment and afflictions await me. But I do not account my life of any value nor as precious to myself, if only I may finish my course and the ministry that I received from the Lord Jesus, to testify to the gospel of the grace of God. And now, behold, I know that none of you among whom I have gone about proclaiming the kingdom will see my face again. Therefore I testify to you this day that I am innocent of the blood of all, for I did not shrink from declaring to you the whole counsel of God" (Acts 20:20-27).

People like Paul and Sharoon and the other martyrs in heaven testify that God is better than life. And they bear witness to that belief by sealing their confession with their blood. In this way they bear witness to the supreme value of God and knowing him.

If you are wondering how common martyrdom is, best estimates are that more than 100,000 Christians have died for their faith during the past ten years. This means that on average there was one Christian killed every five minutes. Martyrdom has been a common experience for believers for the past two-thousand years, but especially in the twentieth century. Experts tell us *more have died for their Christian faith in the twentieth century than in all previous nineteen centuries combined.*

(4) They know *God is in control*. It is to the "Sovereign Lord" that they cry out. This confession is their acknowledgement that their deaths didn't catch God by surprise or disrupt his plans. They suffered martyrdom while the Sovereign Lord over all was in complete and utter control of what the enemies of Christ did and what the people of Christ suffered. Yes, Sharoon likewise lost his life under the sovereign control of a good and just God. And he knows it.

(5) They also know that *God is holy*. Yes, God is sovereign, and he could have intervened to protect their lives. He could have intervened to protect Sharoon. But in his infinite wisdom, he didn't. The suffering of the martyrs does not impeach or call into question God's holiness. His majesty is not marred or disfigured when his people die for their faith.

(6) They also know that *God is true*. He hasn't broken his promises. Their martyrdom is not a violation of anything God said to them. In fact, they were keenly aware of what Paul had said to Timothy, his spiritual son, that all who desire to live godly in Christ Jesus will suffer persecution (2 Tim. 3:12).

Sadly, when we suffer even a tiny bit for being a Christian, we immediately question whether God is good. We begin to doubt whether or not he can be trusted. Has he lied to us? Is he incapable of stepping in and stopping those who oppress us? If he were truly good and holy, would he not put an end to persecution once and for all? Well, one day he will. But to suffer for Christ now is never a cause to question God's goodness or his greatness. In fact, it is an honor to be considered worthy to endure persecution for his name's sake.

At least, that is what Peter and the other apostles believed. We read in Acts 5 that after they were severely beaten for refusing to stop preaching about Jesus, "they left the presence of the council, rejoicing that they were counted worthy to suffer dishonor for the name [of Jesus]. And every day, in the temple and from house to house, they did not cease teaching and preaching that the Christ is Jesus" (Acts 5:41-42).

(7) We now come to their prayer. It is a cry for justice: "O Sovereign Lord, holy and true, how long before you will judge and avenge our blood on those who dwell on the earth?" (v. 10). There are several things of great importance here. For example, they are conscious of the passing of time. They ask, "how long?" until God acts on their behalf. They were sensible of what it means to wait and to hope for something yet to come.

They also have a keen sense of divine justice. They wait in anticipation of God's justice and vengeance on the enemies of his kingdom. Clearly, they understand that it is not their responsibility or right to avenge the blood on those who had killed Christians (see Rom. 12:19). They knew that it was God's prerogative to determine when and where and how. There is nothing wrong or unchristian to desire that God's enemies and those who persecute God's people be held accountable and judged for their wicked deeds (Ps. 94:1-6).

A similar cry for vengeance is found in Psalm 79:5-6 and may provide the background for John's language: "How long, O Lord? Will you be angry forever? Will your jealousy burn like fire? Pour out your anger on the nations that do not know you, and on the kingdoms that do not call upon your name!"

God doesn't tell them they are misguided, that they shouldn't desire justice on the enemies of Christ. In fact, they are simply turning back into prayer a promise that God made to them about what he would do to those who persecute the church. Here is how Paul put it:

> "This is evidence of the righteous judgment of God, that you may be considered worthy of the kingdom of God, for which you are also suffering—since indeed God considers it just to repay with affliction those who afflict you, and to grant relief to you who are afflicted as well as to us, when the Lord Jesus is revealed from heaven with his mighty angels in flaming fire, inflicting vengeance on those who do not know God and on those who do not obey the gospel of our Lord Jesus. They will suffer the punishment of

eternal destruction, away from the presence of the Lord and from the glory of his might, when he comes on that day to be glorified in his saints, and to be marveled at among all who have believed, because our testimony to you was believed" (2 Thess. 1:5-10).

(8) The response is for them to be given "a white robe" as they are "told to rest a little longer." The white robe is a symbol or sign of the righteousness of Christ imputed or reckoned to them through faith. This is the truth of justification by faith alone. John Bunyan, author of *Pilgrim's Progress*, put it this way:

> "Faith wraps the soul up in the bundle of life with God; it encloses it in the righteousness of Jesus, and presents it so perfect in that, that whatever Satan can do, with all his cunning, cannot render the soul spotted or wrinkled before the justice of the law. Yea, though the man, as to his own person and acts, be full of sin from top to toe, Jesus Christ covers all. Faith sees it, and holds the soul in the godly sense and comfort of it. The man, therefore, standing here, stands shrouded under that goodly robe that makes him glisten in the eye of justice."[2]

The command to "rest" means they should not worry or be fearful that perhaps justice will never come. We need to hear this as well. We, too, are restless and impatient and wonder if God will ever step into history and bring justice to bear on those who hate him and his people. There is a reason why God has not done so up to this point in history. And that brings me to my last point.

(9) God's delay in bringing justice against the unbelieving world is simply an expression of his sovereign purpose and decree that many more shall suffer martyrdom. There is a complete and explicitly specified number who must suffer martyrdom as these have. And the fact that Jesus has not yet returned is an indication that the total of those whom God has ordained will die in this manner has not yet been reached. In other words, God has it well

---

2. John Bunyan, "Justification by an Imputed Righteousness," in *Works*, 1:331.

within his perfect plan that a specified number, not one more or one less than he has willed, shall die for their faith.

Note well: (a) God has determined that many of his people should be killed at the hands of unbelievers; their deaths are neither an accident to them nor a surprise to God. (b) God has also determined to hold morally accountable those unbelievers who he knows will sin by persecuting his people.

Some say that what John means is simply that the mission of their fellow believers has not yet been fulfilled. But most argue that John's point is that the full number of those Christians whose destiny is to die for their faith has not yet been reached. This not only indicates that there is a specified number, ordained by God, who will suffer death, but also that God knows precisely who they are. This is why Jesus cannot yet come back. The full number of martyrs ordained by God has not yet been fulfilled. The restraint of God is thus due both to his longsuffering (granting extended opportunity to repent) and the fulfillment of his pre-ordained purpose. Only when all have been killed in accordance with God's plan will he act in judgment.

Conclusion

I grieve for the parents of Sharoon Masih. Their pain and suffering and sense of loss must be incredible. But if there is any comfort for them it is in knowing that their son was counted "worthy" to suffer for the name of Christ. Like the martyrs in Revelation 12, Sharoon did not love his life even unto death. And as horrific as his death was, he "conquered" Satan "by the blood of the Lamb" and "by the word" of his "testimony" (Rev. 12:11).

Chapter Seventeen

The Second Coming of Christ: Blessed Hope or Dreaded Nightmare?

(Revelation 6:12-17; 8:1-5)

There are several good reasons why the Apostle Paul described the second coming of Jesus Christ as our "blessed hope" (Tit. 2:13). It is a "blessed hope" because it will mean the end of all sin and suffering in our lives. No more battles with temptation. No more feelings of guilt when we fail. No more diagnoses of cancer or heart disease or arthritis. No more sadness upon hearing of the death of a loved one. No more funerals. No more anger or resentment or unforgiveness or lust or greed. No more jealous rivalries. No more division between Christians. No more friction between husbands and wives or parents and their children.

But even better than all these glorious truths is what Paul says in 2 Thessalonians 1:10. There he tells us that "when" Jesus "comes on that day" it is to "be glorified in his saints and to be marveled at among all who have believed." In yet another passage Paul says that when Jesus returns, he will "transform our body to be like his glorious body, by the power that enables him even to subject all things to himself" (Phil. 3:21).

And perhaps the most "blessed" thing of all in the coming of Jesus is what John said in 1 John 3:2: "Beloved, we are God's children now, and what we will be has not yet appeared; but we know that when he appears we shall be like him, because we shall see him as he is" (1 John 3:2). John recorded for us this same truth in the final chapter of the final book of the Bible, Revelation. In Revelation 22:4 he says: "They will see his face, and his name will be on their foreheads."

It is a "blessed hope" indeed. But it is far from blessed for many. And it is not something for which unbelievers should "hope". For them, for those who persist in their unrepentant idolatry and rejection and hatred of God, it is a "dreaded nightmare."

I know that you probably don't want to hear about this. And to be honest, I'm not sure I do either. But we cannot claim to be people of the book, people of the Bible, people who believe that this is God's inspired and inerrant revealed Word, and ignore, far less, deny what it says about the fate of those who reject Jesus as Lord and Savior.

The sixth seal judgment, as described in Revelation 6:12-17, is the first detailed description of what will happen at the end of this present age when Jesus returns. We know what will happen for God's people. But here we read of what happens to those who persist in unbelief.

The Sixth Seal

In the previous chapter of this book we heard the voice of the martyrs, their passionate prayer to God that the evil perpetrated against Christians be avenged and judged. Here in verses 12-17 we find the answer to their request. The judgment of the sixth seal must be associated with the final or consummate wrath that comes at the end of human history.

There is in verses 12-17 a description of massive, global, indeed cosmic upheaval and disruptions. There is a "great earthquake" in verse 12a. The sun becomes black as sackcloth and the moon becomes red like blood in verse 12b. In verse 13 the stars are described as falling to the earth. In verse 14 the sky vanishes, and "every mountain and island" are removed from their places.

What is this all about? Is John describing something that is physically literal, or could he be using natural calamities and cosmic disturbances to symbolically portray the turmoil of earthly nations and the judgment that is to befall this world at the time of Christ's return?

The way to answer that question isn't to read the Drudge Report or the Wall Street Journal. You won't get much help by turning to your favorite cable news network or whatever website or blog you typically read when you want to know what is happening in the world around us. The only way to answer that question is to realize, first of all, that John lived in the first century, not the twenty-first. John was a Jewish Christian, not a Gentile. John was immersed in the Old Testament, not in Fox News or CNN or the Huffington Post.

John's language, his terminology, his worldview was shaped by the biblical perspective of what we know as the Old Testament and the teaching of Jesus. I therefore concur with Andrew Perriman that we should try "to read forwards from the first century rather than backwards from the twenty-first century. One of the reasons why the apocalyptic language of the New Testament can be so puzzling to the modern interpreter is that we cannot help but read it retrospectively and with the advantage, which more often than not turns out to be the disadvantage, of hindsight."[1]

This is a tremendous challenge for most Christians. We aren't accustomed to thinking in biblical terms. We aren't sufficiently familiar with the way language worked in biblical times and how biblical authors expressed themselves. We expect them to think like us, to talk like us, and to explain the future in the same way we would. What we simply have to do is to learn how to think, talk, and make use of language in the way they did.

In the Old Testament, the sort of language we find in Revelation 6:12-17 was used to portray not what was going on in the heavens but what was happening on the earth. Natural disasters, political upheavals, and turmoil among the nations are often described figuratively through the terminology of cosmic

---

1. Andrew Perriman, *The Coming of the Son of Man: New Testament Eschatology for an Emerging Church* (Waynesboro: GA, Paternoster Press, 2005), 3.

disturbances. The ongoing and unsettled, turbulent state of affairs among earthly world powers is portrayed symbolically by reference to incredible events in the heavens. In other words, astronomical phenomena are used to describe the upheaval of earthly dynasties as well as great moral and spiritual changes. Once we learn to read this language in the light of the Old Testament, we discover that great upheavals upon earth are often represented with the imagery of commotions and changes in the heavens. As we shall see, when the sun and moon are darkened or the stars fall from heaven, the reference is to the disasters and distresses befalling nations on the earth.

Let me give you some examples. In Isaiah 13:9-10 we read of the impending judgment of God on Babylon, which he describes in this way: "For the stars of the heavens and their constellations will not give their light; the sun will be dark at its rising, and the moon will not shed its light" (v. 10). Clearly, these statements about celestial bodies no longer providing light are figurative of the convulsive transformation of political affairs in the Ancient Near East, on earth. The destruction of earthly kingdoms is portrayed in terms of a heavenly shaking.

We find much the same thing in Ezekiel as he describes the impending destruction of Egypt:

> "When I blot you out, I will cover the heavens and make their stars dark; I will cover the sun with a cloud, and the moon shall not give its light. All the bright lights of heaven will I make dark over you, and put darkness on your land, declares the Lord GOD.... When I make the land of Egypt desolate, and when the land is desolate of all that fills it, when I strike down all who dwell in it, then they will know that I am the LORD" (Ezek. 32:7-8, 15).

The destruction of Idumea (Edom) is described in this way:

> "All the host of heaven shall rot away, and the skies roll up like a scroll. All their host shall fall, as leaves fall from the vine, like leaves falling from the fig tree. For my sword has drunk its fill in

the heavens; behold, it descends for judgment upon Edom, upon the people I have devoted to destruction" (Isa. 34:4-5).

Thus, as William Kimball points out, "when Israel was judged, or when Babylon was subdued by the Medes, or when Idumea and Egypt were destroyed, it was not the literal sun, moon, and stars that were darkened. The literal stars of heaven did not fall from the skies, and the literal constellations were not dissolved or rolled up as a scroll. These figurative expressions were clearly presented in a purely symbolic manner to characterize the destruction befalling nations and earthly powers."[2] Language that describes the collapse of cosmic bodies, therefore, was often used by "OT prophets to symbolize God's acts of judgment within history, with the emphasis on catastrophic political reversals."[3]

In summary, it reflects a failure to read the Bible on its own terms to insist that these words refer to the physical collapse of the space-time world. As one author has said, "This is simply the way regular Jewish imagery is able to refer to major socio-political events and bring out their full significance."[4] In other words, Revelation 6:12-14 is stock-in-trade Old Testament prophetic language for national disaster. John, therefore, is not prophesying that bizarre astronomical or geological events will occur. Instead, he is predicting that the judgment of God will soon fall decisively on the entire earth and on those who refuse to repent and believe the gospel.

OK, but what about verse 14 where John says that "every mountain and island was removed from its place"? This language is repeated in conjunction with the seventh bowl judgment in Revelation 16:20. There we read that "every island fled away, and no mountains were to be found." Is this physically literal, or is it another

---

2. William R. Kimball, *What the Bible says about The Great Tribulation* (Grand Rapids: Baker Book House, 1984), 166.

3. R. T. France, *The Gospel of Matthew* (Grand Rapids: Eerdmans, 2007), 922.

4. N. T. Wright, *Jesus and the Victory of God* (Minneapolis: Fortress Press, 1996), 361.

example of prophetic hyperbole? Probably the latter. "Mountains" are often symbolic of evil forces and/or earthly kingdoms (cf. Jer. 51:25-26; Zech. 4:7) and "islands" (or "coastlands") often represent pagan Gentile nations or kings (Pss. 72:10; 97:1; Isa. 41:1; 49:1; 51:5; 60:9; Jer. 31:10; Ezek. 26:18).

I should also point out, however, that "mountains" and "islands" here may be symbolic simply of the most stable features of the world, all of which are portrayed in the Old Testament as being displaced, cast aside, shaken, moved, etc. as a result of the presence of the Lord and especially the manifestation of his judgments. See Judges 5:5; Psalms 18:7; 46:2-3; Isaiah 5:25; 54:10; 64:1; Jeremiah 4:24; Ezekiel 26:18; 38:20; Micah 1:4; and Nahum 1:5. Few, if any, commentators would suggest that these Old Testament texts describe literal or physical displacement or movement of mountains and islands. Why, then, would they insist on it here in Revelation?

If you insist on interpreting these descriptions in physically literal terms, you have a problem. If, as Revelation 16:20 says, "every island fled away" and "no mountains were to be found," and if, as Revelation 6:14 says, "every mountain and island was removed from its place," how could the kings and all other unbelievers hide in "caves and among the rocks of the mountains, calling to the rocks and mountains and rocks" to fall on them and protect them from the wrath of God? How could they hide in the mountains and call on them for protection if every mountain has already been literally removed and no longer exists?

So here is my point. Or rather, here is John's point. When Jesus returns, he will judge and destroy every political organization that opposes him. He will bring devastation on every government, every army, every nation, every philosophical movement, and every financial institution that refuses to submit to his Lordship. That is what John is describing here. The point is that this celestial (heavenly) and terrestrial (earthly) phenomena are prophetic hyperbole for national and global catastrophe. God's judgment of earthly unbelief and idolatry is described in terms of heavenly disasters.

Let's turn our attention to those on whom this judgment falls. The language of Revelation 6:15-16 in which the people of the earth seek refuge from God's wrath in caves and mountains is taken from Isaiah 2:10, 18-21 and Hosea 10:8, all of which may yet be a further allusion to Genesis 3:8 where Adam and Eve are described as hiding from the presence of the Lord.

I find it interesting that John describes the destruction of seven facets of physical creation: (1) the earth, (2) the sun, (3) the moon, (4) the stars, (5) the heavens or the sky, (6) mountains, and (7) islands. In similar fashion, there are seven groups of humanity who come under judgment: (1) kings, (2) great ones, (3) generals, (4) the rich, (5) the powerful, (6) slaves, and (7) those who are free. It seems clear that the use of the number seven in each instance points us to the universality or the completeness or the comprehensiveness of the disasters and judgments that are to befall the earth.

Be it noted that judgment comes upon all, regardless of their status in society or their wealth or their influence. Kings and slaves alike are accountable to God. The manifestation of God's wrath is a leveler of humanity. The rich and the powerful can't appeal to their earthly achievements to escape judgment. Generals can't call upon their troops to fight the Lamb.

Thus, I conclude that the first five seals portray different aspects of the whole of church history, in particular what believers will suffer in a world overrun with unbelief and opposition to Christ, whereas the sixth seal (and eventually the seventh as well) describes the hour that will end it. What we have seen, therefore, in these seal judgments is "the succession of woes which will sweep to and fro across the world throughout the course of history, and which often cause men to wonder whether the forces of evil are not altogether out of control."[5]

But perhaps the most important and instructive thing for us to see is the reaction of all these individuals to the undeniable presence and power of the risen Lord Jesus Christ. Would it not be the easiest thing in the world, the most sensible thing in the

---

5. Wilcock, *The Message of Revelation*, 76.

world, for these people simply to stop and take account of what is happening and who it is who is bringing this judgment? Is it not the height of folly to think that you could hide from God in caves and under rocks? It is utter insanity and evidence of the spiritual blindness and foolishness of sinful man to think that he can escape the coming judgment of God.

They clearly recognize that this final judgment is being poured out by "him who is seated on the throne," a reference to God the Father, and "the Lamb" who is clearly the Lord Jesus Christ. They just as clearly acknowledge that this is the final day of judgment (v. 17) and that it is inescapable. No one can avoid it. No one can stand against it (v. 17).

So why don't they repent? All they need to do to avert eternal disaster is to bow in repentance before the Lamb and confess him as Lord of all. Their recalcitrant, hard-hearted determination to stand defiantly against Jesus all the way to the end, is repeated yet again in even greater detail in Revelation 9:20-21. And here we see that it isn't the case that they weren't given time and opportunity to repent, as if to suggest that these final judgments came too fast and did not provide them with the chance to bow the knee and believe and acknowledge their need of a Savior:

> "The rest of mankind, who were not killed by these plagues, did not repent of the works of their hands nor give up worshiping demons and idols of gold and silver and bronze and stone and wood, which cannot see or hear or walk, nor did they repent of their murders or their sorceries or their sexual immorality or their thefts" (Rev. 9:20-21).

Observe that these individuals are witnesses to the first six trumpet judgments. That is what John is referring to with the words, "these plagues." They see them. They suffer from them. There is no escaping or denying the reality of what is taking place. They survive them, but still refuse to repent!

There are still many in our world today who insist that human beings are by nature good. They are inherently upright and not sinful. But here we see a stinging indictment and refutation of that optimistic view of human nature. Could there be any more graphic and explicit description of what theologians call total depravity?

In the final analysis, they don't want to look at God. "Hide us from the face of him who is seated on the throne." If it were not for God's sovereign saving grace and mercy, you and I would be numbered among these people. The only reason you desire and hunger for the opportunity to look on the face of infinite beauty and majesty and goodness is because God saved you: by grace alone, through faith alone, in Christ alone.

You and I look upon the Lamb and we see one who has been slain and whose blood "ransomed people for God." We love the Lamb. The Lamb loves us. We will never have to suffer the wrath of the Lamb, because the Spirit has led us to put our confidence and faith in what the Lamb did for sinners on the cross. By the way, does the image of a lamb filled with wrath strike you as odd? It seems to be a contradiction in terms. A lamb is by nature calm, docile, gentle, and easy-going. So, too, is the Lamb of God, until such time as unrepentant and defiant sinners spit in his face and mock him and ridicule his claim to be God.

[Parenthetical Interlude – 7:1-17]

The Seventh Seal

Following the parenthetical interlude in Chapter 7, which we'll look at in the next chapter, we come to Revelation 8:1-5 and John's description of the seventh seal judgment. After the jarring and disruptive nature of the sixth seal it feels a bit anticlimactic for John to say that with the seventh seal there is "silence" in heaven. So what does this mean?

A few scholars have argued that there is no content to the seventh seal, as indicated by the reference to "silence" in 8:1. To them, the seventh seal appears empty. This has led some to posit that the seven trumpets themselves, and perhaps also the seven bowls, constitute the content or substance of the seventh seal. Before drawing this conclusion, however, we must discern the meaning of "silence". Various options are available:

- Some see the "silence" as a temporary suspension of divine revelation (for what purpose is not stated).

- This silence may be indicative of mankind's awestruck reverence in view of the revelation of God's wrath and the imminence of the end.

- Others think the silence is that of the heavenly hosts, i.e., angels as they stand witness to God's redemptive purpose unfolding.

- Some suggest that this is an allusion to the silence that preceded creation and which now precedes the new creation.

- Perhaps this silence indicates God's rest from the judgments that began with the first six seals. Again, however, this is speculative and lacks explicit biblical precedent.

- Others see it as no more than a dramatic pause in the narrative, preparatory to the introduction of the seven trumpets.

- Closer to the correct view is the fact that silence in the Old Testament is often a prelude to some divine manifestation (Job 4:16; Zeph. 1:17; Zech. 2:13).

Many, however, myself included, contend that the meaning of "silence" must be found in the Old Testament where it often points to divine judgment.[6] To be even more specific, perhaps the silence is an indication that God has heard the prayers of the martyrs for vengeance (Rev. 6:10) and is now prepared to respond. In this way the seventh seal is linked to 8:3-5 where the silence is related to God's heavenly temple and sacrificial altar, from which judgment comes forth.

The imagery of the smoke of incense (see Psalm 141:1-2) rising before God (8:4) points to a positive answer to the martyrs' request. Indeed, 8:5 would constitute the actual historical execution of

---

6. See, for example, Psalms 31:17; 115:17; Isaiah 47:5; Lamentations 2:10-11; Amos 8:2-3; Habakkuk 2:20 (cf. Isaiah 23:2; 41:1-5).

God's verdict on behalf of his people. Bauckham even suggests that "the silence is that during which the angel burns the incense on the altar to accompany the prayers of the saints."[7] Thus "at the climax of history, heaven is silent [figuratively speaking, of course] so that the prayers of the saints can be heard, and the final judgment occurs in response to them (v. 5)."[8]

It would be a mistake, however, to conclude that "the prayers of all the saints" refers exclusively to the request by the martyrs whose souls John saw beneath the altar (the fifth seal of Revelation 6:9-11). Although surely inclusive of their request, "all the saints" must be a reference to the totality of God's people throughout the course of the present church age. Thus we see in Revelation 8:3-4 that our prayers are taken seriously by God, are heard by him, and undoubtedly are one of the primary means by which God brings his purposes in history (including his judgments on an unbelieving world) to fulfillment.

While the incense rises up to God, the fire of the altar is directed toward earth, the latter a metaphor anticipating the trumpet judgments that immediately follow in John's vision. There is no need for 8:5 to elaborate on the essence or extent of that judgment, insofar as several subsequent texts will do that in great detail (see 11:14-19; 14:14-20; 16:17-21; 18:9-24; 19:19-21; 20:11-15). Note that "peals of thunder and sounds and flashes of lightning and an earthquake" (8:5) are elsewhere found in texts that undeniably describe the final judgment of the unbelieving world (11:18; 16:18). It may even be that John envisions the trumpets and bowls themselves as part of the answer of God to the prayer of the martyrs.

There is no clear reason why the silence lasts only "for about half an hour" (8:1). The use of the word translated "as" or "about" indicates that John is giving us only an approximation of time. It could be slightly less than half an hour or slightly more. Often in Revelation the time reference "one hour" is used to refer to a sudden

---

7. Bauckham, *The Climax of Prophecy*, 70.
8. Ibid., 71.

and swift crisis in the judgment of the unrepentant or ungodly (see 3:3, 10; 11:13; 14:7, 15; 18:10, 17, 19). There is no reason to believe that a literal thirty minutes is in view.

Conclusion

The fact that the second coming of Jesus Christ will witness a simultaneous outpouring of both divine wrath and saving mercy strikes many as inconceivable. But it isn't about mercy that people voice their objections. It is the notion that God is angry with enemies of the gospel and will hold them eternally accountable for their rejection of Jesus Christ. The Revelation given to John, however, cannot be ignored. There is a "great day" (Rev. 6:17) when the "wrath of the Lamb" (Rev. 6:16) will be seen and felt, and I would be in utter dereliction of my duty as a teacher of God's Word if I conveniently skipped over this vitally important truth just so that some among you might feel better.

I strongly suspect that opposition to the concept of divine wrath is likely due to a misunderstanding of what it is. Wrath is not the loss of self-control or the irrational and capricious outburst of anger. Divine wrath is not to be thought of as a celestial bad temper or God lashing out at those who "rub him the wrong way." Divine wrath, as it is described in this passage, is righteous antagonism toward all that is unholy. It is the revulsion of God's character to that which is a violation of God's will.

And I say this without the slightest hint of contradiction, that there is a very real sense in which divine wrath is a function of divine love. God's wrath is his love for holiness and truth and justice. It is because God passionately loves purity and peace and perfection that he reacts angrily toward anything and anyone who defiles them. J. I. Packer explains:

> "Would a God who took as much pleasure in evil as He did in good be a good God? Would a God who did not react adversely to evil in His world be morally perfect? Surely not. But it is precisely this adverse reaction to evil, which is a necessary part

of moral perfection, that the Bible has in view when it speaks of God's wrath."[9]

And we must never forget that if we don't believe that humans deserve to have God visit upon them the painful consequences of their sin, we empty God's forgiveness of all meaning. If there is no punishment that sin warrants, then God should overlook our transgressions. Forgiveness is real and precious and glorious only because our sin has betrayed us into a situation in which justice demands that God inflict upon us the most serious and eternal consequences. But he has instead visited that judgment on his Son, our Savior, Jesus Christ. That is the glory of saving grace, that the infinitely holy God, who should take action against us, instead has taken action for us.

---

9. J. I. Packer, *Knowing God* (Downers Grove: IVP, 1993), 151.

Chapter Eighteen

The Servants of God: Sealed and Safe

(Revelation 7:1-17; 14:1-5)

The song, *King of My Heart* has become a favorite among many Christians. The way in which it declares that God is good is both biblical and reassuring. But there is a line in the chorus that often times sticks in the throat of some believers. It goes something like this: "You're never gonna' let, never gonna' let me down." Some struggle to sing this because deep down inside they don't really believe it. They think there have been times in their lives when God really did let them down, and they are afraid there may well be more instances in the future when he'll do so again.

When people have asked me about this line in the song and what it means I always direct their attention to Romans 8:28 where we are assured that "for those who love God all things work together for good, for those who are called according to his purpose." In other words, God never lets us down because he takes even the worst of tragedies and setbacks and turns them for good in our lives. He mysteriously and mercifully uses them to change us more and more into the image of Jesus.

There is yet another sense in which God never lets us down. He never fails to fulfill his promises. But the problem with this is that we all too often think God has promised to do something for us that in point of fact is nowhere stated in Scripture.

Perhaps the best and most common example of this is physical suffering and persecution from our enemies. When we endure pain and suffering and opposition and unjust treatment at the hands of the world, we immediately jump to the conclusion that God has quite obviously "let us down" by not protecting us from such attacks. But God never in Scripture promises that his children will be insulated against or protected from the devastating consequences of physical harm or persecution or natural calamities. Never. To suggest then, when you are fired from your job for no reason, that God has let you down is to misunderstand what he does and does not promise us in the Bible. When you suffer financial hardship because of the immoral behavior of someone else, or when you lose your house and possessions in a tornado or when you are slandered at work or are thrown in jail simply for being a Christian, there is no indication that God has failed you or has let you down or has not come through on a promise he made to you in the Bible.

This is critically important for us to understand if we are going to make sense of what we read in Revelation 7 and 14. Here in these two chapters we read of 144,000 individuals being "sealed" by God. Who are these people and what does it mean that they are "sealed"? Is this a promise that God will make certain they never suffer at the hands of the non-Christian world or from the attacks of Satan? If not, what does it mean and how does it apply to you and me? That's where we're going in this chapter. So let's get started.

The Sealing of the Saints

Revelation 7 is a parenthetical pause in which John explains the vision of Revelation 6 in more detail and provides a background against which it may be better understood. Thus, when he begins in verse 1 with the words, "After this," he does not mean that the events of Chapter 7 are chronologically subsequent to or follow those of Chapter 6, but only that the vision of Chapter 7 appeared to him after the vision of Chapter 6. This is confirmed when we observe that the task of the four angels is to prevent any harm being done to "the earth" or "the sea" or "any tree" (7:1), until the servants of God can be sealed. Since the seal judgments of

Chapter 6 describe considerable, indeed catastrophic, harm to the earth, sea, and trees, it seems best to understand Chapter 7 as descriptive of what occurred prior to the events of Chapter 6, and not subsequent to them.

Revelation 7:1-8 answers a question that everyone asks: "If the world is the object or focus of God's wrath, as seen in the seal, trumpet, and bowl judgments, how will Christians survive?" That's a great question! Verses 1-8 of Chapter 7 explain how believers can persevere through these judgments, while verses 9-17 provide us with a description of the heavenly rewards and blessings that will be theirs. There is a sense, then, in which Revelation 7 is the answer to the question posed at the close of Revelation 6. In 6:17, as the wrath of God falls on the unrepentant, they cry out, "Who can stand?" (6:17b). Revelation 7 gives the answer: "Only those who are sealed and thus preserved from God's wrath can stand and persevere."

Before we go any further let me remind you of something that I emphasized and explained at the start of Revelation 6. This book does not merely tell us what will happen in the future leading up to the second coming of Christ. It tells us what has happened in the past nineteen centuries of the history of the church, and it tells us what is happening right now in our lives, in our own day, and it also tells us what will happen in the days and years ahead before Jesus returns. In other words, the book of Revelation portrays for us in highly symbolic and graphic imagery the course of events in all of church history, the conflict between good and evil, the battle between Christ and the enemies of his kingdom, spanning the time from the first coming of Jesus to his second coming. So what we read in Revelation 7 isn't only about the future. It's also about what God has done in the past and is doing in the present for all his redeemed people.

Let's look now at a few of the details in these opening verses of Chapter 7.

The references in 7:1 to the "four corners of the earth" and the "four winds of the earth" points to the cosmic nature of this vision: four being the number in Revelation that consistently symbolizes the entire earth and its inhabitants (see also Ezek. 37:9; Jer. 49:36; Dan. 7:2; 8:8; 11:4; and Zech. 2:6; 6:5). The fact that the four winds must be held back or prevented from "harming" the earth indicates they are probably evil, wicked, rebellious angelic (demonic) agents whom God is using to bring judgment against the world (Jeremiah 49:36 describes "the four winds" as God's agents of judgment against a nation).

In verse 2 John sees "another angel" who is portrayed as issuing a command to other angelic beings, perhaps pointing to a hierarchy within the angelic host. He has a divine and gracious commission: he comes with the "seal of the living God" designed to protect God's people from the "seal" judgments that are imminent. The purpose of this "seal" is not to protect believers from physical harm that comes as a result of the "seal/trumpet/bowl" judgments or by persecution or from the attacks of Satan. Let's never forget that John has described himself as our "partner in ... tribulation" (Rev. 1:9). And Jesus told the Christians in the church in Smyrna to "be faithful unto death" (Rev. 2:10), given the fact that they were about to "suffer" because "the devil is about to throw some" of them "into prison" (Rev. 2:10). You will also recall from what we saw in Revelation 6:9-11 that many had been martyred for their faith and many more would follow. As far as I can tell, nowhere in the New Testament are the people of God ever promised protection from physical suffering at the hands of unbelievers or from the ravages of living in a fallen world. Certainly God often does providentially and mercifully protect his people, but there is no guarantee that he will always do so.

God nowhere says we are invulnerable to Satan's attack, but he does promise us that nothing Satan or anyone else might do can ever separate us from the love he has for us in Jesus (Rom. 8:37-39). What we are reading about here is divine preservation and protection of a spiritual nature. It is God's gracious provision of persevering faith in the midst of intense persecution and suffering. The seal strengthens our faith so that the trials through which we pass serve not to separate us from God but only to refine and purify our commitment to him. In other words, persecution and pain and suffering have the tendency to weaken an individual's resistance. What safeguard or assurance do we have that when faced with this we won't crater under pressure and deny Jesus? The safeguard is the seal of God imposed on the foreheads of God's people.

The verb "to seal" can also mean to authenticate and to designate ownership of something or someone. This is surely in view insofar as in 14:1 the seal is identified as the Name of the Lamb and the Father (cf. 22:4). Indeed, the "mark" of the beast on the forehead of his followers is identified as "the name of the beast" (14:9-11).

I am persuaded that the entire imagery of the "seal" is simply a reference to the Holy Spirit himself, whose abiding presence in Christians is likened unto "sealing" which marks them out as God's and protects them from spiritual harm:

> "And it is God who establishes us with you in Christ, and has anointed us, and who has also put his seal on us and given us his Spirit in our hearts as a guarantee" (2 Cor. 1:21-22).

> "In him you also, when you heard the word of truth, the gospel of your salvation, and believed in him, were sealed with the promised Holy Spirit, who is the guarantee of our inheritance until we acquire possession of it, to the praise of his glory" (Eph. 1:13-14; cf. 4:30).

Thus, when we read in Revelation that God has "sealed" his people and put his name on their foreheads we should immediately think of the gift of the Holy Spirit and his work in our hearts to mark us out as belonging to God and protected and preserved in faith no matter how much tribulation or suffering we face. It's God's way of saying: "You're mine! I will never let you go! I will sustain and preserve and uphold you in faith no matter what the enemy may attempt to do."

By the way, this is the clearest indication that *the so-called "mark of the beast" is not a literal, physical mark on the bodies of unbelievers, either on their forehead or their right hand* (Rev. 13:16). All through Revelation we see Satan making every effort to copy whatever God does. So, for example, the three persons of the Holy Trinity, Father, Son, and Holy Spirit, have their evil counterparts in Satan, the Beast, and the False Prophet. Just as Jesus died and rose again from the dead, so the Beast is portrayed as dying and rising to life again.

My point is simply that the so-called "mark" of the Beast that unbelievers receive on their forehead or their right hand is a demonic rip-off, a depraved parody, a counterfeit imitation of the "mark" that believers receive on their foreheads. Look at the texts where the people of God are "sealed" on their foreheads:

> "Do not harm the earth or the sea or the trees, until we have sealed the servants of our God on their foreheads" (Rev. 7:3).

> "They were told not to harm the grass of the earth or any green plant or any tree, but only those people who do not have the seal of God on their foreheads" (Rev. 9:4).

> "Then I looked, and behold, on Mount Zion, stood the Lamb, and with him 144,000 who had his name and his Father's name written on their foreheads" (Rev. 14:1).

> "They will see his face, and his name will be on their foreheads" (Rev. 22:4).

No one that I know of believes that all Christians will literally and physically have the name of Jesus Christ and the name of the Father tattooed on their foreheads. This is simply a way of describing the fact that those who are born again and redeemed by the blood of Christ belong to him and to his Father and are preserved in faith by the indwelling Holy Spirit.

So we later read that the False Prophet causes everyone who isn't a Christian to have the mark of the Beast written on his/her forehead as a sign that they belong to the Beast and are loyal to him. This "mark" on their foreheads or on their right hand is simply Satan's way of mimicking the seal of God that is on the foreheads of God's people. If you have the name of Jesus and God the Father written on your forehead it simply means they own you, you belong to them, you are loyal to the Lord God Almighty. But if you have "the name of the beast" (Rev. 13:17) written on your forehead it signifies that he owns you, you belong to him, you are loyal to the Antichrist. My point is that if you don't argue that the name of Jesus and God the Father is literally tattooed on the foreheads of Christians you have no reason to argue that the name of the Antichrist (or his number, 666) is literally tattooed on the foreheads of non-Christians.

Some have found the background for the "mark" of the Beast in the Jewish practice of wearing *tephillim* or phylacteries. These were leather boxes containing Scripture passages (Ex. 13:9, 16; Deut. 6:8; 11:18; Matt. 23:5) that were worn either on the left arm (facing the heart) or the forehead. The mark of the Beast, however, was to be placed on the right hand. Others have pointed out that the word "mark" was used of the emperor's seal on business contracts and the impress of the Roman ruler's head on coins. Perhaps, then, "the mark alludes to the state's political and economic 'stamp of approval,' given only to those who go along with its religious demands."[1]

Thus it seems quite clear that the "mark" of the Beast on his followers is the demonic counterpart and parody of the "seal" that is placed on the foreheads of the people of God (see 7:3-8; 14:1; 22:4). "Just as the seal and the divine name on believers connote God's ownership and spiritual protection of them, so the mark and Satanic name signify those who belong to the devil and will undergo perdition."[2] Since the seal or name on the believer is obviously invisible, being symbolic of the indwelling presence of the Holy Spirit, it seems certain that the mark of the Beast is likewise a symbolic way of describing the loyalty of his followers and his ownership of them. If you're wondering why the seal on God's people and the mark on the non-Christian is placed on the forehead of each, it may be that the forehead points to one's ideological commitment, and that the mark on the hand points to the practical outworking or manifestation of that commitment.

---

1. Beale, *Revelation*, 715.
2. Ibid., 716.

The 144,000

The list of tribes here in Revelation 7 corresponds to none of the nearly twenty different variations found in the Old Testament. Judah, listed first here, is found in that position in the Old Testament only when the tribes are arranged geographically, moving from south to north (Num. 34:19; Josh. 21:4; Judg. 1:2; 1 Chron. 12:24). The only exception to this is Numbers 2:3 (followed by 7:12; 10:14). Perhaps Judah's priority here "emphasizes the precedence of the messianic king from the tribe of Judah (cf. Gen. 49:10; 1 Chron. 5:1-2) and thus refers to a fulfillment of the prophecy in Genesis 49:8 that the eleven other tribes 'will bow down' to Judah."[3]

One can hardly fail to note that the tribes of Dan and Ephraim are omitted. One tradition believed that the Antichrist was to come from the tribe of Dan (based on a misinterpretation of Jeremiah 8:16 and first found in Irenaeus, c.200). Dan was also closely associated with idol worship (Judg. 18:16-19; 1 Kgs. 12:28-30; cf. Gen. 49:17; Judg. 18:30; Jer. 8:16), as was Ephraim (Hos. 4:17–14:8). In Revelation 7, Joseph and Manasseh substitute for Dan and Ephraim. In the final analysis, there is no clear reason for this and we may never know why.

Who are the 144,000 who receive the seal of the living God? I believe that they are actually representative of all God's people, whether Jew or Gentile, who have put their trust in Jesus. Several things should be noted about them that confirm this identification.

First, there are several noticeable differences between the 144,000 in verses 4-8 and the great multitude in verses 9-17. The most obvious difference is that the first group is specifically numbered (144,000) whereas the second is innumerable. Furthermore, the members of the 144,000 are all taken from but one nation, Israel, whereas those in the innumerable multitude are taken from "every nation and tribe and people and language" (7:9). Another difference is their location: the 144,000 appear to be on earth, whereas the multitude is in heaven, before the throne of God (7:9). Finally, the 144,000 are in imminent peril and thus

---

3. Ibid., 417.

require divine protection, whereas the multitude are in a condition of absolute peace and joy.

Do these differences mean that the two groups are entirely different, or is it the same group viewed from different perspectives, at different stages of their existence and experience? I believe it is the latter and reasons for this will follow below.

Second, these in 7:4-8 are surely identical with the 144,000 mentioned in Revelation 14:1-5. In both cases it is said that they received the seal of God on their "foreheads" (7:3 and 14:1). In 14:3 they are described as those who had been "redeemed from the earth" and again in 14:4 they were "redeemed from mankind". This echoes Revelation 5:9 where the Lamb is said to have "ransomed" or "redeemed" for God people from every tribe, tongue, people, and nation. This same phrase is used again in Revelation 7:9 to describe the innumerable multitude. This would seem to indicate that the 144,000 = the innumerable multitude = the redeemed of all ages, and not some special remnant of humanity.

Third, in Revelation 14:4 the 144,000 are described as "first fruits" (*aparchē*) to God and to the Lamb. The idea would appear to be that the 144,000 were an initial group, perhaps a remnant, of believers whose salvation was a foreshadowing of a yet greater ingathering or harvest of believers in the end time. Thus the 144,000 represent the totality of God's redeemed at that time, and thus "first fruits" of the remainder of all the redeemed who will be gathered in the final harvest at the close of history.

Fourth, these 144,000 are called the "servants" (*douloi*) of God (7:3). Whenever the word "servants" is used in Revelation (2:20; 19:5; 22:3) it refers to the entire community of the redeemed. Also, if Satan puts a seal or mark on all his followers (13:16-17; 14:9-11), it seems reasonable that God would do likewise for all his people.

Fifth, if you're wondering why the 144,000 are numbered and the multitude is innumerable, it is probably because the numbering (144,000) is being used to evoke images of the Old Testament census, which was designed to determine the military strength of the nation (see Num. 1:3, 18, 20; 26:2, 4; 1 Chron. 27:23; 2 Sam. 24:1-9). The point is that these in Revelation 7 constitute a Messianic army called upon, like Jesus himself, to conquer the enemy through sacrificial death. In the Old Testament those counted were males of military age (twenty years and over). This explains why the 144,000 in Revelation 14:1-5 are adult males, i.e., those eligible for military service.

Sixth, this "military force" in 7:4-8 conquers its enemy in the same way that Jesus has conquered at the cross. When Jesus died it appeared that Satan had won. But in an ironic twist it was precisely by dying that Jesus gained the victory. Likewise, when God's people die for their faith without renouncing Jesus, they conquer the enemy. In other words, the people of God are portrayed as engaging in holy war, but in a spiritual, non-violent way. John's aim is to show that the decisive battle in God's eschatological war against all evil has been won by the sacrificial death and resurrection of Jesus and by his followers who faithfully persevere in the face of death when they refuse to deny that Jesus is Lord. It may look like Satan has won, but the martyrs are the real victors. They conquer by dying in their faith, committed to the end to Jesus.

So, precisely who are the 144,000? Are they different from or one and the same with the innumerable multitude? Most dispensational, pretribulational, premillennialists, that is, most who read the book of Revelation in a futurist sense, understand the 144,000 to be a Jewish remnant saved immediately after the rapture of the church. Many then argue that, in the absence of the church, they serve as evangelists who preach the gospel during the Great Tribulation. In other words, these are literally 144,000 (arithmetically speaking, neither 143,999 nor 144,001) ethnic descendants of Abraham, Isaac, and Jacob. The innumerable multitude, some go on to argue, are Gentiles saved in the tribulation through the evangelistic efforts of the 144,000. Be it noted, however, that there is nothing whatsoever said in this passage about these people functioning as evangelists or being responsible for the salvation of the multitude.

My problem with this perspective begins with the fact that it depends entirely on a futurist interpretation of the book. Furthermore, why would God protect only Jewish believers and leave Gentile believers to endure such horrific judgments? And why would God protect only 144,000 Jewish believers? Why would he not protect all of them? In Revelation 9:4 we read that only those with the seal of God on their foreheads are exempt from the demonic torments that are so horrible and agonizing that men will long to die. Is it feasible or consistent with the character of God that he would protect only a select group from such wrath while afflicting the rest of his blood-bought children with it? The answer is a resounding No. Therefore, the 144,000 who are sealed on their forehead in 7:4-8 (and 14: 9:4) must be all the redeemed, not a select few.

My understanding is that the number 144,000 is symbolic (as is the case with virtually every number in Revelation). "12" is both squared (the twelve tribes multiplied by the twelve apostles? Cf. 21:12, 14) and multiplied by a thousand, a two-fold way of emphasizing completeness. Hence, John has in view all the redeemed, all believers, whether Jew or Gentile, i.e., the church.

Thus the 144,000 in Revelation 7:3-8 and 14:1-5 and the innumerable multitude in 7:9-17 refer to the same group of people viewed from differing perspectives. The 144,000 are the redeemed standing on the brink of battle while still on earth, while the innumerable multitude are the redeemed enjoying their heavenly reward. So again, the 144,000 and the innumerable multitude are the same. The 144,000 are portrayed as a Messianic army waging spiritual war while yet on earth while the multitude are the redeemed of all ages in heaven enjoying their reward in the presence of the Lord Jesus Christ.

I need to briefly address an accusation that has come against me. Since I believe the 144,000 from the twelve tribes of Israel is a reference to the totality of the church of Jesus Christ, a church comprised of both believing Jews and believing Gentiles, some have insisted that I embrace what is called "replacement" theology. Replacement theology argues that believing Gentiles who comprise the church have replaced or perhaps even displaced Jews from ever inheriting the promises made to Abraham. But I do not believe that.

Note carefully. No believing Jewish man or woman will ever be deprived of the inheritance that God promised to Abraham, Isaac, and Jacob. The New Testament clearly teaches that Jews who believe in Jesus together with Gentiles who believe in Jesus together comprise the true Israel of God, the church. They will together, equally, inherit all the promises. Believing Gentiles are described in the New Testament as being made members of the commonwealth of Israel (Eph. 2:11ff.) and of being grafted into the one olive tree alongside believing Jews (Rom. 11).

What the New Testament has done is to *expand* the meaning of a true Jew. A true Jew, a true Israelite, is no longer someone who merely has the blood of Abraham coursing through his veins. A true Jew, a true seed of Abraham, is the man or woman who is in Christ. It doesn't matter if he/she is a Gentile or Jew. The only thing that matters is whether or not he/she is in Christ by faith. And all who are in Christ by faith are heirs of the promises made to the patriarchs. No one is replaced. No one forfeits their inheritance. Thus the relationship between Israel and the church isn't one of replacement but of *fulfillment*. Let me simply ask you this question: "Does the butterfly replace the caterpillar?" No. The butterfly is the organic fulfillment of the caterpillar, just as the church is the continuation and fulfillment of Israel.

The 144,000 in Revelation 14:1-5

On occasion in the Old Testament, Zion could refer to the hilly area in southeast Jerusalem, to the temple mount, to the historical city of Jerusalem, and even to the entire nation of Israel. In Psalm 2:6, Zion is the "holy mountain" of God on which he installs Messiah as King. In other words, Zion may be the eschatological city where God dwells with and protects his people. Hebrews 12:22-23 (cf. Gal. 4:25-27) refers to Zion as the ideal, heavenly city to which believers even now aspire (and in which they hold citizenship; see Philippians 3:20) during the course of the church age. In certain texts, Zion is indistinguishable from the redeemed who dwell there (see Is. 62:1-12). Many contend that it is, in fact, a reference to the New Jerusalem (Rev. 21) which "comes down out of heaven" as a dwelling for God's people. In any case, it is where the Lamb and his redeemed share fellowship and the authority of the kingdom.

The "new song" (14:3) is most likely a hymn of praise for the victory God has secured on their behalf over the Dragon and his two beastly cohorts. You may recall that back in Revelation 2:17 Jesus said he would give to the overcomers "a new name written on the [white] stone that no one knows except the one who receives it." Now we are told that only the redeemed, the 144,000, can "learn" the new song and sing it.

They are described as "ones who have not defiled themselves with women, for they are virgins" (14:4a). Some have taken this literally as a group of celibate men. However, if the 144,000 is a symbol for the entire people of God, as I believe it is, this would mean he envisions all Christians as celibate! This may then be an allusion to the Old Testament requirement that an Israelite soldier preserve ceremonial purity before entering battle (Deut. 23:9-10; 1 Sam. 21:5; 2 Sam. 11:8-11). Others see in the word "virgins" (*parthenoi*) a metaphor of all saints, including women, who have not compromised with the world system or yielded to its idolatry. They have remained loyal as a "virgin bride" to their betrothed husband (see 19:7-9; 21:2; 2 Cor. 11:2). Remember that often times idolatry and injustice are figuratively pictured as "harlotry" or "sexual immorality" (see Jer. 3:1-10; 13:27; Ezek. 16:15-58; 23:1-49; 43:7; Hos. 5:4; 6:10). Israel's idolatry was also described as "defilement" (Isa. 65:4; Jer. 23:15; 51:4). This is similar to what we find in Revelation 2:14, 20-22. In other texts in Revelation, to "fornicate" (*porneuō*) and its cognates usually are metaphorical for spiritual apostasy and idol worship (14:8; 17:1, 2, 4, 5, 15, 16; 18:3, 9; 19:2). When these words are used literally, they are part of vice lists (9:21; 21:8; 22:15). In summary, the "virginity" in view here and the refusal to "defile" themselves with women is a figurative description of all believers, male and female, who resist the temptation to compromise morally with the system of the beast or to yield to its idolatrous ways.

They are also said to "follow the Lamb wherever he goes" (14:4b), a likely allusion to the statements found in the synoptic gospels about believers "following" Jesus (e.g., Matt. 8:19; 10:38; Mark 8:34; Luke 9:57; cf. 1 Pet. 221-22). One element in following the Lamb is that "in their mouth no lie was found, for they are blameless" (v. 5). This is an allusion to Isaiah 53:9 where it is said of the suffering Messiah that "there was no deceit in his mouth." This may be more than a reference to general truth-telling and point also to "the saints' integrity in witnessing to Jesus when they are under pressure from the Beast and the 'false prophet' to compromise their faith and go along with the idolatrous lie (so 13:10, 18; 14:9-12)."[4] They are "blameless" in the sense that they maintain a truthful witness concerning Jesus. They resist the temptation to embrace the "lie" of the Beast.

Conclusion

To sum up simply, I believe Revelation 7:1-8 and 14:1-5 are John's symbolic portrayal of the truth of Romans 8:35-39. "Who shall separate us from the love of Christ? Shall tribulation, or distress, or persecution, or famine, or nakedness, or danger, or sword? [Or perhaps even Satan himself or the Beast or the False Prophet?]... No, in all these things we are more than conquerors through him who loved us." And the way we conquer and persevere and endure is through the Holy Spirit whom Christ has sent to us, who seals us as God's own, in whose strong and loving arms we live securely in the face of all evil.

---

4. Ibid., 746.

Chapter Nineteen

When We've Been There Ten Thousand Years!

(Revelation 7:9-17)

It has always struck me as bizarre that some Christians, or at least those who profess to be Christians, don't think it is spiritually beneficial or helpful or encouraging to think about heaven. Many of them have bought into the old saying that such people are "so heavenly minded they're of no earthly good." Yes, I have known a few people along the way who have used the promise of heaven's blessings as an excuse for neglecting earthly responsibilities. Some seem to think that their primary task is to meditate on the age to come and it leaves them no time to get a job or mow the grass or take a meal to a bed-ridden neighbor. I have no patience for people like that. But I still believe that meditating on the life to come and developing a healthy obsession for the blessings that God has in store for us is of immense practical benefit for how we live now. I am persuaded that we must take steps to cultivate and intensify in our souls an ache for the beauty and blessings of the age to come.

The consistent witness of Scripture is that we should make heaven and its beauty the object of our contemplative energy, not for the purpose of fueling theological speculation, but to equip us for life here and now. Evidently there is something about heaven that makes our anticipation of its experience profoundly lifechanging. And the reason isn't hard to discern. The essence of heaven is the vision of God and the eternal increase of joy in him. Heaven might well be summed up in the declaration: "They will see his face" (Rev. 22:4)!

Why Think About Heaven?

So why should we think about heaven? Why should we bother with a passage like Revelation 7:9-17 that quite clearly describes the incredible experience of God's people in the new heavens and new earth in eternity future? Before I delve into the nature of this passage, consider the immediate and practical impact of the soul's intense longing for it.

First, setting our hearts on the blessings and joys of heaven frees us from excessive dependence upon earthly wealth and comfort. If there awaits us an eternal inheritance of immeasurable glory, an experience like that portrayed in these verses, it makes no sense to expend effort and energy here, sacrificing so much time and money, to obtain for so brief a time in corruptible form what we will enjoy forever in consummate perfection.

The Apostle Paul made this point in Philippians 3:20-21. "Our citizenship," says Paul, "is in heaven" (3:20a). He reminds the Philippians of this because knowing it to be true enables the soul to escape the grip of "earthly things" (Phil. 3:19) and to "stand firm" (Phil. 4:1). Paul in no way denies or minimizes the reality of our earthly obligations. He reminds the Philippians that their bodies were in Philippi. Their names were enrolled as Roman citizens. They had voting rights. They owed their taxes to an earthly king. They were protected by the laws of a this-worldly state. And the same could be said of you and me.

Yet their fundamental identity, ours as well, the orientation of their souls, the affection of their hearts, and the focus of their minds was in heaven! Paul appeals to their patriotic pride, not in Philippi, but in the New Jerusalem, their real residence! Therefore, be governed by its rules, its principles, its values. Paul is careful to insist that our citizenship "is" (present tense) in heaven, not "will be". We are already citizens of a new state. We are resident aliens here on earth.

Peter said much the same thing in his first epistle. There he contends that the ultimate purpose of the new birth (1 Pet. 1:3-4) is our experience of a heavenly hope, an inheritance that is "imperishable," by which he means incorruptible, not subject to decay or rust or mold or dissolution or disintegration. This heavenly inheritance is "undefiled" or pure, unmixed, untainted by sin or evil. Best of all, it is "unfading." Not only will it never end, but it will also never diminish in its capacity to enthrall and fascinate and impart joy. It is "reserved in heaven" for us, kept safe, under guard, protected and insulated against all intrusion or violation. This hope is the grounds for your joy (v. 6) that sustains you in trial and suffering.

A few verses later Peter exhorts his readers to "set your hope fully on the grace that will be brought to you at the revelation of Jesus Christ" (1 Pet. 1:13). This is a commanded obsession. Fixate fully! Rivet your soul on the grace that you will receive when Christ returns. Tolerate no distractions. Entertain no diversions. Don't let your mind be swayed. Devote every ounce of mental and spiritual and emotional energy to concentrating and contemplating on the grace that is to come.

The author of the book of Hebrews echoes this emphasis. He tells us that the expectation of a "city that has foundations" energized Abraham's heart to persevere in a foreign land. All the patriarchs are described as "seeking a [heavenly] homeland" (Heb. 11:14). Their determination in the face of trial was fueled by their desire for a "better country, that is, a heavenly one" (Heb. 11:16). As pleasant as it may be now, what we see and sense and savor in this life is an ephemeral shadow compared with the substance of God himself. Earthly joys are fragmented beams, but God is the sun. Earthly refreshment is at best a sipping from intermittent springs, but God is the ocean!

Here is a second reason why thinking about the blessings of eternal life in the future is so helpful. A contemplative focus on heaven enables us to respond appropriately to the injustices of this life. Essential to heavenly joy is witnessing the vindication of righteousness and the judgment of evil. Only from our anticipation of the new perspective of heaven, from which we, one day, will look back and evaluate what now seems senseless, can we be empowered to endure this world in all its ugliness and moral deformity.

Apart from a contemplative fixation on the glories of heaven, you will always struggle to read the newspaper righteously! If you insist on taking the short view of things you will be forever frustrated, confused, and angry.

We will see this principle later in our study of Revelation when we come to 19:1-8. There we read of the perspective of those surrounding the heavenly throne of God. Their declaration of praise is in response to the judgment on Babylon described in Revelation 18. God is to be praised and all power and glory ascribed to him precisely because he has "judged the great harlot" (Rev. 19:2). Far from the outpouring of wrath and the destruction of his enemies being a blight on God's character or a reason to question his love and kindness (as unbelievers so often suggest), they are the very reason for worship! God's judgments against the unbelieving world system and its followers are "true and righteous" (see 15:3-4 and 16:5-7), for the harlot was corrupting (cf. 17:1-5; 18:3, 7-9) the earth with her immorality, thereby meriting divine vengeance.

Would you like another, third, reason why it's so important for us to spend time in Revelation 7:9-17? A contemplative focus on heaven produces the fruit of endurance and perseverance now. The strength to endure present suffering is the fruit of meditating on future satisfaction! This is the clear message of several texts such as Matthew 5:11-12; Romans 8:17-18, 23, 25b; Hebrews 13:13-14; and 1 Peter 1:3-8.

Romans 8:18 is Paul's declaration that "the sufferings of this present time are not worth comparing with the glory that is to be revealed to us." We do not lose heart because we contemplate the unseen things of the future and nourish our souls with the truth that whatever we endure on this earth is producing a glory far beyond all comparison! Christians are not asked to treat pain as though it were pleasure, or grief as though it were joy, but to bring all earthly adversity into comparison with heavenly glory and thereby be strengthened to endure. The exhortation in Hebrews 13:13-14 to willingly bear the reproach of Christ is grounded in the expectation of a "city which is to come," namely, the heavenly New Jerusalem.

Nowhere is this principle better seen than in 2 Corinthians 4:16-18. Gazing at the grandeur of heavenly glory transforms our value system. In the light of what is "eternal", what we face now is only "momentary". Suffering appears "prolonged" only in the absence of an eternal perspective. The "affliction" of this life is regarded as "light" when compared with the "weight" of that "glory" yet to come. It is "burdensome" only when we lose sight of our heavenly future. The key to success in suffering, as odd as it sounds, is in taking the long view. Only when juxtaposed with the endless ages of eternal bliss does suffering in this life become tolerable.

There is yet another contrast to be noted. In verse 18 Paul juxtaposes "transient" things "that are seen" with "eternal" things "that are unseen." Paul says that our "inner nature" is being renewed as we look or while we look at the unseen, eternal things of the age to come. If you don't "look" you won't change! The process of renewal only occurs as the believer looks to things as yet unseen. As we fix the gaze of our hearts on the glorious hope of the age to come, God progressively renews our inner being, notwithstanding the simultaneous decay of our outer frame! Inner renewal does not happen automatically or mechanically. Transformation happens only as or provided that we "look not to the things that are seen, but to the things that are unseen" (v. 18).

Heavenly Healing and Happiness

The way John begins his portrayal of the immeasurable greatness and glory of heaven is something we've already encountered in Revelation. Back in Revelation 5:9-14 we read about men and women from every tribe and people and language and nation encircling the throne of God and of the Lamb, Jesus Christ, singing their endless praises and adoration of the One who has saved us.

We also saw back in Revelation 4–5 the presence of millions and millions of angels, together with the twenty-four elders and the four living creatures. They together fall on their faces and worship God, giving him all credit and praise for being who he is and doing what he has done.

Only the angels are described as "standing" (no angel in Revelation is described as seated). There was an ancient Jewish tradition, based on Ezekiel 1:7 ("and their legs were straight"), that angels always stood because they have no knees! Well, I don't know about that, but everyone else who has knees is bowing before our great Triune God!

The "great multitude" that John sees are precisely those in Revelation 5:9 whom Jesus redeemed "from every tribe and language and people and nation." The language John uses, "a great multitude, that no one could number," sounds remarkably similar to the promise given to Abraham. That promise consisted primarily of two elements.

First, Abraham was promised that he would have innumerable descendants, described as "the dust of the earth," "the stars of the sky," and "the sand of the sea" (Gen. 13:16; 15:5; 22:17-18). In Genesis 16:10 God said to Abraham: "I will surely multiply your offspring so that they cannot be numbered for multitude." This promise was repeated to Isaac (Gen. 26:4) and to Jacob (Gen. 28:14; 32:12), and it is found in numerous other Old Testament texts (Ex. 32:13; Deut. 1:10; 10:22; 28:62; 2 Sam. 17:11; 1 Kgs. 3:8; 4:20; Neh. 9:23; Isa. 10:22; 48:19; 51:2; Hos. 1:10).

Second, God promised Abraham that he would be the father of many nations (Gen. 17:4-6, 16), a promise also repeated to Isaac and Jacob (Gen. 28:14; 32:12; 35:11; 48:19). In these Old Testament texts it is the physical progeny of Israel who are in view. But amazingly here in Revelation 7:9 it is the church in whom those promises appear to be fulfilled. Verse 9a points to the fulfillment of the first promise above, while verse 9b points to the fulfillment of the second. It may well be, then, that John views the innumerable multitude of Revelation 7:9 as the consummate fulfillment of the Abrahamic promise. And those who inherit these promises include all believing Jews, all those who have descended physically from

Abraham, Isaac, and Jacob, and have put their trust in Christ, as well as all believing Gentiles.

In verse 10 the saints attribute their "salvation" to God and to the Lamb. In Paul's writings this noun normally refers to deliverance from sin and guilt. In this context, however, something more may be in view. John is describing the preservation and protection of the saints in the midst of suffering. Their "sealing" is designed to safeguard their souls, lest they deny Jesus under the pressures of persecution. The focus of Revelation 7:9-17 is the heavenly reward for those who do, in fact, persevere. Therefore, it may be that by "salvation" John refers not only to the forgiveness of sins but also to their preservation in faith in the midst of trials.

One more comment is in order before we go any further. There has been a debate raging in the church for two thousand years about whether the number of those who will be saved is small or large, or perhaps somewhere in between. Of course, those who call themselves universalists insist that every human being will ultimately be saved, regardless of whether or not they believe in Jesus or in any concept of God. Needless to say, this is profoundly unbiblical. It may even be heretical!

Others argue that the number of those who will finally be saved is very small. They appeal to the concept in Scripture of the believing remnant. The remnant is that small portion of the whole of mankind who truly trust Christ. But perhaps the best and most biblical answer to this question is here in Revelation 7:9. John describes a "great multitude that no one could number." That sure sounds to me like a whole bunch of people! I don't know how many. I don't know if this means the majority of people will ultimately be saved. What I do know is that it is far more than a tiny remnant. It is a multitude of men and women that is so great, so large, so numerous, that it was impossible for John to count them. They are "innumerable"!

A Rhetorical Question

I'm assuming you know what a rhetorical question is. It's a question asked by someone who doesn't want you to answer because they already know it. Here in verses 13-14 one of the twenty-four elders speaks to John and asks him: "Who is this 'great multitude that no one can number?' Where did they come from?" John responds by saying, "Uh, well, you tell me!" The elder is only too happy to provide an answer: "These are the ones coming out of the great tribulation" (v. 14b).

Now, let me say a few words about the "great tribulation." This phrase also appears in our Lord's Olivet Discourse in Matthew 24:21. There he is referring to the destruction of Jerusalem and its temple, an expression of the judgment of God against Israel for its calloused rejection of the Messiah. Most of you have grown up thinking that the so-called "great tribulation" refers exclusively to a short period of time in the future immediately preceding the second coming of Jesus. That, I am forced to tell you, is yet another "sacred cow" that I must slay.

The first thing to remember is that in all likelihood the events that transpired in the first century, in the years 33–70, were a microcosmic foreshadowing of what happens on a macrocosmic scale throughout the present age. If that is true, and I suspect that it is, the use of such terminology here in Revelation 7 is understandable.

On the other hand, "tribulation" is nothing new or unexpected for Christians in any age. John's presence on the island of Patmos is described as "tribulation" (1:9). Back in Revelation 2:9 Jesus said to the Christians in first-century Smyrna, "I know your tribulation." Again in verse 10 he said, "Do not fear what you are about to suffer. Behold, the devil is about to throw some of you into prison, that you may be tested, and for ten days you will have tribulation" (Rev. 2:10). Tribulation is the normative experience for all believers, as several texts indicate (John 16:33; Acts 14:22; Rom. 5:3; 8:35-36; 2 Tim. 3:12). In fact, twenty-one of Paul's twenty-three uses of this term (*thlipsis*) refer to an on-going, present-day experience of the Christian. The tribulation we suffer is "great" because of the intensity of opposition from the world and its god, the Devil.

In any case, nothing requires us to think of the "great tribulation" as a special period of time reserved exclusively for the end of the age through which only the last generation of believers might pass. All Christians in every age face the reality of what John describes. Yes, those who are alive just before the second coming of Jesus will endure "great tribulation" and persecution. But countless millions of Christians throughout church history already have. Tribulation is what characterizes this entire church age in which we live.

There is nothing to indicate that only martyrs are in view here in Chapter 7, only those who actually lost their lives because of their faith. If they are the focus of John's comments, they could also serve to represent all believers who must suffer, whether or not they actually lose their lives. That "they have washed their robes and made them white in the blood of the Lamb" (7:14) would mean that "despite resistance, they have continued believing in and testifying to the Lamb's death on their behalf, which has taken their sin away and granted them salvation."[1]

There may also be here an allusion to the Exodus event of the Old Testament. More than allusion, it may be John's way of saying that the church is the true Israel in whom the Old Testament exodus event finds its typological fulfillment. Consider these parallels: (1) a great multitude comes out of trial and tribulation (*thlipsis* is used in the LXX of Exodus 4:31 to describe Israel's experience); (2) Israel is portrayed as washing their garments (Ex. 19:10, 14) and (3) being sprinkled with blood (Ex. 24:8) to (4) prepare them for God's tabernacling among them, (5) as a result of which they receive food, water, protection, and comfort.

Eternal Life in the Presence of God, the Lamb, and the Holy Spirit

Before I unpack these incredible blessings of heaven in God's presence, I want you to take note of a critically important word. It's actually two words in the Greek text that are translated as one word in English. It is the word "therefore" that opens verse 15. It is John's way of alerting us to the reason or cause or ground or basis on which these people are before the throne of God. It points us back

---

1. Beale, *Revelation*, 436.

to the last sentence in verse 14. In other words, the only reason why these people are before the throne of God and enjoy these remarkable blessings is because "they have washed their robes and made them white in the blood of the Lamb."

Stop for a moment and ask yourself this eternally important question. If you are confident that in eternity future you will stand joyfully "before the throne of God" and enjoy these incredible blessings, on what basis do you believe this? What is the ground for your hope? What is the cause that accounts for this? To what or to whom would you point and say: "That's why."

If your answer is: "It is because I've lived a fairly decent life on earth. I've done the very best I could. I tried to be a good father, mother, son, daughter, friend, and employee. I've been really sincere in my religious life. I attended church on a fairly regular basis. I was baptized and I partake of the Lord's Supper and I'm a covenant member of my local church. Yeah, that's why I anticipate standing before the throne of God." If that is your answer, I pity you. More than that, I appeal to you to look at the reason John gives. The only reason anyone in any age or anywhere on earth can have hope of standing before the throne of God is because by God's grace alone, through faith alone, they have washed their robes and made them white in the blood of Jesus. Have you? Well, have you?

As I read verses 15-17, I see no fewer than eight blessings that we will experience in heaven. (1) The first one is that we will stand "before the throne of God" (v. 15a). Whether we will be able to stand upright for very long is doubtful. My guess is that we, like the twenty-four elders before us, will fall on our faces in adoration and joy and love and gratitude.

(2) Second, we will have the pleasure of serving him "day and night in his temple" (v. 15b). Our service will not be to shore up any weakness in God or to perform tasks that he's too tired to get done on his own. Our service is that of worship and praise. The word translated "serve" is not the ordinary Greek word that means to do work for someone or to come to their aid. It is the word that refers to sacred service in the temple of lifting up prayers and praise. And notice that it will be endless: "day and night"!

(3) Then we are told that God "will shelter" us "with his presence" (v. 15c). The word "shelter" literally means he will set his tabernacle over us. This is a clear allusion to Ezekiel 37:26-28, a passage that in its Old Testament context is a prophecy of Israel's restoration. There God says, "I will make a covenant of peace with them. It shall be an everlasting covenant with them. And I will set them in their land and multiply them, and will set my sanctuary in their midst forever. My dwelling place shall be with them, and I will be their God, and they shall be my people." You won't need a home or a tornado shelter or a mansion of any sort to keep you safe. God's very personal presence will be your shelter! You and I will quite literally live in, with, and under him in all his glory!

(4) The fourth, (5) fifth, (6) sixth, and (7) seventh blessings are all drawn from Isaiah 49:10, yet another text that refers to the results of Israel's restoration: "They shall not hunger or thirst, neither scorching wind nor sun shall strike them, for he who has pity on them will lead them, and by springs of water will guide them [or be their shepherd]" (Isa. 49:10).

What does he mean by all this? This is the prophet's way of summarizing every form of physical harm or deprivation or suffering that we might endure in this life. And God will guarantee that no such harm or pain or loss will ever be experienced by his people in the new heavens and new earth! They shall not hunger or thirst, which is to say that whatever your deepest desires may be, he will fulfill them; whatever it takes to fill you and satisfy you and bring you greatest happiness, he will provide.

(8) As if that were not enough, another prophetic promise tied to Israel's restoration is appended to this list of blessings now applied to the church. In Isaiah 25:8 the prophet declared that God "will swallow up death forever; and the Lord God will wipe away tears from all faces, and the reproach of his people he will take away from all the earth." There seems to be no escaping the fact that John sees the Old Testament hope of Israel's restoration and all its attendant blessings fulfilled in the salvation of the Christian multitudes who comprise the church, both believing Jews and Gentiles.

Conclusion

Is there any practical benefit in thinking on these things? Does it help you face today's loss and tomorrow's pain? Oh, my Yes! A thousand times, Yes!

Chapter Twenty

The Trumpet Blasts of Divine Judgment
(Revelation 8:6-13; 9:1-12)

Why do people struggle with the book of Revelation? By that I don't mean why do people have differing interpretations of what will happen when Christ returns, or why do people disagree on the identity of the Beast and the False Prophet. The struggle I have in mind is the difficulty people have with the unrelenting display of divine wrath and judgment on the world of unbelievers and idolaters. In other words, the single greatest problem people have with this book isn't its symbolism or its view of history or the meaning of the number 666. The single greatest challenge that people face when reading Revelation is the extent and intensity of the judgments that unbelievers and idolaters endure.

Let me put it this way. There is a test that each of us can apply to ourselves to determine whether or not we have a biblical view of God. If you want to know what God thinks of his own glory and honor and whether or not you share his perspective, all that is needed is for you to ask yourself this question: "When I read of the devastating judgments in the book of Revelation, that is to say, when I read of the seven seal judgements, the seven trumpet judgments, and the seven bowl judgments, do I think God is overreacting? Do I find myself saying: 'These judgments are unwarranted. They are extreme. They exceed the boundaries of what is just and right. The seal, trumpet, and bowl judgments are excessive and unjustified.'"

If that is your reaction, then I suggest you need to revisit and reevaluate not only your view of God but also your view of the horror and wickedness of human sin. What I'm suggesting is simply this. If you cringe when you read about the seal, trumpet, and bowl judgments, it can only be due to one thing: You have too high a view of humanity and too low a view of God.

Once the human heart has seen, sensed, or come to understand but a fraction of the immeasurable glory and majesty of God, nothing will make more sense than the intensity of the display of divine wrath that we read about in Revelation. So let me ask the question again in a slightly different way. "How serious an act of cosmic treason is it that human beings whom God made to know and glorify him have instead selfishly exploited his gifts and rebelled against him? Do you find it inexpressibly deplorable that men and women have dishonored the only honorable Being in the universe and have treated with calloused contempt the only beautiful and praise-worthy Being in the universe? And do you think that human sin warrants the kind of judgment that we read about in the book of Revelation?"

If you find yourself increasingly bothered and unsettled by the portrayal of judgment in Revelation, my recommendation is that you spend considerable time re-evaluating your view of God. Once you comprehend the immeasurable height of his infinite worth and value, you will understand the immeasurable depth of human sin and idolatry, and the book of Revelation will no longer be an enigma to your mind or an offense to your soul. With that in mind, let's turn our attention to the first five of the seven trumpet judgments. As we do there are four observations that need to be made.

First, let me briefly remind you of something I set forth when we first looked at the seal judgments in Revelation 6. It concerns the way in which Revelation as a whole is structured. In an earlier message I argued that John's perspective in Revelation is analogous to the multiple camera angles at a football game. Imagine, if you will, several different camera locations. One is thirty rows up on the fifty-yard line of the home team. Another records the game from the south end zone, while yet another is located on the visitor's side, at field level. Finally, there is one more camera directly overhead in the MetLife Blimp. My point is that each camera records the same game from beginning to end, but with each one focused on a different facet of the game. One records the offense; another the defense. Yet another concentrates its lens on a particular player. The camera overhead in the blimp records the game from a more comprehensive point of view.

John does something similar in Revelation. He is describing for us the ongoing conflict between the kingdom of Christ and the kingdom of Satan that occurs between the first and second comings of Jesus. At one time he may concentrate on a particular event, while at another time his focus is on a specific person. But what we have in Revelation, at the end of the day, is a somewhat repetitive portrayal of the commonplace occurrences that transpire throughout the course of church history, leading up to the return of Christ at the end of the age.

I believe John does this multiple times in Revelation. *He describes the commonplaces of church history spanning the time between the two comings of Christ.* By "commonplaces" I mean the conditions, circumstances, situations, environments in which people find themselves between the two comings of Christ. As he finishes one section, concluding with the Second Coming of Christ and the end of history, he circles back around to start all over again at the start of the game. Once he concludes yet another journey he circles back around and recapitulates the same period of time from yet another vantage point.

As you know, the book of Revelation is built around three series of seven judgments. There are seven seal judgments, followed by seven trumpet judgments, and finally seven bowl judgments. According to the principle of recapitulation, the seven seal judgments, together with the seven trumpet and bowl judgments, are descriptive of events throughout the course of history between the two advents of Jesus. The only difference in the way John portrays what is happening is that at one time he may describe a preliminary, introductory and somewhat moderate or limited aspect of God's judgment, and then at another time portray that judgment in its more complete and devastating expression.

The fact that the trumpet judgments are partial and somewhat limited and the bowl judgments are more complete and final simply indicates that what can occur in a limited or partial manner at any point in history between the two advents of Christ can also occur at any point in history between the two advents of Christ in a universal or more thorough-going manner. The effect or impact of these plagues of judgment on the unbelieving world is at one time and in one place restricted, while at another time in another place, widespread.

Thus, Revelation is not concerned merely with events at the close of history, immediately preceding the second coming of Christ. Rather, there are multiple sections in the book, each of which *recapitulates* the other, that is to say, each of which begins with the first coming of Christ and concludes with the second coming of Christ and the end of history. Each of these sections provides a series of progressively parallel visions that increase in their scope and intensity as they draw nearer to the consummation.

Try to think of it using the analogy of that football game I just described. Each section of John's book is like each of the many cameras placed throughout the stadium or in the blimp hovering above. In each section John is describing, generally speaking, the same period of time, just as each camera is recording for us the same football game. But each section and each camera provide their own distinctive points of emphasis.

Second, trumpets have always played a significant role in God's purposes in history. When Israel laid claim to the promised land the priests were instructed to blow the trumpets of holy war seven times for seven days. On the final day Israel encircled Jericho seven times. When the seven trumpets blew after the seventh trip around the city, the walls of the city crumbled. We also see in the Old Testament that the feasts of Israel were hailed "with [a] blast of trumpets" (Lev. 23:24). Trumpets were blown to declare Solomon's ascension to the throne (1 Kgs. 1:34, 39). The prophet Joel describes the blowing of trumpets in preparation for God's coming in judgment: "Blow a trumpet in Zion; sound an alarm on my holy mountain..., for the day of the Lord is coming" (Joel 2:1). Most important of all, Israel's trumpets pointed to the coming of the Lord to wage war on the nation's behalf. Thus, when we read in Revelation of the sounding of seven trumpets, we can justifiably expect to see God intervening in history to defeat his enemies.

Third, you can't help but notice that the trumpet judgments are limited in the devastation they bring on the earth. In 8:7 "a third of the earth" is affected. In 8:8 "a third of the sea" became blood. In 8:10 "a third of the rivers" and "the springs of water" were judged. In 8:12 it is "a third" of the sun, moon, and stars that are darkened. The repetition of the fraction ⅓ is important. He isn't trying to be precise arithmetically, as if to say that exactly one third of each element in creation is destroyed. His point is that the judgments are partial. They are preliminary to the final and universal judgment that comes at the end of history. As one commentator put it, "the Trumpets are sounding not doom, but warning. The majority of mankind is allowed to survive, being shown God's wrath against sin, and given the chance to repent."[1] Thus, at one time in human history the judgment of God may be extensive and severe, while at another time it may be limited and partial.

Fourth, we must resist the temptation to interpret these trumpet judgments in a woodenly literal way. The purpose of Revelation is to describe reality through symbolic images. No fewer than twelve times in our passage John uses the word "like". His point is that what he saw was "like" or "resembled" or was in some sense similar to things with which he and his original readers were familiar. But, for example, he isn't saying that the demonic hordes in Revelation 9 are literally locusts or that they literally sting people with their tails. And please don't conclude, as some have, that these locusts are John's way of describing Cobra attack helicopters!

---

1. Wilcock, *The Message of Revelation*, 95.

The First Trumpet

According to Exodus 9:22-25, in the seventh plague God rained down on the land of Egypt "hail and fire", somehow strangely mixed together: specifically, on land, trees, and plants. Here in Revelation 8:7 the "trees" and "grass" are affected. The element of "blood" in this trumpet may derive from the first Egyptian plague in which the Nile turned to blood. Are the "hail and fire mixed with blood" literal (8:7)? The hail and fire in the Exodus plague were literal, indicating that such a phenomenon here would not be inconsistent with divine activity. The reference to "blood" may simply point to the color of the hail under such conditions, or more likely to its effect on earth among men. Elsewhere in Revelation "fire" is often symbolic (see 1:14; 2:18; 9:17; 10:1; 11:5; 19:12). Many believe that the fire in 8:7 that burns a third of the earth, trees, and grass is a metaphorical portrayal of judgment by famine (something we saw in the third seal judgment). Whatever the case, the reference to only one third being destroyed indicates that the judgment here is partial, with the climactic, final judgment yet to come.

Some find a problem in the fact that, according to Revelation 9:4, neither grass nor any green thing is to be hurt. They wonder how this can be if, according to 8:7, "all the green grass" has already been "burned up." But as Leon Morris has said, "it is a great mistake to read this fiery, passionate and poetic spirit as though he were composing a pedantic piece of scientific prose. He is painting vivid pictures and it does not matter in the slightest that the details do not harmonize readily."[2] Perhaps the best explanation is to remember that these judgments are sometimes partial and limited in their scope and at other times are more expansive and universal. So there is no reason to think John has contradicted himself.

The Second Trumpet

Something "like" a great mountain burning with fire is now said to be thrown into the sea. Is this literal? It may be that we have here another example of *prophetic hyperbole*, descriptive of seasons

---

2. Leon Morris, *The Book of Revelation* (Downers Grove: IVP, 1987), 120.

in history of devastation, personal loss, and instability. Let us remember the words of the psalmist: "Therefore we will not fear, though the earth should change, and though the mountains slip into the heart of the sea; though its waters roar and foam, though the mountains quake at its swelling pride" (Ps. 46:2-3). No one believes the psalmist is describing multiple mountains literally slipping into the sea. It is a proverbial expression for times of devastation and turmoil among nations on the earth. We must also keep in mind that a "mountain" in Revelation is often a metaphorical description for an earthly "kingdom" (see 14:1; 17:9; cf. 21:10). Perhaps this trumpet is a reference to the judgment of evil kingdoms on the earth that oppose the kingdom of Christ. Those evil kingdoms in Revelation are symbolically identified with the name Babylon.

Jeremiah 51:25 equates Babylon with a mountain and prophesies her judgment in similar language: "Behold, I am against you, O destroying mountain, declares the LORD, which destroys the whole earth; I will stretch out my hand against you, and roll you down from the crags, and make you a burnt mountain." Could it be that since the mountain is a metaphor for the judgment of Babylon in Jeremiah 51, "mountains" function in the same way in Revelation 8? The description of a third of the sea becoming blood is a direct allusion to Exodus 7:20 and the plague against the Nile River. In both cases, the fish obviously die.

The Third Trumpet

The presence of famine appears to be included in the third trumpet, as it was in the first two. Here we read of the waters becoming bitter and ultimately fatal. Psalm 78:44 also describes this plague: God "turned their rivers to blood, so they could not drink of their streams." The waters are polluted by a "great star ... blazing like a torch" (8:10). It would be difficult to interpret this literally, for how could one star fall on one third of all the rivers and springs of the earth? The star may be symbolic of an angel, as in 1:19, which thus serves as an instrument of divine judgment (for similar language describing the judgment of the king of Babylon in the Old Testament, see Isaiah 14:12-15).

The star is called "Wormwood" (echoing Jeremiah 9:15 and 23:15). There God says, "Behold I will feed this people with bitter food, and give them poisonous water to drink" (Jer. 9:15; cf. 8:13-14). Wormwood is a bitter herb and can be poisonous (although not known to be fatal) if drunk to excess (it is so powerful that a single ounce diluted in over five hundred gallons of water can still be tasted). Israel's sin was having "polluted" herself with idolatry. With poetic justice, God "pollutes" them with bad water. Other Old Testament texts where wormwood is associated with judgment are Deuteronomy 29:17-18; Proverbs 5:4; Lamentations 3:15, 19; and Amos 5:7 and 6:12. Again, the question is raised: Are the waters literally affected by a literal star making them literally bitter and fatal? Or is this a metaphorical portrayal of severe judgment that might conceivably express itself in any number of ways, perhaps primarily in the pollution of our drinking water as well as in famine (in keeping with the thrust of the first two trumpets)?

The Fourth Trumpet

This judgment is strikingly similar to the sixth seal in Revelation 6:12-13. The major difference is that whereas this judgment is partial (again, one third), the other is complete. This judgment also seems to reflect the ninth plague in which darkness covers the land of Egypt (Ex. 10:21-23). Again, is this literal or symbolic? If the latter, symbolic of what? Also, in numerous biblical texts the darkening of heavenly bodies and other similar celestial phenomena typically symbolize chaos on earth and especially divine judgment against national entities. Is that in view here?

Note also that the elements affected by the trumpet judgments to this point include light, air, vegetation, sun, moon, stars, sea creatures, and human beings. Some have suggested that, although the order is different from that in Genesis 1, the basic content and structure of creation itself is being systematically undone. This notion of "de-creation" is supported by the fact that the book of Revelation itself climaxes in the new creation: a new heavens and a new earth!

Conclusion to the First Four Trumpets / Introduction to the Last Three Trumpets

The Old Testament often employs the image of an "eagle" when describing judgment (Deut. 28:49; Jer. 4:13; 48:40; 49:22; Lam. 4:19; Ezek. 17:3; Hos. 8:1; Hab. 1:8). Aside from that we really don't know what meaning there is in the eagle. But note well on whom the impending judgments fall: "those who dwell on the earth." Although Christians themselves also dwell on the earth, this descriptive phrase always in Revelation refers to unbelievers and idolaters.

The Fifth Trumpet

There is no mistaking the fact that the locusts released from the abyss or the bottomless pit are demonic spirits whose purpose is to torment and destroy the lives of unbelieving men and women. We know this because they come out of the "bottomless pit" or "abyss" (vv. 1-3). The Greek word translated "bottomless pit" or "abyss" (*abussos*) is used nine times in the New Testament, seven of which are in Revelation (9:1, 2, 11; 11:7; 17:8; 20:1, 3). The word literally means "without depth," i.e., boundless, or bottomless. Here the shaft of the abyss is portrayed as blocked by a door to which God alone has the key. The demons whom Jesus expelled from the Gadarene entreated him "not to command them to depart into the abyss" (Luke 8:31). Here in Revelation 9 the bottomless pit appears to be the abode of the demonic hosts. The idea of a "pit" with a "shaft" that is "opened" or "locked shut" ("sealed") by a "key" held by an angel is obviously figurative language.

The "angel of the bottomless pit [abyss]" in verse 11, the being who exercises authority over the demonic hordes that dwell there (he is called their "king"), the one called "Abaddon" and "Apollyon", is certainly evil and is most likely Satan himself. As disturbing as this portrayal of demonic activity may be, and as much as you may be inclined to look away and ignore it, please don't. John's vision is designed to let us see beyond the material realm to the spiritual dynamics that alone make sense of what is happening in our society.

"Smoke" emerges from the abyss when it is opened so that the sun and air are darkened by it (cf. Joel 2:10, 31; 3:15; cf. Ex. 10:15; in these texts such darkening is a sign of judgment). Smoke here likely points us to the deception and moral darkness in which most of our world is languishing.

Demonic beings are here portrayed as "locusts" to whom "authority" or "power" "was given". This use of the passive voice is typical both in Revelation and in the rest of the New Testament. We see it again in verse 4 ("they were told") and in verse 5 ("they were allowed"). These verbs in the passive voice point to divine activity. In other words, it is God (or the risen Christ) who has commissioned and authorized them. This authority is likened to that possessed by "scorpions." People greatly fear scorpions because of their venomous sting, which is extremely painful and sometimes lethal.

The literal plague of locusts in Exodus 10:12-15 (the eighth of ten) also brought darkness on the land. There we read that "they ate all the plants in the land and all the fruit of the trees that the hail had left. Not a green thing remained, neither tree nor plant of the field, through all the land of Egypt" (v. 15).[3] But here the locusts are commanded not to harm the "grass ... or any green plant or any tree" (v. 4). They are commanded only to hurt unbelievers, i.e., those who don't have the seal of God by which one might be protected from such a plague.

This is an encouraging reminder that God has taken steps to protect his people against the devastating impact of these plagues, be they literal or symbolic. God's people will never, ever suffer God's wrath! This also proves yet again that the 144,000 in Revelation 7 and 14 who are "sealed" on their foreheads must refer to all God's people, Jewish believers in Jesus and Gentile believers in Jesus. It would be wholly inconsistent with the character of God that he would protect only 144,000 Jewish believers from this horrid

---

3. See also Deuteronomy 28:38; 1 Kings 8:37; 2 Chronicles 6:28; 7:13; Psalms 78:46; 105:34-35; Joel 1:4; 2:25; Amos 4:9; 7:2; and Nahum 3:15.

demonic attack and leave all the millions of other believers in Jesus to suffer this torment.

There is an additional twofold limitation on their activity. First, they are not allowed to kill anyone (in contrast with verses 15-20), but only to "torment" them (which sounds similar to what God allowed Satan to do to Job). Second, the torment will last for only "five months". Some take this literally, but they have no explanation for why such an odd number should be chosen. More likely the five months alludes to the five-month life cycle of the locust. Or "five" may simply be a round number meaning "a few." We can't be certain.

The "torment" they inflict is likened to that of a scorpion when it stings a man. Scorpions are a metaphor for punishment in 1 Kings 12:11, 14. The word "torment" is used in Revelation for spiritual, emotional, or psychological pain (see 11:10; and perhaps 18:7, 10, 15). It comes as no surprise that John describes the suffering inflicted by demons as like that inflicted by scorpions, given the fact that Jesus himself referred to demons as "scorpions" (and "snakes") in Luke 10:19.

The anguish of those tormented by the demonic hordes is any form of psychological or emotional suffering (physical too?) that provoked in them a desire for death. Yet they are unwilling actually to commit suicide, for surely if someone truly wants to die, they can find the means to end their life. John appears to be describing that emotional and psychological depression, frustration, anger, bitterness, and sense of futility and meaninglessness and lack of value, etc. that drives people to the point of utter despair. They prefer death to life but lack the courage to take their own lives, perhaps for fear of the unknown beyond the grave. All of this, says John, is the result of demonic activity (cf. Heb. 2:14-15), like unto that of a plague of locusts unleashed into the earth!

Perhaps John is describing the horrid realization in the human heart that one's belief system is false, that one's philosophy is vain, that one's values are empty, that one's destiny is bleak, and thus that one lacks purpose in living, that one is thus helpless and hopeless. Contrast this with the "peace of God that surpasses all understanding" (Phil. 4:8) granted unto believers who bring their burdens and anxieties to God in prayer. People without Jesus are desperate to find meaning and dignity and happiness in any number of ways: complex philosophies, a self-indulgent hedonism, the New Age movement with its endless remedies for what ails the human soul, reincarnation, radical feminism, political agendas, homosexuality, drugs, sexual immorality, materialism, selfism, etc. Demonic "locusts" lead them into such pursuits, all of which are, at the end of the day, empty and lifeless.

The description of these demonic spirits (vv. 7-11) reflects what we see in Joel 1–2 where a plague of locusts devastates Israel's land. There, as here, a trumpet is sounded to herald their arrival (Joel 2:1, 15). There, as here, the locusts are said to have "the appearance of horses" (Joel 2:4) prepared for battle. This judgment in Joel is itself based on the plague of locusts in Exodus 10. However, whereas the locusts in Exodus were literal (though they certainly symbolized something beyond themselves), and perhaps also in Joel (although there it may be a literal army that is compared to a swarm of locusts), here in Revelation they symbolize demonic spirits unleashed throughout the earth.

Let's take each element one at a time. Their appearance was "like horses prepared for battle" (9:7; cf. Jer. 51:27). On their "heads were what looked like crowns of gold" (9:7), a likely reference to their sovereign authority to afflict the non-Christian world. "Their faces were like human faces" (9:7), perhaps pointing to their intelligence. They had hair like "women's hair" (9:8). In the Old Testament, long and disheveled hair had at least three meanings: (1) it was a sign of uncleanness for people with leprosy (Lev. 13:45); (2) it was a sign of mourning (Lev. 10:6; 21:10); and (3) it was part of the sacrificial protocol for a woman accused of adultery (Num. 5:18). Their teeth were like "lions' teeth" (9:8). The "teeth of a lion" is a proverbial expression for something irresistibly and fatally destructive (cf. Job 4:10; Ps. 58:6). They had "breastplates like breastplates of iron" (9:9), pointing to their invulnerability. The sound of their wings "was like the noise of many chariots, with horses rushing into battle" (9:9). This is strikingly similar to Joel 2:4-5. They have "tails and stings like scorpions" (9:10), a vivid way to portray the torment they inflict on the souls of mankind. And they have a "king" over them, "the angel of the bottomless pit [abyss]" (9:11). This is either the Devil himself or his representative.

First Explanatory Interlude
In saying that "the first woe has passed" (v. 12) John does not mean that the events themselves have already occurred in history but only that the vision in which they are portrayed is now past.

Conclusion

As we look across the vast expanse of human history since the first coming of Christ, and in anticipation of his second coming, we see the concrete and all-too-real effects of God's wrath against human sin, idolatry, immorality, and unbelief: widespread famine, devastating tornadoes, floods, infectious diseases, war, psychological and emotional torment, pollution of our natural resources, and the list could go on seemingly without end. And to what purpose? To warn mankind that God will not ignore the defilement of his glory or the callous disregard for his mercy and longsuffering.

Yet in the midst of this earthly carnage and demonic assault, God's children are kept safe and secure, having been "sealed" by the indwelling presence of the Holy Spirit. We may well suffer at the hands of the unbelieving world. Persecution, slander, imprisonment, even martyrdom may come our way. But we will never endure the wrath of God, for Jesus has satisfied God's justice in our place on the cross!

Chapter Twenty-One

He Shall Reign Forever and Ever!
(Revelation 9:13-21; 11:14-19)

It was on December 10, 2018, the second Sunday in the season we call Advent, that I preached a sermon on the text cited above. It is the season of the year in which we turn our collective attention to the truths of Christmas, which is to say, the truth of the Incarnation of the Son of God, his conception in the womb of the Virgin Mary, and the ultimate purpose for which the Father sent his Son into this world.

At the time, I suspected that some in my church were wondering, "Why is Sam preaching from the book of Revelation during Advent? That seems so inappropriate. After all, what does the message of Revelation have to do with Christmas?" The short answer to that question is: Everything! Let me now explain to you what I explained to them.

When I began this commentary on Revelation, I told you that the theme or overriding emphasis in the book is actually quite simple: God wins! Revelation is all about a conflict between good and evil, between the Christ and the Antichrist, between the Lamb of God and the Beast, between the kingdom of our Lord Jesus Christ and the kingdom of Satan and all his demons. And the good news is that God wins!

Now, what does this have to do with Christmas, you ask? Simply this. Whenever we talk about the Incarnation of the Son of God, we have in mind the act whereby the second person of the Trinity took to himself human flesh and became a man. As John put it in his gospel, chapter one, verse fourteen, "The Word became flesh!" But it isn't enough merely for us to assert this glorious and deeply mysterious truth. We need to press in more deeply and ask a follow-up question: Why did the Word become flesh? What was the purpose in God the Father sending God the Son in the power of God the Spirit to this earth to live and die and rise again? In other words, I'm asking the question: What is the purpose of Christmas?

You can't answer that question by saying, "Well, the purpose of Christmas is to give us a good excuse to take off some extra time from work." Nor can you say, "The purpose of Christmas is to provide us with an opportunity to give gifts to people we love and to receive gifts from them." That may be the purpose of Christmas in the minds of non-Christians who simply don't know what the Bible teaches, but for you and me Christmas means something far deeper and more profound than that.

We could answer the question about the purpose of Christmas and why the Word was made flesh by pointing to any number of biblical texts. I could direct your attention to John 3:16 which tells us that the reason God the Father sent God the Son in the power of God the Spirit was to demonstrate his love for a fallen world and make it possible for us to inherit eternal life. And that would be perfectly true. But there is more to it than that. I could point you to what Jesus himself said about the purpose of his coming to earth. In Matthew 20:28 he said, "the Son of Man came not to be served but to serve, and to give his life as a ransom for many." And that, too, would be altogether true and accurate.

I could go on and on citing numerous biblical texts that describe the reason why Jesus came to earth through the womb of a young virgin girl in first century Israel. But here I want us to consider one other reason that most people would just as soon ignore. And this is the reason that ties in most directly to the overall theme or emphasis of the book of Revelation. For this we must turn our attention to something else that the Apostle John wrote. In his first epistle, chapter three, he said this: *"The reason the Son of God appeared was to destroy the works of the devil"* (1 John 3:8).

Yes, Jesus came to live a sinless life, the life that you and I should have lived but are unable to do so perfectly. But in order to live this sinless life Jesus had to successfully resist the temptation of Satan and defeat the Enemy's efforts to undermine that obedience. Yes, Jesus came "to take away sins" (1 John 3:5) and did so by dying in our place on the cross. But it was by means of the cross, as Paul says in Colossians 2:15, that Jesus "disarmed the rulers and authorities [i.e., Satan and his demons] and put them to open shame, by triumphing over them in him [or better still, in or through "it", that is, through the cross]" (Col. 2:15).

And of course it was by rising again from the dead that Jesus overcame and defeated the power of death and guaranteed for us that we too will one day be raised to an entirely new life in a new and glorified body. The author of Hebrews tells us that by dying and rising again Jesus destroyed "the one who has the power of death, that is, the devil, and deliver[ed] all those who through fear of death were subject to lifelong slavery" (Heb. 2:14-15).

So I hope you can now see that whatever else Christmas may mean, it means that God the Father sent God the Son in the power of God the Spirit to defeat and overthrow and ultimately destroy Satan and all his works. And that, I suggest, is also the primary emphasis or theme of the book of Revelation. And nowhere do we see this with greater clarity in Revelation than in Revelation 9 and 11. So let's turn our attention to John's vision of the sixth and seventh trumpet judgments, for in them we find a graphic and highly symbolic description of the activity of Satan in the earth and the ultimate triumph of Jesus Christ and his kingdom.

The Sixth Trumpet

Whose "voice" is it that John hears (v. 13)? Is it that of Jesus (as in 6:6), or an angel (as in 16:7), or is it the voice of God the Father? We can't be certain, but the fact that the voice emanates from the golden altar connects this sixth trumpet judgment with the saints' prayer for vindication in Revelation 6:10-11. People in the Old Testament "sometimes expressed a desire to seek safety and protection from others by holding on to the horns of the altar (1 Kgs. 1:50-51; 2:28-34). Could the 'four horns of the golden altar' here refer to the full power of God that will be expressed in answering the cry of the saints by judging the wicked in the following trumpets?"[1] Perhaps.

We see in verse 14 that "four angels" have been bound *deō*; cf. 20:2) "at the great river Euphrates," apparently restrained against their will. This would strongly suggest that these "four angels" are demons (cf. 9:1-3). It may be that what we read here is a rescinding of the command given back in 7:1-3 where "four angels standing at the four corners of the earth" were restrained from doing damage in the earth until the people of God had been sealed and made secure in their relationship with God.

In the time of John's writing, the Euphrates was the eastern border of the Roman Empire, beyond which were the terrifying and greatly feared horsemen of the Parthian Empire. But the Jewish people viewed the Euphrates as the northern frontier of Palestine, across which "Assyrian, Babylonian, and Persian invaders had come to impose their pagan sovereignty on the people of God. All the scriptural warnings about a foe from the north, therefore, find their echo in John's blood-curdling vision."[2]

These demonic invaders are coming at God's appointed time: they had been "prepared for the hour, the day, the month, and the year." This clearly reminds us that contrary to what you may think, and contrary to all appearances, God is in complete control not only of what Satan and demons are allowed to do but also the precise time when they have been ordained by God to do it. Their aim is to kill a third of mankind. Is this numerically literal, such that precisely one third of humanity are killed? Or is it John's way of describing a preliminary, partial judgment that will only later, at the end of history, reach its consummation? I think it is the latter.

---

1. Beale, *Revelation*, 506.

2. Caird, *Revelation*, 122. On this see especially Isaiah 5:26-29; 7:20; 8:7-8; 14:29-31; Jeremiah 1:14-15; 4:6-13; 6:1, 22-23; 10:22; 13:20; Ezekiel 38:6, 15; 39:2; and Joel 2:1-11, 20-25; as well as Isaiah 14:31; Jeremiah 25:9, 26, 46-47; 46:4, 22-23; 50:41-42; and Ezekiel 26:7-11.

A Massive Demonic Army Unleashed

Although it isn't explicitly stated, it appears from verses 16-19 that these four "angels" have power over a massive demonic army of horsemen. The number of mounted troops is "twice ten thousand times ten thousand" or 200,000,000 (in all likelihood, symbolic of an incalculable number, an innumerable, indefinite group; see Gen. 24:60; Lev. 26:8; Num. 10:35-36; Deut. 32:30; 33:2, 17; 1 Kgs. 18:7-8; 21:12; Dan. 7:10). There is no basis whatsoever for trying to identify this "army" with the military forces of Red China that allegedly stand poised to invade Israel. It seems clear from what we saw in Revelation 9:1-11 and from the description of these horsemen that we are dealing with a symbolic portrayal of demonic hosts, not human soldiers.

Again, let us take each descriptive item in turn. In doing so, however, we must be careful not to let our concern for the particular elements of their makeup obscure the overall visceral impact that John intends. In other words, John's point in piling up these monstrous metaphors is to underscore "that the demons are ferocious and dreadful beings that afflict people in a fierce, appalling, and devastating manner."[3]

- The riders of the horses (and perhaps the horses themselves) "had breastplates the color of fire and of sapphire (or hyacinth) and of sulfur" (9:17).

- The heads of the horses "were like lions' heads" (9:17). Again, this points to their fierceness.

- Out of the mouths of the horses came "fire and smoke and sulfur" (9:17). Elsewhere in Revelation "fire and brimstone" or "fire and sulfur" are descriptive of scenes of the final judgment of unbelievers (14:10; 21:8) and of the dragon, the Beast, and the False Prophet (19:20; 20:10). See also "fire, sulfur, smoke" in several Old Testament texts relating to judgment (Gen. 19:24,28; Deut. 29:23; 2 Sam. 22:9; Isa. 34:9-10; Ezek. 38:22).

---

3. Beale, *Revelation*, 510.

- In verse 19 the power of the horses is said to be in their tails, "for their tails are like serpents with heads." John likens their tails to serpents, the heads of which are the source of the harm inflicted. That these are demonic armies is thus confirmed, for elsewhere in Revelation the "serpent" (*ophis*) is always a reference to Satan (12:9, 14-15; 20:2). This reference to the serpent-like tail of the horses may specifically allude to their deception of unbelievers, for "the sweeping of the Serpent's 'tail' [in Rev. 12] is symbolic of his [Satan's] deception of the angels whom he caused to fall."[4]

Again, the four angels who were bound at the river Euphrates, who are then released, employ this massive demonic army to kill one third of mankind (cf. 9:15), utilizing the "fire and the smoke and the brimstone" that proceeded out of their mouths (9:18). The similarities with the destruction of Sodom and Gomorrah are obvious (Gen. 19:24,28). Note that these three elements are now called "three plagues" (v. 18).

Whereas the demons, portrayed as locusts, in Revelation 9:5 were not permitted to kill anyone, but only to torment, this demonic army from beyond the Euphrates is permitted to kill. Is this a literal, physical termination of human life, or is it figurative for spiritual or emotional or psychological "death"? The verb translated "kill" (*apokteinō*) generally refers to literal physical death in Revelation. That would seem to be confirmed by verse 20 ("the rest ... who were not killed"). If that is the meaning here, John envisions this demonic host (under and subordinate to God's sovereignty) killing a sizeable number of earth dwellers (i.e., unbelievers), whether through illness (perhaps outbreaks of infectious diseases), accident, natural disaster, famine, suicide, etc.

In verse 19 these demonic horses/horsemen are said to "wound" or to do "harm" (*adikeō*), the same Greek word used in 9:4, 10 where demonic "locusts" torment, but do not kill, those who lack the seal of God (cf. also its use in 2:11; 7:3). Perhaps, then, the "wound/

---

4. Ibid., 514.

harm" here (v. 19) is not physical death but a variety of forms of spiritual and psychological torment and emotional anguish short of, but a prelude to, death itself.

Unrepentant!

Verse 20 does not explicitly say that the purpose of the demonic plagues was to induce or stir up repentance. Certainly such plagues serve as a warning, but one that goes unheeded. This highlights the hardness of heart of those who lack the seal of God on their foreheads. Michael Wilcock adds this insightful comment:

> "The death-dealing horsemen of Trumpet 6 are not tanks and planes. Or not only tanks and planes. They are also cancers and road accidents and malnutrition and terrorist bombs and peaceful demises in nursing homes. Yet 'the rest of mankind, who were not killed by these plagues', still do not repent of their idolatry, the centering of their lives on anything rather than God, or of the evils which inevitably flow from it. They hear of pollution, of inflation, of dwindling resources, of blind politicians, and will not admit that the first four Trumpets of God are sounding. In the end they themselves are affected by these troubles, and for one reason or another life becomes a torment: the locusts are out, Trumpet 5 is sounding, but they will not repent. Not even when the angels of the Euphrates rise to the summons of Trumpet 6, and the cavalry rides out to slay – by any kind of destruction, not necessarily war – a friend or a relative, a husband or a wife: not even in bereavement will they repent."[5]

Here we have a typical Old Testament list of idols according to their material composition: gold, silver, bronze, stone, and wood (see Dan. 5:4, 23; Pss. 115:4-7; 135:15-17; Deut. 4:28). John portrays the worship of idols, in whatever form that idolatry might take, as the "worship" of "demons". We should probably translate verse 20 – "so as not to worship demons, that is, the idols..." On this he agrees with Paul (1 Cor. 10:20) as well as several Old Testament

---

5. Wilcock, *The Message of Revelation*, 99-100.

texts (Deut. 32:17; Ps. 96:5; 106:36-37), that all idolatry, whatever form it may assume, is ultimately energized by and representative of demonic activity. In verse 21 they are described as not repenting of yet additional sins, a list obviously derived from the Ten Commandments. These particular four vices are often associated with idol worship in both the Old Testament and New Testament (Jer. 7:5-11; Hos. 3:1–4:2; Isa. 47:9-10; 48:5; Mic. 5:12–6:8; Rom. 1:24-29; Gal. 5:20; Eph. 5:5; Col. 3:5).

Second Explanatory Interlude (11:14)
Just as there was an interlude, a parenthetical pause, in 7:1-17 between the sixth and seventh seals, so also there is a similar parenthesis in 10:1–11:13 between the sixth and seventh trumpets.

The Seventh Trumpet

I can only speak for my wife and me, but when we are expecting company at the house we get a bit frantic. We divide up responsibilities, whether it be vacuuming the carpets, cleaning up the kitchen, wiping down the bathroom, taking out the trash, dusting furniture, etc. I have to confess that we don't do this on a daily basis. It usually only takes place when we have reasonably high expectations that visitors are on their way. That isn't to say my wife doesn't keep a clean and tidy house! She does. But I trust you understand my point.

Preparing ourselves for the second coming of Jesus Christ ought to have a decidedly different effect on us. There is no doubt whatsoever that he's on his way. I don't know when that will be, but I'm absolutely certain it is certain to occur. Unlike friends here in Oklahoma City and elsewhere, who might call at the last minute to cancel their plans or reschedule them for a later date, Jesus is coming, and he won't be a millisecond behind schedule. Our problem, as you know, is that we have no idea when this will be. My point is simply that in the case of Christ's return to this earth, we need to be ready every minute of every day. I suspect that if you were told that the King of Britain planned on visiting you sometime in the next two weeks, you would go home and immediately get things in order, even if it turned out that he didn't arrive until the last hour of the last day. Knowing that Jesus is assuredly coming again ought to exert on our souls the most powerful sense of urgency to get our lives in order, to stir up our hearts in expectation, and to turn our eyes toward heaven as we await his appearing.

I say all this because the certainty of Christ's coming again is clearly in view in Revelation 11:15-19 and the description of the seventh trumpet judgment. In his commentary on Revelation, Joel Beeke rightly points out that "the passage in Revelation describing what will happen after the blowing of the last trumpet is proleptic or anticipatory. John is so certain of the fulfillment of what he prophesies that he speaks of it in the past tense, as though it were already an accomplished fact."[6]

Some contend that these verses do not describe the content of the seventh trumpet but simply anticipate it. The content of the seventh trumpet is then identified as the seven bowls. They argue that these verses portray no action but merely songs or hymns of God's reign. But action is, in fact, portrayed in these verses. A song or hymn can depict the content of a "woe" or trumpet judgment as easily as a vision can. Also, what could possibly be more severe or demonstrable than the last, climactic, judgment itself, regardless of how long it lasts? Also, the most natural interpretation of 11:14, where the third woe or seventh trumpet is "soon to come," is that 11:15-19 form its content.

How could John have heard these "loud voices" if they occurred "in heaven" (v. 15a)? See also 12:10 and 19:1. Elsewhere he speaks as if from an earthly perspective and uses the phrase "from heaven" (10:4, 8; 11:12; 14:2, 13; 18:4). It would seem that on a few occasions John was either in a visionary trance state or bodily/spiritually present in heaven when he received his revelations. The "loud voices" are either those of the angelic hosts worshiping God, or perhaps the saints in heaven (7:9; 19:1, 6), or perhaps the twenty-

---

6. Joel Beeke, *Revelation* (Grand Rapids: Reformation Heritage Books, 2016), 327.

four elders who are then portrayed as falling down in worship and speaking their praises in verses 17-18.

The declaration is that what Satan formerly ruled, in a manner of speaking, as the "god of this world" (2 Cor. 4:4) and "the prince of the power of the air" (Eph. 2:2; cf. 6:12) and "the ruler of this world" (John 12:31; 14:30; 16:11), has now finally and wholly been taken by the Lord and his Christ! Note that in verse 15 we read of the "kingdom of the world" (singular) not "kingdoms" (plural). All the secular empires of this earth are actually one earthly kingdom ruled by Satan, but now under the sovereign sway of Jesus.

Whereas in 1 John 5:19 we are told that now, in some sense, in this present age, "the whole world lies in the power of the evil one," a day is coming (this day, described in 11:15-19) when such shall no longer be! This is the consummate overthrow of all God's enemies and the manifestation of the universal and cosmic extent of his rightful rule! Whereas the "world" could refer to the totality of creation it more likely has in view the world of humanity that stood in opposition to God and at odds with his purposes. Interestingly, the only other verbal parallel to this phrase is found in Matthew 4:8 where Satan offers dominion of "the kingdoms of the world" to Jesus if he will only bow before him. The implication is that such dominion was, at that time, Satan's to offer. But no longer! G. B. Caird explains:

> "In one sense God's sovereignty is eternal: he entered on his reign when he established the rule of order in the midst of the primaeval chaos (Ps. xciii. 1-4); he has reigned throughout human history, turning even men's misdeeds into instruments of his mercy; and above all he reigned in the Cross of Christ (xii. 10). But always up to this point he has reigned over a rebellious world. A king may be king de jure, but he is not king de facto until the trumpet which announces his accession is answered by the acclamations of a loyal and obedient people."[7]

---

7. Caird, *Revelation*, 141.

Four additional observations are called for. First, as I said earlier, the past tense "has become" in verse 15 is used proleptically, that is to say, a future event is so certain to occur that it is described as a reality of the past. Second, who is the "he" in verse 15 that "will reign forever and ever"? Is it God the Father, the "Lord" of verse 15, or God the Son, i.e., "his Christ"? Or is it both, as John envisions them as an inseparable unity? Third, a phrase parallel to "he shall reign forever and ever" is found in Revelation 22:5 where it refers to us in the New Jerusalem! God will reign forever and ever, but so will we ... with him! Finally, this verse is not saying that political parties and positions of earthly power and authority will be taken over by Christians so that the world will finally be Christianized. Verse 15 does not refer to what will happen before Christ returns but what will happen when and after he returns. It describes not this present age in which we live but the future age of eternity.

The Declaration of the Twenty-four Elders

The twenty-four elders once again resume their familiar posture: face down in the presence of God! Their cry is one of gratitude. They address God as the "Lord God, the Almighty" (cf. 19:6). The word "Almighty" (*pantokratōr*) means sovereign ruler or ruler over all. The Roman Caesars presumptuously adopted this title for themselves. But this day will expose them as charlatans and usurpers as God exerts his rightful Lordship over all.

But something is missing. Their declaration "who is and who was" (v. 17) lacks the third element found earlier, "who is to come" (1:4; 4:8). In all likelihood this means that the final part of the threefold name for God ("is, was, is to come") is not merely a reference to his sovereignty over the future or of his timeless nature, but specifically speaks of the end time, when God, by means of the return of Christ, will break into world history and overthrow once and for all every opposition. The God who "is to come" has come! The promise of ultimate victory is so utterly immutable that John speaks of it as if it had already arrived.

The rage of the nations is provoked by the inception of God's rule through his Christ. This is a clear reference to Psalm 2:2 –

"The kings of the earth set themselves, and the rulers take counsel together, against the LORD and against his anointed" (see also vv. 5, 10-12). The word translated "wrath" (*orgē*), which is said to have come, is always used in Revelation of the final outpouring at the end of history (6:16-17; 14:10-11; 16:19; 19:15). Note well: "the nations were enraged (lit., *ōrgisthēsan*) and God's wrath (*orgē*) came." This is an example of how the punishment fits the crime: their rage against God is met by God's rage against them!

The fact that this is the time "for the dead to be judged" and the faithful rewarded proves that John has in view the end of history. The parallel in Revelation 20:12-13, which all acknowledge speaks of the final judgment, makes this inescapable. Again in verse 18 we see that the punishment fits the crime (sin), for God "destroys" (*diaphtheirai*) those who have sought to "destroy" (*diaphtheirontas*) the earth (the "earth" here is probably a reference to God's people).

Believers, on the other hand, now receive their heavenly "reward", part of which, perhaps, is bearing witness to the judgment of those who have persecuted them (and thus this, too, is God's positive answer to the prayer of 6:9-11). For the response of God's people (described in almost identical terms) to judgment of the wicked, see 18:24–19:5. For other elements of this "reward", see 2:7 (22:14); 2:11; 2:17; 2:26-27; 3:5 (7:14); 3:12; 3:21; 7:15-17; 22:3-4; and 22:14.

A Concluding Vision of Heaven Opened

Was the ark of the covenant somehow translated into heaven before the fall of Jerusalem in 586 B.C.? There is no way to know. There is a tradition in Judaism that some expected the return of the ark of the covenant at the end of history when God would once again graciously dwell among his people. Indeed, one legend had it that Jeremiah removed the ark to safety in a cave or buried it on Mt. Sinai where it would remain hidden until the final restoration of Israel (see 2 Macc. ii.4-8; cf. 2 Bar. vi. 5-10; lxxx.2). But no such expectation is found in the biblical literature.

People couldn't look upon the ark in the Old Testament. Those who transported it were given special instructions for how to cover the ark without looking upon it. The reason was because the ark represented or embodied God's holiness and the object lesson was to awaken and alert people to their sin. But the fact that the ark is now open to be "seen" indicates that sin has been forgiven and the barrier to God's presence has been torn down. Thus, most likely "the ark is shown here as a symbol, representing God's covenant with his people."[8]

This, then, is the glorious purpose of Christmas. God the Father sent God the Son in the power of God the Holy Spirit to defeat and overthrow the works of the Devil, and by doing so to deliver his people from the guilt and condemnation of their sin. And this marvelous and majestic description of the seventh trumpet judgment is a reminder to us all that God will win! Not all the nuclear power on earth can thwart the full and final revelation of his kingdom authority. Not all the backroom shenanigans of conspiratorial politicians and power-brokers can delay the ultimate judgment of all unbelievers. Not all the immoral chaos and vain philosophy of a world gone mad can prevent the ultimate rule and reign of King Jesus.

---

8. Richard D. Phillips, *Revelation* (Phillipsburg: R & R Publishing, 2017), 336.

Chapter Twenty-Two

Knowing Who's in Charge Makes all the Difference in the World

(Revelation 10:1-11)

We earlier saw that a parenthesis or dramatic interlude (7:1-17) stands between the sixth and seventh seal judgments. Here, too, we have a parenthetical pause or digression (10:1–11:13) between the sixth and seventh trumpets. The parenthesis in 10:1–11:13 explains the relationship between the unbeliever and the believer during that same time. There is also a theological parallel between the two parentheses (i.e., between the content of 7:1-17 and the content of 10:1–11:13). In Chapter 7 believers are sealed or protected against the spiritually destructive impact of the first six seals. Likewise, in Chapter 11 believers are protected ("measured") against the spiritually destructive impact of the trumpets and the Beast.

It's not easy today to remain hopeful and encouraged and confident about the future of our society and the world as a whole. Things are a mess. For every one step forward, it seems like we take two steps backwards. For every victory that is won for truth and morality and the Christian faith, it seems as if there is a multitude of defeats. In his excellent commentary on Revelation, Dennis Johnson puts it this way:

"When evil is everywhere and the world is ripe for judgment, can God protect his own? When economies crash, when civil order falters and the social fabric frays, when restraint and respect give way to rude aggression and random violence, when greed and animal appetite reign supreme, this question weighs on the hearts of God's people: Can God keep Jesus' little flock safe as they stand, it seems, defenseless in the crossfire? On the one hand, Christian believers will be targeted for attack by people who hate our King, his purity, and even his mercy; on the other, God calls us to stay involved in the broader community, even as it rushes pell-mell toward its rendezvous with God's wrath."[1]

It's an important and pressing question, but I don't want to dwell on the dark and discouraging elements in our world. I don't need to. The simple truth is that all of you are as aware of how bad it is as I am. It wouldn't accomplish much for me to rehearse the countless ways in which the fabric of society as a whole is unraveling right before our eyes. No, my aim is to speak words of encouragement, words that remind us that no matter how dismal the prospects for society may appear, we know who is in charge. We know that the risen Lord Jesus Christ is sovereign over every man and molecule in existence. And we know it because the Bible over and over again tells us so.

Take for instance the natural calamities, whether it be the hurricanes that strike Florida, or the wildfires in California, or the snow and ice in the northeast, or volcanic eruptions and earthquakes that we read about on almost a daily basis. What are we to make of such phenomena? Here is what Scripture says:

"He covers the heavens with clouds; he prepares rain for the earth; he makes grass grow on the hills. He gives to the beasts their food, and to the young ravens that cry.... He makes peace in your borders; he fills you with the finest of the wheat. He sends out his command to the earth; his word runs swiftly. He gives snow like wool; he scatters

---

1. Dennis Johnson, *The Triumph of the Lamb: A Commentary on Revelation* (P & R Publishing, 2001), 155-56.

frost like ashes. He hurls down his crystals of ice like crumbs; who can stand before his cold? He sends out his word, and melts them; he makes his wind blow and the waters flow" (Ps. 147:8-9, 14-18; see Ps. 148:1-12).

There are several passages in Job that affirm God's complete sovereignty over all of nature, both on earth and in the heavens above:

"[It is God] who removes the mountains, they know not [how,] When he overturns them in his anger; who shakes the earth out of its place, and its pillars tremble; who commands the sun not to shine, and sets a seal upon the stars; who alone stretches out the heavens, and tramples down the waves of the sea; who makes the Bear, Orion, and the Pleiades, and the chambers of the south; who does great things, unfathomable, and wondrous works without number" (Job 9:5-10).

"He stretches out the north over empty space, and hangs the earth on nothing. He wraps up the waters in his clouds; and the cloud does not burst under them. He obscures the face of the full moon, and spreads his cloud over it. He has inscribed a circle on the surface of the waters, at the boundary of light and darkness. The pillars of heaven tremble, and are amazed at his rebuke. He quieted the sea with his power, and by his understanding he shattered Rahab. By his breath the heavens are cleared; his hand has pierced the fleeing serpent. Behold, these are the fringes of his ways; and how faint a word we hear of him! But his mighty thunder, who can understand?" (Job 26:7-14)

"Keep listening to the thunder of his voice and the rumbling that comes from his mouth. Under the whole heaven he lets it go, and his lightning to the corners of the earth. After it his voice roars; he thunders with his majestic voice, and he does not restrain the lightnings when his voice is heard. God thunders wondrously with his voice; he does great things that we cannot comprehend. For to the snow he says, 'Fall on the earth,' likewise to the downpour, his mighty downpour. He seals up the hand of every man, that all men whom he made may know it. Then the beasts go into their lairs, and remain in their dens. From its chamber comes the whirlwind, and cold from the scattering winds. By the breath of God ice is given, and the broad waters are frozen fast. He loads the thick cloud with moisture; the clouds scatter his lightning. They turn around and around by his guidance, to accomplish all that he commands them on the face of the habitable world. Whether for correction or for his land or for love, he causes it to happen" (Job 37:2-24; see also Pss. 104; 105:16; Job 38:8-41; Jer. 10:12-13; 14:22; and Amos 4:7).

Or consider God's sovereignty over our daily lives and the plans we make for each day:

> "A man's steps are from the Lord; how then can man understand his way?" (Prov. 20:24)

> "Many are the plans in the mind of a man, but it is the purpose of the Lord that will stand" (Prov. 19:21)

> "Come now, you who say, 'Today or tomorrow we will go into such and such a town and spend a year there and trade and make a profit'—yet you do not know what tomorrow will bring.... Instead you ought to say, 'If the Lord wills, we will live and do this or that'" (Jas. 4:13-15).

Many are ready to concede that God is sovereign over the beginning of life, but they do not like the idea that God is sovereign over the time and manner of its end. But note the following:

> "See now that I, even I, am he, and there is no god beside me; I kill and I make alive; I wound and I heal; and there is none that can deliver out of my hand" (Deut. 32:39)

> "The Lord kills and brings to life; he brings down to Sheol and raises up" (1 Sam. 2:6)

> "Your eyes saw my unformed substance; in your book were written, every one of them, the days that were formed for me, when as yet there was none of them" (Ps. 139:16).

God is sovereign over everything:

> "[God] works all things according to the counsel of his will" (Eph. 1:11).
>
> "Our God is in the heavens; he does all that he pleases" (Ps. 115:3).
>
> "I know that you can do all things, and that no purpose of yours can be thwarted" (Job 42:2).
>
> "All the inhabitants of the earth are accounted as nothing, and he does according to his will among the host of heaven and among the inhabitants of the earth; and none can stay his hand or say to him, 'What have you done?'" (Dan. 4:35)

Many are happy to concede that God is in charge when it comes to events in nature, but what about the choices and decisions made by us, by human beings? Consider these texts:

> "Then God said to him [Abimelech] in the dream, 'Yes, I know that you have done this in the integrity of your heart, and it was I who kept you from sinning against me. Therefore I did not let you touch her" (Gen. 20:6).

Here we see that God exerts control over the decision-making of Abimelech and restrains him from having illicit sexual relations with Sarah, Abraham's wife. Some argue that God cannot do that. They say he cannot intrude on the human will and prevent a free moral agent from committing abuse or an atrocity. Yet we see from this story that God can surely prevent someone from sinning against someone else if he so chooses.

> "The king's heart is a stream of water in the hand of the LORD; he turns it wherever he will" (Prov. 21:1).

Again, God's sovereignty over the will/heart of the king is seen in his determination to turn that will or to direct the king's choices in accordance with whatever God pleases. And yet the king (or any person) is still morally responsible to God for the decisions he/she makes.

"In the first year of Cyrus the king of Persia, that the word of the LORD by the mouth of Jeremiah might be fulfilled, the LORD stirred up the spirit of Cyrus king of Persia, so that he made a proclamation throughout all his kingdom and also put it in writing ..." (Ezra 1:1).

God moved on ("stirred up") the heart of the pagan king Cyrus to issue a decree that the Jews should be free to return to Jerusalem and rebuild the temple (see also Ezra 6:22; 7:27). There are numerous other texts that describe how God exerted his will on and over the will of others so that his ultimate purpose might be achieved.[2]

So why bring this up here? What does it have to do with Revelation 10? Everything! Revelation 10 is first and fundamentally about the sovereignty of God over the nations and peoples and events on earth and in heaven. If ever a passage of Scripture should speak encouragement into your life, it is Revelation 10.

Who is the "mighty angel" in Revelation 10?

In verses 1-2 John describes "another mighty angel coming down from heaven". This isn't the first time he has seen a mighty angel. Back in Revelation 5:2 the same terminology appears. In both instances they cry out "with a loud voice" (5:2; 10:3). Some believe this "angel" in Chapter 10 is, in fact, the person of Christ himself or perhaps "the angel of the Lord" referred to often in the Old Testament (see Gen. 16:10; 22:11-18; 24:7; 31:11-13; Ex. 3:2-12; 14:19; Judg. 2:1; 6:22; 13:20-22). Against this suggestion is the fact that the word translated "angel" (*angelos*) is never used elsewhere in Revelation of anyone but a created, heavenly being (whether good or evil). Also, the "angel of the Lord" was a distinctly pre-incarnate manifestation of God. Now that the Son of God has appeared (permanently) in the flesh, it would be unlikely, if not impossible, for him to assume the guise or form of an "angelic" being. But let us note how the angel is portrayed.

---

2. See Deuteronomy 2:30; Joshua 11:20; Judges 7:2-3, 22; 1 Samuel 14:6, 15, 20; 2 Samuel 17:14; 1 Kings 12:15; 20:28-29; 2 Chronicles 13:14-16; Acts 4:27-28; 2 Corinthians 8:16-17; and Revelation 17:17.

(1) The angel is "wrapped in a cloud." In the Old Testament the "clouds" are often the vehicle or means by which God makes an appearance. (2) There was also a "rainbow over his head." This is probably an allusion to Ezekiel 1:26-28 where God is described in similar terms. The only other reference in Revelation to the "rainbow" is in 4:3 where God is pictured on his throne, surrounded by a rainbow. (3) We also read that "his face was like the sun." This recalls the description of the risen Jesus in Revelation 1:16 (cf. Matthew 17:2 and the transfiguration of Jesus). (4) His legs were "like pillars of fire." This also points back to Revelation 1:15 and the description of the risen and glorified Jesus. This also may point to Exodus 13:21 and the "pillar of fire" by which God guided Israel at night. (5) We should also note that in verse 3 his voice is compared to "a lion roaring". You will recall that Christ is compared to a lion in Revelation 5:5.

These factors would appear to indicate that the "angel" in Chapter 10 is the risen Christ. However, it may simply be that the angel is portrayed in such terms because he represents Christ and speaks authoritatively on his behalf. Because the angel is doing Christ's will and speaking on his behalf and portraying his sovereign rule, he is described in terms that apply directly to the Lord Jesus. He reflects the Lord's majesty and glory and sovereignty. If this being is in fact an angel it may well be Gabriel whose name literally means "mighty one of God".

(6) We read in verse 2 that "he had a little scroll open in his hand." There has been a lot of fruitless debate about the identity of this so-called "little scroll." The Greek word is the one from which we derive our word for "Bible." The question is whether or not this "little scroll" in Chapter 10 is identical with the "scroll" of Chapter 5. You may recall from Chapter 5 that the scroll was sealed with seven seals. It couldn't be opened and its contents revealed until the seven seals were broken. The seventh and final seal was broken in Revelation 8:1. Now, here in Revelation 10:2, it makes sense that the scroll is finally said to be "open." The content of the scroll is God's sovereign purpose for establishing his kingdom on earth. Therefore, in all likelihood, the "little scroll" in Chapter 10 is

identical with the "scroll" in Chapter 5 and contains the substance of the book of Revelation itself. But why is it called "little"? Perhaps the scroll is "little" in comparison with the massive "mighty" angel who straddles land and sea (10:2). Also, perhaps the scroll is portrayed as "little" because it must be small enough for John to eat (10:9). Perhaps the scroll in Chapter 10 is called "little" precisely because its contents are smaller than the scroll in Chapter 5. That is to say, the scroll or book of Chapter 10 describes a smaller portion of God's eternal purpose in Christ, the whole of which is found in the larger book of Chapter 5.

(7) We read in verse 2 that "he set his right foot on the sea and his left foot on the land." This points to Jesus Christ's unchallenged dominion over all creation (see Psalm 8:6). When you put your foot on something it means you have absolute and ultimate authority over whatever is under it.

We should also be encouraged to remember that the mighty angel's sovereignty over sea and land demonstrates that God is also ultimately in control over Satan and all his activities. We read in Revelation 12:18 that when the dragon, or Satan appears, he stands "on the sand of the sea." It is from there that he beckons forth the "beast" who is described as "rising out of the sea" (13:1). And in 13:11 there is "another beast," often called the False Prophet, who is said to rise up "out of the earth" (13:11). The point is that Jesus Christ rules supremely and sovereignly even over the enemies of the church. Satan may well call forth the Beast and False Prophet from the sea and earth, but Christ stands over Satan and anything that might emerge from sea or land.

David Aune suggests that the imagery of this "angel" is similar to what we know of the Colossus of Rhodes, one of the seven wonders of the ancient world. The Colossus was a bronze statue erected in 280 B.C. by Charles of Lindos. It was destroyed by an earthquake in 224 B.C. It was approximately seventy cubits high (one hundred and five feet). "According to a popular but erroneous view, the Colossus stood astride the harbor of Rhodes permitting ships to pass through its legs; actually it stood on a promontory overlooking the harbor."[3]

The Seven Thunders

We then read that when the "mighty angel" spoke he called out with a loud voice and "the seven thunders sounded" (Rev. 10:3). What are the "seven thunders" and why was John prohibited from writing down in Revelation their content? In a book that is designed to "reveal" things to God's people, this demand for secrecy is surprising. The presence of the definite article with the phrase "the seven thunders" may be referring back to something familiar to John's audience. In other words, it may imply that "the seven thunders" are something already known to John's original readers.

But why the command not to write it down? We can't be certain, but here are some possible answers. This may be God's way of telling John and us that some things in the future are not for us to know. God is telling us to live in complete dependence upon him, especially when we feel ignorant and lacking information. God obviously knows far more about the future than he has chosen to reveal to us. Some things are for him to know and for us to trust. This, then, would be a reminder that we should avoid undue speculation and certainly undue dogmatism about the future.

Then, of course, there is Deuteronomy 29:29, where we read that "the secret things belong to the LORD our God, but the things that are revealed belong to us and to our children forever." It's also possible that we have here something similar to what we read in 2 Corinthians 12:4. There the Apostle Paul describes his translation into the third heaven where "he heard things that cannot be told, which man may not utter." In other words, some things are so extraordinary and overwhelming and glorious that it is not for us to know, at least for now.

It may be that the "thunders" are, like the seals, trumpets, and bowls, judgments that have been entrusted to seven additional

---

3. David Aune, *Revelation 17-22* (Nashville: Thomas Nelson, 1998), 2:556.

angels. By telling John not to write them down he is saying that God has cancelled or in some way restricted the judgments they contain. In other words, not writing them down is an expression of God's mercy in giving people an opportunity to repent. John is not allowed to write down the seven peals of thunder because they will never occur. But we have already seen that people in that day refuse to repent, notwithstanding the massive judgments that fall on the earth.

The Mystery of God's Purposes is Fulfilled!

What we read in verses 5-7 is clearly an allusion to Daniel 12:7 where Daniel encountered a "man [angel?] clothed in linen, who was above the waters of the stream; he raised his right hand and his left hand toward heaven and swore by him who lives forever." It would appear that "raising the right hand to heaven when an oath is taken is a gesture that symbolically appeals to God, who dwells in heaven and therefore sees and knows everything, as a witness to the oath (Deut. 32:40; Ps. 106:26)."[4]

Note the three spheres: heaven, earth, and sea, hence encompassing all that God has made. There is no place over which God's sovereignty doesn't exist and no place where his word doesn't apply. God "created heaven and what is in it," which means that every single one of the seemingly countless trillions and quintillions of galaxies, each of which contains billions and trillions of stars, was created by our God! Everything on the earth, whether grass or grasshoppers, whether flowers or the country of Finland, whether rocks or human rulers, everything that is exists because God said so. And everything in the sea he created: sharks and dolphins and swordfish and seals and eels and snakes and every species of the multitude of creatures at the bottom of the ocean, many of which no human eye has ever seen.

This "mighty angel" who is the ambassador and representative of the risen Christ swears an oath by God that "there would be no more delay, but that in the days of the trumpet call to be sounded

---

4. Ibid., 2:564.

by the seventh angel, the mystery of God would be fulfilled." Literally it reads, "the time will be no longer." But this doesn't mean that when Christ returns time will be abolished and clocks will be obsolete, as if to say that timelessness ensues. "The idea here is that there is a predetermined time in the future when God's purposes for history will be completed.... The point is that when God has decided to complete his purposes and to terminate history, there will be no delay in its termination."[5]

Be very encouraged by the word "fulfilled" in verse 7. It is a firm reminder to us all that there is no doubt about whether or not God's purposes will come to pass. The angel "swears" that what God has revealed is true and will be fulfilled. In other words, don't despair. Don't fret. Don't worry. Don't be eaten up with anxiety. Don't live in fear about who wins. Only if God himself can lie is this declaration not true. And if God can lie, he isn't God and we're all a bunch of fools for having trusted him in the first place! This is our hope, our confidence, our joy, in knowing that God has sworn that he will judge wickedness and we will be saved. No terrorist attack, no nuclear assault (whether by North Korea or any other country), no corruption in government, no sexual scandal, no military power, or economic collapse will stand in the way of God's word being fulfilled.

Eat the Scroll and Prophesy Again

Although John has already been instructed to prophesy in Revelation 1:10 and 4:1-2, here in verses 8-10 we find a formal recommissioning. The instructions given to John by the angel are patterned after Ezekiel's experience where he, too, is commanded to eat the scroll (Ezek. 2–3). The eating of the scroll symbolizes the spiritual "assimilation" of the message it contains and the prophet's personal identification with and submission to its truth. The point is that it is not enough merely to own a Bible or hold it in your hand or carry it to church or display it on the coffee table in your

---

5. Beale, *Revelation*, 538-39.

den. We must digest it, take it in to our innermost being, and assimilate it:

> "Your words were found, and I ate them, and your words became to me a joy and the delight of my heart" (Jer. 15:16).

The book is sweet in his mouth because of the joy and delight which God's word brings to the believer (see Ezek. 3:3; Jer. 15:16; Pss. 19:10; 119:103; Prov. 16:21-24; 24:13-14) and also because of the blessings to God's people that the outworking of the divine purpose will bring. Its bitterness, however, is more difficult to interpret. Generally, two reasons have been suggested as to why the book turns bitter in John's stomach. Although salvation is certain for the people of God, the book contains a prophecy of harsh persecution they must suffer at the hands of Satan and the Beast before entrance into the bliss of eternal fellowship and joy with Christ. Perhaps the book is bitter because it contains a prophecy of the judgments which must soon fall upon unbelievers. But is this bitterness simply a reflection of what they will experience, or is it also an expression of John's personal feelings as he contemplates their ultimate demise? Believing and living according to the Bible is a "bittersweet" experience. It brings joy and life and hope and peace and also brings division and incurs the hatred and opposition of others.

In verse 11 John is addressed by a plurality of beings. The translation in the ESV, "I was told," is literally, "they said to me." Up till now, John has heard only a singular voice. These who now speak may be the angel of 10:1-3 together with the "voice from heaven" in 10:4, 8. Or the plural may represent the consensus of all the angelic hosts surrounding the throne. What's important for us to note is that John is given authority and under the inspiration of the Holy Spirit to "prophesy" of what the future holds. This is yet another reminder of God's sovereignty over all the affairs of men and angels and demons. He knows what is going to happen and communicates this to John by revelation, who in turn communicates it to us by prophecy. Prophecy is the believer's comfort and assurance that God controls the present and the future and that we can rest comfortably in knowing he is in charge. When the world speaks scornfully of what God has said in Scripture, we may rest assured that the word of the Lord will stand firm and be fulfilled. When the world demands that we alter our views on human sexuality or gender or marriage or minimize the claims of exclusivity, we must call to mind that God has spoken.

Conclusion

You may remember the story from Greek mythology of Atlas. He and his brother Menoetius sided with the Titans in their war against the pantheon of Greek gods. When the Titans were defeated, many of them (including Menoetius) were confined to Tartarus, but Zeus condemned Atlas to stand at the western edge of Gaia (the Earth) and hold up the sky on his shoulders, to prevent the two from resuming their primordial embrace. A common misconception today is that Atlas was forced to hold the Earth on his shoulders, but Classical art shows Atlas holding the celestial spheres, not a globe.

As you look at pictures of Atlas, he is shrugging. He appears almost to be buckling under the weight of the world, barely able to maintain his grip and keep things in place. But not Jesus Christ. By his omnipotent power and infinite wisdom he easily upholds all things in place and is guiding this crazy world to its proper consummation when he will be glorified and honored as Lord over all! That is what Revelation 10 is all about. Christ wins!

Chapter Twenty-Three

The Church: Prophesying and Persecuted

(Revelation 11:1-13)

What are the prospects for the church of Jesus Christ all across the earth, as we await the second coming of our Lord? What I mean by that is, what should we expect in terms of our relationship to the broader culture and the world of unbelievers as a whole? What should we do as we look to the end of human history and the establishment of God's eternal kingdom?

Those are the two questions I want you to consider: what should we expect and what should we do? My belief is that those questions are answered in Revelation 11. It's important for you to know that Revelation 11 is generally the subject of more interpretive mysteries and disagreements than any other chapter in the book. As you can see from our reading of the text, it is filled with strange images of a temple and two unnamed witnesses and odd references to forty-two months or 1,260 days and fire and blood and a sadistic beast and death and resurrection and the ultimate triumph of God's kingdom.

We could easily spend several chapters unpacking all the details of this chapter and debating the various attempts to make sense of it. But I don't think that is the wisest thing for us to do. Instead, I will simply present to you what I think this chapter is all about. I won't spend much time describing alternative views or refuting them but rather focus on what I believe John is describing for us. And what I believe is that we have here a description in highly figurative and extremely graphic language of what the church of Jesus Christ can expect during the time between the first and second comings of Jesus and also what the church should do as we await our Lord's appearance. The church can expect persecution and severe opposition but in the midst of its prophetic witness to the gospel of Jesus Christ it will be protected and preserved.

Measuring the Temple of God

Many of you have probably been led to believe that the temple, altar, and outer court in verses 1-2 all refer to a literal physical temple in geographical Jerusalem that will be built just before the second coming of Christ. You've been taught that the worshipers are faithful, believing Jews of the so-called tribulation period who will have reinstituted the sacrifices and rituals of the Mosaic economy. Their activity, however, will be terminated by the Beast who will bring desolation to the temple service and subject the holy city of Jerusalem to severe affliction for the last (literal) three-and-a-half years (or forty-two months) of the (literal) seven-year tribulation period. Thus the "outer court" refers to Gentiles who will persecute the remnant during a literal forty-two-month period. The two witnesses are either Elijah and Moses themselves or individuals who are characterized in their persons and ministries by the elements and activities of those two figures as recorded in the Old Testament narratives. Their witness will span the three-and-a-half-year period, after which they will be martyred by the Beast, only to be resurrected three and a half days later.

I have tremendous respect for the many who believe that is what John is describing, but I humbly disagree. *I believe that all of 11:1-13 describes symbolically the mission and fate of the church during the entire present inter-advent age, culminating in the final period of opposition and persecution by the Beast.* On this view, the temple or sanctuary, together with the altar and the worshipers, are a reference to the *church* as God's people. All throughout the New Testament, the temple of God is, first, the person of Jesus Christ in whom God dwelt and manifested his presence, and then, second, Christ's body, the church of Jesus Christ. We, the church, are the only temple in which God will ever again dwell. Among the many texts that indicate this (cf. 1 Cor. 3:16-17; 2 Cor. 6:16; 1 Pet. 2:5), I'll mention only one, Ephesians 2:19-22:

> "So then you are no longer strangers and aliens, but you are fellow citizens with the saints and members of the household of God, built on the foundation of the apostles and prophets, Christ Jesus himself being the cornerstone, in whom the whole structure, being joined together, grows into a holy temple in the Lord. In him you also are being built together into a dwelling place for God by the Spirit."

But is it plausible, you ask, to believe that the temple, the altar, the worshipers, the outer court, and the holy city, here in 11:1-2, all refer figuratively or symbolically to the church, i.e., the believing community of God's people now on earth? Yes! Let us remember that in Revelation 3:12 the church, the believing community of God's people now on earth, are promised that they will be "a pillar in the temple" of God. They will have written on them the name of God and "the name of the city" of God, "the New Jerusalem"!

The measuring of the temple has nothing to do with ascertaining its size or width or height. To "measure" speaks of spiritual preservation from God's wrath, but not from physical persecution and martyrdom. Thus this "measuring" is equivalent to the "sealing" of Chapter 7, and the "worshipers" in 11:1 are the same as the "144,000" in 7:4.[1] The point of the imagery is to remind us that we, the people of God, are sustained and protected and kept secure in our faith while we suffer greatly at the hands of the Beast. To be "measured" means to be known and loved and preserved secure by God against all opposition.

---

1. See 2 Samuel 8:2b; Isaiah 28:16-17; Jeremiah 31:38-40; Ezekiel 40:1-6; 42:20; and Zechariah 1:16 for Old Testament examples of "measuring" as "protection."

So what does it mean that the inner sanctuary is protected but the outer court is trampled or persecuted? Some say that the inner sanctuary is the true church of Jesus Christ while the outside "court" refers to only nominal, but not true believers in Jesus. One is protected by God and the other is not. That's entirely possible, but I'm inclined to think that this is John's way of describing the church's experience viewed from two different perspectives. The church is spiritually protected from God's wrath (the inner sanctuary) but is physically oppressed by pagan forces (outer court). According to this view "the holy city" must be yet another symbolic designation of the church. In Revelation, "city" (*polis*) is used four times of the future heavenly city, the New Jerusalem (3:12; 21:2, 10; 22:19). This is similar to what we read in Hebrews 11:10; 12:22; and 13:14. The people of God on earth are members and representatives of the heavenly Jerusalem (cf. Gal. 4:26).

42 Months, 1,260 Days, 3½ Years, a time, times, and half a time (vv. 2-3)

What is the meaning of forty-two months and twelve hundred and sixty days and three and a half years? Are these references to some chronologically precise period of time that you might mark on a calendar, or are they a symbolic reference to any period of time, regardless of duration, in which certain characteristic features and events are prominent? Once again, dispensationalists who take Revelation in a strictly futuristic sense argue that this is a reference to three and a half years of the so-called seven-year Great Tribulation that is yet to come.

I would contend, instead, that *the period forty-two months = twelve hundred and sixty days = three and a half years = time, times, half a time, is a reference to the whole of this present church era, spanning from the exaltation and ascension of Christ to his second advent/coming, during which time the beast oppresses and persecutes the people of God.* In other words, the question before us is this: is the period of *forty-two months = twelve hundred and sixty days = three and a half years = time, times, half a time,* chronological (hence, literal) or theological (hence, symbolic)? Does it refer to a quantity of time or to the quality of a period of time? I believe it is the latter.

The first thing we observe is that the expression in Daniel 7:25 is not in terms of years, days, months, weeks or any such chronological measure. Rather, we read of a "time, times, and half a time," by which we may take Daniel to mean one plus two plus a half equals three and a half. But three and a half of what? In Revelation there are several texts in which a similar if not identical designation is found:

- 11:2 = forty-two months = the period during which the nations will trample the holy city.
- 11:3 = twelve hundred and sixty days (or forty-two months of thirty days each) = the period during which the two witnesses will prophesy.
- 12:6 = twelve hundred and sixty days = the period during which the "woman" is nourished by God in the wilderness.
- 12:14 = a time, times, and half a time = the period during which the "woman" is nourished in the wilderness.
- 13:5 = forty-two months = the period during which the beast acts with authority and blasphemes.

One's understanding of these time references will depend on how one interprets the events predicted to occur within each respective period. Suffice it to say that in my view these designations (forty-two months = twelve hundred and sixty days = time, times, and half a time = three and a half years) all refer to the entire present age intervening between the two comings of Christ. In other words, they are but literary variations for the same period. It is the period of persecution and tyranny, during which the people of God are oppressed and martyred. I do not believe that either Daniel or John intended us to take these references as chronologically precise periods that may be specified on a calendar.

In the Old Testament book of Daniel the number three and a half is described as "a time, times, and half a time." But that isn't what we expect, is it? We expect there to be a "time", after which comes two "times", after which comes "four times." But instead of the expression four times, we read of half a time. The point is that the "beast" will hold sway for a time. His tyranny will increase in strength and intensity. This is represented by the word *times*. We then naturally would expect that the strength and scope of his rule will double. However, we read that it will then only be for half a time. This suggests that his power is curtailed at the very time it seemed to be increasing.

There is evidence both in the Old Testament and outside of it that the number three and a half gradually became a stereotypical or stock designation in apocalyptic literature for a period of persecution and distress, regardless of its chronological duration. As for references to this time frame in biblical literature, note the three and a half years of drought during the ministry of Elijah and the rule of Ahab and Jezebel in 1 Kings 17-18; Luke 4:25; James 5:17. It was also approximately for three and a half years that Antiochus Epiphanes persecuted the Jewish people by defiling the temple.

The reference to forty-two months is possibly taken from the forty-two years of Israel's wilderness wandering (the initial two years followed by the forty God inflicted upon her). Or it may allude to the forty-two stations or encampments of Israel while in the wilderness (Num. 33:5ff.). Others suggest that three and a half signifies a broken seven, and thus becomes a symbol for the interruption of the Divine order by the malice of Satan and evil men, a period of unrest and trouble.

In the light of this, I believe that the period is simply an expression for the time of tyranny until the end comes, the period of eschatological crisis, the age of persecution and pilgrimage for the people of God however long it may be. "The figure [thus] becomes a symbol like the red cross or the swastika, a shorthand way of indicating the period during which the 'nations,' the unbelievers, seem to dominate the world, but the 'people,' God's people, maintain their witness in it."[2] Therefore, John is not attempting to tell us how long the Beast will hold sway, as if by three and a half, forty-two, twelve hundred and sixty, etc., he is specifying a period that is chronologically precise. It is not the length but the kind of time that is meant. In other words, three and a half, forty-two, and twelve hundred and sixty are not a description of the chronological quantity of the period but rather of its spiritual and theological quality.

Who are the Two Witnesses?

Once again, probably contrary to what you've been taught before, I do not believe the two witnesses are real or historical individuals, but rather symbolize the entire church of Jesus Christ in its missionary and prophetic role during the present age and particularly at the close of history.

I count as many as nine possibilities for who might have served as models for the "two witnesses", but for the sake of time I'll only mention three. (1) There is Enoch and Elijah. This view is based on the belief that Enoch (Gen. 5:24) and Elijah (2 Kgs. 2:10-11) were the only two Old Testament figures who did not experience physical death. Thus, theologically speaking, they would be the most likely candidates to return to earth and to complete the ministries which their heavenly translations cut short.

(2) Another view is that they represent Joshua and Zerubbabel. Since Revelation 11:3ff. is clearly patterned after Zechariah 4:1-14 where these two figures are mentioned, they are seen as likely candidates.

(3) The most popular and likely view is that they are patterned after Moses and Elijah. It was Elijah who called down fire from heaven on Mt. Carmel (1 Kgs. 18:38) to consume his enemies (2 Kgs. 1:10-14; cf. Luke 9:54). In Revelation 11, however, the imagery is changed and the fire proceeds from the mouths of the witnesses. Elijah also prevented rain from falling for three and a half years (1 Kgs. 17:1). Moses was responsible for turning water

---

2. Wilcock, *The Message of Revelation*, 106.

into blood (Ex. 7:14-24) and for striking the Egyptians with "every sort of plague" (1 Sam. 4:8). And the two appeared together with Jesus on the Mount of Transfiguration (Matt. 17:3). However, this does not mean that the two witnesses literally are Moses and Elijah.

First of all, the powers of each of these two Old Testament figures are attributed to both of the two witnesses, not divided between them (11:5-6). Look at all the references to "them" and "they" and "their." In other words, they are, as Beale notes, "identical prophetic twins".[3]

Second, and even more important, is the fact that they are called "two olive trees and two lampstands" (11:4). The reference to "two olive trees" most likely points to the fact that they are empowered by the Holy Spirit (Zech. 4:2-6). Olive oil was often associated with anointing, and anointing is associated with the ministry of the Holy Spirit. "Lampstand" in Revelation is used as a symbol for the church. We saw in Revelation 2 and 3 that the seven lampstands are representative of the whole church, since seven is the number of completeness. Jesus himself said in Revelation 1:19 that "the seven lampstands are the seven churches." Therefore, the two lampstands stand for the church exercising its role as witness to the gospel and Jesus Christ. But why two and not seven? Don't forget that all through Scripture it was required that evidence be accepted only on the testimony of two witnesses.[4] When Jesus sent his followers "into every town and place" he did so "two by two" (Luke 10:1). The "two witnesses" then are not a mere part of the church, but the whole church insofar as it fulfills its role as faithful prophetic witness in the power of the Holy Spirit.

Notice that according to verses 9-13 "the entire world of unbelievers will see the defeat and resurrection of the witnesses. This means that the witnesses are visible throughout the earth," which makes sense if they are symbolic of the entire global church

---

3. Beale, *Revelation*, 575.
4. Numbers 35:30; Deuteronomy 17:6; 19:15; cf. Matthew 18:16; John 5:31; 8:17; 15:26-27; Acts 5:32; 2 Corinthians 13:1; 1 Timothy 5:19; Hebrews 10:28.

of God.[5] Hal Lindsey, the author of the bestselling book, *The Late Great Planet Earth*, had a quick answer for this: he appealed to the availability of worldwide television to make this possible.[6] I suppose today Lindsey would also appeal to the internet! So, simply put, you are the two witnesses! All Christians collectively as they bear witness to the gospel and the Lordship of Jesus are represented by the two witnesses of Revelation 11.

The Ministry of the Two Witnesses

The "harm" mentioned in verse 5, from which they are protected, is a result of the church having been "measured" back in verse 1. Christians who comprise the church will undoubtedly suffer bodily harm and economic oppression and political harassment and spiritual persecution, but nothing can threaten their eternal relationship with God. They may kill the body, but they cannot destroy the soul. Notwithstanding the worst imaginable efforts of the Beast, the church will fulfill its mission of bearing witness to Jesus.

That "fire" should proceed "out of their mouths" points again to the symbolic nature of both the witnesses and the ministry they are described as fulfilling. In Revelation 1:16 and 19:15, 21, Jesus is portrayed as judging his enemies by means of a "sharp sword proceeding from his mouth" (cf. 2:16). This is clearly a metaphor of the effect and fruit of his spoken word, whether it be of judgment or blessing. We read of this same imagery in Jeremiah 5:14: "Therefore, thus says the LORD, the God of hosts: 'Because you have spoken this word, behold I am making my words in your mouth a fire and this people wood, and the fire shall consume them.'"

But precisely what is meant, practically speaking, by the imagery of the church, through her prophetic ministry, stopping the rain, turning water into blood, and smiting the earth with plagues? The "power to shut the sky" so that "no rain may fall" was the hallmark of Elijah's ministry. But in James 5:16-17, James mentions this facet

---

5. Beale, *Revelation*, 574.
6. Hal Lindsey, *The Late Great Planet Earth*, Zondervan, 1970.

of Elijah's ministry and tells us that our prayers can be as powerful and effective as those of Elijah. I suggest, then, that this "power" to halt the rain is simply a reference to the impact of the prayers of God's people in this age.

Or it could be that God will, in response to the preaching, praying (cf. James 5:16-17), and prophesying of the church, pour out his judgments on an unbelieving world. We read in verse 10 that the two witnesses are described as having "tormented" the earth-dwellers. Is the torment a reference to the seal, trumpet, and bowl judgments? Is the church and its ministry one of the means by which these judgments are poured out? On this, see especially Revelation 8:3-5.

The reference to water being turned into blood and plagues striking the earth evokes the memory of what Moses did in securing the liberation of Israel out of bondage in Egypt. Perhaps the declaration in verse 6 that the church has this power means that we have "the necessary power to liberate people from bondage, to enable people to experience the new exodus" from sin through Jesus Christ.[7] This, then, is what the church is to do in this present age. But what should we expect? For this we turn to verses 7-10.

Persecution and Oppression

The opening words of verse 7 indicate that John is now describing what will occur at the end of history. Clearly, the "measuring" of verse 1 has succeeded in preserving the church and its prophetic witness intact until all has been accomplished.

The "beast" is mentioned here for the first time in Revelation, although it appears that John expected his readers to know of whom/what he spoke. Note two things. First, the Beast does not now, at the end of history, for the first time rise up out of the bottomless pit. The phrase, "the beast that rises from the bottomless pit" describes what is characteristic of the Beast, most likely throughout the course of the church's witness during the inter-advent age. The Beast has been actively engaged in persecuting God's people for

---

7. Hamilton, *Revelation*, 239.

the last two thousand years and will continue to do so up until the end of the age when Christ will destroy him at his second coming. This is the first indication that the Beast is far more than the end-of-the-age Antichrist. But for this we will have to wait until we come to Revelation 13.

The description in verse 8 is not intended to suggest that the entire church is destroyed. However, as Wilcock explains, "Scripture does seem to envisage a time... when at the very end of history an unexampled onslaught will be mounted against the church, and she will to all appearances 'go under.'"[8] It will appear that the public and official witness of the church has been smothered. The previous influence of the church will have diminished and be treated with indignity and open contempt (which is surely the point of their bodies being left unburied; on the latter see 1 Samuel 17:44, 46; 2 Kings 9:10; Psalm 79:1-5; Isaiah 14:19-20; Jeremiah 8:1-2; 9:22; 16:4-6; and 22:19).

Is the "great city" in verse 8 literal Jerusalem? Many think so. But this could only be the case if the two witnesses are, in fact, two literal individuals, contrary to what I argued above. In every instance in Revelation where the words "great city" are used they refer to Babylon the Great (Rome?), not Jerusalem (see 16:19; 17:18; 18:10, 16, 18, 19, 21; and possibly 14:8). The "great city" is, then, the ungodly world as a whole where earth-dwellers live.

This "great city" is "symbolically" or more accurately "spiritually" (*pneumatikos*) called "Sodom and Egypt" [cf. Joel 3:19] (v. 8). Thus the ungodly world is likened not simply to Babylon but to other embodiments and corporate expressions of wickedness in the ancient world. The word "symbolically" indicates "that the city is not to be understood in a literal, earthly manner, but figuratively through spiritual eyes.... The city is ungodly and is not to be located in any one geographical area but is any ungodly spiritual realm on earth."[9] Or as Richard Phillips says, these cities "represent not a place in the world but the world itself in its sensual harlotry, violent

---

8. Wilcock, *The Message of Revelation*, 106.
9. Beale, *Revelation*, 592.

persecution, and idol-worshiping false religion as it militantly opposes the gospel."[10]

The concluding phrase of verse 8, "where their Lord was crucified," has led some to insist that literal Jerusalem is meant. But I think John is saying that Jesus was crucified in, throughout, and by the ungodly of the entire earth. In other words, the world city is spiritually like Jerusalem in having turned its back on Jesus, accounting for his crucifixion and its continuing hostility to him and those who bear witness to his life, death, and resurrection.

The apparent demise of the church will captivate the attention of the unbelieving world, but only for a brief season. The "three and a half days" of their shame is to be contrasted with their "three and a half years" of invincible witness (the former to be taken as no more literal than the latter). The point is simply that the "victory" of the Beast and his/its followers "is brief and insignificant in comparison to the victorious testimony of the witnesses."[11] Their refusal to place the bodies "in a tomb" is again a powerful symbolic heightening of the indignity and contempt to which the unbelieving world subjects the church.

The happiness and merriment of the earth-dwellers in verse 10 is due to their belief that the message of the church, which brought them so much discomfort and emotional anguish, has been silenced. Perhaps their joy is due to their belief that the ultimate judgment which the church proclaimed will now never come to pass. Simply put, verses 7-10 are designed to portray symbolically the global scope of all the persecution and eventual martyrdom of Christians throughout the present church age in which it appears that God's people are destroyed and evil has triumphed over truth and righteousness. But appearances can be deceiving!

Resurrection or Vindication?

This portrayal of "resurrection" is an echo of Ezekiel 37:5 and 10, where we read of God's restoration of Israel out of the Babylonian

---

10. Philips, *Revelation*, 324.
11. Beale, *Revelation*, 595.

exile. The nation in exile is described as corpses of which only dry bones remain: "Thus says the Lord God to these bones, 'Behold I will cause breath to enter you, and you shall live.... So I prophesied as he commanded me, and the breath came into them, and they lived and stood on their feet, an exceeding great army."

Some believe that the "resurrection" in Revelation 11:11 is literal and refers to the bodily resurrection of the dead in Christ which occurs at the time of the rapture of the church (cf. 1 Thess. 4:16-17), the latter being the focus of 11:12. Others contend that this scene is simply a symbolic portrayal of vindication. Perhaps both ideas are in view.

Is the "great fear" that "fell upon" (v. 11) the unbelievers who saw them a saving fear, descriptive of their repentance and salvation (as, for example, in Revelation 14:7; 15:4; 19:5)? Or is it merely the reversal of their joy and merriment (v. 10) as they suddenly realize that they must face the wrath of the God whom the witnesses proclaimed (for "fear" of this sort, see 18:10, 15; Psalm 105:38; Exodus 15:16; Jonah 1:10, 16)? It's hard to say.

Events of the Last Day

Four things are said in verse 13 that occurred at "that hour", i.e., at the time undoubtedly of Christ's return when God's people are vindicated and resurrected.

(1) First, *"there was a great earthquake."* Similar terminology occurs in 6:12 (the sixth seal) and 16:18 (seventh bowl) where the last judgment is beginning to unfold. Is it a literal earthquake or a symbolic portrayal of the fall of earthly kingdoms as Christ brings his judgment to bear upon them? I don't know.

(2) Second, *"a tenth of the city fell."* (3) Third, *"seven thousand people were killed in the earthquake."* If the two witnesses are linked to the ministry of Elijah, the seven thousand who die may be the just equivalent of the seven thousand faithful who "did not bow the knee to Baal" (cf. Rom. 11:4). But these are odd numbers. If this is a global judgment at the time of Christ's return, why does only one-tenth of the world city fall and why are only seven thousand people killed? Ah, be patient, the answer is coming!

(4) Finally, *"the rest were terrified and gave glory to the God of heaven."* The question once again is whether this "terror" or "fear" and the subsequent "glorifying" of God describes an expression of saving repentance and faith in the God of heaven. I believe it does! Almost identical terminology occurs in Revelation 14:7 ("fear God and give him glory") and 15:4 ("Who will not fear, O Lord, and glorify your name?"). Both of these texts have in view saving fear and acknowledgement of God.

We should also take note of Revelation 16:9 where the unrepentant are described in these terms: "they did not repent and give him glory," the point being that "to give God glory" is to repent. In fact, in Revelation "to give God glory" always refers positively to a saving response on the part of people (see 4:9; 14:7; 16:9; 19:7).

Global Revival?!

There is yet one more thing we must note, and I owe these observations to Richard Bauckham. He believes, and I am inclined to agree with him, that the numbers "one-tenth" and "seven thousand" indicate that the conversion portrayed here is of the vast majority of the lost, not a paltry few. That is to say, there is in the events of Revelation 11:11-13 an indication of *a great, vast final global harvest or revival of souls!*

In the Old Testament God's judgment typically falls on the vast majority of people and only a tiny remnant is saved or delivered. That remnant is often described as only a tenth (Amos 5:3; cf. Isaiah 6:13, where in its present context the tenth part is the righteous remnant). The figure of seven thousand alludes more specifically to Elijah's prophetic commission to bring about the judgment of all except the seven thousand faithful Israelites who had not bowed the knee to Baal (1 Kgs. 19:14-18; cf. Rom. 11:2-5). In other words, John in verse 13 reverses the arithmetic! It is typically a small number whom God saves and a large percentage that God judges. But here in Revelation 11:13 it is a small percentage that God judges and a vastly larger percentage that God saves! So, if only a tenth of the city falls under judgment, nine-tenths of the city fears God and gives him glory. If only seven thousand are killed in the judgment of the earthquake and the rest fear God and give him glory, it would seem that John is describing a vast global harvest of souls coming into the kingdom at the end of the age.

Conclusion

When we were in Kansas City two young ladies from Canada came to visit our church. I engaged in conversation with them and asked why they had come so far south. They responded: "We came to prophesy because we are the two witnesses of Revelation 11!"

Needless to say, virtually everyone standing with us had to muffle their laughter. I, on the other hand, said: "Well, of course you are! And so are all of us! And so are all of God's people, the church, through this present age in which we live." They were not comforted by that answer and returned to Canada. You, Christian brother or sister, are the two witnesses. And what is it that we should expect: persecution. And what is it that we should do: prophesy! And in the end we will be vindicated. In the end we will live!

Chapter Twenty-Four

War in Heaven and on Earth: How the Church Conquers the Devil

(Revelation 12:1-17)

Having described the seven trumpet judgments, but before explaining the seven bowls, John inserts three parenthetical chapters (Revelation 12–14). The purpose of Chapter 12 is to provide us with a deeper perspective on the spiritual conflict between the world and the church. At the heart of its message is that, although Satan is the principal source of the persecution of God's people, he has been decisively defeated by Christ, a victory in which we now share even in the midst of suffering and martyrdom.

If you ever had any doubts about the reality of spiritual warfare, by which I mean the battle that rages between Satan and the people of God, Revelation 12 should forever put your concerns to rest. The Apostle Paul wrote in Ephesians that "we do not wrestle against flesh and blood, but against the rulers, against the authorities, against the cosmic powers over this present darkness, against the spiritual forces of evil in the heavenly places" (Eph. 6:12). Here in Revelation 12 we find the most graphic portrayal of that battle, albeit in the highly symbolic and graphic imagery that we have come to expect from apocalyptic literature.

At the heart of Revelation 12 is its message that, although Satan is the principal source of the persecution of God's people, he has been decisively defeated by Christ, a victory in which we now share even in the midst of suffering and martyrdom.

The Woman and the Dragon

Who is the woman described in verses 1-6? Countless interpretations have been suggested. Some believe she is the first woman Eve, whose offspring was to be the serpent's great enemy (Gen. 3:15). Roman Catholic commentators, as expected, have generally argued that the woman symbolizes Mary, the literal birth mother of Jesus. But it's hard to then understand how, according to verse 6, Mary was specifically persecuted after Christ's enthronement, requiring protection for twelve hundred and sixty days. Various cults have claimed that the woman is one of their own number. For example, Christian Scientists insist that the woman is Mary Baker Eddy. The child to which she gives birth is her unique doctrinal teachings, and the dragon is the modern mind that disdains and seeks to destroy her influence!

Some have said the woman symbolizes Old Testament Israel while others argue she stands for the New Testament church. I'm convinced that *the woman symbolizes what we might call the believing messianic community: both Old Testament Israel and the New Testament church*. Later in the chapter we read, that when the woman is persecuted, she flees into the wilderness and has other children who are described as faithful Christians. In other words, the woman is both Israel, the community of faith that produced the Messiah, and the church, the community of faith that subsequently follows and obeys him. John clearly envisioned an organic and spiritual continuity between Old Testament Israel and the church. They are one body of believers. If that interpretation is correct, the twelve stars in her crown would seem to stand both for the twelve tribes of Israel and the reconstitution and continuation of true Israel in the twelve apostles of the church.

The woman is pregnant and suffering birth pangs. On the one hand, this represents the longing, expectation, and anticipation of the Messiah's birth on the part of those in the Old Testament community of faith (cf. Luke 2:25-38). But it is also a symbolic reference to the persecution of God's people during the period of the Old Testament leading up to Christ's coming. That persecution is in view is evident from the word translated "in birth pains" (v. 2, *basanizō*). This term is used in the New Testament of suffering, punishment, trial, and persecution (Matt. 8:6, 29; 14:24; Mark 5:7; 6:48; Luke 8:28; 2 Pet. 2:8) and in Revelation of torment inflicted by demons (9:5) or by God (11:10; 14:10; 20:10). Nowhere in the Bible is this particular Greek word used to describe merely a woman suffering birth pains.

We then read in verse 3 that John sees yet another "sign" in heaven: a great red dragon with seven heads, seven diadems, and ten horns. In the book of Revelation, the "dragon" is typically a symbol for Satan, the one who both represents and energizes all individual and corporate opposition to the kingdom of Christ and persecution of the people of God (see 12:9; 20:2, 10). That there are "seven" heads and "ten" horns probably should not be pressed (after all, how do you distribute ten horns onto only seven heads?), except to indicate and emphasize the fullness of his oppressive power. The diadems or crowns probably point to the earthly kings and rulers through whom the devil works.

Contrary to what most of you have probably been led to believe, the "stars of heaven" in Revelation 12:4 which Satan throws to the earth are probably not those in the angelic host who fell with him in some pre-temporal rebellion and subsequently constitute the demonic hosts of which we read in both the Old and New Testaments. There are two reasons for this.

First, the time of the event described in verse 4 is immediately before the birth of Jesus, whereas most believe that the angelic rebellion occurred prior to creation. Second, it seems reasonable that the "stars" of verse 4 that are swept down by Satan must be related to the "stars" of verse 1 which are found in the crown of the woman. Thus the "stars" of verse 4 are not to be identified with the dragon's "angels" in verses 7-8. Instead, Revelation 12:4 is probably describing the persecution by Satan of God's people, perhaps even their martyrdom.

What is far more important for our purposes is the second half of verse 4 where we read of Satan's determination to kill Jesus upon his birth. Surely this has in view the barbaric and heartless command from King Herod that all the male infants in Bethlehem, two years and younger, be killed (Matt. 2:16-18). I don't want to minimize the horror of this event, but people have often believed that this was a mass slaughter when in fact the population of Bethlehem in those days would have allowed for at most two dozen young boys who were the victim of Herod's wrath. It may also be the case that this has in view the many times when Satan tried to thwart Jesus' work in his earthly ministry (see Luke 4:28-30).

Verse 5 provides us with a synopsis or snapshot of Christ's entire life. Such abbreviations are not uncommon in the New Testament.[1] His being "caught up to God and to his throne" in verse 5b is not protection from death but a reference to the resurrection and ascension of Jesus. The reference to Jesus ruling "all the nations with a rod of iron" is an allusion to the prophecy of Psalm 2:7-9 and indicates that, whereas this will be consummated at the end of the age (see Rev. 19:15), an inaugurated fulfillment has already begun (see Rev. 2:26-28). Jesus has "already" received the authority spoken of in the Psalm and is now ruling the nations from his heavenly throne, but he has "not yet" manifested that authority in its fullness.

Whereas the woman in verse 1 was primarily the covenant community of believers prior to the incarnation of Jesus, the woman in verse 6 is the covenant community of believers subsequent to his resurrection. But it is the same, one people of God, the one olive tree. The "flight" of the woman into the "wilderness" is simply a symbolic way to describe God's supernatural protection of his people, the church, throughout the course of the present age in which we live.

You will recall, I'm sure, from our study of Revelation 11, that the twelve hundred and sixty days (v. 6b) is a stock or proverbial

---

1. See John 3:13; 8:14; 13:3; 16:5, 28; Romans 1:3-4; 1 Timothy 3:16; see also Revelation 1:5, 17-18; 2:8.

way of referring to the time of persecution and tyranny. It is equivalent to three and a half years or forty-two months or a time, times, and half a time. In every case where this number of days appears it refers to the present church age, from the first coming of Christ extending to the second coming at the end of history. It is during this time that the church is engaged in battle with the Devil and suffers oppression at the hands of his henchmen, the Beast and False Prophet. More on them when we come to Revelation 13.

War in Heaven and Victory on Earth

Revelation 12:7-11 are introduced by John to explain why the Woman (the church) had to flee into the wilderness (vv. 1-6). The reason why Satan's fury is now unleashed against the church of Jesus Christ on earth is because he has lost his place and position in heaven; his power has been curtailed.

What kind of "war" does John have in mind? What kind of "weapons" might have been employed, if at all? Was there some sort of contact, appropriate to spiritual beings, which occurred? Could such war have resulted in some form of injury to the combatants, even death? Or is the use of the terminology of "war" simply a metaphor designed to paint a theological picture? If so, what is that picture?

So, when did (or when will) this expulsion of Satan and his demons from heaven occur? Three answers have figured prominently among evangelicals. (1) According to dispensationalists who read Revelation as applying almost exclusively to the future, it will occur just before or during the so-called seven-year "great tribulation" period. (2) Others say it is timeless. No specific moment in history is in view. It is simply a highly symbolic description of Satan's downfall. (3) I, on the other hand, believe *it is because of the incarnation, life, death, and resurrection of Jesus in the first century that this defeat of the Devil occurs, indeed, has already occurred.* Michael and his angels are given the task of expelling Satan consequent to the victory of Jesus at the time of his first coming (we see a whisper of this event in the words of Jesus in Luke 10:18). Christians carry on this victory over Satan (v. 11) as they stand on the achievements of the cross and boldly proclaim the authority of Jesus' name. In other words, this war was provoked by the victory of Jesus Christ over sin and death. Michael and his angels are here portrayed as enforcing the results of Christ's victory over his enemies, namely, Satan and his demons. Michael and his angels win because Christ won.

Satan's accusations no longer have any legal or moral force following his defeat at the cross. This, I believe, is the meaning of his being "thrown down" and there no longer being "any place for them in heaven." In other words, this is not a description of a literal or spatial or geographical change in the devil's dwelling place. Rather we should understand that this is John's way of describing the glorious fact that Satan's power was broken through Christ's atoning sacrifice on the cross and his bodily resurrection. The result is that Satan can no longer successfully bring accusations against God's people. Prior to the cross the accusations and slander of Satan had legal force, for the sin of those against whom he spoke had not been fully expiated. But now, subsequent to the cross, "there is no condemnation for those that are in Christ Jesus" (Rom. 8:1). Whatever ongoing work of accusation Satan may attempt is countered by the intercessory ministry of Jesus (Rom. 8:33-34; Heb. 7:25; 1 John 2:1-2).

The word "devil" in verse 9 is used thirty-five times in the Bible and literally means "slanderer" or "accuser" (*diabolos*). See 1 Samuel 29:4; 1 Kings 11:14. In Luke 4:2, 13 and Revelation 12:9, 12 it is the devil's aim to defame. He is a constant source of false and malicious reports (1) to God, about you (Rev. 12:10; but cf. 1 John 2:2; Rom. 8:33-39); (2) to you, about God (Gen. 3; Matt. 4); and (3) to you, about yourself (Eph. 6:16; he seeks to undermine and subvert your knowledge of who you are in Christ).

The title "Satan" in verse 9 is used fifty-two times in the Bible and literally means "the adversary," the one who opposes.[2] According

---

2. See Zechariah 3:1-2; cf. Numbers 22:22, 32; 1 Samuel 29:4; 2 Samuel 19:22; 1 Kings 5:4; 11:14, 23, 25. In Psalm 109:6 it has the sense of "accuser" or "prosecuting attorney".

to verse 10, the fact that Satan has been defeated, that the atoning death and resurrection of Jesus have stripped him of his legal right to accuse the brethren is evidence that the "kingdom" of God and the "authority" of Christ have been inaugurated. Thus verse 10 does not merely anticipate the final and consummate coming of God's kingdom but celebrates the presence of the kingdom in the here and now. The point of verse 11 is to reassure the people of God, then and now, that suffering and even martyrdom at the hands of the devil is not defeat for them, but for him! It is an ironic victory, but a victory, nonetheless.

What does it mean to "conquer" the Devil?[3]

It does not mean that we destroy him (not until Revelation 20). In fact, note well that the victory of these believers only serves to intensify the wrath of Satan directed against the earth (v. 12)! It does not mean we put a permanent end to his attack of us (cf. Jesus after temptation). It does not mean Satan cannot kill you (through persecution; cf. Revelation 2:10; 6:9-11). Here is what it does mean.

You overcome the Devil when you stand firmly in your faith in Christ and thereby find the strength to say No to sin. How is this done? Paul refers to the "the shield of faith" in Ephesians 6:16 that protects us against "the flaming darts of the evil one." What are these "missiles/darts/arrows" that Satan launches against us? We would have to include here the sudden and unexpected eruption in our minds of vile images and thoughts that shock and surprise us (such that are obviously and undeniably contrary to our most basic desires). Paul may also have in view words and pictures that disgust you and violate your God-given sense of propriety/morality. These often leap into your mind without warning or provocation. This may include blasphemous thoughts about Jesus; revolting images of sexual perversity; suicidal urges; compulsive thoughts of doing horribly violent things to family/friends; unaccountable

---

3. Much of what follows has been adapted from my book, *Understanding Spiritual Warfare: A Comprehensive Guide* (Grand Rapids: Zondervan, 2021), and is used here with permission.

impulses to rebel against God, against one's family, against one's church; subtle insinuations against God's character/goodness; and false feelings of guilt. Frequently, people report these things to occur while reading the Bible (not newspapers or magazines), while praying and while praising God. This aggravates feelings of personal guilt and worthlessness, insofar as such occasions are regarded as spiritual ("What kind of person am I that I would have such thoughts/fantasies at precisely the time I should be loving and worshiping God?").

So how does faith function as a shield of protection against these "flaming darts" of Satan? Several things should be noted. First, putting our faith in the superior pleasures of God extinguishes the flaming darts of Satan. For example, we read in Hebrews 11:24-26 that it was Moses' faith in the glory of the coming Christ and the rewards of obedience that enabled him to say No to the powerful temptation presented by the wealth and treasures of Egypt.

Second, there is faith in the steadfast promises of God. When Satan whispers, "God may have cared about you once before, long ago, but his interest in who you are is gone," you lift up the shield of faith and say, "That is impossible. God is immutable. He cannot change. His concern for me is eternal. What he has promised to me he will fulfill."

Third, when Satan whispers, "God doesn't love you anymore; not after you've failed him so many times," you lift up the shield of faith and say, "That is impossible. God's love for me cannot cease to exist, for he demonstrated it when he gave his Son to suffer in my place." Thus, the shield of faith functions whenever we say to the enemy, "I'm going to believe God when he tells me that there is great gain in godliness and therefore I will not fall prey to your seductive temptations."

The shield of faith functions each time we hold up the truth of the Scriptures under the onslaught of Satan's lies. Satan knows he can gain a major strategic advantage over us if he can sow the seeds of doubt in our minds concerning our relationship with God. In every instance of serious and sustained demonic attack that I have encountered, the individual was plagued with doubt concerning his/her salvation. Thus when Paul tells us in Ephesians 6:17 to put on the "helmet of salvation" he is instructing us to live in the knowledge and assurance of the truth expressed in Romans 8:1, 31-38 and Hebrews 13:5-6.

There is nothing Satan can do to alter or undermine the fact that we are saved. Not "angels, nor principalities, nor things present, nor things to come, nor powers, nor height, nor depth, nor any other created thing, shall be able to separate us from the love of God, which is in Christ Jesus our Lord" (Rom. 8:38-39). But what he can do is erode our assurance and confidence that we are saved. Our salvation, our standing with God, does not fluctuate or diminish with our success or failure in spiritual battles. Yet Satan is determined to convince us that it does.

By what means did they (we) overcome him?

John answers this question by mentioning three things in particular. First, they conquered Satan "by the blood of the Lamb" (v. 11a). How is this done? It is done when we stand on the truth of Romans 8:1, that there is no condemnation for those in Christ Jesus. It is done when we proclaim the truth of Colossians 2:13-15 and Christ's triumph over Satan and his forces by means of his cross. It is done when we declare and trust in the truth that the cross/resurrection of Jesus has secured for us the presence and power of the Holy Spirit. Thus, the phrase "the blood of the Lamb" is simply a way of referring to Jesus in his capacity as Lord and Savior, the one who triumphed over sin and death. Simply put, Satan's only hope for victory in your life is the presence of unforgiven sin. But Christ's blood cleanses us from the condemning power of our guilt, guilt incurred by our sin (1 John 1:7) and thus forever removes any and all grounds on which Satan might have a legal basis for launching his attack.

Second, they conquered Satan "by the word of their testimony." This starts with the confident proclamation of our identity in Christ. One of Satan's primary weapons is the lie. He is committed to deceiving you into believing you are not what, in fact, you are, and that you cannot do what, in fact, you can. Satan will try to persuade you that you are: a failure, a fool, of no use to God or other Christians, worthless, an embarrassment to Christ, that you are wasting your time to confess your sins (God won't listen), that you are inferior to other believers, destined always to fall short of their successes, that you are a hopeless victim of your past and helpless to change your future, that you are a pathetic excuse for a Christian, that you are owned by Satan, that you are now what you will always be (there's no hope for improvement), that you are stupid and beyond the reach of prayer, etc. You must respond to such deceitful, destructive slander by remembering and standing firmly on the truth of 2 Corinthians 5:17; Ephesians 2:1-7; 5:8; 1 John 3:1-3; etc.

The "word" of our "testimony" is also expressed when we engage in heartfelt, passionate worship of the Son of God. The power to repel the enemy, the authority to overcome, is not to be found in the physical elements of music per se, i.e., volume, melody, rhythm have no inherent spiritual power. Power to repel and overcome the enemy resides in the truth of what is sung or played and the heart of the singer/player. The devil pays no attention to decibels or sweat or physical gestures. But he is compelled to submit to the proclamation of truth and the presence of the Spirit and the authenticity and intensity of heart devotion to Jesus. Intimacy in worship (God's love and ours) together with our adoration, declaration of God's power, grace, kindness, justice, etc., as well as the affirmation of our commitment to Christ, do more to repel the enemy than anything. That is warfare worship. *Nothing will do more to drive away demons than the intensity of intimacy with Jesus!*

The "word" of our "testimony" is also expressed in prayer. This involves praying for ourselves and for others to be given insight and understanding into who we are in Christ and what is ours through faith (Eph. 1:15ff.). There are also prayers of resistance and rebuke of the enemy. For example:

> "Satan, I rebuke you in the authority of Jesus Christ. I declare your works in my life destroyed. Jesus triumphed over you in the wilderness, on the cross, and in the grave. His resurrection

has sealed your fate. I triumph over you now in the strength of his name. I resist and rebuke your efforts to oppress, afflict, or deceive me. I remove from you the right to rob me of the joy and fruit of my salvation. Through the power of the blood of Calvary, I command all powers of darkness assigned to me, sent to me, or surrounding me now, to leave. Go where Jesus Christ orders you to go, never to return."[4]

Third, and finally, they conquer Satan by not loving their lives "even unto death." What is being described in this little phrase is a value judgment, a prioritizing that affected every aspect of their lives. They loved Jesus more than their earthly welfare, more than earthly pleasures, more than earthly convenience, more than peace, prosperity, comfort, etc.

Here he means the willingness to give up good things for the sake of better things; the willingness to sacrifice all in life, even life itself, because life isn't the most valuable thing to us; they would rather die than yield one inch of their hearts to the world or Satan; no earthly pleasure was worth denying Jesus. No promise of peace or power was deemed of greater value than the value of remaining steadfast. We read in Hebrews 10:34: "For you … accepted joyfully the seizure of your property, knowing that you have for yourselves a better possession and an abiding one." They had refused to let anything in life get a grip on their hearts in such a way that it might diminish their devotion to Jesus. "Jesus is more valuable to us than anything life can offer. Jesus is greater treasure than life itself. We will gladly die before we renounce him!"

Don't you see that Satan has absolutely no chance of winning when he confronts a heart like that! Simple, unqualified, unconditional devotion to Jesus! That is why even in their death they overcame him (Rev. 2:10). Satan only wins when we love our lives more than we love God. When we allow our hearts to be captured by earthly comfort and find that we would do anything and everything to procure more, preserve what we have, promote

---

4. Thomas B. White, *The Believer's Guide to Spiritual Warfare* (Ventura, CA: Regal, 1990), 116.

it, make it comfortable, insulate it, etc. Too many of us love our lives illegitimately; there is a good and legal love of life (I'm not talking about that; celebrate life, enjoy it, etc.). This is an overprotective concern for personal comfort and convenience and peace and prosperity and the resultant energy and lifestyle designed to perpetuate it. Satan wins whenever we treasure anything more than Jesus.

So, how does this perspective on life overcome the enemy? When you prioritize your life so that nothing means more to you than Jesus, you deprive Satan of any legal right to your heart or mind; you undermine and short circuit his power to influence your soul. How? If this (Rev. 12:11) is your life, what can he possibly latch hold of? What is there in your life to which he can affix himself? To what can he appeal in your soul that would give him a power base from which to operate?

The Church, the Dragon, and Divine Protection

Verses 12-13 pick up where verse 6 left off. Failing to destroy the "child" (Jesus), Satan turns his wrath and destructive attention to the "woman", i.e., the people of God, the church. Verse 14 is a vivid and obviously figurative portrayal of how God has taken steps to protect his people and preserve them against Satan's attacks during this present church age. As you know, Hal Lindsey and other dispensationalists believe this refers to something that has yet to occur. It will take place, so Lindsey says, during the time of the so-called Great Tribulation. He suggested that some kind of massive airlift will transport these fleeing Jews across the rugged terrain to their place of protection. He then points to the eagle as the national symbol of the United States and argues that it is possible that the airlift will be made available by aircraft from the U.S. Sixth Fleet in the Mediterranean. Says Craig Keener, "fortunately for both Lindsey and other Americans, Ben Franklin failed in his attempt to make the national bird a turkey."[5]

---

5. Craig S. Keener, *Revelation* (The NIV Application Commentary), (Grand Rapids: Zondervan, 2000). 329.

The devil's persecution of the church is described in the vivid imagery of water pouring forth from the serpent's mouth in an effort to drown the woman. The imagery of an overflowing flood or torrential waves of water is used throughout the Old Testament in two primary ways: (1) it points to the persecution of God's people by his enemies;[6] and (2) it is also used to portray the judgment that God brings against those who resist him.[7]

It may be that since the waters pour forth from the serpent's "mouth" the idea is particularly of Satan's attempt to destroy the church through deception and false teaching/doctrine.[8] Recall the numerous times in church history (past and present) where the rise of heresy threatened the purity (and even existence) of the church: Gnosticism and Marcionism in the second-third centuries, anti-Trinitarian Monarchianism in the third century, Arianism in the fourth century, Pelagianism in the fifth century, the various false teachings in Roman Catholicism throughout the middle ages, Socinianism in the sixteenth and seventeenth centuries, Deism in the seventeenth and eighteenth centuries, the emergence of Darwinian evolution and religious liberalism in the nineteenth and twentieth centuries.

And do you remember how God's defeat of Pharaoh's armies at the Red Sea is portrayed? We read in Exodus 15:12, "You stretched out your right hand; [and] the earth swallowed them." Later in the wilderness "the earth opened its mouth and swallowed" the families of Korah, Dathan, and Abiram because of their resistance to Moses' leadership (Num. 16:12-14; Deut. 11:5-6; Ps. 106:17). The devil's fury and wrath is now directed at the "rest of her offspring." That's you and me! Satan hates you. He hates everything about the church, the people of God. He hates those "who keep the commandments of God and hold to the testimony of Jesus" (v. 17).

---

6. See 2 Samuel 22:5; Psalms 18:4, 16; 46:3; 66:12; 69:1-2, 14-15; 124:4-5; 144:7-8, 11; and Isaiah 43:2.

7. See Isaiah 8:7-8; 17:12-13; Jeremiah 46:8; 47:2; 51:55; and Hosea 5:10.

8. See Revelation 2:14-16, 20-22; 3:15-17; Romans 16:17-20; 1 Timothy 4:1; 5:15; and 2 Timothy 2:23-26.

Conclusion

The church, the people of God, have been engaged in a war with Satan for more than two thousand years. It is a staggering testimony to the wickedness of our Enemy that "he knows that his time is short" (12:12b) yet continues to assault, accuse, and do everything in his power to undermine our faith in Jesus. But we have been guaranteed victory, not because of our righteousness or spirituality, but because of the victory secured for us by Jesus, whose blood cleanses from all sin. Praise be to God!

Chapter Twenty-Five

The "Beast" of Revelation: Who, What, Why?

(Revelation 13:1-10)

I'm guaranteed of one thing when it comes to this chapter. Most, if not all of you, will pay very close attention. The reason is that there is hardly a more fascinating and controversial topic in eschatology than that of the Antichrist. Is the Antichrist the same as the Beast of Revelation? Is there more than one Antichrist? Is he a figure of past history or of the future? Is the Antichrist a person or a power or a movement, or a combination of all? These and other questions will arise as we try to understand this concept.

To make sense of Revelation 13 we need to back up to the concluding verse of Chapter 12. *In Revelation 12:17 we find the most precise and riveting explanation for virtually everything we see in our world today*: whether that be the rise of militant Islamic fundamentalism, the angry atheism that has erupted in recent years, global persecution of the church of Jesus Christ, rampant sexual immorality, oppressive laws that seek to restrict what Christians can say and do, just to mention a few. Look again at John's words: "Then the dragon became furious with the woman and went off to make war on the rest of her offspring, on those who keep the commandments of God and hold to the testimony of Jesus. And he stood on the sand of the sea."

We cannot afford to overlook the crucial relationship between Revelation 12:17b and 13:1. We read that Satan "stood on the sand of the sea" (17b). What an odd way to conclude a chapter! Odd indeed, until you realize what happens in Revelation 13:1-18. Satan stands on the shore in order that he might beckon forth from the sea the "Beast" with "ten horns and seven heads, with ten diadems on its horns and blasphemous names on its heads" (Rev. 13:1).

Who or what is this "Beast" and what relevance does it have for us today? Many mistakenly think that the "Beast" is only the end-time Antichrist. He is surely that. But he is more. When you read the description of the Beast in Revelation 13:2 and following you discover that John has taken the four world kingdoms described in Daniel 7 and combined them in one composite figure: the Beast from the sea.

In Daniel 7 we read about four beasts who rise up out of the sea. The "sea" is often symbolic of evil, chaos, and anti-kingdom powers with whom Yahweh must contend.[1] We should also note that the image of an evil sea monster always symbolizes kingdoms that oppose and oppress God's people (especially Egypt and Pharaoh).[2]

Most believe that the four earthly kingdoms symbolized by the four beasts in Daniel were four successive empires in ancient history: Babylon, Medo-Persia, Greece, and Rome. It seems obvious that whereas the four beasts of Daniel 7 represent four historical successive world empires, *the sea-beast of Revelation 13 is John's creative composite of them all.* All the evil characteristics of those four kingdoms are now embodied in the one sea-beast who becomes Satan's principal agent in persecuting the people of God. The point would seem to be that the "Beast" of Revelation 13 is corporate in nature as well as personal. That is to say, *the Beast is a symbol for the very real system of Satanically inspired evil, and thus opposition to the kingdom of God, that throughout history has manifested itself in a variety of forms, whether political, economic,*

---

1. On the symbolic significance of the "sea", see Isaiah 17:12, 13; 51:9-10; 27:1; 57:20; Revelation 17:8; 21:1; Jeremiah 46:7ff.; and Job 26:7-13.

2. See especially Psalms 74:13-14; 89:10; Isaiah 30:7; 51:9; Ezekiel 29:3; 32:2-3; and Habakkuk 3:8-15.

military, social, philosophical, or religious. Anything and anyone that seeks to oppress, persecute, or destroy the church is the Beast!

What I'm saying, then, is that although the Beast is very much involved in earthly events, *the Beast is also a trans-cultural, trans-temporal symbol for all individual and collective, Satanically-inspired, opposition to Jesus and his people.* It is anything and everything (whether a principle, a person, or a power) utilized by the enemy to deceive and destroy the influence and advance of the kingdom of God. Thus, the Beast at the time when John wrote Revelation was the Roman Empire. At another time, the Beast was the Arian heresy in the fourth century that denied the deity of Jesus Christ. The Beast is, at one time, the emperor Decius (third century persecutor of the church); at another, evolutionary Darwinism. The Beast is the late medieval Roman Catholic papacy, modern Protestant liberalism, Marxism, the radical feminist movement, the Pelagian heresy of the fifth century, communism, Joseph Stalin, the seventeenth century Enlightenment, eighteenth century deism, Roe v. Wade, the state persecution of Christians in China and North Korea, militant atheism in the twenty-first century and ISIS.

Each of these is, individually and on its own, the Beast. All of these are, collectively and in unity, the Beast. Will there also be a single person at the end of the age who embodies in consummate form all the characteristics of the many previous historical manifestations of the Beast? If so, should we call this person the Antichrist? Probably.

Who or What is the Beast?

A recurring theme both before and during the time of the Protestant Reformation was the identification of the Antichrist either with the Roman Catholic Church in general or the papacy in particular. Among the pre-reformers, John Wycliffe (late fourteenth century) believed the papacy itself, as an institution, rather than any one particular Pope, was the Antichrist. John Hus (1372–1415), the Bohemian reformer who was burned at the stake for his opposition to the Roman Catholic Church, embraced Wycliffe's view as well.

Virtually all the Protestant Reformers, including Martin Luther and his associate Philip Melancthon, together with the English Reformers and most Puritans, identified the Antichrist with the Roman Catholic Church, or more particularly, the office of the papacy. According to John Calvin, "Daniel [Dan 9:27] and Paul [II Thess. 2:4] foretold that Antichrist would sit in the Temple of God. With us, it is the Roman pontiff we make the leader and standard bearer of that wicked and abominable kingdom."[3]

Just so you know, I don't agree with those who would identify the Beast with the Roman Catholic Church. Most evangelicals today, especially those who embrace the futurist perspective on Revelation, refer to the Beast as the eschatological or end-time Antichrist, a literal human being who will deceive the world and persecute the church during the closing few years preceding the second advent of Jesus. Consider this statement by Dave Hunt:

> "Somewhere, at this very moment, on planet Earth, the antichrist is almost certainly alive – biding his time, awaiting his cue. Banal sensationalism? Far from it! That likelihood is based upon a sober evaluation of current events in relation to Bible prophecy. Already a mature man, he is probably active in politics, perhaps even an admired world leader whose name is almost daily on everyone's lips."[4]

If, on the other hand, Revelation 13 and 17 are describing the oppressive reign of the "Beast" and "false prophet" (whoever or whatever they may be) throughout the course of the inter-advent age, these views will need to be re-examined to determine if they have biblical support.

The Sea Beast

It would appear that Revelation 13:1-18 is temporally parallel with Revelation 12:6, 13-17 and explains in more detail the

---

3. John Calvin, *Institutes of the Christian Religion*, edited by John T. McNeill (Philadelphia: The Westminster Press, 1975), Book IV:2:12.

4. Dave Hunt, *Global Peace and the Rise of Antichrist* (Eugene: Harvest House, 1990), 5.

precise nature and extent of the Dragon's (Satan's) persecution of the people of God. In fact, Revelation 13 describes the earthly governmental, political, economic, as well as individual, powers of the earth through whom Satan works. Though Satan has been defeated (12:7-12), he can still oppress the saints (12:12). And the primary way in which he exerts this nefarious influence and wages war against the seed of the woman (Rev. 12:17) is through the activities and oppression of the Beast. Here John narrates his vision of the Dragon standing on the seashore, calling forth his agents through whom he will carry out his persecution of the people of God. The "war" which the Dragon is said to wage with the church (Rev. 12:17) is actually undertaken by his servants as portrayed in Chapter 13. Note carefully how this is stated in verse 2b: "And to it [that is, to the Beast rising out of the sea] the dragon [Satan] gave his power and his throne and great authority" (Rev. 13:2b).

In Daniel 7 the first sea-beast is like a lion, the second resembled a bear, and the third was like a leopard. These three are all now found in the one sea-beast of Revelation 13:2 who is said to be "like a leopard; its feet were like a bear's, and its mouth was like a lion's mouth." Likewise, the fourth sea-beast in Daniel 7 is said to have ten horns, as is also the case with the sea-beast in Revelation 13. In other words, as noted earlier, *whereas the four beasts of Daniel 7 represent four historically successive world empires, the sea-beast of Revelation 13 is John's creative composite of them all.* All the evil characteristics of those four kingdoms are now embodied in the one sea-beast who becomes Satan's principal agent in persecuting the people of God. The point would seem to be that the "Beast" of Revelation 13 is primarily corporate in nature, rather than personal.

The "Dragon" (i.e., Satan) of Revelation 12:3 is said to have "seven heads and ten horns, and on his heads seven diadems." Here in Revelation 13:1 the Beast who is beckoned from the sea to do the Dragon's work likewise has seven heads and ten horns, but he now has ten (rather than seven) diadems that appear on his horns (rather than on his heads). Nevertheless, it is explicitly stated that the sea-beast receives "his power and his throne and great authority" from the Dragon of Revelation 12. The "crowns" or "diadems" point to the Beast's false claim of sovereignty, royalty, and authority, in opposition to the true King, Jesus, who also wears "many diadems" (19:12,16). The "blasphemous names" on his seven heads probably represent the Beast's arrogant claims to divinity/deity.

Because of the figurative use of numbers in Revelation, it is unlikely that "seven" and "ten" are to be identified literally and only with a specific series of rulers or kingdoms, whether in the first century or thereafter. More likely is the suggestion that both "seven" and "ten" emphasize "the completeness of oppressive power and its worldwide effect" as well as "the all-encompassing span of time during which these powers hold sway."[5]

The Johannine Epistles

Interestingly, the only place in the New Testament where the word "antichrist" appears is in the Johannine Epistles (1, 2, 3 John), not in Revelation. Nowhere in Revelation is the "beast" ever called "antichrist". In his first epistle John emphatically states that we may know this is (the) last hour because of the existence and activity of many antichrists. He says: "Children, it is the last hour; and as you have heard that antichrist is coming, so now many antichrists have come. Therefore, we know that it is the last hour" (2:18). Note well that the entire period between the first and second comings of Jesus = the "last days".[6]

Later, in 1 John 2:22, he writes: "Who is the liar but he who denies that Jesus is the Christ? This is the antichrist, he who denies the Father and the Son." The spirit of the antichrist, says John, is found in anyone who denies that Jesus is God come in the flesh (1 John 4:3). Again, in 2 John 7, he writes: "For many deceivers have gone out into the world, those who do not confess the coming of Jesus Christ in the flesh. Such a one is the deceiver and the antichrist." Thus, for John, "antichrist" is:

---

5. Beale, *Revelation*, 684, 686.
6. See Acts 2:17; 2 Timothy 3:1; Hebrews 1:2; and 1 Peter 1:20 (cf.1 Corinthians 10:11).

- Anyone "who denies that Jesus is the Christ" (1 John 2:22).
- Anyone "who denies the Father and the Son" (1 John 2:22).
- "Every spirit that does not confess Jesus" (1 John 4:3).
- "Those who do not confess the coming of Jesus Christ in the flesh" (2 John 7).

The term "antichrist" is a combination of *anti* (against or instead of) and *christos* (Messiah, Christ). It is ambiguous whether the Antichrist is merely one (or anyone) who opposes Christ as his adversary or enemy, or is also a specific person who seeks to take his place. Most have believed that antichrist is a lying pretender who portrays himself as Christ; he is a counterfeit or diabolical parody of Christ himself (see 2 Thess. 2:3-12).

Although John's readers have been told that antichrist's appearance is yet future, "even now" many antichrists have already come. Paul wrote in 2 Thessalonians 2:7 that "the mystery of lawlessness is already at work." In 1 John 4:3 John points out that the spirit of antichrist is "now" "already" at work in the world. Most believe that what John means in 1 John 2:18 is that the "many antichrists" (those who in the first century were denying the incarnation of Jesus) are forerunners of the one still to come. Because they proclaim the same heresies he/it will proclaim, and oppose Christ now as he/it will oppose him then, they are rightly called antichrists (especially in view of their denial of Christ in 1 John 2:22-23).

The antichrists of 1 John 2:18 are the false teachers against whom the epistle is directed. In 1 John 2:19 John indicates that at one time they were "members" of the community which professed faith in Christ. They were actively involved in the ministry of the church and until the moment of separation were hardly distinguishable from the rest of the Christian society. The essence of antichrist, the height of heresy and the lie "par excellence" is the denial that Jesus is the Christ (1 John 2:22).

Some have argued that John's point is that there is no other "antichrist" than the "one" even then operative in his day or the "one" who takes up and perpetuates this heresy in subsequent history. In other words, anyone in general can be "antichrist", if he or she espouses this heresy, but no one in particular, whether in the first or the twenty-first centuries, is the antichrist as if there were only one to whom the others look forward. In other words, the "antichrist" who his readers were told was yet to come is "now" with them in the form of anyone who espouses the heretical denial of the incarnation of the Son of God. But I'm not persuaded by this. I believe that the "spirit" of the future Antichrist was already present in the first century among those who denied that Jesus was God come in the flesh. That same "spirit" of Antichrist exists today, but that does not mean there will not be a final, personal embodiment in one particular individual.

The question still remains: Is the Beast of Revelation the same as the Antichrist of 1 and 2 John?

The Forty-two Months of the Beast's Authority

The identity of the Beast in Revelation 13 is revealed to some degree by the reference to the duration of its (his?) reign. According to 13:5-8, the Beast makes war with the saints for a period of forty-two months, the same length of time, according to Revelation 11:2, that the "holy city" [i.e., the people of God] is trampled upon. Therefore, if the period three and a half years = forty-two months = twelve hundred and sixty days = time, times, half a time, all refer to the entirety of the present inter-advent age, the Beast cannot be merely an individual living at the end of human history. Rather, the Beast would be a symbol for the system of Satanically inspired evil, and thus opposition to the kingdom of God, that throughout history has manifested itself in a variety of forms, whether political, economic, military, social, philosophical, or religious. Alan Johnson provides this excellent explanation. The Beast

> "is not to be identified in its description with any one historical form of its expression or with any one institutional aspect of its manifestation. In other words, the beast may appear now as Sodom, Egypt, Rome, or even Jerusalem and may manifest itself

as a political power, an economic power, a religious power, or a heresy (1 John 2:18,22; 4:3) .... This interpretation does not exclude the possibility that there will be a final climactic appearance of the beast in history in a person; in a political, religious, or economic system; or in a final totalitarian culture combining all these. The point is that the beast cannot be limited to either the past or the future."[7]

The "blasphemous names" on the Beast's heads (Rev. 13:1) indicate that he/it challenges the supremacy and majesty of God by denying and defying the first commandment: "You shall have no other gods before me" (Ex. 20:3). Therefore, says Johnson,

> "whatever person or system – whether political, social, economic, or religious – cooperates with Satan by exalting itself against God's sovereignty and by setting itself up to destroy the followers of Jesus, or entices them to become followers of Satan through deception, idolatry, blasphemy, and spiritual adultery, embodies the beast of Revelation 13. The description John gives of the beast from the sea does not describe a mere human political entity such as Rome. Rather, it describes in archetypal language the hideous, Satan-backed system of deception and idolatry that may at any time express itself in human systems of various kinds, such as Rome. Yet at the same time John also seems to be saying that this blasphemous, blaspheming, and blasphemy-producing reality will have a final, intense, and, for the saints, utterly devastating manifestation."[8]

The Beast, then, is a trans-cultural, trans-temporal symbol for all individual and collective, Satanically-inspired, opposition to Jesus and his people. It is anything and everything (whether a principle, a person, or a power) utilized by the enemy to deceive and destroy the influence and advance of the kingdom of God.

---

7. Alan Johnson, *Revelation* (Grand Rapids: Zondervan, 1996), 129.
8. Ibid.

The Beast's "mortal wound"

John sees the Beast with a wound on one of his heads. The word translated "wound" (*plēgē*) is used throughout Revelation (eleven times) for the "plagues" that God inflicts on an unbelieving world. In other words, the likelihood is that God is the one who strikes this blow in judgment against the Beast. Although we must not seek to identify or reduce the Beast to any one historical event, institution, or person, John seems to use the historical career of the Roman emperor Nero as a way to illustrate in graphic terms the character and agenda of this archenemy of the kingdom. Nero horribly persecuted the early church and most believe he was responsible for the martyrdom of both Peter and Paul. Nero committed suicide in the year 68, although some thought he never died and would soon return to take up once again his rule over Rome. Others believed he died but was raised from the dead.

Although Nero is nowhere explicitly mentioned in Revelation, many believe that John makes use of him and his story to craft his image of what the Beast is like. That is to say, John uses Nero because he was the first and most obvious and hideous example of the antichristian imperial power that threatened the people of God. The legend of Nero's return thus proved helpful to John because he could adapt it to serve his own portrayal of the conflict between the Beast and the church. Nero's own "death", "resurrection," and "return" provided a perfect canvas on which John could paint both the character and course of the Beast's attempt to rival God. In John's day that Beast was Rome. In subsequent centuries it is any and all individual and collective attempts to oppose the kingdom of God and his purposes in Christ.

Those who find in Revelation 13 the legend of Nero's return point to verse 3 as one particular historical manifestation of this death-wound/healing scenario. As I said, whereas Nero committed suicide in the year 68, some thought he never died while others believed he died but was raised from the dead. It may have appeared that the Beast (i.e., Rome) was slain with Nero's death, since it brought a dramatic decrease in the persecution of Christians.

However, the Emperor Vespasian soon solidified the empire once again, so that the Roman Beast appeared to have fully recovered. Thus, whereas we read in 13:3 that only one of the Beast's heads was wounded, we read in 13:12, 14 that it is the Beast itself that recovers from the wound.

Of great importance is the way John describes the Beast in terms that echo the person and work of Christ. In other words, for John *the Beast is an imitation or satanic parody of Jesus Christ*. For example, in Revelation 13:3 the phrase "seemed to have a mortal wound" should probably be translated "as though slain unto death." This is almost the precise language used in Revelation 5:6 to describe Jesus, the Lamb of God. "It is clearly intended to create a parallel between Christ's death and resurrection, on the one hand, and the beast's mortal wound and its healing, on the other."[9] This also may suggest that the "wound" or "plague" suffered by the Beast was inflicted by Jesus through the latter's death and resurrection. It appeared as though the wound was a fatal one. In one sense, it really was. The devil suffered a spiritually fatal blow at Calvary. Despite defeat, however, the devil and his forces, as manifest in and through the "Beast", continue to exist. The imagery of a "fatal" blow followed by continued life ("its mortal wound was healed") may well point to what we see in Revelation 12:7-12. There Satan is defeated. He loses his legal grounds for accusing the saints. His moral authority over them is gone. Yet he continues to thrive on earth and to persecute, and oftentimes kill, the people of God. It is this continuing presence of Satan, in and through the Beast, in spite of his apparent defeat at Calvary, which amazes the unbelieving world and wins their allegiance and worship.

There is yet another parallel between the Beast and the Lamb in Revelation 13:14. There John says the Beast "yet lived" and uses a verb (*ezēsen*) that is found in Revelation 2:8 with reference to the resurrection of Jesus (cf. 1:18). Note also that the universal worship of the Beast (13:4, 8) following its "death and resurrection", parallels the universal worship of the Lamb (5:8-14) following his

---

9. Bauckham, *The Climax of Prophecy*, 432.

death and resurrection! In 13:2 we read that the dragon (Satan) gives the Beast his power, throne, and authority. This parallels the Father's gift to the Lamb of authority and a place on his throne (2:28; 3:21). We should also note that both Jesus and the Beast have swords (13:19; 20:4), both have followers who have their names written on their foreheads (see 13:16-14:1), and both have horns (5:6; 13:1, 11).

It would seem, then, that the Beast is primarily Satan himself "as he repeatedly works through his chosen agents throughout history [Nero certainly being one]. Therefore, whenever any major opponent of God reaches his demise, it appears as if the beast has been defeated, yet he will arise again in some other form, until the end of history. Such revivals make it appear as if Christ's defeat of the devil was not very decisive. But such revivals are under the ultimate hand of God, who 'gives authority.'"[10]

Worship of the Beast

Revelation 13:4 refers to the devotion of the unbelieving world to anything and anyone other than Jesus. The power and influence of the Beast, in whatever form it manifests itself, is grounds for their declaration concerning what they perceive to be the Beast's incomparable authority: "Who is like the beast, and who can fight against it?" Indeed, this is the precise terminology found throughout the Old Testament that is applied to YHWH.[11]

The Beast's Persecution of the People of God

Verses 5-10 simply portray yet again what we see throughout Revelation: the Beast's (Satan's) blasphemy of God and persecution of his people throughout the present church age. The statement "to make war" (v. 7) doesn't necessarily mean that the Beast organizes literal armed conflict with the church but rather has in view the Beast's hatred of the church and his/its efforts to undermine

---

10. Beale, *Revelation*, 691.
11. See Exodus 8:10; 15:11; Deuteronomy 3:24; Isaiah 40:18, 25; 44:7; 46:5; Psalms 35:10; 71:19; 86:8; 89:8; 113:5; and Micah 7:18.

everything the church does and believes. Thus, when John says the Beast will "conquer" the saints he doesn't mean the people of God lose their faith in Christ but that many of them suffer martyrdom at the hands of the Beast and his cohorts.

The mistake of dispensational interpreters of Revelation is to project these events into a future "tribulation" period unrelated to the situation, circumstances, and practical needs of all those believers resident in the late first century in the seven churches of Asia Minor. Whatever Revelation 13:1-10 means, it applies to the people of John's day to whom the book was written. Confirmation of this is found in verse 9, where we find the familiar exhortation, "If anyone has an ear, let him hear." The only other place this exhortation appears is at the conclusion of each of the seven letters in Revelation 2 and 3. Thus, verses 9-10 describe the appropriate response of Christians to the deception and persecution portrayed in verses 1-8. Revelation 13:10 is a paraphrase that combines Jeremiah 15:2 and 43:11. John's point is that believers are not to offer physical or violent resistance to their persecutors but are to faithfully submit to whatever destiny awaits them as they persevere in their trust in Jesus.

The People of God and the Lamb's Book of Life

There are two ways of translating Revelation 13:8, both of which are grammatically possible: (1) "whose name has not been written before the foundation of the world in the book of life of the Lamb who was slain" (ESV); or, (2) "whose name has not been written in the book of life of the Lamb who has been slain from the foundation of the world."

The almost parallel statement in 17:8 would indicate that (1) is correct. Also, whereas it can certainly be said that the Lamb of God was "foreknown before the foundation of the world" (1 Pet. 1:20) and that he was "delivered up [to die] by the predetermined plan and foreknowledge of God" (Acts 2:23), what can it possibly mean theologically to say that the Lamb of God was "slain from the foundation of the world"? The point of the text is that the people who worship the beast do so because their names have not been written in the book of life. That is why they are deceived by the Beast.

In sum, what we see here in verse 8 is the declaration that whoever does not worship Jesus Christ as God is guilty of idolatry. Anytime anyone worships or gives their life, energy, and devotion to themselves or to money or to political power or to military strength or to educational achievements or to any philosophy or religion or to any individual leader anywhere in the world that does not acknowledge Jesus Christ as Lord and Savior is guilty of worshiping the Beast.

Chapter Twenty-Six

666

(Revelation 13:11-18)

In his final two letters written not long before he was beheaded in Rome under orders from the Emperor Nero, the Apostle Paul was clearly energized and concerned about the emergence of false teaching that he obviously believed would pose a great threat to the health and well-being of the church. In 1 Timothy 4:1 he wrote: "Now the Spirit expressly says that in later times some will depart from the faith by devoting themselves to deceitful spirits and teachings of demons." Later he exhorted his young protégé, Timothy, to keep a close watch on himself and especially "on the teaching" of biblical truth (1 Tim. 4:16).

In his final letter, written perhaps only days before his execution, he again said to Timothy: "Follow the pattern of sound words that you have heard from me, in the faith and love that are in Christ Jesus. By the Holy Spirit who dwells within us, guard the good deposit entrusted to you" (2 Tim. 1:13-14). He again warned Timothy that "the time is coming when people will not endure sound teaching" but "will turn away from listening to the truth and wander off into myths" (2 Tim. 4:3-4). And it was the invasive and influential presence of false teachers that prompted Jude to say in his short epistle that we should "contend for the faith that was once for all delivered to the saints" (Jude 3).

Let me be as clear and straightforward as I can: *false teaching, deceptive doctrines, distortions of biblical truth are perhaps the single greatest threat to the health and flourishing of the church in this present age.* If you ask me for explicit biblical support for this notion, we need go no further than what we read here in Revelation 13:11-18.

The So-Called "False Prophet"

We read in verse 11 that John saw yet another beast, this one arising from the earth (cf. Daniel 7:17). Like the first beast it too is a demonic parody of Jesus, for it has two horns "like a lamb" (v. 11b). Perhaps it has "two" horns instead of seven in order to mimic the two witnesses, the two lampstands, and the two olive trees of Revelation 11:3-4. There have been numerous suggestions as to the identity of this "earth beast".

Some argue that this refers to the Jewish religious system of the first century that conspired with the Roman state to suppress and persecute the early church. Others point to the Roman imperial priesthood that sought to enforce worship of Caesar as god. Many of the Protestant Reformers and Puritans believed this is descriptive of the priesthood of the Roman Catholic Church or perhaps even the Pope himself. Most dispensationalists believe the "false prophet" is a literal individual living and working in conjunction with the Antichrist at the end of the age.

But I'm persuaded that John is describing, once again in highly figurative language, the presence and influence of false teachers, particularly false prophets, throughout the course of church history (see especially Matthew 7:15-23). This beast is later called "the false prophet" (16:13; 19:20; 20:10) and together with the Dragon (Satan) and the sea-beast forms the unholy trinity of the abyss. Thus, there is a sense in which even as the Devil seeks to imitate and take the place of God the Father, and the Beast imitates and seeks to usurp the role of God the Son, so the earth Beast or the False Prophet claims to fill the role of the Holy Spirit. Thus, we see in verse 12 that even as the true Holy Spirit empowers and sustains our worship of Jesus Christ, the False Prophet of Revelation 13 empowers and directs unbelievers to worship the Beast.

False prophets and deceivers were prevalent throughout the early church as evidenced by the consistent apostolic (Peter, Paul, John) warning concerning their influence (see especially 1 John 4:1-6). The aim of false prophets is to mislead the people of God by diverting their devotion from Jesus to idols. They aim to make the claims of the first Beast plausible and appealing and, as is especially the case in Revelation 2 and 3, to encourage ethical compromise with the culture's idolatrous and blasphemous institutions (cf. the Nicolaitans, the false apostles, Jezebel, etc. in Revelation 2–3). Thus the "false prophet" or land-beast stands in immediate opposition to the true prophets of Christ symbolized by the two witnesses in Revelation 11. It is clearly the purpose of the false religious systems of the world to seduce people into idolatry, into worshiping and devoting their lives to anything or anyone other than Jesus Christ. That is the point of John in saying what he does in verse 12.

Idolatry!

So what does it mean when John says in verse 13 that the so-called "false prophet," this beast from the earth, "performs great signs, even making fire come down from heaven" and again in verses 14-15 says that he even enables the image of the beast to speak? Clearly, this (these) False Prophet (prophets) tries to mimic the ministries of both Moses and Elijah. As you will recall, it was Elijah who called down fire from heaven to destroy the prophets of Baal. Even in Exodus (7:11) Pharaoh's court magicians, with their secret arts, performed many of the same "great signs" as did Moses (see also Matthew 7:22; 2 Thessalonians 2:9).

Jesus warned that "false christs and false prophets will arise and perform signs and wonders, to lead astray, if possible, the elect" (Mark 13:22). We know from numerous sources that priests of some cults in John's day were experts in magical arts and sleight of hand and were able to make it appear as if statues could talk and seemingly could produce thunder and lightning. Of course, we must not forget that most of what they do is energized by demonic spirits. The Apostle Paul spoke of the coming "lawless one" as someone who by "the activity of Satan" would perform false signs and wonders (2 Thess. 2:9).

Verses 13-15 describe vividly and in highly figurative terms the idolatrous aims of the false prophet. The picture is clearly drawn from Daniel 3 and the command that all should worship the image of Nebuchadnezzar. Perhaps also the command to engage in idolatrous worship of the Beast alludes in part to the pressure placed on the populace and the churches in Asia Minor to give homage to the image of Caesar as god. To say that "it was allowed to give breath" to the image of the Beast "is a metaphorical way of affirming that the second beast was persuasive in demonstrating that the image of the first beast (e.g., of Caesar) represented the true deity."[1]

With the story of Daniel's three friends still in mind, John portrays Christians of his day as being pressured by this latter-day Babylon (Rome) to worship the image of Caesar, i.e., the state (as inspired and energized by the dragon, from whom the state/beast receives its authority and power). Whereas the immediate idea in John's mind may well be the attempts by the imperial priesthood to seduce the people of God into worshiping the image of a Roman ruler, Johnson reminds us that "the reality described is much larger and far more trans-historical than the mere worship of a bust of Caesar."[2] Using the well-known story of Nebuchadnezzar, "John describes the world-wide system of idolatry represented by the first beast and the false prophet(s) who promotes it. John describes this reality as a blasphemous and idolatrous system that produces a breach of the first two commandments (Ex. 20:3-5)."[3]

---

1. Beale, *Revelation,* 711.
2. Alan Johnson, *Revelation,* 135.
3. Ibid.

The "Mark" of the Beast

I will draw attention one more time to an issue that continues to inflame debate concerning the end times and contributes greatly to the overall hysteria that serves only to discredit the Christian community in the eyes of the world. I have in mind the belief by many that the "mark" of the Beast is a literal tattoo, or perhaps a chip implant, or imprint of sorts, or perhaps some other physiological branding by which his/its followers are visually identified. The popular notion among many Christians (usually of the dispensational, futurist school of interpretation) is that some such designation, whether "the name of the beast" or "the number [666] of its name" (Rev. 13:17) will be forcibly imposed on people living in the final few years prior to the coming of Christ. If one wishes to buy or sell and thus survive in the days ahead, he/she must submit to this means of identification.

Needless to say, this interpretation is entirely based on a futurist reading of Revelation, such that what John describes pertains largely, if not solely, to that last generation of humanity alive on the earth just preceding the second coming of Christ. If, on the other hand, as I have argued, the book of Revelation largely portrays events that occur throughout the entire course of church history, this view is seriously undermined. As I argued earlier in our study of Revelation 7, *we should understand the "mark" of the Beast on the right hand or forehead of his/its followers to be a Satanic parody (a religious rip-off, so to speak) of the "seal" that is placed on the foreheads of God's people (Rev. 7:3-8; 14:1; cf. 22:4).*

Many believe the reference to receiving a "mark" (*charagma*; found in 13:16, 17; 14:9, 11; 16:2; 19:20; 20:4) is an allusion to the ancient practice of branding or tattooing. David Aune[4] has documented several purposes for the latter:

- Barbarian tribes in antiquity practiced tattooing as a means of tribal identification.

---

4. Aune, *Revelation,* 2:457-59.

- The Greeks used tattoos primarily as a way to punish both slaves and criminals. As such, it was a mark of disgrace and degradation, thus accounting for the methods of removal discussed in ancient medical literature.
- Tattooing could also be a mark of ownership, similar to the branding of cattle.
- In a number of ancient religions, tattooing indicated dedication and loyalty to a pagan deity.

That being said, I do not believe that the so-called "mark of the Beast" is a literal, physical mark on the bodies of unbelievers, either on their forehead or their right hand. All through Revelation we see Satan making every effort to copy whatever God does. So, for example, the three persons of the Holy Trinity, Father, Son, and Holy Spirit, find their evil counterpart in Satan, the Beast, and the False Prophet. Just as Jesus died and rose again from the dead, the Beast is portrayed as dying and rising to life again.

My point is simply that *the so-called "mark" of the Beast that unbelievers receive on their forehead or their right hand is a demonic rip-off, a depraved parody, a counterfeit imitation of the "mark" that believers receive on their foreheads.* Look at the texts where the people of God are "sealed" on their foreheads:

> "Do not harm the earth or the sea or the trees, until we have sealed the servants of our God on their foreheads" (Rev. 7:3).

> "They were told not to harm the grass of the earth or any green plant or any tree, but only those people who do not have the seal of God on their foreheads" (Rev. 9:4).

> "Then I looked, and behold, on Mount Zion, stood the Lamb, and with him 144,000 who had his name and his Father's name written on their foreheads" (Rev. 14:1).

> "They will see his face, and his name will be on their foreheads" (Rev. 22:4).

No one that I know of believes that all Christians will literally and physically have the name of Jesus Christ and the name of the Father tattooed on their foreheads. This is simply a way of describing the fact that those who are born again and redeemed by the blood of Christ belong to him and to his Father and are preserved in faith by the indwelling Holy Spirit.

So when we read that the False Prophet causes everyone who isn't a Christian to have the mark of the Beast written on his/her forehead we are to understand this as a sign that they belong to the Beast and are loyal to him. *This "mark" on their foreheads or on their right hand is simply Satan's way of mimicking the seal of God that is on the foreheads of God's people.* If you have the name of Jesus and God the Father written on your forehead it simply means they own you, you belong to them, you are loyal to the Lord God Almighty. But if you have "the name of the beast" (Rev. 13:17) written on your forehead it signifies that he owns you, you belong to him, you are loyal to the Antichrist. My point is that if you don't argue that the name of Jesus and God the Father is literally tattooed on the foreheads of Christians you have no reason to argue that the name of the Antichrist (or his number, 666) is literally tattooed on the foreheads of non-Christians.

Some have found the background for the "mark" of the beast in the Jewish practice of wearing *tephillim* or phylacteries. These were leather boxes containing Scripture passages (cf. Ex. 13:9, 16; Deut. 6:8; 11:18; Matt. 23:5) that were worn either on the left arm (facing the heart) or the forehead. The mark of the Beast, however, was to be placed on the right hand. Others have pointed out that the word "mark" was used of the emperor's seal on business contracts and the impress of the Roman ruler's head on coins. Perhaps, then, "the mark alludes to the state's political and economic 'stamp of approval,' given only to those who go along with its religious demands."[5]

Thus it seems quite clear that the "mark" of the beast on his followers is the demonic counterpart and parody of the "seal"

---

5. Beale, *Revelation*, 715.

that is placed on the foreheads of the people of God (see 7:3-8; 14:1; 22:4). "Just as the seal and the divine name on believers connote God's ownership and spiritual protection of them, so the mark and Satanic name signify those who belong to the devil and will undergo perdition."[6] Since the seal or name on the believer is obviously invisible, being symbolic of the indwelling presence of the Holy Spirit, it seems certain that *the mark of the Beast is likewise a symbolic way of describing the loyalty of his followers and his ownership of them.* If you're wondering why the seal on God's people and the mark on the non-Christian is placed on the forehead of each, it may be that the forehead points to one's ideological commitment and the hand to the practical outworking or manifestation of that commitment.

666

Two issues need to be addressed as a prelude to our study of the mark of the Beast. First, we need to be familiar with the legend of Nero's return, which was circulating in more than one form when John wrote his book. Second, we need to examine the meaning of the number 666 and its relation to the Beast. That these two matters are closely intertwined will become evident as we proceed.

The Legend of Nero's Return[7]

Nero was the great, great grandson of Caesar Augustus. He was born on December 15, A.D. 37. Following the death of Nero's father, his mother married her paternal uncle who subsequently adopted Nero at the age of twelve. In A.D. 53 he married Octavia, daughter

---

6. Ibid., 716.

7. The best treatment of Nero is found in Richard Bauckham, *The Climax of Prophecy: Studies on the Book of Revelation* (Edinburgh: T & T Clark, 1993), on which I have relied for the following portrayal. Two more recent, in-depth treatments of Nero are by Mary Beard, *Emperor of Rome: Ruling the Ancient Roman World* (New York: Liveright Publishing Corporation, 2023), and Tom Holland, *Pax: War and Peace in Rome's Golden Age* (New York: Basic Books, 2023).

of the emperor Claudius. The latter died on October 13, A.D. 54, leading to Nero's accession to the throne.

The first seven to eight years of Nero's reign were remarkably good and productive. Things began to change when in the year 62 he divorced Octavia (who had failed to bear him a child) and married Poppaea Sabina. In the early hours of June 19, A.D. 64, a devastating fire broke out around the Circus Maximus and spread north through the valley between the Palatine and the Esquiline. Unable to silence rumors that he himself had set the fire, Nero found a scapegoat in the emerging Christian community, which he persecuted with intense cruelty. It is generally believed that both Peter and Paul were martyred as a result of Nero's rage against the church. In addition to the numerous political murders for which he was responsible, Nero killed his own mother, bringing him the unwelcome title "The Matricide" (mother-killer). His dictatorial style of leadership, combined with his self-indulgent personality, provoked the opposition of the Roman senate and aristocracy, although he remained popular with the general population of Rome.

Suspicion was only intensified by Nero's love for the east and its cultural expressions. He toured Greece in 66–67 and was especially popular in Parthia. The Jewish War broke out during Nero's reign and he sent Vespasian to quell it (the latter's son, Titus, was responsible for the final destruction of both city and temple). Nero was declared a public enemy by the Senate in mid-68 and troops were sent to arrest him. On hearing this, he fled to the villa of his ex-slave where he committed suicide by thrusting a dagger into his throat.

As noted earlier, whereas the name "Nero" nowhere appears in Revelation, *John most likely would have seen in this historical figure the perfect prototypical embodiment of that anti-Christ, anti-Christian spirit which is characteristic of the entire church age.* I agree with Bauckham that "the impending confrontation between the beast and the followers of the Lamb would appear to John as an apocalyptic extension and intensification of the Neronian persecution."[8]

It may well be that the mysterious circumstances surrounding Nero's death gave rise to rumors that he was actually still alive and would soon return to seek revenge on his enemies. Several Nero impostors emerged. The first appeared one year after his death in July, 69. This one not only physically resembled Nero but was also, like the emperor, an accomplished musician. "He appeared in Greece, where he mustered some support, set sail for Syria, but was forced by a storm to put in at the island of Cythnos in the Cyclades, where he was captured and killed. His dead body was taken to Rome via Asia (Tacitus, Hist. 2.9)."[9] A second impostor by the name of Terentius Maximus, who also resembled Nero, appeared in the year 80. It is not known how he came to an end. At least one more pretender appeared during the reign of Domitian in 88–89 and must have been fresh in John's mind as he wrote Revelation.

The legend of Nero's return is first found in the Jewish Sibylline Oracles. One of the important features is how Nero is portrayed as identified with the Parthians whose armies he will lead in an invasion of the Roman west. He is also portrayed as the eschatological adversary of the people of God who will destroy both them and the holy city.

As I said earlier, in conjunction with our study of Revelation 13:3, *John has adapted the legend of Nero's return to paint his portrait of the oppressive career of the Beast.* Nero constituted the most obvious and ready-at-hand embodiment of that antichristian power which opposes and oppresses the people of God. Against the backdrop of Nero's "death, alleged resurrection, and return" John is able to portray the Beast's career of persistent persecution of the church. For the people of God in the first century, that "Beast" was the Roman imperial power. In subsequent centuries and in our own day it is seen in any and all attempts, whether by individuals, institutions, or movements, to thwart God's kingdom

---

8. Bauckham, *The Climax of Prophecy*, 412.
9. Ibid., 413.

in Christ. Whether or not this "Beast" is also to manifest itself at the end of the age in a single individual, popularly known as the Antichrist, is yet to be determined. That John used the Nero legend to paint his portrait of the Beast is also evident from the reference in Revelation 13:16-18 to the "mark" of the Beast or the "number" of his name: 666. To that we now turn.

The Mark of the Beast

The meaning of the number 666 has puzzled students of the Scriptures ever since John first wrote Revelation 13:8. There are essentially three schools of thought on the problem.

First is the Chronological View. Some have thought that the number refers to the duration of the life of the Beast or his kingdom. Very few, if any, hold this view today.

Second is the Historical View. According to this school of thought, the number is believed to refer to some historical individual, power, or kingdom. This is easily the most popular interpretation and is based on a practice in ancient times called Gematria (from the Greek *geomatria*, from which we derive our English word "geometry"). This practice, found in both pagan and Jewish circles, assigns a numerical value to each letter of the alphabet. For example, using the English alphabet, the first nine letters would stand for numbers 1 through 9 (A = 1; B = 2; C = 3; etc.), the next nine letters for numbers 10 through 90 (J = 10; K = 20; L = 30; etc.) and so on. If one wished to write the number "23", for example, it would appear as "KC" (K = 20 + C = 3). There is a well-known and oft-cited example from a bit of graffiti found in the city of Pompeii which reads: "I love the girl whose number is 545". Apparently, the initials of her name were phi = 500; mu = 40; epsilon = 5.

Third is the Symbolic View. Virtually all other numbers in the book of Revelation are figurative or symbolic of some spiritual or theological reality and give no indication that the calculations entailed by gematria are in view. *Thus, according to this view, the number refers to the Beast as the archetype man who falls short of perfection in every respect.* Triple sixes are merely a contrast with the divine sevens in Revelation and signify incompleteness and imperfection. 777 is the number of deity and 666 falls short in every digit. Again, "three sixes are a parody of the divine trinity of three sevens. That is, though the beast attempts to mimic God, Christ, and the prophetic Spirit of truth, he falls short of succeeding."[10] Thus, *the number does not identify the Beast, but describes him. It refers to his character. It isn't designed to tell us who he is but what he is like.*

Furthermore, if a particular historical individual were in view, why didn't John use the Greek *anēr/andros* instead of *anthrōpos/anthrōpon*? The former means "man" as over against woman, child, etc. The latter, however, is generic, i.e., it speaks of "man" as a class over against, say, animals or angels (see also Revelation 21:17 for the use of the generic "man's measure"/"angel's measure"). Also, if a particular historical person were in view, John could have made that explicit by saying a "certain" (*tinos*) man or "one" (*henos*) man. If this view is correct, we should translate: "for it is man's number." This stresses the character or quality of man as apart from Christ forever short of perfection, completely epitomized in the Beast.

Having Fun with Gematria

People have tried to identify the Beast of Revelation by some form of Gematria. Here are some examples.

The name of Jesus is said to be 888, the sum of the Greek letters of the name Jesus (Iesous). It has then been pointed out that since 777 stands for completeness or perfection, 888 stands for more than perfection (i.e., Jesus), and thus 666 stands for imperfection, which is Antichrist.

In case you were wondering, the numerical equivalent of my name, Charles Samuel Storms is 1303. None of the other variations work either: Sam Storms = 740; C. Samuel Storms = 1069; Dr. Storms = 684 (we're getting closer!), Pastor Sam = 662, and Pastor C. Sam = 665! Almost!

---

10. Beale, *Revelation*, 722.

If we use English letters, such that A = 100, B = 101, C = 102, etc., we come up with some interesting discoveries. Take for example Adolph Hitler: H = 107, I = 108, T = 119, L = 111, E = 104, R = 117. Add them up and you get 666! If A = 6, B = 12 (i.e., 6x2), C = 18 (i.e., 6x3), and so on, and you apply that to the name of [Henry] Kissinger, Secretary of State under President Richard Nixon, you also get 666.

Someone has pointed out that there are six letters in former President Reagan's first, middle, and last names (Ronald Wilson Reagan), hence 666! This same individual also points to the fact that when Reagan moved to Los Angeles the address of his home had to be changed from 666 to 668 St. Cloud Drive! I wonder, since Reagan and I share the same birthday (February 6), could I be the False Prophet?!

Craig Keener points out that if one adds up the potential Roman numerals in "Cute Purple Dinosaur" (counting "U" as "V", hence as 5), one ends up with 100 + 5 + 5 + 50 + 500 + 1 + 5, for a total of 666! Poor Barney! Others who have been singled out as potential candidates for Antichrist, even if their names did not add up to 666 include: Benito Mussolini, Anwar Sadat, Yasser Arafat, Ayatollah Khomeini, King Juan Carlos of Spain, Pope John Paul II, Saddam Hussein, Muammar Gaddafi, Mikhail Gorbachev, Jimmy Carter, and other U.S. Presidents!

When one uses Hebrew letters there is an interesting result. Nero's name in Greek (Neron Kaisar) yields 1005. But his name in Hebrew letters adds up to 666! It should also be noted that the Greek word for "beast" (*therion*), when transliterated into Hebrew letters, also adds up to 666.

Recall that in Revelation 13:18 John said, "Let him who has intelligence calculate the number of the beast (*tou theriou*), for it is the number of a man." It may be that John is telling us that the number of the word "beast" is also the number of a man. If so, says Bauckham, "the gematria does not merely assert that Nero is the beast: it demonstrates that he is. Nero's very name identifies him by its numerical value as the apocalyptic beast of Daniel's prophecy."[11]

Conclusion

If there is one lesson that we must learn from Revelation 13, it is the ever-present danger and threat of false teaching and the urgent need for Christians to be fully informed by God's Word. "But be on guard," said Jesus (Mark 13:23). Satan is ever seeking to devour and destroy us by sowing the seeds of heresy in our hearts. Stand firm, having "fastened on the belt of truth" (Eph. 6:14).

---

11. Bauckham, *The Climax of Prophecy*, 389.

Chapter Twenty-Seven

Must We Speak of Hell?

(Revelation 14:6-13)

Let me say this up front and get it out of the way. I really don't want to write on this text. It isn't because I don't understand it. I do. In fact, it is precisely because I understand what it is saying that makes me reluctant to write about it. Neither is my reluctance to address this topic because I don't believe it is true. I do believe it is true. I do believe that there is a place called hell and that people are going there.

My hesitation or reluctance is due to what I have seen repeatedly through the years whenever this text or others like it speak so definitively and inescapably about the reality of hell. What I've observed is that some are immediately offended to such a degree that they simply walk away from the Christian faith. I have a close friend whose son has abandoned Christianity because he cannot bring himself to believe that God would consign anyone to hell. This topic is also emotionally explosive. It's hard to read words like those in verses 9-11 and maintain one's composure. People hear these verses and they grimace and flinch and recoil and sometimes shut their ears so that they don't have to think about what is being said.

And then there are those whose reaction is one of distortion or denial. They perform every manner of exegetical gymnastics to jump over or around or in some way evade the implications of what is said. Others shake their heads in dismay and deny that whatever

I may say this text means it simply cannot mean. It must mean something else. Why? Because it is too emotionally disturbing to contemplate the fact that people we know and love will be among those who are "tormented with fire and sulfur" and who "have no rest, day or night" from the suffering that is here described.

So, you may be asking yourself: "Sam, how do you get past your gut reaction to a text like this? How do you bring yourself to embrace it as true and how do you get the consent of your own soul to write about it?" That's a good question. There are three short answers to it.

First, I have such unshakable and robust confidence in the inerrant truth of every word in this book, the Bible, that the matter is already settled before I even read the text. I believe, as the Apostle Paul said in 2 Timothy 3:16, that "all Scripture is breathed out by God and [is] profitable for teaching, for reproof, for correction, and for training in righteousness." Second, by God's grace I have come to understand the immeasurable magnitude and majesty of God's holiness and beauty and authority and the honor that is due to him from all of his creatures, including you and me. Third, by God's grace I have come to understand the immeasurable horror and ugliness and self-centeredness of humanity's sin and depravity and wickedness.

So I can honestly say that to the degree that you and I struggle with the concept of hell and eternal punishment is the degree to which we don't understand God's holiness and honor, on the one hand, or the horror and depravity of mankind's sin, on the other. In other words, if hell strikes you as unreasonable or unfair or disproportionate, it can only be due to the fact that either you don't believe this book is inspired and true, or you don't believe that God is infinitely holy and just, or you don't believe that mankind is morally depraved and has committed cosmic treason and is thus deserving of eternal condemnation.

Myths about hell

Perhaps it would help if I mentioned some of the myths in our culture about the nature and reality of hell.

Myth #1. Hell is a place where we are united with our unbelieving friends and drink beer all the time in an endless party. The fact is that hell is a place of utter isolation, loneliness, and deprivation.

Myth #2. Hell is the place where Satan and his demons exercise their authority to rule and reign. The fact is that hell is the place where Satan and his demons suffer eternal punishment. Satan and his demons are inmates in hell, not its warden or guards.

Myth #3. Directly related to the previous myth, there is the notion among many that in hell Satan and his demons torment human beings who also are there. No. There is not one text in the Bible that suggests Satan and his demons afflict or torment human beings. They themselves, instead, are the object of God's punishment.

Myth #4. There are people in hell crying out for mercy who want to reconcile with God. Nothing in Scripture indicates this is so. Instead, those in hell are eternally defiant of God and hate him all the more with each passing moment.

Myth #5. There are people in hell who don't deserve to be there. Nothing could be farther from the truth. God's justice is impeccable and he never consigns anyone to punishment in hell who does not fully deserve to suffer there.

Myth #6. There are people in hell who wanted to go to heaven while they were still alive, but God wouldn't let them. That is utterly false. Jesus himself made this clear when he said, "I am the bread of life; whoever comes to me shall not hunger, and whoever believes in me shall never thirst.... whoever comes to me I will never cast out.... For this is the will of my Father, that everyone who looks on the Son and believes in him should have eternal life, and I will raise him up on the last day" (John 6:35, 37b, 40).

Myth #7. There are people in hell who will eventually be released and granted entrance into heaven. As much as we might wish this were true, it isn't. The Bible does not teach the doctrine of universalism, that is, the idea that everyone will eventually be saved and given eternal life in the new heaven and new earth.

Myth #8 - In hell people will finally be rid of God and have no experience of him. That is not true. It is true they will have no experience of God's loving and gracious presence, but they will most assuredly experience his presence in justice and wrath. In fact, we read here in Revelation 14:10 that they will be tormented "in the presence of the Lamb," that is, in the presence of Jesus Christ. As John Piper once said, verse 14 is not saying that "those in hell have the privilege of seeing what they enjoy, but that they have the remorse of seeing what they rejected."

Just a few more introductory comments are in order. There simply is no way around the truth of God's wrath against sin. There are, in fact, more than six hundred references to God's wrath in Scripture. And when it is described, there is no hesitation or embarrassment or the nervous shuffling of feet that we so often witness today. Furthermore, as someone has said, "In the Bible, God's wrath is not the problem but the solution.... [It is] not the offensive doctrine needing defense but the long-awaited vindication of justice after" the suffering endured by God's people at the hands of the followers of the Beast.

Context

Insofar as the majority of Chapters 12 and 13 focused on the persecution of believers by the Dragon (Satan) and his earthly agents, the sea-beast and the land-beast, it is understandable that Chapter 14, together with 15:2-4, should describe the reward of the persecuted faithful and the final punishment of their enemies. In other words, "chapter 14 briefly answers two pressing questions: What becomes of those who refuse to receive the mark of the beast and are killed (vv. 1-5)? [And] What happens to the beast and his servants (vv. 6-20)?"[1]

The Eternal Gospel of God

Is the "gospel" preached by this angel designed to lead to conversion? Or is it simply the declaration of final judgment on those who have rejected it? Those who favor the latter point to what follows: verses 8-11 proceed to describe the eternal judgment of unbelievers. They also point to the similarity between this angel and his gospel, on

---

1. Alan Johnson, *Revelation*, 141.

the one hand, and the messenger of the three woes in 8:13. Both speak "with a loud voice" (8:13; 14:7) while "flying in mid-heaven" (8:13; 14:6). Both also address unbelieving earth-dwellers (8:13; 14:6). Thus, many conclude that the command to "fear" God, "give him glory," and "worship" is a compulsory edict for hostile humanity, signifying that they will be compelled to acknowledge the reality of who God is in Jesus (cf. Phil. 2:9-11). But that doesn't mean they are saved.

On the other hand, these verses are similar to Revelation 11:13 where we concluded that the possibility of conversion is in view. However, even if the angel is holding out one final opportunity to repent and be saved, the subsequent context would seem to indicate it goes unheeded. This "gospel" is referred to as "eternal" because it is the fulfillment of God's saving purposes for mankind from the foundation of the world, but also because the consequences of either believing it or rejecting it are eternal (heaven or hell).

The Fall of Babylon

The repetition of the verb "fallen" (v. 8) is probably intended for emphasis, to highlight the certainty of Babylon's judgment. But who or what is "Babylon"? In its original concrete historical manifestation, Babylon was a city, then an empire under which Israel lived in captivity (see Gen. 10:1–11:9; Isa. 13-14; Jer. 50-51; Zech. 5:5-11). Jeremiah spoke of ancient Babylon in graphic terms: "Babylon was a golden cup in the LORD's hand, making all the earth drunken; the nations drank of her wine; therefore the nations went mad" (Jer. 51:7).

Just as ancient Babylon destroyed the temple and oppressed God's people, so also Rome destroyed the temple in Jerusalem (A.D. 70) and continued to oppress the people. Thus, in Revelation, all wicked world systems, including Rome, were called by the symbolic name "Babylon the Great". Babylon is the symbol of human civilization with all its pomp and circumstance organized in opposition to God. It is the sum total of pagan culture: social, intellectual, commercial, political, and religious. It is the essence of evil, the "Mecca", if you will, of heathenism, the symbol for collective rebellion against God in any and every form. It is the universal or world system of unbelief, idolatry, and apostasy that opposes and persecutes the people of God.

Although the word translated "sexual immorality" is the Greek term *porneia*, in view of what we read in Revelation 18 the particular kind of immorality in verse 8 may well be commercial in nature (see 18:3, 9; cf. Isaiah 23:15-18). "Babylon's promise of prosperous earthly welfare for its willing subjects is an intoxication that the majority of the world's inhabitants also want to imbibe."[2]

Eternal Punishment and the Nature of Hell

This third angel also announces judgment. The verbs translated "worships" and "receives" are both in the present tense, perhaps pointing to a continual, obstinate, and thus final allegiance to the Beast, in spite of the warnings issued in verses 6-8. Several things should be noted.

First, those who choose to "drink the wine of the passion of her [Babylon's] sexual immorality" (v. 8) will, appropriately, be forced to "drink the wine of God's wrath" (v. 10; i.e., the wine which is his wrath). The image of pouring intoxicating wine from a cup often points to the experience of divine wrath and the suffering it inevitably brings.[3]

The intoxicating effect of drinking Babylon's wine is only temporary; it will wear off. But the effect of drinking the wine of God's wrath is eternal. The phrase "poured full strength" in verse 10 is literally, "mixed unmixed." There are two options here. It may mean that, contrary to normal practice, the wine that is prepared ("mixed") will not in any way be diluted with water (hence, "unmixed"). That is, God's wrath is utterly undiluted, being poured out in full strength, unmitigated, unmixed with mercy or longsuffering. Or John may be alluding to Psalm 75:8 where wine is mixed with spices to increase its intensity (cf. Jer. 31:2).

---

2. Beale, *Revelation*, 756.
3. See Psalms 60:3; 75:8; Isaiah 51:17, 21-23; 63:6; Jeremiah 25:15-18; 51:17; Lamentations 4:21; Ezekiel 23:31-33; Habakkuk 2:16; Zechariah 12:2.

Thus "mixed" would refer to the addition of spices to increase the potency of the wine and "unmixed" to the fact that it is not diluted with water. On either reading, God's wrath is penal and in no way remedial. Longsuffering and patience have given way to the consummation of a promised day of reckoning.

Second, they will be "tormented with fire and sulfur" (v. 10b). Punishment with "fire and sulfur" is also found in Genesis 19:24 (Sodom and Gomorrah); Psalm 11:6; Isaiah 30:33; and Job 18:15. The combination of fire and sulfur (or brimstone) as a means of torment occurs four times in Revelation (14:10; 19:20; 20:10; 21:8). Sulfur or brimstone was a type of asphalt found in volcanic deposits that produced extreme heat and a noxious smell. However, the nature of the "torment" is primarily spiritual and psychological (cf. Revelation 9:5-6; 18:7, 10, 15; 20:10), and thus the "fire and sulfur" are probably figurative. In other words, as literal fire and sulfur cause physical pain and extreme discomfort to the body, so the infliction of divine judgment on unbelievers will cause spiritual or psychological anguish to their souls. But could there also be a "physical" dimension to eternal punishment (see especially John 5:28-29)?

Third, public exposure is an added insult to the torment of the wicked, for we read that their punishment is in the presence of the holy angels and the Lamb (cf. Revelation 19:1-10). One can't help but wonder: What will the angels and Jesus be thinking and feeling at that time?

The Duration of Hell

That is the nature of hell. But the question of its duration is where we enter into controversy.

First, the "smoke" of their torment, i.e., the smoke of the fire and sulfur (v. 10) "goes up forever and ever" (v. 11; see Isaiah 34:9-10). It is almost as if there is a smoldering testimony to the consequences of sin and the justice of God's wrath. The duration of this phenomenon is said to be "forever and ever" or, more literally, "unto the ages of the ages". This terminology occurs thirteen times in Revelation: three times with reference to the duration of praise, glory, and dominion given to God (1:6; 5:13; 7:12); five times with reference to the length of the life of God or Christ (1:18; 4:9,10; 10:6; 15:7); once referring to the length of God's reign in Christ (11:15); once referring to the length of the saints' reign (22:5); once referring to the ascension of the smoke of destroyed Babylon (19:3); once referring to the duration of torment of the Devil, Beast, and False Prophet (20:10); and, of course, once here in 14:11.

Second, "they have no rest, day or night" (the latter phrase being parallel to "forever and ever"). In Revelation 4:8 the same terminology occurs with regard to the duration of worship on the part of the four living creatures. That from which they have "no rest" is, presumably, the torment caused by the fire and brimstone. But do texts such as this speak of eternal *punishing* (with focus on the *act* of judging) or eternal *punishment* (with focus on the *effect* of judgment)? In other words, what is it that is eternal or unending: the act of punishing unbelievers, or the effect of their punishment? Again, is the torment of the lost a conscious experience that never ends? Or is the punishment a form of annihilation in which, after a just season of suffering in perfect proportion to sins committed, the soul ceases to exist?

Does the ascending smoke of their torment point to the unending conscious experience of suffering they endure? Or does it signify a lasting, irreversible effect of their punishment in which they are annihilated? Those who argue for the latter view contend that there will be no rest "day or night" from torment while it continues or as long as it lasts. But whether or not it lasts forever or eternally must be determined on other grounds.

Annihilation or Eternal Conscious Suffering?

Do not confuse annihilationism with universalism. Universalists believe that after unbelievers have suffered, they will be saved and reconciled to God in heaven. According to the doctrine known as annihilationism, once unbelievers have suffered in hell in proportion to their sin, they will be annihilated as the final act of judgment. That is to say, God will simply cause them to cease to be.

(1) Those who argue for annihilation appeal to the biblical language of hell, primarily the words "to destroy", "destruction", and "perish" (Phil. 3:19; 1 Thess. 5:3; 2 Thess. 1:9; 2 Pet. 3:7). The "fire" of hell burns up, consumes, and utterly "destroys" its object, leaving nothing (Matt. 10:28). Thus, they interpret "destroy" to mean deprive of life and existence, hence the extinction of being.

However, the word group which includes "destroy" and its synonyms is used in a variety of ways, some of which do not require or even imply the cessation of existence. In other words, a careful examination of usage indicates that destruction can occur without extinction of being. Likewise, with the imagery of "fire" in hell, we must acknowledge that this is metaphor, and thus not press the terms to prove something about hell's duration they were never intended to communicate. Just think of hell in the New Testament being described at one time as "utter darkness" and at another time as "a lake of fire". How do these two coexist if they are strictly literal? Thus, we must be cautious in drawing rigid doctrinal conclusions about the supposed "function" of fire in hell. One cannot help but wonder about Matthew 18:8 which speaks of those who are thrown into the "eternal" fire. This forces me to ask why the fires should burn eternally or forever and why the worms do not die (cf. Mark 9:47-48) if their purpose comes to an end.

(2) Those who argue for annihilation appeal to the Greek word often translated "forever" (*aiōn*), which literally means "age". Whereas in some contexts the "age" may be endless, in others it may not be so. But there are as many texts where *aiōn* means eternal as there are where it refers to a more limited period of time. This argument is indecisive on both sides of the debate.

(3) Those who argue for annihilation appeal to an argument from justice: A "just" penalty will be in proportion to the crime or sin committed. How can sins committed in time by a finite creature warrant eternal, unending torment? In response I must say that we humans are hardly the ones to assess the enormity of our sins. "Is the magnitude of our sin established by our own status, or by the

degree of offense against the sovereign, transcendent God?"⁴ Says Piper: "Degrees of blameworthiness come not from how long you offend dignity, but from how high the dignity is that you offend."⁵ In other words, our sin is deserving of infinite punishment because of the infinite glory of the One against whom it is perpetrated.

(4) To suggest that hell lasts forever is to say that God does not, in actual fact, achieve victory over sin and evil. How can God be said to "win" if his enemy continues to exist forever? Would not the eternally continuous existence of hell and its occupants mar the beauty and joy of heaven? My answer is No, I don't think so. Only sin that goes unpunished would indicate a failure of justice and a defeat of God's purpose. The ongoing existence of hell and its occupants would just as readily reflect on the glory of God's holiness and his righteous opposition to evil.

(5) Those who argue for annihilation find it morally repugnant and emotionally abhorrent to suggest that a God of love and mercy and kindness would torment people in hell forever and ever. No matter how grievous the sin(s), horrific pain, whether spiritual or physical or both, that goes on and on for billions of years, and after that for billions of years, *ad infinitum*, is more than they can tolerate. John Stott put it this way:

> "I find the concept [of eternal conscious punishment in hell] intolerable and do not understand how people can live with it without either cauterising their feelings or cracking under the strain. But our emotions are a fluctuating, unreliable guide to truth and must not be exalted to the place of supreme authority in determining it. As a committed Evangelical, my question must be – and is – not what does my heart tell me, but what does God's word say?"⁶

---

4. D. A. Carson, *The Gagging of God: Christianity Confronts Pluralism* (Grand Rapids: Zondervan, 1996), 534.

5. John Piper, *Let the Nations Be Glad! The Supremacy of God in Missions*, Second Edition Revised and Expanded (Grand Rapids: Baker Academic, 2003), 122.

6. John Stott, *Evangelical Essentials: A Liberal-Evangelical Dialogue*

I feel the force of this point, but there are other considerations as well. Perhaps the idea of endless punishing is less offensive when the idea of endless sinning is considered. In other words, if those in hell never cease to sin, why should they ever cease to suffer? Consider Revelation 22:11. There we read: "Let the evildoer still do evil, and the filthy still be filthy, and the righteous still do right, and the holy still be holy." On this latter text Carson comments: "If the holy and those who do right continue to be holy and to do right, in anticipation of the perfect holiness and rightness to be lived and practiced throughout all eternity, should we not also conclude that the vile continue in their vileness in anticipation of the vileness they will live and practice throughout all eternity?"[7]

The point here is that although we don't have a strong biblical basis for asserting that those consigned to hell will continue to sin, neither do we have any indication that they won't. And it seems reasonable to think that with the withdrawal of God's common grace and restraint on their sin they will sin ever more and more throughout eternity. It makes sense, then, that they will suffer throughout eternity. If one should reject this notion and argue that people pay fully for their sins in hell and at some point cease to sin, why can't they then be brought into heaven (thereby turning hell into purgatory)? If their sins have not been fully paid for in hell, on what grounds does justice permit them to be annihilated?

In addition, one must explain Matthew 25:46 and Revelation 20:10-15. Regardless of what one thinks about the identity of the Beast and the False Prophet, no evangelical denies that Satan is a sentient or feeling being. Thus, here is at least one such "person" who clearly suffers eternal conscious torment. "We may not feel as much sympathy for him as for fellow human beings, and we may cheerfully insist that he is more evil than any human being, but even so, it is hard to see how the arguments deployed against the notion of eternal conscious suffering of sinful human beings would be any

---

(Downers Grove: IVP, 1989), 314-15.

7. Carson, *The Gagging of God,* 533.

less cogent against the devil."⁸ See especially Revelation 20:15 ("if anyone's name", not just the Beast and False Prophet) and 21:8.

I must confess that I wish the doctrine of annihilation were true. But at this time in my life and my study of God's Word, I don't believe it is. But I'm open to being persuaded otherwise!

The Endurance of the Saints (vv. 12-13)

These verses provide a motivation to believers to persevere, whether by pointing to the reality of judgment (v. 12) or to the promise of reward of eternal rest (v. 13). Could it be that verses 6-11 and the description of hell are intended to motivate believers to persevere? In other words, one of the ways believers are stirred to persevere in faith and obedience is by contemplating the eternal destiny of those who choose instead to worship the Beast.

To "die in the Lord" means to die physically yet spiritually united to Christ by faith. All those Christians we have known and loved who have died are freed from the burden of painful striving and the struggle of resisting sin and the agony of brokenness of life on this earth. It is reassuring to know that their "deeds follow them" rather than precede them. Our deeds do not pave the way into heavenly rest, as if they are the grounds for our acceptance with God. Instead they "follow" us in the sense that they bear witness to our faith in Christ, deeds for which rewards will be granted in the new heaven and new earth (2 Cor. 5:10).

Conclusion

I have two heartfelt and altogether sincere reactions to this passage and others like it. On the one hand, I can't read it or think about it without feeling a deep and unrelenting agony in my heart. We should never talk about hell without weeping, for it is real and people are going there. This is not a subject for joking or lighthearted banter. It is an issue that should provoke within us both anguish and an urgent commitment to share the gospel with those who remain in unbelief.

---

8. Ibid., 527.

My second reaction is one of unfathomable gratitude. *When I read about hell in a passage like Revelation 14, I'm reading about what I deserve.* God would have been perfectly just and righteous had he chosen to consign me to eternal torment. But in mercy he has drawn me to faith in his Son. In mercy he has poured out his wrath on Jesus in my place, a wrath and judgment that Jesus lovingly and willingly embraced and endured. Every single one of us deserves damnation. God owes us nothing but justice. The fact that he has given us mercy instead, and forgiveness instead of condemnation, ought to awaken in us the most heartfelt and passionate gratitude and praise.

Chapter Twenty-Eight

Great and Amazing are the Deeds of God!

(Revelation 14:14-20; 15:1-8)

In the preceding chapter we immersed ourselves in what is undeniably one of the most emotionally challenging passages in all the Bible. The portrayal in Revelation 14:9-11 of eternal punishment in hell is terrifying and sobering. Now we come to a passage that is only slightly less foreboding.

There is no doubt whatsoever that what we read in this final paragraph of Revelation 14 is a symbolic portrayal of the final judgment that will come when Jesus Christ returns to this earth at the end of history. People don't want to hear that. They prefer to think that life will simply continue on as it currently exists and that when it comes time for them to die, they will go to a place in the sky called "heaven" and be reunited with their loved ones and friends, regardless of whether or not they have ever trusted and treasured Jesus Christ as their Lord and Savior. To suggest that judgment will occur when Christ comes, to suggest that not everyone who is "religious" or "spiritual" or "good" or "law-abiding" will enjoy eternal fellowship with God, is politically incorrect to the highest degree. But the words of this passage are unmistakable and unavoidable. In it we find two harvests that will take place at the return of Christ: one of the saved unto eternal life, and the other of the lost unto eternal condemnation.

The Harvest of the Saved

Who is this person or being who is "like a son of man"? Some have argued that this is simply another angel, in light of the fact that in the previous paragraph we saw three angels bringing a message of judgment against unbelieving nations in the earth. However, the likelihood is that this is an allusion to Daniel 7:13 which all acknowledge is a portrayal of God the Son, and therefore it is the risen and exalted Son of God, Jesus Christ, who is in view in verse 14.

I can understand why some conclude this is yet another angel. As I said, we've just witnessed the appearance of three angels in Revelation 14:6-13. You can also see that the one "like a son of man" in verse 14 and the angel in verse 17 both have a "sharp sickle." Perhaps the strongest evidence that the being in verse 14 is an angel is the fact that the angel in verse 15 issues a command to him to "put in your sickle and reap." It does seem odd that an angel would be portrayed as giving a command to the risen and exalted Lord Jesus Christ. However, be it noted that if the "command" is one that the angel received from the Father in heaven (note reference to his coming from the heavenly "temple"; this is typical of angelic responsibility), the idea of his then passing this on to Jesus is not objectionable. So, I am inclined to think that the one "like a son of man" is in fact Jesus Christ.

As we'll see in a moment, there is no debate about the meaning of verses 17-20. Everyone agrees that those verses describe the final judgment of unbelievers only. But what about verses 15-16? Those who argue that verses 15-16 refer to judgment only appeal to the fact that both verses 15-16 and verses 17-20 are a clear allusion to Joel 3:13, a passage that deals only with divine judgment: "Put in the sickle, for the harvest is ripe. Go in, tread, for the winepress is full. The vats overflow, for their evil is great" (Joel 3:13).

Also, the "sickle" is more normally viewed as a negative instrument of judgment, designed to inflict harm, not to provide help. And then there is the phrase "the hour to reap has come" (v. 15). This sounds similar to "the hour of his judgment has come" in verse 7, the latter clearly referring to the final judgment. And of course, the image of a "harvest" is common in the Bible for divine judgment.[1]

But I'm not convinced that verses 15-16 describe only, or even primarily, judgment. I think what we read here is *a portrayal of the harvest of those who are saved.* Here is why. First, you may remember that the 144,000 are described as "first fruits" (Rev. 14:4) in the sense that they are an initial redemptive ingathering that anticipates or serves as a pledge of a final redemptive harvest. Verses 15-16 describe the latter. Second, it is no less the case that the image of a harvest (especially "reaping") can be used in a positive sense as a metaphor of the gathering of God's elect.[2] Third, there is no reference in verses 15-16 to the metaphors of threshing and winnowing (common images of judgment). Therefore, I'm inclined to believe that verses 14-16 describe the glorious ingathering of God's elect from the four corners of the earth. *The "reaping" of the earth (v. 16) is John's poetic way of describing how Jesus at his second coming will differentiate between believers and unbelievers, separating them and taking into his presence all who have trusted him as Lord and Savior.*

The Harvest of the Condemned

In biblical times a winepress would be constructed of either brick or some form of rock. The grapes would be placed in an upper trough where they would be trampled upon by workers. The juice from the grapes would then flow down a channel into a lower trough. This practice of treading upon a cluster of grapes in a wine press is without exception a vivid metaphor of divine judgment in the Bible. In the description of the second coming of Christ in Revelation 19:15 it says that "he will tread the winepress of the fury of the wrath of God," and all agree that this is a portrayal of final judgment. Verses 17-20 also echo what we saw concerning

---

1. See Isaiah 17:5; 18:4-5; 24:13; Jeremiah 51:33; Hosea 6:11; Joel 3:13; Matthew 13:24-30, 36-43; and Mark 4:29.

2. See Luke 10:2; Matthew 13:30, 43; John 4:35-38.

Revelation 14:9-10 where being compelled to drink wine is a metaphor of divine punishment. The Old Testament background is probably Isaiah 63:1-6.

Thus we are reading here of the final judgment that will come upon all who have rejected Jesus. Just as one would take grapes and tread upon them to produce wine, God will tread in wrath and judgment upon an unbelieving, Christ-hating world. But let's slow down and look more closely at verse 20.

First, the wine press was trodden "outside the city" (20a), most likely a reference to the holy city, i.e., the new Jerusalem (fifteen times in Revelation). In Revelation 20:8-9 we read of unbelieving enemies of the saints being judged outside the "beloved city" (see also 21:8 in conjunction with 21:27 and 22:14-15). It may be that this judgment of unbelievers constitutes what might be regarded as "poetic justice," given the fact that Jesus was himself executed "outside of Jerusalem" (Matt. 27:33; Mark 15:22; Luke 23:33; cf. Heb. 13:12-13).

Second, blood rising "as high as a horse's bridle" is stock, figurative language in prophetic and apocalyptic literature designed to emphasize wartime slaughter of exceptional proportions and the unqualified nature of the judgment in view. It is most often used of the last battle in history in which sinners will destroy each other on an unprecedented scale. Thus, it should not be taken in some physically literal way, as if one could actually quantify the amount of blood that will be spilt![3]

Third, the distance of "1,600 stadia" (which was equivalent to about 184 miles) probably bears some symbolic importance. The number four in Revelation is symbolic of the four corners of the earth, thus pointing to the global scope of this judgment. When four is squared one gets sixteen. Sixteen is then multiplied by the number one thousand which stands for the completeness of judgment. Others have argued that the number forty is itself

---

3. Craig Keener (*Revelation,* 378, notes 39-41), David Aune (*Revelation,* 2:848), and especially Richard Bauckham (*Climax of Prophecy,* 40–48) provide extensive listing of ancient sources that document this unique verbal form.

symbolic of judgment, as when Israel was compelled to wander in the wilderness for forty years. 1600 is forty squared. In other words, verses 17-20 are a highly symbolic, intensely graphic way of describing the desolation and destruction that awaits the unbelieving world at the time of Christ's return. I know this isn't popular and one typically won't increase church attendance by speaking on it, but it is true. And because it is true, we should be increasingly energized with passion to proclaim to all, "Repent and believe the gospel!"

The Wrath of God

Many would prefer that we only speak of God's love and grace. But apart from the reality of divine wrath neither love nor grace makes much sense. Some less-than-evangelical theologians and pastors have argued that the doctrine or concept of wrath is beneath the dignity of God. The late C. H. Dodd, for example, spoke for many when he said that the notion of divine wrath is archaic and that the biblical terminology refers to no more than an inevitable process of cause and effect in a moral universe. In other words, for these folks, divine wrath is an impersonal force operative in a moral universe, not a personal attribute or disposition in the character of God. Wrath may well be ordained and controlled by God, but is clearly no part of him, as are love, mercy, kindness, etc.

Opposition to the concept of divine wrath is often due to a misunderstanding of what it is. Wrath is not the loss of self-control or the irrational and capricious outburst of anger. Divine wrath is not to be thought of as a celestial bad temper or God lashing out at those who "rub him the wrong way." Divine wrath is righteous antagonism toward all that is unholy. It is the revulsion of God's character to that which is a violation of God's will.

I know this may strike you as odd, but there is a very real sense in which one may speak of divine wrath as a function of divine love. God's wrath is an expression of his love for holiness and truth and justice. It is because God passionately loves purity and peace and perfection that he reacts angrily toward anything and anyone who defiles them. We earlier noted the words of J. I. Packer in this regard. They bear repeating:

> "Would a God who took as much pleasure in evil as He did in good be a good God? Would a God who did not react adversely to evil in His world be morally perfect? Surely not. But it is precisely this adverse reaction to evil, which is a necessary part of moral perfection, that the Bible has in view when it speaks of God's wrath."[4]

Leon Morris agrees:

> "Then, too, unless we give a real content to the wrath of God, unless we hold that men really deserve to have God visit upon them the painful consequences of their wrongdoing, we empty God's forgiveness of its meaning. For if there is no ill desert, God ought to overlook sin. We can think of forgiveness as something real only when we hold that sin has betrayed us into a situation where we deserve to have God inflict upon us the most serious consequences, and that is upon such a situation that God's grace supervenes. When the logic of the situation demands that He should take action against the sinner, and He yet takes action for him, then and then alone can we speak of grace. But there is no room for grace if there is no suggestion of dire consequences merited by sin."[5]

Wrath isn't something reserved exclusively for the future. It is even now, presently, being revealed and expressed by God. We read in Romans 1:18 that God's wrath is being revealed (present tense). Paul probably has in mind the disease and disasters of earthly life. It is also true that God's wrath is revealed in the content of Romans 1:24-32 where God is portrayed as giving over sinners to a deeper and more intense cultivation of the sinful behavior that they have chosen for themselves. In other words, God's wrath is

---

4. Packer, *Knowing God*, 151.
5. Leon Morris, *The Apostolic Preaching of the Cross* (Grand Rapids: Eerdmans, 1972), 185.

seen even today in his abandonment of people to their chosen way of sin and its consequences.

When we envision God as filled with wrath against sin and evil we should also understand this as an expression of his justice. When we speak about the justice of God, we have in mind the idea that God always acts in perfect conformity and harmony with his own character. Justice, therefore, is God acting and speaking in conformity with who he is. To say that God is just is to say that he acts and speaks consistently with whatever his righteous nature requires.

When we speak of divine wrath as one facet of divine justice our primary concern is with what has been called the *retributive justice* of God, or that which God's nature requires him to require of his creatures. Retributive justice is that in virtue of which God gives to each of us that which is our due. It is that in virtue of which God treats us according to our deserts. Retributive justice is thus somewhat synonymous with punishment. This is a necessary expression of God's reaction to sin and evil.

Retributive justice is not something which God may or may not exercise, as is the case with mercy, love, and grace. Retributive justice, i.e., punishment for sin, is a matter of debt. It is something from which God cannot refrain from doing lest he violate the rectitude and righteousness of his nature and will. Sin must be punished. It is a serious misunderstanding of Christianity and the nature of forgiveness to say that believers are those whose guilt is rescinded and whose sins are not punished. Our guilt and sin were fully imputed to our substitute, Jesus, who suffered the retributive justice in our stead.

An excellent illustration of this principle is found in Psalm 103:10. Retributive justice is that in God's nature which requires him to deal with us according to our sins and reward us according to our iniquities. But in Psalm 103:10 we are told that God "does NOT deal with us according to our sins, NOR repay us according to our iniquities!" Indeed, according to verse 12, we are told that "as far as the east is from the west, so far does he remove our transgressions from us."

Does this mean, then, that God has simply ignored the righteous requirements of his nature, that he has dismissed or set aside the dictates of divine justice? Certainly not (see Romans 3:21-26). All sin is punished, either in the person of the sinner or in the person of his/her substitute. God's retributive justice was satisfied for us in the person of Christ, who endured the full measure of punishment which the justice and righteousness of God required. Thus, the reason we can confidently declare that God has not dealt with us according to our sins is because he has dealt with Jesus according to our sins. He will not repay us according to our iniquities because he has repaid Jesus for them, by punishing him, for them, in our place.

And don't let anyone tell you that this is an example of cosmic child abuse. What a horribly blasphemous way of describing the splendor and beauty and joy of substitutionary atonement! Jesus, because of his love for us, voluntarily and willingly gave himself in our place on the cross. He wasn't compelled against his will or forced to do something contrary to his desires. Jesus himself said in John 10:17-18: "For this reason the Father loves me, because I lay down my life that I may take it up again. No one takes it from me, but I lay it down of my own accord. I have authority to lay it down, and I have authority to take it up again." As Paul said, "the life I now live in the flesh I live by faith in the Son of God, who loved me and gave himself for me" (Gal. 2:20b).

The reason we can read Revelation 14:17-20 and not tremble in fear is because the cup of the wine of the wrath of God has been drunk in our place by Jesus, our substitute.

The Seven Angels with the Seven Bowls of Wrath

Whereas it may initially seem strange that John introduces the seven bowl judgments in 15:1, only then to change subjects in 15:2-4, returning again to the bowls in 15:5-8, we have seen it before. In Revelation 8:1-2 the seven trumpets are introduced only to be followed by the parenthetical transition in 8:3-5, after which the trumpets are then described in detail (8:6ff.).

This "sign" John now sees in heaven is the third that he has mentioned, the first two being that of the pregnant woman in 12:1ff. and the great red dragon in 12:3ff.

These seven "plagues" or bowl judgments are said to be "the last" (*eschatos*; from which we derive our word "eschatology", the study of "last things"). Futurist interpreters of Revelation, who see the trumpets as chronologically subsequent to the seals, and the bowls as chronologically subsequent to the trumpets, take this to mean that the bowl judgments are the concluding events in history, clustered, as it were, just prior to the second coming of Jesus.

More likely is the suggestion that the bowls are "the last" in a formal series of visions. In other words, the vision of the bowl judgments occurred "last" in the order of visions presented to John. Thus John is saying, in effect, "The vision I had of the seven bowls is the last such vision in a series that began with the seals." Others suggest that the bowl judgments are "last" in that whereas the trumpets primarily warned unbelievers of impending wrath, still holding forth the possibility of repentance, the bowls mark the end of any opportunity to be saved.

Note also that in the bowls, says John, "the wrath of God is finished" (v. 1a). In other words, the seven bowl judgments round out and complete the portrayal of divine wrath that began with the seven seal judgments. The full portrait of God's wrath will have been painted, so to speak, when the vision of the seven bowls is finished. Or it could be that we should translate it this way: "in them [i.e., the seven bowls] was filled up with the wrath of God." If so, it would be similar to the statement in 15:7 where we read of "seven golden bowls full of the wrath of God" and again in 21:9, "seven bowls full of the seven last plagues." In these latter two texts the imagery is of bowls being filled, metaphorically speaking, with the "liquid" of divine judgment. Thus the meaning of the metaphor in 15:1 would be "that the seven bowls are 'last' in that they portray the full-orbed wrath of God in a more intense manner than any of the previous woe visions."[6] Also, it can't be the case that the wrath

---

6. Beale, *Revelation*, 788.

of God is altogether finished, as if there is no more wrath to come, because we read of God's wrath yet again in Revelation 20:10-15 and we know that God's wrath will continue to be poured out and experienced by unbelievers in hell.

The Song of Moses

This intervening paragraph beginning with verse 2 looks back to the theme of final judgment in 14:14-20 and portrays the consummated defeat of the Beast which the victorious and vindicated saints now celebrate in song. They "conquered the Beast" and Satan himself, as 12:11, tells us, "by the blood of the Lamb and by the word of their testimony" and by loving Jesus and treasuring him more than their own earthly lives. They are described as holding harps and standing on "a sea of glass mingled with fire" (v. 2a). Given the "new/second exodus" motif in this chapter, this "sea" probably alludes to the Red Sea through which the Israelites were delivered. Others have seen it as identical with the "sea of glass like crystal" (4:6) which stands before the throne in heaven. It may also be that the "sea" here connotes cosmic evil and the chaotic powers of the Dragon resident within it, over which the saints have now emerged victorious.

The victorious saints now sing in praise of God for defeating the Beast on their behalf. They sing "the song of Moses" and "the song of the Lamb." Are these two different songs, or one and the same? There's no way to be certain. Given the background for this in Exodus, perhaps we are to understand Moses as the source or author of a song he and the Israelites sang about God, in praise for deliverance at the Red Sea during the time of the exodus. But the Lamb of God has secured for his people an even greater exodus, one that delivers not simply from physical slavery out of Egypt but from spiritual slavery out of sin. The song is thus about the Lamb. He is the content and the focus and the principal theme of their singing!

The lyrics that follow in verses 3-4 do not appear to be drawn from the song of Moses in Exodus 15, but rather come from a variety of Old Testament texts. However, the themes in 15:3-4 most assuredly do derive from the song in Exodus 15. As for the lyrics here in verses 3-4: "Great and amazing are your deeds" (see Ps. 111:2-4).

All God's works are stunning. There is nothing bland or boring about what God does. All his deeds are the sort that amaze and shock us because they exceed anything that a human being might produce. They are awe-inspiring. None of his deeds are computer generated facsimiles of reality. They are reality! The psalmist declared something similar: "Great are the works of the LORD, studied by all who delight in them. Full of splendor and majesty is his work, and his righteousness endures forever. He has caused his wondrous works to be remembered: the LORD is gracious and merciful" (Ps. 111:2-4). "O Lord God the Almighty" is found repeatedly in the prophets Haggai, Zechariah, and Malachi. "Just and true are your ways" echoes Deuteronomy 32:4. It would seem that this phrase parallels the first, "showing that God's sovereign acts are not demonstrations of raw power but moral expressions of his just character."[7]

We may not immediately recognize the justice in all that God does, but we can trust that he never violates what is morally proper. His judgments against an unbelieving world are both true and just. No one is treated unfairly. We find almost identical language in Revelation 16:7: "And I heard the altar saying, 'Yes, Lord God the Almighty, true and just are your judgments!'" (see also Rev. 19:2). And clearly this is said with regard to the final judgment poured out against those who oppose God and his kingdom (see 16:5-6).

I know there is much that God either does or permits that is confusing to you. You wonder why he strikes down a godly man in his youth and allows the wicked to live a hundred years. You wonder, as I do, why he tolerates one earthly tyrant who persecutes the church and at the same time brings another crashing down in humiliation and shame. But one day we will see all God's deeds and we will marvel and declare that everything he has ever done was both just and true!

---

7. Ibid., 795.

In particular, the saints are singing about the punishment of God's (and their) enemies, not only in terms of the seal, trumpet, and bowl judgments which they endure but also the everlasting torment inflicted upon them as described in 14:9-20.

"O King of the nations! Who will not fear, O Lord, and glorify your name?" This echoes Jeremiah 10:7. If the answer to this question is, "No one," i.e., everyone will fear and glorify God's name, does this imply universalism? No. See Philippians 2:8-11. Even unbelievers will be compelled to acknowledge that God is to be feared and is deserving of all glory and honor and praise.

"For you alone are holy. All nations will come and worship you, for your righteous acts have been revealed" (all comes from Psalms 86:8-10 and 98:2). Again, those among the nations who do not respond voluntarily in saving faith will be divinely and justly compelled to acknowledge this truth. Others take a more positive approach, seeing in this text (v. 4) a reference to the conversion of the nations as they behold the vindication of God's people and the righteousness of God's ways.

Seven Golden Bowls

Verses 5-8 are clearly an introduction to the seven bowls of divine wrath that we will read about in Revelation 16. We should probably read the phrase in verse 5 as "the sanctuary which is the tent of witness." This is the heavenly counterpart to the tabernacle in which God manifested his presence during Israel's wandering in the wilderness. The "witness" or "testimony" here is a reference both to the ten commandments which Moses placed in the ark of the tabernacle (Ex. 16:34; 25:21; 31:18; 32:15) and the "testimony of Jesus" (Rev. 12:17) who is the fulfillment of the Old Testament law.

The Old Testament background to the concept of "seven plagues" is probably Leviticus 26 where four times it is said that God will judge Israel "seven times" if she is unfaithful (vv. 18, 21, 24, 28). Here, too, in Revelation we have four sets of seven judgments (seals, trumpets, thunders, bowls). The verbal similarity between "the seven golden bowls full of the wrath of God" here in

15:7 and the "golden bowls full of incense, which are the prayers of the saints" in 5:8, together with 8:3-5, suggests that the saints' prayers for vindication in 6:9-11 are now being fully answered. The point is that *God's judgments on an unbelieving world come in response to the intercessory prayers of his people.* See especially Revelation 6:9-11.

Smoke in the temple is a familiar biblical theme.[8] Here it is a tangible token or sign of God's glory and power as revealed in the activity of judgment. But no one can enter the heavenly sanctuary or temple until the bowl judgments are completed. Why? Perhaps God is temporarily unapproachable because his presence is at this time revealed only in judgment and wrath. Others suggest that it is too late for any angelic or human mediator to present prayers of intercession for God to have mercy on the world. Or it may simply be that, as in Exodus 19:9-16 at Sinai, such a powerful manifestation of divine glory and strength is more than either humanity or the angelic community can bear.

Conclusion

In closing this chapter I have but one question for you. Is God's grace still amazing? After hearing in Revelation 14 of the justice of God's judgment and wrath against a sinful world, are you not shocked and overwhelmed by the reality of his saving grace and mercy, given that you and I only deserve judgment and condemnation? If grace has ceased to be anything less than amazing, it can only be due to your failure to properly grasp the justice of God's wrath.

---

8. See Exodus 40:34-35; 2 Chronicles 5:13; Isaiah 6:1; cf. 1 Kings 8:10-11

Chapter Twenty-Nine

Armageddon! The War to End All Wars
(Revelation 16:1-21)

Theories about the end of the world have become big business in recent years. Certain environmentalists tell us that unrestrained global warming will bring about the end of the world as we know it. Certain politicians tell us that the world will likely end in a nuclear conflagration, perhaps instigated by North Korea, Iran, or Russia. Certain astronomers tell us that one day a massive meteorite will break through our atmosphere and crash headlong into the earth, setting in motion a series of climate changes and floods and earthquakes that will mark the world's end. Then, of course, we've got hundreds of movies coming out of Hollywood that are making a fortune by promoting the idea that in some form or other aliens from a distant galaxy will invade us and either colonize or cannibalize our world, bringing an end to life on this planet.

It all makes you stop and give more serious consideration to that bearded hippie walking the sidewalks of our streets with a sandwich board which declares: "Repent! The world is coming to an end!" But there are others who insist that the world will never come to an end. Life on earth will simply continue to evolve and expand and develop with ever increasing technological sophistication. Life ten thousand years from now will be noticeably different, but human beings will still be here doing their thing, whatever that "thing" might be.

So, what does the Bible say? Does Scripture give us a hint as to whether the world will end, and if so, how? Yes, it does. Of course, as you already know, it doesn't tell us what everyone really wants to know, namely, when will it end? That is a mystery that God has chosen to keep hidden within his own heart. But make no mistake about it: God, in Scripture, has very clearly told us how the world will end.

One more word of clarification about the so-called "end" of the world. In speaking this way neither the Scriptures nor I are suggesting that human existence on earth will ever end. What the Bible tells us is that human history in its present form or shape will come to an end. But God's people will continue to live forever on a new and redeemed earth, an earth that is free from pollution, free from corruption, free from natural disasters, free from the effects of sinful human beings, free from war and pestilence and disease, free from the presence of Satan and his demonic forces, an earth that will be glorified and transformed to serve as the habitation in eternity for those whom Jesus Christ has redeemed and saved by his cross and resurrection. In fact, the final two chapters in Revelation go into considerable detail about the New Heavens and New Earth. If you're interested, go ahead and spend some time reading and meditating on Revelation 21 and 22.

So, if the Bible doesn't tell us when this will happen, what does it say about how it will happen? Aside from the wide variety of alternative beliefs about what will happen at the end of the age, I think I can sum up what most if not all Bible-believing followers of Jesus will agree on. Let me sum it up this way. The Scriptures, and in particular the book of Revelation, tell us that there will be ever-increasing expressions of demonic activity, ever-increasing expressions of idolatry and immorality, and ever-increasing persecution of Christians by the world system that hates God and his truth. Eventually, at some point in the future, perhaps in our lifetime, perhaps not, Satan will orchestrate a global assault on the church of Jesus Christ in one last-ditch attempt to crush the kingdom of Christ. But Jesus will return in the clouds of heaven and together with the angelic hosts and the multitudes of saved men and women will destroy his enemies and bring final and decisive judgment against those who have resisted, defied, and blasphemed his name.

As I said, Christians differ on a lot of other details about what will or will not happen in conjunction with the return of Christ, but most will agree on the basic truths that I just stated about how human history in its present expression will come to an end.

The good news for us today is that Revelation 16 speaks to this very point. This chapter brings us to the final seven expressions of divine wrath and judgment against an idolatrous and immoral world. We looked closely at the seven seal judgments and the seven trumpet judgments. In this chapter we turn our attention to the seven bowl judgments. You will be happy to hear that apart from the final paragraph of Revelation 19, this is the last time the book of Revelation speaks in detail of the wrath of God. If that doesn't make you happy, I assure you it makes me happy!

Let me briefly remind you that all three series of seven judgments (seals, trumpets, bowls) portray events and phenomena that occur repeatedly throughout the course of history between the first and second comings of Christ. All three series of seven judgments bring us to the consummation at the close of human history where we see the final judgment of unbelievers, the salvation and vindication of God's people, and the full manifestation of the kingdom of Christ.

I'm repeating what I've already written in preceding chapters, but I think it's important enough to continue to bring this to your attention. *According to my understanding of the text in Revelation, all (or at least the first six) of the seal, trumpet, and bowl judgments are released by the Sovereign Christ at the beginning of the present inter-advent age, at the time when Jesus was exalted to the right hand of the Father on high. These judgments and plagues are thus descriptive of the commonplaces of human history, i.e., they can and do occur at any and all times throughout the course of the present age and do not necessarily sustain a temporal relationship to each other.*

It is only with the seventh in each series (and perhaps with the sixth trumpet and bowl) that we are assuredly at the close of history.

Thus, I believe that the seal, trumpet, and bowl judgments are temporally parallel. The fact that the trumpet judgments are *partial* and the bowl judgments are *complete* simply indicates that what can occur in a limited or partial manner at any point in history between the two advents of Christ, can also occur, at any point in history between the two advents of Christ, in a universal or more thorough-going manner. The effect or impact of these plagues of judgment on the unbelieving world is at one time and in one place restricted, while at another time in another place, widespread.

Thus, contrary to the futurist interpretation, Revelation is not concerned merely with events at the close of history, immediately preceding the second advent. Rather, there are multiple sections in the book, each of which recapitulates the other, that is to say, each of which begins with the first coming of Christ and concludes with the second coming of Christ and the end of history. Each of these sections provides a series of progressively parallel visions that increase in their scope and intensity as they draw nearer to the consummation. This is what is called the principle of *recapitulation*.

That being said, there can be no questioning or doubting the fact that the sixth and seventh bowl judgments that we read about in Revelation 16 bring us all the way up to the Second Coming of Jesus Christ, the end of human history as we now know it, and the inauguration of the eternal state.

The First Bowl

This first bowl judgment is based on the Egyptian plague of "boils breaking out with sores" (Exodus 9:9-11; see the summary in Deuteronomy 28:27, 35). Are these "harmful and painful" sores physically literal, or do they represent some form of suffering similar to that in the fifth trumpet (9:4-6, 10) where men are psychologically and emotionally tormented by something likened to the sting of a scorpion? Probably both. Of course, this may simply be a metaphorical way of summing up the wide variety of infectious diseases with which mankind has been afflicted throughout the course of human history. May I once again remind you that during the few short years in the middle of the fourteenth century more than half of the entire population on the continent of Europe died from the Bubonic plague or Black Death, as it was known. In any case, the description of people as those who "bore the mark of the beast and worshiped its image" is John's way of telling us that anyone who worships and serves anyone or anything other than the one true God of the Bible is the object of God's wrath.

The Second Bowl

This bowl, like the second trumpet, is based on Exodus 7:17-21 and the plague that turned the waters of the Nile River to blood. Unlike the trumpet judgment that affected a third of all in the sea, the plague here affects all. Thus "the second bowl shows that what can be applied partially can also be applied universally at times throughout the inter-advent age. That is, at times the ... plague extends throughout the entire earth and not merely part of it."[1] In any case, this likely points to the variety of ways in which our oceans and seas have become polluted.

The Third Bowl

Once again, this bowl judgment is similar to the plague on the Nile River in Exodus 7:17ff. Similar to the third trumpet in 8:10-11, this bowl judgment most likely portrays the suffering and death incurred by those who rely on maritime commerce.

Notice in verse 5 that John refers to "the angel in charge of the waters" (16:5). Could this be a hint that the various elements in the material creation on earth are presided over by particular angelic beings? Possibly. On the other hand, the "angel of the waters" (literally translated) may simply refer to an angelic being who was given sovereignty over the waters by God to carry out his judgment against the economic prosperity that it produced. The precise nature of this judgment ("you have given them blood to

---

1. Beale, *Revelation*, 815.

drink") is not stated. Presumably it would be any form of suffering commensurate with what unbelievers had inflicted on believers.

And isn't it interesting that the angel of the waters isn't in the least upset or confused about what is happening and who is behind it? This is God's doing and what he does is an expression of his holiness. True and just are his judgments.

Some have argued that the statement, "it is what they deserve" should be rendered more literally, "They are worthy," and applies to the "saints and prophets" of verse 6. The idea would be that the latter were innocent of that for which they were persecuted. More likely, however, is that "it is what they deserve" refers to unbelieving oppressors and the justice of God's judgment against them.

Make no mistake about what we are reading here in 16:6. Both the individuals and nations that persecute and kill Christians will be held accountable before God. They may not suffer retributive justice in this life, but they will most certainly face it when they stand before God's throne in the final judgment. And as verse 7 makes clear, you can rest assured that there will be no miscarriage of justice. God's punishment of those who have oppressed and slaughtered his people will be in perfect harmony with truth and justice.

The Fourth Bowl

If one should ask what sort of suffering this judgment brings, Revelation 7:16 may provide the answer. There the reward of the righteous in heaven is the reversal of their deprivation while on earth: "They shall hunger no more, neither thirst anymore; the sun shall not strike them, nor any scorching heat" (7:16; cf. Isa. 49:10; Ps. 121:5-6). Perhaps, then, this judgment in which they are scorched with heat from the sun entails economic hardship resulting in thirst and starvation, for which they blaspheme God.

Notwithstanding the tendency for people to resist the idea that God is the source of such judgments against unbelievers and the resultant suffering, verse 9 makes it clear that it is "God who had power over these plagues" (whether seal, trumpet, or bowl plagues). It bears witness to the hardness of the human heart in sin that not even the inescapable recognition that God is the source of their misery leads to repentance! We will see this again in verse 11.

The Fifth Bowl

We are told in Exodus 10:21ff. that one of the plagues that Moses brought against Egypt was complete darkness throughout the land for three days. This plague of darkness was likely a rebuke or refutation of the sun god Ra, of whom Pharaoh was believed to be an incarnation. This fifth bowl judgment is obviously parallel to the plague in Exodus.

The "throne of the beast" most likely symbolizes the seat or center of the world-wide dominion of the great satanic system of idolatry. The "darkness" into which it is plunged is probably spiritual darkness and intellectual confusion that brings chaos to those who were dependent on the world system and its idolatrous ways. Darkness in Scripture almost always symbolizes judgment (1 Sam. 2:9; Amos 5:20; Joel 2:2; Zeph. 1:15), as well as ignorance and wickedness (Ps. 82:5; Prov. 2:13; Eccles. 2:14) and death (Ps. 143:3). The impact of darkness on the Beast's sovereignty could entail internal strife, rebellion, or loss of political power. A symbolic interpretation of the "darkness" is necessary, insofar as literal darkness of itself cannot account for the intense "pain" that leads to the gnawing of their tongues. The latter could well include both emotional as well as physical anguish, the former in particular being the result of their experience of spiritual "darkness" and the realization of their separation from God.

The Sixth Bowl

In the Old Testament God's deliverance of his people was achieved by the drying up of the Red Sea which allowed them to escape Pharaoh's armies. A similar phenomenon later occurred with the Jordan river, allowing Israel to enter the promised land. It may then be that "the drying up of the river Euphrates to allow the kings of the east to cross over it is the typological antithesis" of these earlier deliverances.² The point is that whereas in these two Old Testament cases the water is dried up to make possible the deliverance of God's people from his enemies, in Revelation the water is dried up to facilitate the attack on God's people by his enemies.

On yet another occasion, God's judgment of historical Babylon in the sixth century B.C. was achieved by the diversion of the Euphrates River which allowed the armies of Cyrus to enter the city and defeat it.³ God raised up Cyrus "from the east" (Isa. 41:2-4, 25-27; 46:11-13), "from the rising of the sun" (41:25) and used him to destroy Babylon. It seems clear that the language of Revelation 16:12ff. is based on this familiar Old Testament pattern which John now universalizes. That is to say, what happened to one nation (ancient Babylon) on a local and restricted geographical scale in the Old Testament was a type or foreshadowing of what will happen to all nations on a global and universal scale at the end of history.

The imagery of kings coming from the east, from the vicinity of the Euphrates, was standard Old Testament prophetic language for the enemies of Israel coming to invade and destroy. For those in the Roman Empire, the Euphrates River marked the boundary on the other side of which was their bitter enemy, the Parthians. But for the Jewish people the Euphrates served as the boundary across which their enemies would come, namely the Assyrian, Babylonian, and Persian invaders.⁴

The *"kings from the east" therefore does not refer to the armies of Red China.* It was a standard expression among the Jewish people for anyone that sought to invade and conquer Israel. You will notice that in verse 14 John refers to "the kings of the whole world" who assemble to wage war against God's people. So, the "kings from

---

2. Aune, *Revelation*, 2:891.

3. See Isaiah 11:15; 44:24-28; Jeremiah 50:33-38; 51:13, 36; an event corroborated by the secular historians Xenophon and Herodotus.

4. On this see especially Isaiah 5:26-29; 7:20; 8:7-8; 14:29-31; Jeremiah 1:14-15; 4:6-13; 6:1, 22; 10:22; 13:20; Ezekiel 38:6, 15; 39:2; and Joel 2:1-11, 20-25; as well as Isaiah 14:31; Jeremiah 25:9, 26; 46–47 (esp. 46:4, 22-23); 50:41-42; and Ezekiel 26:7-11.

the east" is simply his way of describing the global conspiracy just before Christ's return in which Satan and his demons try to destroy the kingdom of the Lord Jesus Christ.[5]

Whereas verse 12 summarizes the sixth bowl, verses 13-16 provide the details. Here again we see the unholy "trinity" of Satan, the Beast, and the False Prophet (called that for the first time here). Their deceptive influence is portrayed through the imagery of three unclean, obviously demonic, spirits in the form or appearance of frogs, which obviously alludes to the frogs in the Exodus plague (Ex. 8:1-15). In ancient Jewish literature frogs were viewed not only as ceremonially unclean but also as agents of destruction. Beale suggests that "the frogs and their croaking represent the confusion brought about by deception."[6] That the frogs are metaphorical is seen from the fact that they "perform signs" (v. 14). In other words, these demonic spirits utilize supernatural phenomena to deceive and thereby influence humans to follow after the Beast (cf. 13:11ff.). The primary target of their deception is the kings of the earth, i.e., political leaders and authorities who align themselves with the principles of the Beast in opposition to God.

This is a clear and unmistakable reminder once again that the oppression and persecution of Christians all around the globe is energized and driven by Satan and his demonic hosts. But these demonic spirits do more than merely persecute the church. They

---

5. I want to mention in passing one intriguing interpretation put forth by Hans La Rondelle in his book *Chariots of Salvation: The Biblical Drama of Armageddon* (Washington, D.C.: Review & Herald Publ. Association, 1987). La Rondelle contends that the "kings from the east" (Rev. 16:12) are in fact the celestial or angelic armies whom Christ himself will lead on that final day in judgment against his enemies. Thus the "kings of the east" are the same as the "armies which are in heaven" (Rev. 19:14) that accompany Jesus at his second coming. He explains: "As the commander of the angelic legions of heaven, Christ will descend from the eastern skies to wage war against the united 'kings of the earth' and their armies ([Rev. 19:] verse 19). The 'kings from the East' thus appear in opposition to the 'kings of the earth,' a cosmic contrast between heaven and earth" (119). That's an intriguing interpretation, but not the correct one, in my opinion.

6. Beale, *Revelation*, 832.

work to orchestrate a conspiracy among the kings and leaders of all nations designed to utterly destroy the people of God.

Look at verse 14 where they are described as gathering or assembling the kings and nations of the earth "for battle." But that translation isn't helpful. It is literally, "for the war" (cf. 19:19; 20:8). The use of the definite article ("the") points to a well-known war, the final, end-of-history, eschatological war often prophesied in the Old Testament between God and his enemies (cf. Joel 2:11; Zeph. 1:14; Zech. 14:2-14).

Verse 15 is a parenthetical exhortation addressed to believers to be vigilant lest they be caught unprepared on that great day. The picture is of a person who stays spiritually awake and alert, clothed in the righteous garments of Christ. For the image of physical nakedness as a symbol of spiritual shame often brought on by idolatry, see Revelation 3:18; 17:16 (cf. also Ezekiel 16:36; 23:29; Nahum 3:5; Isaiah 20:4). This is God's counsel to us all: don't buy into the deceptive lies of the world regarding peace, prosperity, and material success; don't listen to the false teachers who would have you believe that Christ won't return because he never rose from the dead in the first place. Be alert! Be watchful! For you don't know when the Master of the house will appear!

The place of this eschatological war is called Har-Magedon (v. 16). "Har" is the Hebrew word for "mountain." This poses a problem for those who believe a literal battle at the literal site is in view, insofar as there is no such place as the Mountain of Megiddo. Megiddo was itself an ancient city and Canaanite stronghold located on a plain in the southwest region of the Valley of Jezreel or Esdraelon. Although situated on a tell (an artificial mound about seventy feet high), it can hardly be regarded as a mountain! The valley of Megiddo was the strategic site of several significant battles in history (two hundred, according to Johnson[7]). It makes sense that the vicinity would become a lasting symbol for the

---

7. Alan Johnson, *Revelation*, 155. See also Judges 4:6-16; 5:19; Judges 7; 1 Samuel 29:1; 31:1-7; 2 Kings 23:29-30; and 2 Chronicles 35:22-24

cosmic eschatological battle between good and evil. As Mounce accurately notes,

> "geography is not the major concern. Wherever it takes place, Armageddon is symbolic of the final overthrow of all the forces of evil by the might and power of God. The great conflict between God and Satan, Christ and Antichrist, good and evil, that lies behind the perplexing course of history will in the end issue in a final struggle in which God will emerge victorious and take with him all who have placed their faith in him. This is Har-Megedon."[8]

To help you understand this, think about how we have come to use the words Gettysburg or Waterloo or Dunkirk to refer not simply to those specific battles but to any major time or event of great conflict, perhaps even a global war. Be it also noted that the plain around Megiddo was barely large enough for one army to occupy. It could hardly accommodate all the armies of the entire earth. To put it simply, Armageddon is *prophetic symbolism* for the whole world in its collective defeat and judgment by Christ at his second coming. The imagery of war, of kings and nations doing battle on an all-too-familiar battlefield (Megiddo), is used as a metaphor of the consummate, cosmic, and decisive defeat by Christ of all his enemies (Satan, Beast, False Prophet, and all who bear the mark of the Beast) on that final day. That, by the way, is how human history as we now know it will come to an end. It won't be due to environmental catastrophes or a large meteorite or alien invasions but by the decisive and dramatic re-entrance into history of the King of the Universe, Jesus Christ!

Thus we see that demonic spirits will be unleashed in an unprecedented way at the end of the age to stir up and mobilize the leaders of all nations to unite their forces in an effort to crush the church and to wipe Christianity from the face of the earth. But to no avail, as we shall see.

---

8. Mounce, *Revelation*, 302.

The Seventh Bowl

The imagery of "lightning, rumblings, peals of thunder, and a great earthquake" points to the final, consummate judgment at the end of the age (see 8:5 and 11:19). Whether or not there will be literal, physical lightning, thunder, and an earthquake is basically irrelevant and unrelated to John's point. After all, how could these natural phenomena cause the downfall and judgment of principles and ideas and unholy opposition in the souls of men to the things of God? John is describing the final judgment that will come against both individual and collective resistance to the kingdom of God and his Lamb. Typical of Old Testament prophetic literature, John uses the imagery of geographical and astronomical upheaval to make the point.

The "great city" (v. 19) is neither historical Jerusalem nor Rome, but trans-historical "Babylon the great," the trans-cultural, trans-temporal collective embodiment of all cities of the earth, together with every political, economic, philosophical, moral, religious, and sociological power base that opposes Christ and his kingdom (cf. 17:18; 18:10, 16, 18, 19, 21).

Additional dissolution of the cosmos is described in verse 20, a passage that is strikingly similar to Revelation 6:14 and 20:11. Is this displacement of islands and mountains physically literal, or is it another example of prophetic hyperbole? Probably the latter. "Mountains" are often symbolic of evil forces and/or earthly kingdoms (cf. Jer. 51:25-26; Zech. 4:7) and "islands" often represent Gentile nations or kings.[9] I should also point out, however, that "mountains" and "islands" here may be symbolic simply of the most stable features of the world, all of which are portrayed in the Old Testament as being displaced, cast aside, shaken, moved, etc., as a result of the presence of the Lord and especially the manifestation of his judgments.[10] Few, if any, commentators would suggest that

---

9. Psalms 72:10; 97:1; Isaiah 41:1; 45:16; 49:1, 22; 51:5; 60:9; Jeremiah 31:10; Ezekiel 26:18; Zechariah 2:11.

10. See Judges 5:5; Psalms 18:7; 46:2-3; Isaiah 5:25; 54:10; 64:1; Jeremiah 4:24; Ezekiel 26:18; 38:20; Micah 1:4; Nahum 1:5; Habakkuk 1:6; Zechariah 14:4.

these Old Testament texts describe literal or physical displacement or movement of mountains and islands. Why, then, would they insist on it here in Revelation?

In verse 21 the Exodus plague of hail is replicated, but with two significant changes: first, not merely one nation (Egypt) but the whole earth suffers from the plague, and second, the size of the hailstones is said to be "one hundred pounds" (lit., "the weight of a talent"). Cf. also Ezekiel 38:19-22. Is this "hailstorm" (and the size of the stones) physically literal, as it was in ancient Egypt, or should it be interpreted symbolically as is the case in verses 18-20?

Conclusion

As we conclude this chapter, I want to return to verse 15 and speak a word of exhortation to those reading this commentary who are not Christians. One day you will stand in the presence of your Creator, the Triune God of Scripture: Father, Son, and Holy Spirit. With what will you be clothed? Your righteousness? Your good works? Your good intentions? Do you honestly believe that anything you do in this life is sufficient to secure your place in God's eternal kingdom? Do you honestly believe that the forgiveness of your sins will come based on your collective "good deeds"? No. Christians will stand in God's presence then, even as we do now, clothed in the righteousness of Jesus Christ.

That can be yours today! Today, before you finish reading this chapter, you can be finally and forever clothed in the only righteousness that will avail in the presence of an infinitely holy God. Hear the words of the Apostle Paul, who spoke of his desire to "be found in him [that is, in Christ], not having a righteousness of my own that comes from the law, but that which comes through faith in Christ, the righteousness of God that depends on faith" (Phil. 3:9).

Chapter Thirty

The Great Prostitute, the Scarlet Beast, and the Conquering Lamb!

(Revelation 17:1-18)

I hope that this chapter will help you make sense of the world in which we live. In particular, I have in mind the multiple ways in which our society and every society on earth conspires to oppose and oppress the kingdom of Jesus Christ. I imagine there are any number of ways in which people try to make sense of what is happening around the globe, but I want to do my best to account for it in terms derived from the book of Revelation.

In Revelation we are given a highly symbolic but very real portrayal of the forces that stand in opposition to Jesus Christ and his kingdom. We have already been told repeatedly that standing behind the anti-Christian sentiment that we so often see is Satan himself. He is described symbolically in Revelation 12:3 as a "great red dragon" and in Revelation 20:2 as "that ancient serpent." But Satan does not work alone. He is responsible for orchestrating, energizing, and supporting a vast political, social, religious, immoral, idolatrous, and economic network of anti-Christian forces. In Revelation this conspiracy of opposition to Jesus Christ is called the Beast.

Yet another word that is used to identify the Beast is the name *Babylon*. As you will recall, Babylon first appears in history as the name for the ancient kingdom that took Israel into captivity.

Babylon was guilty of all manner of wickedness and oppression and idolatry. Thus, the name "Babylon" came to be used not simply for the historical kingdom in the sixth century B.C. but also for any earthly city or nation or ruler who stands opposed to Jesus. Babylon in Revelation refers to any nation, such as North Korea, any social organization, such as Planned Parenthood, any political movement such as communism under Lenin and Stalin, or the pornography film industry, or false religions such as Islam that denies that Jesus Christ is God incarnate and opposes the teachings of God's Word as revealed in the Bible.

Babylon cannot be limited to any one individual or institution or nation or city. You can't point to any one location or country on a globe and say, "That alone is Babylon." You can't confine Babylon within any particular geographical or territorial boundaries. Babylon is found wherever and whenever there is Satanically inspired deception and idolatry. *Babylon is the symbol of all worldly entrenched opposition to Jesus Christ.* In ancient times Babylon was Sodom and Gomorrah, Egypt, Nineveh, and Rome. More recently, Babylon is Nazi Germany, China under Mao Tse Tung, Soviet Russia under Stalin, North Korea and Iran and even the United States to the degree that it resists the kingdom of Christ. As one author put it, *"Babylon represents the total culture of the world apart from God."*[1]

Earlier in our study of Revelation I summarized it all by saying that, Babylon is the symbol of human civilization with all its pomp and circumstance organized in opposition to God. It is the sum total of pagan culture: social, intellectual, commercial, political, and religious. It is the essence of evil and pagan opposition to Jesus as Lord and Savior. It is the symbol for collective rebellion against God in any and every form. It is the universal or world system of unbelief, idolatry, and apostasy that opposes and persecutes the people of God.

Babylon is every organization or institution that promotes racial supremacy. Babylon is political corruption and economic

---

1. Alan Johnson, *Revelation,* 158 (italics mine).

exploitation. Babylon is Boko Haram and ISIS. Babylon is religious liberalism. Babylon is the self-centered sensual world of Hollywood. Babylon is the symbol for any and all rebellion against Jesus Christ, his revealed Word, and his people, the church.

Babylon has a variety of features and expressions, but the two that are most prominent are its political and religious embodiments. The woman or prostitute of Revelation 17 is a symbol for the religious expression of Babylon while the scarlet beast on which she rides is the political embodiment. And although they appear at first to be aligned, they eventually turn on each other.

We know that the "great prostitute" or "whore" or "harlot" (depending on which translation you are reading) described here is a symbol for Babylon because we are told this explicitly in verse 5 – "And on her forehead was written a name of mystery: 'Babylon the great, mother of prostitutes and of earth's abominations.'" And we know that it is primarily the religious dimension of Babylon that is in view because this "prostitute" is said to commit "sexual immorality" and to have caused those who dwell on the earth to get drunk "with the wine" of her "sexual immorality." As you may recall, in Revelation "sexual immorality" is a metaphorical way of describing religious apostasy and idolatry. That doesn't exclude literal or physical sexual immorality. But the primary point is that to be guilty of sexual immorality means that one has abandoned the one true God and replaced him with an idol or false god.

The Great Prostitute

Here in the opening verses of Revelation 17 John personifies the apostate world culture as a prostitute, an image designed to emphasize the sensual and seductive appeal by which she seeks to lure people away from Jesus. Four times in this chapter she is portrayed as "sitting" (vv. 1, 3, 9, 15), all of which point to enthronement, sovereignty, and influence over the people and the Beast (in 18:7 she says, "I sit as a queen"). The "many waters" (v. 1) on which the harlot sits are explicitly identified in verse 15 as "peoples and multitudes and nations and languages." In other words, this is John's way of describing the global and cross-cultural influence of false religion and all forms of idolatry in which the world is engulfed.

One reason for the harlot's judgment is that the kings of the earth "committed sexual immorality" (v. 2) with her, or more literally, they "fornicated" with her (see almost identical language in 18:3, 9; 19:2). Again, this is not primarily a reference to literal sexual immorality (although the "harlot" undoubtedly encourages it!) but a figurative portrayal of the acceptance of the religious and idolatrous demands of the ungodly earthly order. As noted earlier, in the Old Testament "fornication" is often used in a figurative sense of Israel's spiritual unfaithfulness and her lapses into idolatry.[2] This "sexual immorality" and "intoxication with the wine of her immorality" (see Rev. 14:8; 18:3; 19:2) thus points primarily to the prostitute as an image of all false religions, and especially the apostate or false "church" that claims to be Christian but has abandoned the faith.

According to verse 3, John is "carried ... away in the Spirit into a wilderness." This is very similar to what Ezekiel experienced (2:2; 3:12, 14, 24; 11:1; 43:5). If the presence of "many waters" (v. 1) in the "desert" (v. 3) seems contradictory, remember that this is symbolic geography. We have already seen an overflowing river in the desert (12:15-16), so this should come as no surprise. But why the "wilderness" or more literally the "desert"? You may recall that back in Revelation 12 the wilderness/desert was the place where God took his people to protect them from Satan's destructive plans. "Thus the angel carries John to the wilderness to place him out of reach of the allure of the harlot's deceptive appearance, so that he can see accurately and testify truthfully against her immorality and violence."[3]

The description of the "Beast" here in verse 3 is almost verbatim that of Revelation 13:1. The Beast's scarlet or red color links it with

---

2. See Leviticus 17:7; 20:5-6; Numbers 14:33; 15:39; Deuteronomy 31:16; Judges 2:17; 8:27; 1 Chronicles 5:25; 2 Chronicles 21:11; and Psalm 73:27; see also Hosea 1:2; 2:4; 4:15; 9:1; Jeremiah 2:20; 3:2, 9, 13; 5:7, 11; 13:27.

3. Dennis Johnson, *The Triumph of the Lamb,* 244.

the dragon (12:3) who is also red and may point to the bloody nature of the persecution it inflicts on the people of God. That the woman (i.e., the harlot of verse 1) rides the Beast indicates some form of alliance between the apostate religious world system and the tyranny of the state. Several things are said of the woman/harlot/prostitute in verses 4-6 that point to her identity and nature:

(1) She is clothed in purple and scarlet, adorned with gold and jewels and pearls, all of which is identical with what we read of Babylon in Revelation 18:16. On the one hand this points to her worldly beauty and seductive appeal, but on the other it emphasizes the economic prosperity on the strength of which she lures unbelievers into participation in her religious fornications. There is an obvious contrast between the harlot and the Bride of the Lamb, the latter portrayed as a city adorned with precious stones, pearls, and gold, and clothed in bright, pure linen (21:2, 9-23).

(2) In her hand she holds a golden cup full of "abominations" and the "impurities of her sexual immorality" (v. 4b), both of which are references to the various forms of idolatry in which she and her "lovers" are engaged. Her clothing (v. 4a) and the contents of her cup (v. 4b) provide an interesting contrast between beauty and utter wickedness.

(3) A name is written on her forehead (cf. 7:3; 13:16; 14:1, 9; 20:4; 22:4). The specific part of the name that is a mystery is that this harlot is the "mother" of all prostitutes and the "mother" of the abominations of the earth. That is to say, "she is the fountainhead, the reservoir, the womb" that in a sense gives birth to all the individual cases of historical resistance to God's will on earth.

(4) The woman is guilty of persecuting those who believe in and witness to Jesus (cf. 18:24; 19:2). She is "drunk with the blood of the saints, the blood of the martyrs of Jesus" (v. 6).

This stunning and disturbing image overwhelms John. In verse 6 he confesses that he "marveled greatly" at the sight of this harlot." There is in his response a mixture of fear, perplexity, and perhaps a measure of admiration for her beauty and power. John is both temporarily captivated and awestruck. But more than anything, he is fundamentally repulsed.

The Scarlet Beast

The description of the Beast (see 13:1ff.) and the book of life (see 13:8) have been dealt with elsewhere (see the exposition of those texts). Here we take note of the Beast as one who "was and is not, and is about to rise from the bottomless pit and go to destruction" (v. 8). This is clearly a Satanic parody or idolatrous imitation of God who on several occasions has been described as the one "who was and who is and who is to come" (4:8; cf. 1:4, 8).

Note first of all that the negative middle term "is not" and the third term "is about to rise" are probably a parody of Christ's death and resurrection. That the Beast "is not" points to the continuing effects of his having been decisively defeated at the cross of Christ. That the Beast yet "lives" to persecute the people of God is why the earth-dwellers wonder and follow after him/it. Also observe that "whereas Christ's resurrection results in his being 'alive forever' (1:18), the beast's resurrection results in his 'destruction.'"[4]

On the other hand, some believe that the reference to the Beast's "coming up" or "rising up" is a parody not of the resurrection of Christ but of his second coming. We noted earlier that God's "coming" refers to his coming at the end of the age in the person of Christ to judge the world and consummate the kingdom. The description of the Beast's "coming" thus is a demonic rip-off of the final return of Christ. The Beast comes up from "the bottomless pit" while Jesus comes down from "heaven" (19:11).

The Seven Heads and Ten Horns

There are two primary interpretive approaches to this difficult passage: the historical view (within which are two options) and the symbolic view. The first approach believes that the city and empire of Rome are principally in view. The "seven mountains" (v. 9) are a reference to the seven hills on which Rome sat (Palatine,

---

4. Beale, *Revelation*, 865.

Capitol, Aventine, Caelian, Esquiline, Viminal, and Quirinal). These seven mountains or hills are further identified with seven kings, five of whom are in the past, one presently rules, and the last has not yet come. The debate concerns which seven of the many Roman emperors are in view. I'm not going to explain the many options, but you can read of this in the Addendum at the close of this chapter.

The second option is to interpret the seven mountains of verse 9 as a reference not to Rome or any of its emperors but to seven world empires that oppressed the people of God.[5] Five of these pagan empires belong to past history from John's perspective: Egypt, Assyria, Babylon, Persia, and Greece. A sixth kingdom, Rome, ruled the world when John wrote (hence, Rome is the one who "is"). The seventh, i.e., "the other [who] has not yet come", is the emergence of a world empire at the close of history.

Many futurist interpreters of the book take this view and believe the seventh empire will be a revival of ancient Rome. They appeal to Revelation 13:3 and argue that the "mortal head wound" suffered by the Beast was the fall of ancient Rome and the miraculous recovery (or resurrection) that astounds the world is the modern-day revival of Rome in all its power and glory. According to Revelation 17:11, the Beast not only has seven heads; he also somehow is himself an eighth head. The Beast is an eighth empire and is somehow related to ("of") the first seven. That is to say, out of revived Rome will emerge yet another pagan power related to the previous seven, but nevertheless distinct in its own right. This, then, would be the final manifestation of pagan opposition to the kingdom of God.

One major problem with this view is that in order to make the five + one + one scheme of empires work it unjustifiably omits the devastating persecution of the people of God by the Seleucids of Syria and the evil Antiochus Epiphanes. Also, if the seventh world empire in this list has yet to appear, what does one do with the many major world empires that have come and gone in the past

---

5. Cf. Daniel 2:25; 7:17; Jeremiah 51:25; Isaiah 2:2; 41:15; Psalms 30:7; 68:15-16; Habakkuk 3:6.

sixteen hundred years, especially those that sorely persecuted and oppressed the church?

I believe there is a better solution, one that is more consistent with John's use of numerical symbolism. On this view "seven" is not numerically precise, as if he had in mind seven and not six or eight, but points figuratively to the idea, as it often does, of fullness or completeness (see 1:4, 20; 4:5; 5:6). As in Revelation 12:3 and 13:1-2, notes Beale, "fullness [or totality] of oppressive power is the emphasis here. Therefore, rather than seven particular kings or kingdoms of the first century or any other, the seven mountains and kings represent the oppressive power of world government throughout the ages, which arrogates to itself divine prerogatives and persecutes God's people when they do not submit to the evil state's false claims."[6]

The seven heads of the Beast, therefore, signify totality of blasphemy and evil. "It is much like our English idiom 'the seven seas,' i.e., all the seas of the world."[7] In sum, seven does not point to quantitative number but to qualitative fullness. In John's day the particular manifestation of the Beast was, of course, Rome. This may well have been what influenced him to use the figurative number "seven" (with reference to its hills), although he would have insisted that the Beast is far more than Rome.

Here is the simplest way I know to explain John's symbolic imagery. Seven is the number of totality or completeness. It is John's way of saying that the Beast rules or holds sway over the entire history of fallen, rebellious humanity. But the good news for us is that the Beast's tyrannical reign is coming to an end. Of the Beast's seven heads or kings or mountains, five "have fallen" or come to an end. But the Beast, in the form of one of its seven heads, is still in power, or as John says in verse 10, it "is". And yet one more expression of the Beast's power, the seventh head, "has not yet come," but it will. However, when this final expression of the Beast's tyranny over the earth has appeared, it will rule "only a

---

6. Beale, *Revelation,* 869.
7. Alan Johnson, *Revelation,* 163.

little while" (v. 10b). And just when you might think the Beast is dead and gone, it will come to life yet one more time in the form of an eighth head. But soon it will altogether go into destruction.

This "eighth" head or manifestation of the Beast's power will lead to an unprecedented persecution of the church as Satan makes one final attempt to destroy Christ's kingdom and his church. For a very brief time (John calls it "one hour" in verse 12) the "ten kings" or the totality of pagan rulers throughout the earth will align themselves with the Beast in one last ditch effort to "make war on the Lamb", that is, to destroy Jesus Christ and his people, but all to no avail. Jesus will return from heaven and "conquer them, for he is Lord of lords, and King of kings" (v. 14).

So, in summary, the first six "heads" or kingdoms last a long time, throughout the course of history, in contrast with the seventh, and penultimate earthly incarnation of evil, which will fail to sustain a lengthy tenure. It will remain only a short time. Likewise, the "eighth" head, like the other "seven," has a figurative meaning. The number "eight" in the early church was a symbolic reference to the day of Christ's resurrection, and even of Christ himself (using the method called Gematria, the sum of the Greek letters in the name "Jesus" = 888). Therefore, calling the Beast an "eighth" may be another way of referring to his future attempted imitation of Jesus who in his resurrection inaugurated the new creation.

The Ten Horns

We also need to determine who or what constitutes the "ten horns". Those who embrace the historical view above usually find here ten literal rulers of the ten Roman provinces or perhaps ten specific nations in what they believe will be a revived Roman empire (hence the wild speculation and jubilation of some futurists when it was announced in January 1981 that the European Common Market had admitted its tenth member nation).

In 1950 the six original nations were Italy, France, Belgium, Germany, Luxembourg, and the Netherlands. On January 1, 1973, the number of member nations increased to nine when the United Kingdom, Denmark, and Ireland joined. People began to sense the impending end of the age when Greece became the tenth(!) member in 1981. This excitement (or nervousness!) was short-lived. Spain and Portugal joined in 1986, and Austria, Finland, and Sweden joined in 1995. An additional ten countries joined in 2004 (Cyprus, Czech Republic, Estonia, Hungary, Latvia, Lithuania, Malta, Poland, Slovakia, and Slovenia), and in 2007 Romania and Bulgaria got on board. The EU had twenty-seven member nations in 2010. As you know, the United Kingdom recently withdrew from the European Union ("Brexit").

But as we have seen, the number "ten", like "seven", is figurative. It likely symbolizes the variety and multiplicity of earthly nations and their rulers that join hands with the Beast to enhance its power. These "kings" embody the fullness of Satan's attack against the Lamb in the great eschatological showdown. These "ten kings" are most likely identical with the "kings from the east" (16:12-14, 16). They are also identical with the "kings of the earth" described in Revelation 19:19-21 who align themselves with the Beast in the final battle with the Lord Jesus Christ at his return.

Therefore, I'm inclined to see the ten horns as representing any and all kings, i.e., the totality of the powers of all nations on the earth, which align themselves with the Beast in a final attempt to crush the church. Their unified purpose in giving their power and authority to the Beast (v. 13) is the result of God's providential control (v. 17) pursuant to the fulfillment of God's eternal prophetic purpose. Verses 14-15 answer the question raised in 13:4, "Who is like the beast, and who can fight against it?" The answer is that the Lamb is able! Together with his "called and chosen and faithful" people he will conquer the one who to all outward appearances had himself conquered.

The Sovereign Purpose of God

The scenario portrayed in Revelation 17:16-17 is stunning. Evidently at the end of the age the nations of the earth (i.e., the "ten horns = ten kings") will conspire with the Beast for the purpose of destroying the harlot. Many take this to mean that "the political side of the ungodly world system will turn against the heart of the social-economic-religious side and destroy it."[8] I agree. The harlot, i.e., the apostate church together with every false religious institution and/or system, will be destroyed by a coalition of political and/or military powers. The Old Testament language behind the demise of the harlot comes from Ezekiel 23:25-29, 47. Four metaphors are used to describe this event: they make her "desolate" and "naked" and "devour her flesh" and "burn her up with fire" (v. 16).

The amazing thing is that the ten kings are inspired and energized to do this by God (v. 17)! This incredible internecine conflict between the religious and political spheres of the ungodly world system is so foolish, short-sighted, and ultimately self-destructive that only the hand of God could account for it. This is a theologically fascinating assertion. Clearly, it is against God's will for anyone to assist or align with the Beast, for the Beast's ultimate aim is to wage war with the Lamb. Nevertheless, the angel says (literally), "God gave into their [the ten kings] hearts to do his will, and to perform one will, and to give their kingdom to the beast, until the words of God shall be fulfilled" (v. 17). Therefore, God willed (in one sense) to influence the hearts of the ten kings so that they would do what is against God's will (in another sense).

Conclusion

In the midst of this horrific and ugly portrayal of Satan and the Beast and the Great Prostitute whose aim collectively is to seduce and destroy the people of God and thus to undermine the kingdom of King Jesus, we should be encouraged by the reminder that our Lord is the "Lord of lords" and that our King is the "King of kings" and that he "will conquer" (v. 14) and "his purpose" (v. 17) will be fulfilled.

But more than that, we will participate with Jesus in his defeat of the Beast. Look again closely at verse 14. Jesus isn't alone when he conquers. "With him" are his people, those whom he has "called." We who are the "chosen" of God, we who by God's grace

---

8. Beale, *Revelation*, 883.

are "faithful," are there to share in Christ's victory! Thus we see that in the midst of all this ugliness and idolatry and immorality the people of God stand firmly in their identity. No matter what the Beast may do, he cannot reverse our calling. He cannot negate our being chosen. He cannot undermine our faithfulness to Jesus. No matter how bad conditions may get, no matter how ugly and idolatrous and immoral our society may become, never lose sight of who you are! You are "called and chosen and faithful."

Addendum

The "historical" interpretation of verse 9-11 seeks to identify the seven heads/mountains with a series of Roman emperors. Here is the list of Roman emperors, and the duration of their reigns, beginning with Julius Caesar.

Julius Caesar (101–44 B.C.) / Augustus (27 B.C.–A.D. 14) / Tiberius (A.D. 14–37) / Caligula (37–41) / Claudius (41–54) / Nero (54–68) / Galba (68) / Otho (69) / Vitellius (69) / Vespasian (69–79) / Titus (79–81) / Domitian (81–96) / Nerva (96–98)

(A) According to one scheme, the list begins with Julius Caesar and proceeds through Augustus, Tiberius, Caligula, Claudius, Nero, and finally Galba.

(B) Another scheme believes the first six are the same as above. But the seventh is Vespasian, skipping Galba, Otho, and Vitellius.

(C) In yet another scenario, Julius Caesar is skipped and the series begins with Augustus and runs consecutively through Tiberius, Caligula, Claudius, Nero, Galba, and concludes with Otho.

(D) Finally, others believe the series begins with Augustus and runs through Nero. Galba, Otho, and Vitellius are omitted, making Vespasian the sixth and Titus the seventh.

One key is the statement in verse 10 that "one is", i.e., the sixth king is ruling at the actual time of John's writing of Revelation. If we adopt scheme "A" and begin the series with Julius Caesar, the sixth king is Nero and the seventh is Galba, who according to verse 10 remains only "a little while" (which would be historically true, for Galba ruled only from October 68 to January 69). But this would require a date of composition for Revelation in Nero's reign, a view that is possible, but not likely.

View "B" arbitrarily omits Galba, Otho, and Vitellius. This is justified by appealing to the brevity of their reigns. However, brief though they were, they were still legitimate Roman emperors. As a matter of historical note, Galba was stabbed to death, decapitated, and his corpse mutilated; Otho committed suicide with a dagger (similar to Nero); and Vitellius was beaten to death. On view "B" Vespasian would be the seventh, but his rule was almost eleven years (is that consistent with "a little while"?).

If one begins counting the seven with Augustus, schemes "C" and "D" are possible. On view "C" John would be writing Revelation during Galba's reign (late 68–early 69), making Otho the seventh (whose time in office lasted from January 5th 69 to April 16th 69, which would certainly qualify as "a little while"). View "D" chooses to omit Galba, Otho, and Vitellius, making Vespasian the sixth (during whose reign John wrote Revelation) and his son Titus the seventh (whose reign lasted little more than two years).

The simple fact is, no scheme satisfactorily leads to Domitian as the sixth king who "is" reigning when John wrote Revelation (early 90s). Be it also noted that if the seven hills point to Rome one would hardly need special divine wisdom to figure it out (as verse 9 asserts). In other words, "any Roman soldier who knew Greek could figure out that the seven hills referred to Rome. But whenever divine wisdom is called for, the description requires theological and symbolical discernment, not mere geographical or numerical insight."[9]

---

9. Alan Johnson, *Revelation,* 162.

Chapter Thirty-One

The Fall of Babylon

(Revelation 18:1-24)

In Revelation 17:1 John was promised that he would be shown "the judgment of the great prostitute". Although he was given a brief glimpse in 17:16, the full story is now told in Chapter 18. Alan Johnson reminds us that John "is not writing a literal description, even in poetic or figurative language, of the fall of an earthly city, such as Rome or Jerusalem; but in portraying the destruction of a city [in particular, Rome, since that was the expression of Babylon and the Beast with which the recipients of this letter had to contend], he describes God's judgment on the great satanic system of evil that has corrupted the earth's history. Drawing especially from the Old Testament accounts of the destruction of the ancient harlot cities of Babylon (Isa. 13:21; 47:7-9; Jer. 50-51) and Tyre (Ezek. 26-27), John composes a great threnody [i.e., a song of lamentation for the dead] that might well be the basis of a mighty oratorio."[1]

To say it in slightly different terms, Babylon is the entire unbelieving, Christ-hating, secular system of this present world. Be it the godless educational system, the avarice of financial institutions, Hollywood in all its decadence, the sexual deviance that promotes so-called same-sex marriage and the myth of transgenderism, the countless secular governments throughout

---

1. Alan Johnson, *Revelation,* 169.

the earth, the abortion industry, the numerous philosophical beliefs that stand in opposition to God and his revealed Word, or the many so-called churches and religious movements that have abandoned the foundational truths of Christianity, Babylon is precisely what the apostle John had in view in 1 John 5:19 when he spoke of "the whole world [that] lies in the power of the evil one."

If the language in this chapter seems foreign to the modern reader, it is largely due to John's having drawn on the corrupt and sinful culture of not only ancient Babylon and Tyre but also the oppressive and demonic spirit that permeated the Roman empire with which John's first readers would have been painfully aware.

A working outline for this chapter is as follows: (1) the prediction of Babylon's fall (vv. 1-3); (2) an exhortation to God's people to separate from Babylon before judgment comes (vv. 4-8); (3) the lament of those who cooperate with Babylon (the kings of the earth [vv. 9-10], the merchants of the earth [vv. 11-17a], the mariners [vv. 17b-19]); and (4) the rejoicing of the faithful once Babylon's judgment is complete (vv. 20-24).

The Prediction of Babylon's Fall

Some believe this angelic appearance to be a Christophany (a manifestation of Christ himself), pointing to its "great authority" but especially to its "glory" whereby the earth is "made bright" or "illumined". The same argument was made with regard to the "strong angel" of 10:1ff. Some argue that this must be a Christophany because in every place in Revelation where "glory" is ascribed to a heavenly figure it is either God the Father (4:9, 11; 5:13; 7:12; 11:13; 14:7; 15:8; 16:9; 19:1; 21:11, 23) or Christ (1:6; 5:12-13; see also 21:23). But then perhaps the angelic figure here merely reflects God's glory as his emissary and revelatory agent.

Revelation 18:2b portrays the consequences of Babylon's judgment. It is only fitting that she who promoted idolatry and reveled in demonic power should become the habitation for such following her demise. The Old Testament background for this text is Isaiah 13:21; and 34:11, 14.

> "But wild animals will lie down there, and their houses will be full of howling creatures; there ostriches [or owls] will dwell, and there wild goats will dance" (Isa. 13:21).

> "But the hawk and the porcupine shall possess it, the owl and the raven shall dwell in it. He shall stretch the line of confusion over it, and the plumb line of emptiness" (Isa. 34:11).

> "And wild animals shall meet with hyenas; the wild goat shall cry to his fellow; indeed, there the night bird settles and finds for herself a resting place" (Isa. 34:14).

The word for 'goat' used in these texts elsewhere simply means "male goat" (the sort presented as a sin offering). It is likely, however, that in the two texts from Isaiah it refers to demons. As Sydney Page notes, "in both cases, the word appears in a prophecy of the destruction Yahweh will bring to an enemy of Israel. Chapter 13 describes the devastation of historical Babylon, and Chapter 34 paints a similar picture for Edom. Both passages envisage a time when Israel's enemies will be utterly destroyed, when their centers of power will no longer be inhabited by humans but become a dwelling place for the denizens of the desert. The *se'irim* are included among the future inhabitants of these waste places."[2]

In Isaiah 34:14, another word occurs that probably refers to demons. It is the Hebrew word translated Lilith, rendered "night monster" by the NASB, "night creature" by the NIV, and "night bird" by the ESV. In Babylonian demonology, Lilith could refer to several things: (a) a child-stealing witch; (b) Adam's first wife, before Eve, believed to be the mother of all demons; or (c) a night demon that prowled about in dark and desolate places. In post-biblical times, Lilith became the topic of much speculation in Judaism. "She came to be regarded primarily as a demon who seduced men in their dreams, who murdered young children, and who was a special threat at childbirth. More recently, she has

---

2. Sydney H. T. Page, *Powers of Evil: A Biblical Study of Satan and Demons* (Grand Rapids: Baker Books, 1995), 69.

emerged as a positive symbol for Jewish feminists."[3] Some have argued that the reference to "the terror of the night" in Psalm 91:5 is an allusion to Lilith.

The cause or ground of Babylon's judgment is now stated (v. 3). Again, John is not referring to literal sexual immorality (although all expressions of Babylon certainly promote it!), but he is using the latter to portray religious and philosophical idolatry. To yield to Babylon's demands for allegiance is to insure one's material security. Says Beale,

> "Economic security would be removed from Babylon's subjects if they did not cooperate with her idolatry. Such security is too great a temptation to resist. Therefore, the verb 'drank' refers to the willingness of society in the Roman Empire to commit itself to idolatry in order to maintain economic security. Once one imbibes, the intoxicating influence removes all desire to resist Babylon's destructive influence, blinds one to Babylon's own ultimate insecurity and to God as the source of real security, and numbs one against any fear of coming judgment."[4]

The Exhortation to Separate

The destiny of Babylon just described becomes the reason for the urgency of the exhortation that follows. See Jeremiah 51:45 and Isaiah 52:11 for two Old Testament texts that issue similar exhortations concerning historical Babylon. This separation (certainly ideologically and, if necessary, physically) has two aims: that they might not participate in her sins and that they might not suffer her judgment.

We should remember that the people in the seven churches (Rev. 2–3) "were by no means all poor and persecuted, like the Christians at Smyrna. Many were affluent, self-satisfied and compromising, and for them John intended an urgent revelation of the requirements and the peril of their situation. Most of the seven cities were prosperous communities with significant stakes,

---

3. Ibid., 73.
4. Beale, *Revelation,* 896.

as ports or as commercial, administrative and religious centers, in Roman rule and Roman commerce."[5] The command in verse 4 "is for the readers to dissociate themselves from Rome's evil, lest they share her guilt and her judgment. It is a command not to be in the company of those who are then depicted mourning for Babylon."[6] Keener's comment is worth pondering:

> "'Come out of her' (18:4) also reminds us that we Christians may share in the judgments on our society, in spite of forgiveness for individual sins. Nations and institutions as corporate entities can stand under judgment (e.g., 1 Sam. 15:2-3); we who participate in such institutions share in their responsibility before God unless we explicitly repudiate our complicity with them and declare their activities wrong (Deut. 21:7-9; cf. Amos 4:1-3)."[7]

The imagery of sins "heaped high" or "piling up" or "joining together" or being "lifted up" to heaven is found in the Old Testament with reference to the extreme depths of human sin and the certainty of judgment (cf. Jonah 1:2; Ezra 9:6). That God would "remember" such sin is obviously anthropomorphic (or more accurately, anthropopathic), an echo of Psalm 109:14 and Hosea 9:9.

The principle of punishment fitting the crime is explicitly affirmed in verses 6-7a (an allusion to Psalm 137:8). However, if the punishment fits the crime (or sin), why does verse 6 say that she will be paid back "double" and "twice" what she deserves? Several scholars, appealing to the use of these terms in the LXX, have pointed out that the translation "double/twice" is inaccurate and should be rendered, "give the very equivalent (i.e., produce a duplicate or repeat) according to her deeds."

Babylon's false sense of security and purported immunity to judgment is described in verse 7b, a text that is clearly based on Isaiah 47:7-8.

---

5. Bauckham, *The Climax of Prophecy*, 377.
6. Ibid.
7. Keener, *Revelation*, 437.

"You said, 'I shall be mistress forever,' so that you did not lay these things to heart or remember their end. Now therefore hear this, you lover of pleasures, who sit securely, who say in your heart, 'I am, and there is no one besides me; I shall not sit as a widow or know the loss of children'" (Isa. 47:7-8).

In view of the obvious dependence on the Isaiah text, we see again that "the pride and fall of historical Babylon is taken as a *typological pattern* of the hubris and downfall of the worldwide Babylonian system at the end of history. As with old Babylon, latter-day Babylon sees herself as mother to all her inhabitants, whom she nourishes. She has complete confidence that she will never be without the support of her children."[8] Such confidence is more than delusion; it is idolatry. The warning to the church is evident: beware of trusting in economic security; the world may appear to provide a firewall against future distress, but it is merely an illusion. Recall the warning to the Laodiceans (3:17).

David Aune points out that "the emphasis on widowhood [in verse 7] is appropriate since one of the frequent results of war in ancient times (and all times) was the slaughter of adult males, many of whom were husbands and fathers. Widows (and orphans) were extremely vulnerable and disadvantaged in ancient Israel because they were deprived of the protection and financial support afforded them by husbands and their families, and consequently often experienced extreme hardship and oppression.... 'Widow' was [also] an appropriate metaphor for cities and nations who were defeated in war and consequently desolated" (cf. Isa. 47:9; 54:4; Lam. 1:1; 5:3-4). [9]

In verse 8 John warns of the impending judgment of the world system as similar to that which befalls a literal historical city: pestilence and famine (the common results of a prolonged siege) and destruction by fire will destroy everything and there will be great mourning (cf. Isa. 47:9, 14). Babylon's purported strength

---

8. Beale, *Revelation,* 903 (italics mine).
9. Aune, *Revelation,* 3:996.

and stability will pale in comparison with the God who judges her, for he is truly mighty, indeed omnipotent!

The Lament by the Kings of the Earth

The point of verses 9-19 is to describe how those who prosper from their cooperation with Babylon will mourn when they see the destruction of that on which they have come to rely for their happiness and prosperity. Thus, the principal message of this paragraph is despair over economic loss. For the Old Testament background, see Ezekiel 26 and 27 and the prophetic dirge over the ancient city of Tyre.

These verses make sense only when we remember the close association in Asia Minor of John's day between idolatry and economic prosperity. There "allegiance to both Caesar and the patron gods of the trade guilds was essential for people to maintain good standing in their trades (see esp. on 2:9-10, 12-21). Local and regional political leaders had to support this system to keep their offices and the economic benefits that came with their high positions."[10]

The "smoke of her burning" (v. 9) links this judgment with that of 14:9-11. Are these "kings of the earth" the same as those in 17:16? Probably not. The kings of 17:16 appear to be a smaller and more powerful and elite body whereas those here include anyone who had come to depend on Babylon for economic security. That they "weep" and "lament" and stand "at a distance" (v. 10) from her is due both to the gruesome sight of her judgment and fear that such a destiny will soon be their own. The bottom line is that they are afraid of sharing her suffering. Their fear is also traceable to the suddenness with which the judgment came ("in a single hour", v. 10b).

The Lament by the Merchants of the Earth

Since Babylon has been the principal consumer of all their products (indeed, they "gained wealth from her", v. 15), Babylon's

---

10. Beale, *Revelation*, 905.

demise means the end of the merchants' prosperity. Their lament is not altruistic or sympathetic but entirely self-centered: they can only think of their personal financial loss. Verses 12-13 provide a representative list of trade products, i.e., the commodities that Babylon will no longer purchase. The Old Testament background for this list is Ezekiel 27:7-25 where fifteen of the twenty-eight items listed here are found.[11]

The number four is the number of the world. Thus, it is certainly no accident, notes Bauckham, "that the list of cargoes which Babylon (Rome) imports from 'the merchants of the earth' (18:11-13) comprises twenty-eight (4x7) items. They are listed as representative of all the products of the whole world."[12] Bauckham contends that "while the list includes some items (wine, oil, wheat) which illustrate how the survival of the whole city depended on such imports, it features especially the luxury items which fed the vulgarly extravagant tastes of the rich."[13]

It's important to point out that there is nothing inherently wrong with these products, except for the final one in the list: human slaves. Wealth and possessions, *per se*, are not what John condemns in Revelation 18, but rather the greed and materialistic spirit that energizes their pursuit, as well as the selfish hoarding that ignores the needy and the pride and self-reliance that excessive wealth often produces.

The reference to "slaves" in verse 13 is worthy of comment. It should probably be translated, "slaves, that is, human beings" (literally, "souls of men"). This is not only one item in a list, but John's comment on the slave trade.

> "He is pointing out that slaves are not mere animal carcasses to be bought and sold as property, but are human beings. But in this emphatic position at the end of the list, this is more than

---

11. For the most extensive discussion of the various items in the list, see Bauckham's essay, "The Economic Critique of Rome in Revelation 18" in *The Climax of Prophecy*, 338-83.
12. Ibid., 31.
13. Ibid., 366.

just a comment on the slave trade. It is a comment on the whole list of cargoes. It suggests the inhuman brutality, the contempt for human life, on which the whole of Rome's prosperity and luxury rests."[14]

The phrase, "the fruit for which your soul longed" (v. 14) "expresses that the core of Babylon's being is committed to satisfying herself with economic wealth instead of desiring God's glory."[15] The words translated "delicacies" and "splendors" allude to the false glitter and glory of Babylon's wealth which one day will be replaced by the enduring brilliance and glory of God. Indeed, the word *lampros* in verse 14 ("splendid") is used of those in God's presence in 15:6; 19:8 and of the New Jerusalem in 22:11 and of Jesus in 22:16 (see also 21:11, 23-24). Verse 15 repeats verses 9-11. We see again in verses 16-17 that the strength of Babylon is identified as her wealth (v. 17a). Wealth is transient, unworthy of our soul's trust.

The Lament by the Mariners

The focus in verse 19 is on a particular group of merchants, namely, sailors, who profited from their economic association with Babylon. The language is very similar to that in verses 9-11 with the additional reference to their throwing dust on their heads, not as a sign of true repentance, but as an expression of sorrow for the personal financial loss they will inevitably suffer. For the Old Testament background, see Ezekiel 27:28-33.

The Rejoicing of the Faithful

In Jeremiah 51:48 we read that "heaven and earth and all that is in them will shout for joy over Babylon, for the destroyers will come to her from the north, declares the LORD." Just as the judgment of historical ancient Babylon was cause for celebration, so too will be the judgment of eschatological Babylon. The reason for this celebration is found in a difficult statement at the close of verse 20.

---

14. Ibid., 370-71.
15. Beale, *Revelation,* 910.

Although there are a number of possible translations,[16] it most likely should be rendered either (1) "God has given judgment for you against her" (ESV), or (2) "God pronounced on her the judgment she passed on you." Together with 19:1-5, this passage constitutes the consummation of God's response to the prayer of the martyred saints in Revelation 6:10. God has truly acted to vindicate both the honor of his name and the righteousness of those who were killed for the testimony of Jesus.

The judgment of Babylon which has already been described in graphic detail is here again portrayed with stunning imagery. Based on the judgment of ancient Babylon as found in Jeremiah 51:63 and the judgment of Tyre in Ezekiel 26:12, the end of eschatological Babylon will be like that of a giant millstone flung into the sea to sink into oblivion (v. 21). "One quick gesture becomes a parable of the whole judgment on Babylon the Great! Suddenly she is gone forever."[17] All of Babylon's workers and artisans will be gone. "The various kinds of musicians [v. 22] may be further representatives of crafts or may be merely figurative for the pleasures of an affluent society. Babylon, who removed the joys of life from the saints, will have her own pleasures taken away."[18]

This judgment comes for three reasons: first, because "your merchants were the great ones of the earth" (v. 23), and second, the "nations were deceived by your sorcery." The latter surely refers to Babylon's idolatrous deception, but what of the former? Much of Revelation has been a call to give God alone the glory of which he is worthy, to enjoy and to rest in him alone. The claim to "glory" or "greatness" which Babylon made for herself is fundamentally idolatrous and echoes the sin of Nebuchadnezzar in Daniel 4. The third reason for judgment is her persecution of the people of God (v. 24), where "blood" need not refer exclusively to literal death but, in addition to that, also to any form of oppression and suffering (cf. Rom. 8:36).

---

16. Ibid., 917-18.
17. Alan Johnson, *Revelation*, 172.
18. Beale, *Revelation*, 920.

Conclusion

This chapter, difficult though it be, is a much-needed reminder to us all that the world truly does lie in the power of the evil one (1 John 5:19). There is no such thing as religious neutrality. Be they institutions, organizations, or simply individual men and women, not to be aligned with Christ and his kingdom is to exist in bondage to demonic deception and the numerous sins described by John.

There are times when we all wonder if the rampant wickedness in our society will ever be brought to justice. This chapter is a healthy affirmation of the certainty of divine judgment for those who stand opposed to the reign of our sovereign God and his Christ.

Chapter Thirty-Two

You're Invited to the Marriage Supper of the Lamb (RSVP Required)

(Revelation 19:1-10)

I served as Lead Pastor at Bridgeway Church in Oklahoma City for fourteen years. I was often asked, "Why does Bridgeway exist?" My answer was always the same: "We exist to exalt Christ in the City." We do many things. We preach Scripture. We pray. We evangelize and go on mission trips. We gather in small groups and sing. We serve one another and love one another and sacrifice for one another. We strive for ethnic reconciliation. We strive for biblical justice. But why do we do these things? We do them because of the reason why we exist. We exist to make Christ known, to exalt his beauty and majesty, to act and speak and live in such a way that Christ is seen as preeminent and glorious and worthy of all our heart's affection and joy and delight.

You may think that I have a multiplicity of goals when I preach or teach God's Word. I don't. I have one goal. I have many subsidiary goals that I want to achieve. But I seek to achieve them in order that they might enable me to achieve my highest, singular goal. And that goal is to be an instrument in the hands of the Holy Spirit by which the heart's affections of men and women might be transformed and their mind's thoughts might be aligned with who God is and their spirit's desires might be to praise and magnify Jesus.

My ultimate goal is that God as revealed in Jesus Christ by the power of the Holy Spirit might be treasured and prized and enjoyed and extolled as supreme and altogether satisfying to your soul. Any church that exists for anything less is not aligned with Scripture. Many churches may do many different things, and that is fine. But if the "many differing things" that these churches do doesn't serve the single ultimate aim of exalting God as revealed in Jesus Christ by the power of the Holy Spirit, it has failed to achieve what God had in mind when he called us out of sin and darkness into the light of the kingdom of Christ.

And why should any of us believe that the God of the Bible is the sort of God who deserves this sort of single-minded, whole-hearted admiration and enjoyment? We are given numerous reasons here in Revelation 19:1-10. Our God is ...

- a God of salvation and glory and power (v. 1),
- a God whose judgments are true and just (v. 2),
- a God who vindicates his servants and avenges their blood (v. 3),
- a God of small people and great people (v. 5),
- an Almighty God who reigns in sovereignty over all that he has made (v. 6), and
- a God who ordained from eternity past that his Son, Jesus Christ, would have a Bride, a people whom he redeemed from sin and death, with whom he now celebrates in the great marriage feast (v. 7).

Let's place this paragraph in its proper context. Virtually everything you read in the previous two chapters, Revelation 17 and 18, is a description of the judgment that God will bring to bear against Babylon, that global network of human defiance and unbelief and idolatry. That rebellious, immoral, Satanically-energized conspiracy among the nations of the earth to cast aside and crush

Jesus is finally and forever crushed and destroyed in Revelation 17 and 18.

You may recall that Chapter 17 opens with these words: "Come, I will show you the judgment of the great prostitute who is seated on many waters" (Rev. 17:1b). Then in Chapter 18 we read this: "Fallen, fallen, is Babylon the great!" (Rev. 18:2b). Again, we read in 18:8, "she will be burned up with fire, for mighty is the Lord God who has judged her" (Rev. 18:8b). And again, "Alas! Alas! You great city, you mighty city, Babylon! For in a single hour your judgment has come" (Rev. 18:10b). Then Chapter 19 begins with the words, "After this," that is to say, after the portrayal of the certainty and finality of God's judgment against wicked Babylon, that world city and civilization that opposed him. What follows in Revelation 19:1-10 is the response of God's people and the angelic hosts to the judgment that he will bring on Babylon. "He has judged the great prostitute" (Rev. 19:2b). And for this reason he is to be praised.

Thus, *what we have in Revelation 19 is John's hearing of the worship in heaven as God's creation and the church celebrate their Lord's triumph over wicked Babylon*. In fact, worship of our great Triune God is not only the purpose of the book of Revelation. It is the purpose for all existence. It is why we are here. Revelation 17 to 19 are saying to all: Don't worship the wealth of Babylon. Worship God! Don't worship the power of Babylon! Worship God! Don't worship any of the sensual or worldly pleasures that Babylon offers you. Worship God!

John records for us what he hears in heaven so that we on earth might join in the celebration and admiration and adoration of the God who not only judges Babylon but who also has redeemed men and women from every tongue and tribe and nation and people. John writes this while sitting in exile on the island of Patmos. We listen to it while sitting in luxury and peace and calm in the building of whatever local church you attend. Surely we can join with him in the praise of who God is and what he has done.

Do you realize what is happening when you sing your praises to God? Do you understand what you are saying not only to God but to your city and area? We are saying that we refuse to be seduced by Babylon's treasure and pleasure. We are saying that we refuse to buy into the Satanic lie that there is more satisfaction to be found in the world than in Jesus. We are saying what David said in Psalm 16:11, that it is in God's presence that we find fullness of joy and at God's right hand that we experience pleasures that never end. Here is how John Piper put it:

> "Corporate worship is the public savoring of the worth of God and the beauty of God and power of God and the wisdom of God. And therefore worship is an open declaration to all the powers of heaven and to all of Babylon that we will not prostitute our minds or our hearts or our bodies to the allurements of the world. Though we may live in Babylon, we will not be captive to Babylonian ways. And we will celebrate with all our might the awesome truth that we are free from that which will be destroyed."[1]

Worship is far more than singing. We don't merely sing songs. We sing to celebrate and proclaim the God of heaven and earth. We sing to enjoy him. We sing to savor all that he is for us in Jesus. We sing and pray to connect with God himself. Worship is all about engaging with God, encountering God, extolling God, enjoying God. Now that we all understand the ultimate purpose of this paragraph, let's pull it apart piece by piece.

Eavesdropping on the Worship of Heaven's Inhabitants

I greatly envy John. Here once again he is allowed to eavesdrop, as it were, on what is happening in heaven. He hears a "great multitude" shouting praise and crying out to God. Who is it that he hears? Are these angels, or perhaps the twenty-four elders that we encountered back in Revelation 4 and 5, or maybe these are the voices of the four living creatures? It could be the martyred saints, those who have been killed because of their allegiance to Jesus. My guess is that it is probably all of them, joining together as if they were a heavenly choir.

---

1. John Piper, *Worship God!* September 15, 1991, https://www.desiringgod.org/messages/worship-god.

Note carefully that this declaration in verse 1b is more than a simple doxology. "Salvation" belongs to "our God" in the sense that he alone can provide redemption and forgiveness of sins. Whatever other so-called "god" you may seek, you may find much, but you won't find deliverance from divine judgment. "Glory" belongs to "our God" in the sense that the weighty, priceless beauty and splendor for which our souls long and with which we will be captivated for all eternity are found only in the Christian God. For most in our society God is inconsequential. If he is regarded at all, he is regarded very lowly. When I once heard someone take the Lord's name in vain, cursing wildly with a string of "G-d's," I challenged him. He immediately apologized by saying, "Oh, I'm sorry. I didn't mean anything by it." My response was: "That's precisely the problem! God doesn't mean anything to you. He is inconsequential to your life and your language. He has value to you only to the degree that his name adds punch to your profanity."

And "power" belongs to "our God." Not weakness, not feebleness, not fragility, but omnipotent power to create and uphold the universe and to supply us with everything we need to thrive in a broken world. Their declaration of praise is no doubt in response to the judgment on Babylon described in Chapters 17 and 18. This is confirmed by verse 2 (note the transitional word "for"/"because"). God is to be praised and all power and glory ascribed to him precisely because he has "judged the great prostitute" (v. 2). Far from the outpouring of wrath and the destruction of his enemies being a blight on God's character or a reason to question his love and kindness (as unbelievers so often suggest), they are the very reason for worship!

As we saw earlier in 15:3-4 and 16:5-7, God's judgments against the unbelieving world system and its followers are "true and just". They are true and just because the great prostitute "corrupted [cf. 17:1-5; 18:3,7-9] the earth with her immorality," thereby meriting divine vengeance.

Of all the questions I am asked by people, the one that rings most loudly and consistently is this: "How can God do this and be just? How can God permit that and be just? If God were just, he would do A and not B and most certainly would never permit X or Z." I cannot explain how or why or for what purpose God does all that he does, but this I know with absolute certainty: whatever he does, be that saving a soul or judging another, granting access to heaven or casting into hell, he is always and ever wholly just and true!

You might think that the word translated "Hallelujah" (lit., praise Yahweh) would appear everywhere in the New Testament. It actually occurs only four times in the New Testament, all of which are found here in Revelation 19 (vv.1, 3, 4, 6).

The ESV translates the final phrase in verse 2, "on her," when it literally should read, "from her hand." This may simply be a figure of speech in which a part ("hand") represents the whole (all of Babylon). Or it may be that God "has avenged the blood of his bondservants which was shed by her hand" (cf. 2 Kings 9:7).

Praising God for the Eternal Duration of her Destruction

As if once were not enough, now "once more" the cry of Hallelujah! sounded. The wording here comes from the Old Testament description of God's judgment against Edom (Isa. 34:9-10) and is similar to Revelation 14:11, all of which points to the never-ending nature (or effect?) of Babylon's judgment. Beale suggests that "the portrayal of the city's eternal judgment may be a partial polemic against the mythical name *Roma aeterna* ('eternal Rome'), which was one of the names for the Roman Empire."[2] This verdict is then echoed (note their "Amen", a formal expression of ratification and endorsement) by the twenty-four elders and four living creatures (cf. Psalm 106:48 for this combination of "Amen" and "Hallelujah").

Praising God from both Small and Great

Whose "voice" is this that John hears in verse 5? Is it Jesus? Could it be Michael or one of the other angels, or perhaps one of the four living creatures? The fact that it came "from the throne" has led some to say this is Jesus calling everyone to worship the Father.

---

2. Beale, *Revelation*, 929.

If so, would he say, "Praise our God," "Give praise to your God," or even "Give praise to my God"? In any case, those called on to praise God (again, given the context, for the judgment of Babylon and all God's enemies) include all God-fearing bondservants, both great (powerful and important) and small (weak and unnoticed). Worship is incumbent on us all, regardless of our earthly status, socio-economic achievement, reputation, or accomplishments.

Praising God for his Sovereign Reign

Again, a "great multitude" shouts forth its praise (v. 6). Surely this is the same group, whoever they may be, that began this worship service in verse 1. Only here their voice is even louder (like the "roar of many waters" and "mighty peals of thunder"), gradually increasing as they reflect more deeply on the reasons why God is worthy of praise (as stated in verse 2 and all of Chapter 18).

When we lived in Kansas City, I had the privilege on several occasions of attending football games of the Kansas City Chiefs. Arrowhead Stadium, where the Chiefs play, is famous for being one of the loudest, if not the loudest outdoor sports arena in the country. And I can testify to it. During a typical moment in the game, I could turn to Ann with my lips pressed against her ear and loudly say something, and yet she couldn't hear a thing. Such was the level of excitement among the fans. But that pales in comparison with the roars that are incessantly heard around the throne of God! Would that the worship at every local church be comparable to "the roar of many waters" and "the sound of mighty peals of thunder"!

The judgments of God against Babylon are indicative of God's "reign" (v. 6). This is important, because the wickedness and rebellion of all earthly non-believing people and nations might appear to call into question whether or not God is actually in control. We tend to think that the rampant evil in our world is a sign that God has lost his grip on creation and the affairs of men.

But no! God is to be worshiped precisely because, through it all, he and he alone reigns. His will is done in both heaven and earth. Nothing in Revelation has caught him by surprise. The one thing that will keep you singing your praises and extolling our God is your assurance that he is almighty and sovereign and in control, even if the evil plans of Babylon on earth end up costing you your livelihood or even your life.

Praising God for the Salvation and Sanctification of the Bride of Christ

Do you realize that the way in which God brings glory to himself and gladness to us is by graciously and lovingly securing a Bride for his Son, our Savior, Jesus Christ? The totality of the biblical story, from Genesis to Revelation, is concerned with God's redemptive pursuit of a people for Jesus. All of history consummates here, in the spiritual union and joy and ecstasy of God's people with God's Son.

The image of Jesus as the bridegroom and his people the bride reaches all the way back into the Old Testament. But it was Jesus himself who spoke of this more than any other. Jesus replied to the religious leaders that the reason his disciples were not fasting was because he, the Bridegroom, was present with them (Matt. 9:14-15). When he would depart, then they would fast. He described heaven as being like a wedding feast: "And again Jesus spoke to them in parables, saying, 'The kingdom of heaven may be compared to a king who gave a wedding feast for his son'" (Matt. 22:1-14). He portrayed his Second Coming as the coming of a bridegroom (Matt. 25:1-13). When John the Baptist described himself in relation to Jesus he basically said, "I am the best man but Jesus is the bridegroom" (see John 3:29).

Let's begin by noting her clothing, or as David Aune has put it, "the bridal trousseau."[3]

- The "fine linen, bright and pure" is an obvious and intentional contrast between the clothing of Babylon (where it functions as "a symbol of decadence and opulence,")[4] and the clothing of the bride (where it functions as a symbol of righteousness

---

3. Aune, *Revelation,* 3:1030.
4. Ibid.

and purity; see esp. the Old Testament background for this imagery in Isaiah 61:10).

- The "fine linen" is then said to symbolize "the righteous deeds of the saints" (v. 8b). Some believe this points to the idea repeated throughout Revelation of the saints "holding to the testimony of Jesus" (cf. 19:10), i.e., bearing witness to Jesus in both word and deed (see 1:9; 6:9; 11:7; 12:11, 17; 20:4). Others emphasize the idea of purity that results from persevering faith amidst trials and suffering (cf. 3:5-6).

- Another suggestion is that the phrase "righteous deeds of the saints" points instead to God's act of vindication on behalf of the saints. In other words, God's act of judgment against Babylon and the Beast, persecutors of the saints, is a declaration of acquittal, i.e., God has vindicated them. He has passed judgment on their behalf. If so, the "fine linen" points to the final reward for having lived righteously rather than the righteous living itself.

- Finally, note the classic theological tension between divine sovereignty and human responsibility. On the one hand, the bride "has made herself ready" (v. 7). There is something we must do. We must be prepared for that day. We are responsible to obey what God has called us to do in Scripture. I tremble at the thought of how much time and money were required so that my daughters could be "ready" to meet their respective bridegrooms as they walked down the aisle! They exercised to lose weight, they purchased cosmetics, hired hairdressers, and their wedding dresses,... well, you can only imagine the painstaking process of selecting just the right one and the monetary price that I had to pay! But it was worth every dollar!

Yet on the other hand, "it was granted to her [by God] to clothe herself" (v. 8). On this tension see Philippians 2:12-13. Yes, the bride must actively and willingly pursue purity of life ("work out your salvation with fear and trembling"), yet all the while acknowledging that it is God's grace that makes it possible ("for it is God who is at work in you to work and to will for his good pleasure"). The good deeds, the righteous deeds with which we are clothed, are a gift from God. Paul says in Ephesians 2:10 they have been prepared for us before the foundation of the world that we might walk in them. And this makes it all the more fitting and appropriate that we should give God the glory, as we saw in verse 7.

Praising God for the Marriage Supper of the Lamb

I don't know what will be served at the marriage supper of the Lamb. But contrary to what many of you might otherwise believe, I can assure you that squash will not be on the menu!

There is a slight change in perspective between verses 7-8 and verse 9. In the former verses the bride is viewed corporately, on the verge of marrying the Lamb. But in verse 9 the focus is on individual believers who are portrayed as invited guests at the marriage supper. Both pictures describe the intimacy of communion between Jesus and his people. But this is an invitation to which you and I must personally respond. Many of you, sad to say, ignore the requested RSVP when you receive an invitation to a wedding. But to be a part of this wedding you must respond in repentance and faith and embrace the Bridegroom as your own!

Of all possible scenarios or spiritual metaphors that could have been used to portray the relationship between the Lamb, Jesus Christ, and his people, why was that of marriage and a wedding feast (cf. Isa. 25:6) chosen? What is it in this imagery that John finds particularly appropriate when describing the nature of how we feel about and relate to Jesus? Joy? Celebration? The beginning of a new life together? Intimacy? Trust? Oneness? Commitment? Delight in one another? Yes!

As the father of two daughters, I know what it costs to pay for and host a wedding reception and dinner. I did the best I could for my two girls given the money that was available to me at the time. But nothing will ever compare with the feast that the heavenly Father plans on hosting for his Son, the bridegroom, together with his bride, the church. Not all the wedding cakes and exquisite dinners and luscious desserts that you've enjoyed at the most lavish of wedding feasts can compare with what the Father has planned for his Son!

The angel speaking to John has anticipated our objection that surely this is all too good to be true. It must be a spectacular exaggeration. "Ah," says the angel in verse 9b, "These are the true words of God." So when you hear him say that those who are invited to this wedding feast are "blessed" you had better believe it!

There is an obvious contrast between, on the one hand, the marriage "supper" of the Lamb, to which the Bride is invited, and, on the other, the "great supper" of God (vv. 17-18), to which the birds are invited that they might eat the flesh of his enemies! At the end of history there will be two great suppers, at one of which all people will attend. Either you will eat or be eaten! Either you are a guest who dines, or you are the dinner! One is a reward for faith and righteousness, the other a punishment for unbelief and wickedness.

People have often wondered why John would be so naïve as to fall at the feet of an angel and worship. Some have tried to dismiss the problem by saying that the word "worship" (*proskunesis*) need only refer to a normal gesture of respect, far short of genuine worship. Whereas the word can often have this meaning in the Bible, the angel's response in verse 10b and his advice to John indicate otherwise. There are at least two answers to this problem, both of which bear a measure of truth.

First of all, this is only the first of two such occurrences, the other in Revelation 22:8-9. It may be that John, much like Daniel in Chapter 10 of his prophecy, was overwhelmed with the brilliance and power of this angelic being. Let us remember that in 18:1 an angel is described as "having great authority" and so completely reflecting the glory of God that "the earth was made bright with his glory."

Second, the angel has just pronounced an awesome beatitude or blessing on John and others who are invited to the marriage supper, immediately followed by a powerful declaration that authenticates its reality: "These are true words of God" (v. 9b). The impact of this statement may have been simply more than he could fathom. He may have thought that any spiritual being commissioned from the throne of God with such profound news was deserving of special reverence. But is there any other reason why the Spirit, through John, would include this story? Yes.

- First of all, note that it is the angel as the giver of prophetic revelation (especially seen in 22:8-9) that explains why John prostrates himself in this way. But "in rejecting worship the angel disclaims this status: he is not the transcendent giver of prophetic revelation, but a creaturely instrument through whom the revelation is given, and therefore a fellow-servant with John and the Christian prophets, who are similarly only instruments to pass on the revelation. Instead of the angel, John is directed to 'worship God' (19:10; 22:9) as the true transcendent source of revelation."[5] As 22:16 makes clear, "the angel is a mere intermediary, Jesus is the source of the revelation."[6] The angel makes clear that when it comes to revelation, he belongs on the side of the creatures who receive it, while Jesus belongs on the side of God who gives it.

- Second, it may be that John is reinforcing in this story one of the principal themes of the entire book: namely, the difference between true worship and idolatry. Everyone in Revelation either worships God or the dragon/beast/Babylon. There is no third way or middle ground.

- Third, and related to the above, is the fact that this scenario presents both an example and a warning of how easy it is to be deceived and seduced into idolatry. If someone like John, who has been the recipient of such marvelous revelatory experiences as found in Revelation, can fall prey to this temptation, how much more should we be on the alert!

---

5. Bauckham, *The Climax of Prophecy*, 134.
6. Ibid.

You and I, together with John and all those who have been invited and made fit to attend the marriage supper of the Lamb, have one ultimate responsibility and privilege: "Worship God!" (v. 10b). Why? Because "the testimony of Jesus is the spirit of prophecy" (cf. 1:2, 9; 12:17; 19:10b; 20:4). Let me help you understand the connection between the command to worship God and the declaration that the testimony of Jesus is the spirit of prophecy.

The Greek would allow us to render the first part either of two ways: (1) "the testimony about Jesus," or (2) "the testimony which comes from Jesus," i.e., which Jesus himself bears or declares. The latter option points to the idea that all true prophecy has its origin in the words and acts of Jesus. But I think the former option is more likely. It highlights the idea that all true prophecy consists in testimony or witness to/about Jesus himself. He is its content and focus (whether directly or indirectly). In other words, the reason you should only worship God is because the testimony of all prophecy is about Jesus, not about angels, not about mere human beings, but about and concerning the God-man, Jesus Christ.

The second half of this statement may mean that all true prophecy is inspired by the Holy Spirit (i.e., energized and sustained by him). Or it may mean that the essence of prophecy, the purpose and principle of it all, is bearing witness to Jesus. Or again, it may mean that the (Holy) Spirit is chiefly characterized by prophetic manifestations. And since all of you who know Jesus have the Holy Spirit dwelling within you, all of you therefore potentially may prophesy concerning who Jesus is and what he has done.

Conclusion

The wedding day is near. The bridegroom is coming! Have you betrothed yourself to Christ? Have you made yourself "ready" by turning to him in faith and clinging to him above all others? The invitation has been extended. If you wish to attend the marriage feast of the Lamb, you must respond. RSVP in trust and adoration and confident hope that Jesus alone can save your soul, forgive your sins, and clothe you in fine linen.

Chapter Thirty-Three

Our Blessed Hope!

(Revelation 19:11-21)

I hope ... I hope that all of you reading this book will find it helpful and perhaps share it with someone you know who likewise be strengthened and encouraged by it.

I hope ... I hope my hometown of Oklahoma City will be spared an outbreak of tornadoes in the coming months.

I hope ... I hope my children and grandchildren will flourish spiritually and passionately pursue God all the days of their lives.

I hope ... I hope the Kansas City Chiefs will continue to win the Super Bowl every year, and that the Kansas City Royals will emerge from the cellar of the American League Central Division and compete for another World Series title!

I hope ...

What do all of these "hopes" have in common? Not one of them is guaranteed to come to fruition. Hope can be incredibly painful and frustrating. When what we hope for doesn't come to pass, we hurt, we're confused and disillusioned. But the human soul cannot survive without hope. So it seems best and wisest if we invest our hope in something that is absolutely certain to occur. And the Bible tells us what that is. It is the hope we have that Jesus Christ will return to this earth a second time to consummate his kingdom, to deliver his people, to banish evil from our world, to destroy every enemy that defies him and his lordship, and to create a new heaven and a new earth where we will live with him in indescribable joy forever. This hope is described in the New Testament in several different places. For example:

> "For we know that the whole creation has been groaning together in the pains of childbirth until now. And not only the creation, but we ourselves, who have the firstfruits of the Spirit, groan inwardly as we wait eagerly for adoption as sons, the redemption of our bodies. For in this hope we were saved. Now hope that is seen is not hope. For who hopes for what he sees? But if we hope for what we do not see, we wait for it with patience" (Rom. 8:22-25).

> "But we do not want you to be uninformed, brothers, about those who are asleep, that you may not grieve as others do who have no hope. For since we believe that Jesus died and rose again, even so, through Jesus, God will bring with him those who have fallen asleep. For this we declare to you by a word from the Lord, that we who are alive, who are left until the coming of the Lord, will not precede those who have fallen asleep. For the Lord himself will descend from heaven with a cry of command, with the voice of an archangel, and with the sound of the trumpet of God. And the dead in Christ will rise first. Then we who are alive, who are left, will be caught up together with them in the clouds to meet the Lord in the air, and so we will always be with the Lord. Therefore encourage one another with these words" (1 Thess. 4:13-18).

> "[We are] waiting for our blessed hope, the appearing of the glory of our great God and Savior Jesus Christ, who gave himself for us to redeem us from all lawlessness and to purify for himself a people for his own possession who are zealous for good works" (Titus 2:13-14).

> "Therefore, preparing your minds for action, and being sober-minded, set your hope fully on the grace that will be brought to you at the revelation of Jesus Christ" (1 Pet. 1:13).

> "Beloved, we are God's children now, and what we will be has not yet appeared; but we know that when he appears we shall be like

him, because we shall see him as he is. And everyone who thus hopes in him purifies himself as he is pure" (1 John 3:2-3).

If your hope is not in the concrete, tangible, physical, personal return of Jesus Christ, you have no hope. No other hope makes sense or has any possibility of being of any benefit to anyone if Jesus Christ is not going to return a second time. As Paul said, this is our "blessed hope"! If you think there is yet another option, another hope worthy of your focus and faith, you've been lied to.

I'm not writing to lie to you. I'm writing to tell you the truth: Jesus Christ is coming back, and that and that alone is the only hope worthy of your confidence. It is the only hope that will never put you to shame or disappoint you. In this chapter we are going to see what John says about this hope, especially as it pertains to what Jesus will do to the unbelieving, immoral, and idolatrous world that has denied him.

The Rider on the White Horse

There have been previously in Revelation allusions and somewhat vague references to the return of Jesus Christ and the consummation of his kingdom. We saw this in Revelation 11:15 and again in 14:14-16. But now the veil is lifted and there can be no doubt whatsoever as to what is happening. We see here in verses 11-21 what is undoubtedly a vivid and highly symbolic portrait of Jesus at his second coming. Each of these twelve descriptive phrases is designed to tell us something about who Jesus is, what he has done, and what he will do for his people.

First, Jesus is first portrayed as one sitting upon "a white horse" (v. 11). You may recall from Revelation 6:2 that another white horse has already appeared, but we determined that the rider in Chapter 6 was a Satanic parody or idolatrous rip-off of the Lord Jesus. Someone may push back by saying that in other texts concerning the second coming Jesus is described as coming on the clouds of heaven. So which is it: on a horse or in the clouds or perhaps on a horse that is in the clouds? Probably none of the above. We must never lose sight of the fact that this is apocalyptic language. It is highly symbolic. His appearance here on a white horse is designed to alert us to the fact that he comes to conquer and to rule. I don't think we are supposed to press for a literal or physiological interpretation of this text.

Second, he is called "Faithful and True" (v. 11). He does not usurp to himself a judgment that he does not rightfully own. His faithfulness to the Father in obeying every command and his faithfulness in fulfilling every promise he has ever made are the foundation of his right to bring judgment. Jesus always spoke the truth and never compromised. You can't trust anyone but Jesus. He is the only one who always speaks the truth and never lies. He is the only one who is always faithful to his promises, never breaking his word. He is the only one who will never betray you or break a confidence. He is the only one who will tell it like it is, regardless of how it may make you feel. If Jesus said that your sins are forever forgiven when you repent and trust in his death in your place on the cross, you can believe it. You can bank on it. Why? Because he doesn't lie. He speaks the truth. He is perfectly and altogether faithful.

Third, "in righteousness he judges and wages war" (v. 11). Both verbs are present tense, perhaps pointing to timeless or customary actions of the rider. This judgment and waging of war is not merely against unbelievers but also on behalf of his people. It is in "righteousness" that he judges. Unlike tyrants and rulers throughout history who took bribes and extorted from others, Jesus wields the sword of judgment in perfect harmony with what is right. Unlike generals and armies that waged unrighteous wars for financial or territorial gain, Jesus wages war against all such unrighteousness.

Fourth, his "eyes are a flame of fire" (v. 12). This reminds us of the portrait of the risen Christ in Revelation 1:14 (see also 2:18-23), all of which points to his role as divine judge who sees perfectly and exhaustively into the lives and hearts of people. You can't hide from him. Nothing in your heart, not even the most closely guarded secrets, are unknown to him. His eyes not only see what you do, but why you do what you do.

Fifth, on his head are "many diadems" (v. 12). This is to be contrasted with the dragon who has but seven diadems and the beast who has ten. "The undefined multiplicity of diadems shows Christ is the only true cosmic king, on a grander scale than the dragon and the beast, whose small number of crowns implies a kingship limited in time. Christ should wear more crowns than any earthly king or kings, since he is 'King of kings and Lord of lords' (19:16)."[1] The crowns point to his authority. It was the great Dutch theologian and statesman, Abraham Kuyper, who rightly declared of Jesus: "There is not a square inch in all the universe over which he does not say: Mine!"

Sixth, he has a name written "which no one knows but himself" (v. 12). It initially seems strange since there are three other names of Jesus that are explicitly mentioned in this paragraph: he is called "Faithful and True" (v. 11), "The Word of God" (v. 13b), and "King of kings and Lord of lords" (v. 16). But there is apparently one more name that is too sacred or too profound for any to know.

This clearly echoes Revelation 2:17 as well as 3:12. This statement would contradict verses 11, 13, and 16 only if it is meant to be taken in a strictly literal sense of a literal label. But "the confidential nature of the name here has nothing to do with concealing a name on the cognitive level but alludes to Christ being absolutely sovereign over humanity's experiential access to his character. To some he reveals his name (i.e., his character) by initiating a salvific relationship (as in 2:17; 3:12; 22:3-4; Luke 10:22; Matt. 16:16-17), but to others he reveals his name through an experience of judgment."[2] Thus, most likely his "name" refers to his character as saving Lord and/or judging king.

It may also point to the fact that there are depths to Christ's character and resources in his infinite being that we simply are incapable of grasping or understanding. Also, in the ancient world to know someone's name "was a basis of power over him. Jesus remains beyond the grasp of his foes, but he has their name and

---

1. Beale, *Revelation*, 952.
2. Ibid., 955-56; cf. Ex. 6:3.

number, allowing him to place them wholly under his spell."[3] He is truly inexhaustible!

Seventh, he is clothed in a "robe dipped in blood" (v. 13; see Isaiah 63:1-3). Whose blood is this? Is it the blood of Christ himself, shed at Calvary? Is it the blood of the martyred saints? Is it the blood of Christ's defeated enemies (a common Old Testament image[4])? I'm inclined to believe it is his own blood, the blood he shed on the cross as the basis of his victory over sin.

Eighth, his name is called "the Word of God" (v. 13). He is the Word of God in that through his words and deeds he manifests and reveals the character of God himself. He not only makes known God's will but is also the one who enforces it on his people. He speaks for God. He perfectly embodies all that God is. He is the expression of God's character.

Ninth, he is followed by heavenly "armies ... arrayed in fine linen, white and pure," who were "following him on white horses" (v. 14). Is this an army of angels accompanying Jesus from heaven to execute final judgment?[5] Or are these believers, martyrs, and others in the intermediate state, who accompany him? Revelation 17:14 speaks of the second coming of Christ and identifies those who come "with" him as the "called and chosen and faithful", a clear reference to Christians. Also, in Revelation, with one exception (15:6), only believers wear white garments (see 3:4-5, 18; 4:4; 6:11; 7:9, 13-14). See also 1 Thessalonians 4:14-17 for the idea that the saints accompany Jesus at his second coming. In addition, we read in Revelation 19:8 that the saints, the people of God who have trusted Jesus, are clothed in fine linen, white and pure. This now appears again on those who accompany Jesus at his return.

---

3. Phillips, *Revelation,* 546-47.

4. See Exodus 15; Deuteronomy 33; Judges 5; Habakkuk 3; Isaiah 26:16–27:6; 59:15-20; 63:1-6; and Zechariah 14:1-21.

5. Matthew 13:40-42; 16:27; 25:31-32; Mark 8:38; Luke 9:26; 2 Thessalonians 1:7; and Jude 14-15.

Tenth, a sharp "sword" from his mouth is used to "strike down the nations", which he rules "with a rod of iron" (v. 15). The Old Testament background for this is found in Isaiah 49:2; 11:4; and Psalm 2:9. One word from his mouth, one declaration of judgment, and his enemies are defeated. They are defeated by the proclamation of truth! I find it fascinating, disturbing, and a bit silly to listen to Russia and North Korea and the United States threaten one another with destruction, each claiming to have more nuclear firepower, more manpower, more machines, and more military might than the other. When Jesus returns, he will only have to speak one word with the sword that comes from his mouth and all nations will crumble in defeat.

Eleventh, he treads "the wine press" of the fury of God's wrath (v. 15). This image is drawn from Isaiah 63:2-6 (see also Revelation 14:19-20). Note the piling up of language here. God is the Almighty One. The Almighty One will give vent to his wrath against wickedness and rebellion. This wrath of the Almighty One is characterized by intense and unimaginable "fury." So don't think for a moment that God is indifferent to the immorality and idolatry and arrogance of people today or of people in times past. Fierce, yet righteous, judgment is coming.

Twelfth, the name "King of kings and Lord of lords" is on his robe and thigh (v. 16). An elderly Scottish Christian lady was near death, yet full of peace and comfort and confidence. When asked how she could be like this, she replied: "I'm resting in the truth and power of Christ's good name. If I should awaken in eternity to find myself among the lost, the Lord would lose more than I would, for all that I would lose would be my immortal soul, but he would have lost his good name."[6] According to Proverbs 18:10, "the name of the LORD is a strong tower; the righteous man runs into it and is safe." We are to take refuge and seek our safety and the reassurance of all God's promises by trusting in the truth of what God's name embodies. This means that we must put our confidence and hope for the future in what his many names mean.

---

6. As told by Joel Beeke in *Revelation*, 498.

A Brief Summation of the Order of Events at the Second Coming of Christ

It might be helpful for me to pause here and try to provide you with a step-by-step scenario of what I believe will happen when Jesus returns to this earth.

First, contrary to what many, if not most, of you have been taught for the majority of your life in church, Christians will not be raptured or removed from this earth so that they don't have to endure the persecution and trials that will be imposed by the Beast and by unbelievers. The end-time scenario portrayed by Hal Lindsey in *The Late, Great Planet Earth* or in the many *Left Behind* novels of Tim LaHaye and Jerry Jenkins is simply not biblical. The rapture or translation of the saints is never described in Scripture as a means of escape from tribulation or suffering.

Second, at the close of history Christ will return in the company of his angels and all those who have died in faith. At the sound of the trumpet, those who are with Christ will immediately receive their resurrected and glorified bodies (1 Thess. 4:13-18).

Third, those believers who are alive on the earth when Christ returns will be caught up or raptured and immediately transformed by receiving their glorified bodies. See Philippians 3:20-21 and 1 Corinthians 15:50-55.

Fourth, we will not ascend into some spiritual heaven far beyond this world but will accompany Christ as he continues his descent to the earth and participate in his defeat of all his enemies. See 1 Thessalonians 4:13-18, especially verse 17 and the verb "to meet", which typically refers to people going to the outskirts of their city to "meet" and then accompany back in a visiting dignitary.

The Judgment of Christ's Enemies

One thing that this final battle signals is the end of any opportunity to be saved. There is no hint in Scripture that those who persist in unbelief and idolatry to the end of their lives or until the time that Jesus returns will have another opportunity to recognize the error of their ways and repent.

Here the angel announces the coming destruction of the Beast, False Prophet, and their followers through the same imagery found in Ezekiel 39:4, 17-20 where the defeat of Gog and Magog is described. The picture of vultures or other birds of prey feasting on the flesh of unburied corpses killed in battle (see also Revelation 19:21b) was a familiar one to people in the Old Testament (cf.).[7] *This is obviously highly graphic and evocative symbolism. In the Old Testament to give someone's flesh to be eaten by the birds was an expression of total defeat and their being put to shame.* We see this in David's words to Goliath:

> "This day the LORD will deliver you into my hand, and I will strike you down and cut off your head. And I will give the dead bodies of the host of the Philistines this day to the birds of the air and to the wild beasts of the earth, that all the earth may know that there is a God in Israel, and that all this assembly may know that the LORD saves not with sword and spear. For the battle is the LORD's, and he will give you into our hand" (1 Sam. 17:46-47).

So, we need not think that all the bodies of all unbelievers will literally be eaten by the birds, but rather that God's enemies will suffer complete defeat and devastation and be exposed to the humiliation of judgment. This portrayal also reminds us that judgment is the great leveler of persons. Neither wealth nor influence nor political power nor gender nor ethnicity nor education will exempt anyone from judgment. All are held accountable to God.

Note in verses 19-21 the instantaneous brevity of the battle. There will be no successful resistance. Christ's omnipotent authority brings an immediate and irreversible end to all opposition.

The judgment appears to come in two stages (although note that nowhere is the actual "battle" described; only its outcome). First, the Beast and False Prophet are "seized" and "thrown alive" into the lake of fire. Revelation 20:10 indicates that their torment is eternal. I have argued earlier that the Beast and False Prophet are primarily corporate or collective images and not two particular

---

7. Deuteronomy 28:26; 1 Samuel 17:44-46; 1 Kings 14:11; 16:4; 21:24; 2 Kings 9:10; Jeremiah 7:33; 15:3; 16:4; 19:7; 34:20; and Ezekiel 29:5.

historical individuals (although individuals may at various times in history function as a manifestation of either the Beast or the False Prophet).

Also, if it seems strange to you to speak of throwing non-human, corporate, images into the lake of fire, see Revelation 20:14 where "death and Hades" are also thrown into the lake of fire! Second, all "the rest" of their followers are killed. That they, too, will ultimately be thrown into the lake of fire is evident from Revelation 20:15.

Conclusion

There are two ways to escape the eternal judgment and condemnation that comes when Christ returns. On the one hand, you can live a perfect life: holy, righteous, not only in your deeds but in your thoughts and motivation. Or you can flee to Christ and put your confidence and hope and trust in what he endured on the cross for those who know they could never live a perfect life.

Everyone hopes, even those who deny Jesus Christ. Even atheists. If nothing else, they hope that Christianity is wrong, because if it is right, they will find themselves among those described here in Revelation 19:17-21. Or perhaps their hope is that with death there is oblivion. Eternal unconsciousness. But at minimum they hope with all their hearts that what we read in Revelation is false, a religious fantasy.

Or it may be that some hope that the end result will be some form of universal salvation. They may not believe in Jesus. They may not believe that salvation comes from faith in Christ. But they may live in quiet hope that if they are wrong about whether or not God exists at least there may be the possibility that all mankind will transition into some form of spiritual afterlife where all is well.

But there is only one hope that is sure and solid and certain and that is the hope that Christians have of an eternity of glory and joy and happiness and peace that comes from living as forgiven sinners in the presence of the King of kings and Lord of lords. And that hope can be yours today if you will but cry out to Jesus and invest your belief and trust in his death on the cross for sinners and his bodily resurrection from the grave.

Chapter Thirty-Four

The Millennium, the Final Battle, and the Final Judgment

(Revelation 20:1-15)

In February of 2015, twenty Egyptian Christians were lined up on a beach in Libya, wearing orange jumpsuits. After refusing to renounce their faith in Christ, they were forced to kneel down. One by one, they were each savagely beheaded. It wasn't until three years later, in 2018, that their bodies were returned to Egypt to be properly buried. Although their physical bodies suffered great indignity, their souls immediately entered into the presence of their Lord Jesus Christ where, as priests of God, they joined with him in ruling and reigning over the affairs of heaven and earth. And when Christ returns to this earth at the end of human history, they will accompany him and be among the first to receive their glorified and resurrected bodies.

On what basis do I say this, you ask? The answer is found in the second half of Revelation 20:4 where we read: "Also I saw the souls of those who had been beheaded for the testimony of Jesus and for the word of God, and those who had not worshiped the beast or its image and had not received its mark on their foreheads or their hands. They came to life and reigned with Christ for a thousand years" (Rev. 20:4b).

In other words, I believe what John is describing in Revelation 20:1-6 is the blessed experience of all who have died believing in Jesus as they enter into what is known as the *intermediate state*. The intermediate state is the experience of all believers, but especially martyrs, who die physically and yet spiritually continue to live in the presence of Christ. It is there, in that intermediate state, that they share with Christ, for one thousand years, his reign as King of kings and Lord of lords.

As you probably know, Revelation 20 is the single most debated chapter in the entire book. The debate swirls around the meaning of the "first resurrection" and the thousand years during which believers share Christ's kingly rule. I can't begin to present all the many interpretations of this passage. So I will simply describe for you what I believe this passage is saying. Many of you will disagree, but that's ok. So let me walk you through the various details of what John says.

Amillennialism

When I make known my beliefs about the so-called millennium, after getting over their initial shock and incredulity, it's not uncommon for my friends to say: "But Sam, how can you say you embrace a 'millennial' option when you don't even believe in a millennium?" As you'll soon come to see, I most assuredly do believe in the reality of a literal millennial kingdom. The reason for this misunderstanding is the label most commonly used to describe the view I'm prepared to defend: *amillennialism*.

You've no doubt heard someone described as being "**a**political" or perhaps "**a**moral" and you know what is meant. Similarly, to say that I am "**a**millennial" (where the alpha privative "a" seemingly negates the word "millennial") exposes me and others to the charge that we deny the existence of what is clearly taught in Revelation 20. So in this chapter, I aim to show you that *the "millennium" that I believe John describes in Revelation 20 is concurrent or simultaneous with the church age in which we live and consists of the co-regency with Christ of those believers who have died and entered into the glory of the intermediate state.*

Therefore, contrary to what the term 'amillennialism' implies, amillennialists believe in a millennium. The millennium, however, is now: the present age of the church between the first and second comings of Christ in its entirety is the millennium. While an amillennialist does deny the premillennial belief in a personal, literal reign of Christ upon the earth for a thousand years following his second coming, I affirm that there is a millennium and that Christ rules. This messianic reign is not precisely a thousand years in length, and it is wholly spiritual (in the sense that it is non-earthly, non-visible, non-physical, but no less literal) in nature. "This millennial reign is not something to be looked for in the future;" writes Hoekema, "it is going on now, and will be until Christ returns.... [Thus we must remember] that the millennium in question is not an earthly but a heavenly reign."[1]

I believe that the millennium is restricted to the blessings of the intermediate state; that is to say, the millennium as described in Revelation 20:4-6 refers to the present reign of the souls of deceased believers with Christ in heaven. According to the amillennialist, there will be a parallel and contemporaneous development of good and evil in the world which will continue until the second coming of Christ. History will witness a progressively worsening situation in which the church of Jesus Christ will experience an increasingly widespread and oppressive time of suffering and persecution.

Make no mistake: amillennialists such as myself most certainly believe that the people of God will rule on the earth in fulfillment of the promises made to Abraham, Isaac, and Jacob in the Old Testament. But it will be on the new earth, as described in Revelation 21 and 22, that we will live and reign with Christ forever and ever.

Therefore, Revelation 20:1 is not to be thought of as following Revelation 19 in chronological order (which describes the second coming of Christ). Rather, it takes us back once again to the beginning of the New Testament era and *recapitulates* the entire present age (that is to say, it describes the same period in different but complementary terms). By doing this the amillennialist is able to interpret the binding of Satan in Revelation 20:1-3 as having

---

1. Anthony A. Hoekema, *The Bible and the Future* (Grand Rapids: Eerdmans, 1979), 235.

already occurred during our Lord's earthly ministry, and the thousand-year reign (i.e., the millennium) of Revelation 20:4-6 as describing in symbolic language the entire inter-advent age in which we now live. Therefore, *the thousand-year period is not a chronologically literal piece of history; it is a symbolic number coextensive with the history of the church on earth between the resurrection of Christ and his return.*

One of the primary reasons I don't believe Revelation 20 follows chronologically the events of Revelation 19 is because of what happens at the time of Christ's second coming. We saw in Revelation 19:11-21 that all the unbelieving nations and peoples of the earth were destroyed by the Lord Jesus Christ at the time of his return. We saw in Revelation 19 that when Christ returns, he will utterly defeat and destroy "kings" and "captains" and "mighty men" and "all men, both free and slave, both small and great" (v. 18). Later in verse 21 we read the "rest" of mankind were also slain by the sword of Jesus Christ. In other words, to put it simply, why would Satan need to be bound in Revelation 20 lest he deceive the nations when the nations have all been utterly destroyed by Christ in Revelation 19? My point is that Revelation 20 takes us back to the beginning of the present church age and describes the course of church history up to the end when Christ returns.

The Binding of Satan

Premillennialists insist that Satan's imprisonment in 20:1-3 is not compatible with the dimensions of his present activity as portrayed in the New Testament epistles.[2] However, the question must be asked: *In regard to what is Satan bound? Is the binding of Satan designed to immobilize him from any and all activities? The premillennialist thinks so. But that is not what John says. The premillennial interpretation errs in that it has attempted to universalize what John explicitly restricts.*

---

2. For example, in 1 Corinthians 5:5; 2 Corinthians 4:3-4; Ephesians 6:10-20; 1 Thessalonians 2:18; James 4:7; 1 Peter 5:8-9; and 1 John 4:4; 5:19.

Two statements in Revelation 20 tell us the purpose of Satan's imprisonment. First, in verse 3, John says that Satan was bound "so that he should not deceive the nations any longer." Then second, in verse 8, John tells us that upon his release from the abyss Satan will come out "to deceive the nations which are in the four corners of the earth, Gog and Magog, to gather them together for the war." Note well what John does and does not say. He does not say that Satan was bound so that he should no longer persecute Christians, or so that he should no longer prowl about "like a roaring lion" devouring believers (1 Pet. 5:8). He does not say that Satan was bound so that he should no longer concoct schemes to disrupt church unity (2 Cor. 2:11), or so that he could no longer disguise himself as an angel of light (2 Cor. 11:14). He does not say that Satan was bound so that he could no longer hurl his flaming missiles at Christians (Eph. 6:16), or so that he could be kept from thwarting the plans of the apostle Paul (1 Thess. 2:18) or other church planters.

Rather, John says that Satan was bound so that he should no longer deceive the nations (v. 3), the purpose behind which is to mobilize them in an international rebellion against the people of God (v. 8). And the language John employs in verses 1-3 makes it clear that there is no possible way for Satan to do so during the thousand years. The restriction on this particular aspect of his sinister ministry is absolute and invincible. The intent of the devil is to incite a premature eschatological conflict, to provoke Armageddon before its time, that is to say, before God's time. The exalted Christ, through the agency of an angelic being, has temporarily stripped Satan of his ability to orchestrate the nations of the earth for the final battle.

The final assault against the Lamb and his elect shall come only when the restriction placed on this element of Satan's work is lifted. For the duration of the present Christian era Satan's hand is stayed. Upon release from his imprisonment, just before the second coming of Jesus, he will dispatch his demonic hordes "which go out to the kings of the whole world, to gather them together for the war of the great day of God, the Almighty" (Rev. 16:14).

Although Satan may and will do much in this present age (as the epistles clearly indicate), there is one thing of which John assures us: Satan will never be permitted to incite and organize the unbelieving nations of the world in a final, catastrophic assault against the church until such time as God in his providence so determines. That event, which the Lord will immediately terminate with the fiery breath of his mouth (Rev. 20:9), will come only at the end of this age. John does not say that Satan's activity is altogether eliminated, but that it has been effectively curtailed in *one particular domain*. The binding is absolute and, at least for the duration of a "millennium," unbreakable. It is designed solely for one purpose, *to prohibit and prevent a satanic plot to deceive the nations into a war which, in view of the prophetic plan and power of God, is both premature and futile.*

Yet another form of deception that Satan perpetrated prior to Christ's first advent pertains to the gospel. There is a sense in which prior to Christ's first coming all "nations," with the exception of Israel, were "deceived" by Satan and thus prevented from embracing the truth (with certain notable exceptions, of course). The universal expansion and embrace of the gospel (Matt. 28:19) subsequent to Christ's first coming is the direct result of Satan's being bound. Especially relevant in this regard is Paul's statement in Acts 26:16-18 concerning the mission given him by the exalted Christ:

> "But rise and stand upon your feet, for I have appeared to you for this purpose, to appoint you as a servant and witness to the things in which you have seen me and to those in which I will appear to you, delivering you from your people and from the Gentiles – to whom I am sending you to open their eyes, so that they may turn from darkness to light and from the power of Satan to God, that they may receive forgiveness of sins and a place among those who are sanctified by faith in me."

The Gentiles ("nations") are portrayed as being in darkness with respect to the gospel, having been blinded ("deceived") while under the dominion of Satan. However, as a result of Christ's first coming, such deception no longer obtains. The nations or Gentiles may now receive the forgiveness of sins and the divine inheritance. Thus, the binding of Satan means that throughout this present Gospel Age, which began with Christ's first coming and extends nearly to the second coming, the devil's influence on earth is curtailed so that he is unable to prevent the extension of the church among the nations by means of an active missionary program. During this entire period, he is prevented from causing the nations of the world to destroy the church. "By means of the preaching of the Word as applied by the Holy Spirit, the elect, from all parts of the world, are brought from darkness to light. In that sense the church conquers the nations, and the nations do not conquer the church."[3]

Though Satan still blinds the minds of the unbelieving (2 Cor. 4:4), he is providentially restricted from hindering the pervasive expansion of the gospel throughout the world. Satan may win an occasional battle, but the war belongs to Christ!

So, to sum up thus far, *I believe Revelation 20:1-6 is telling us that during the course of this present church age Satan is prevented from orchestrating a global assault against the church. It is during this time that all who die having believed in Jesus join with him in heaven, in the intermediate state, where they share his reign and rule over the affairs of earth. Just before the return of Christ, the restriction placed on Satan will be lifted and he will once again deceive the unbelieving nations into launching a war against the church. We know this war to be what Revelation calls Armageddon. At that time, Christ returns from heaven with his saints and defeats them all, Satan is judged and cast into the lake of fire, the unbelieving dead are all raised to stand judgment, and are in turn cast into the lake of fire to suffer the second death.*

In this way John encourages all believers who are facing martyrdom to remember that although they may die physically at the hands of the Beast they will live spiritually in the presence

---

3. William Hendrickson, *More Than Conquerors: An Interpretation of the Book of Revelation* (Grand Rapids: Baker, 1939 [the 22nd printing was released in 1977], 226-27.

of the Lamb. This, I believe, is what John means by the "first resurrection." Especially relevant in this regard is the letter to the church at Smyrna in Revelation 2 and its emphasis on the blessedness of Christian death. To the believers in Smyrna Jesus speaks these words of encouragement and comfort:

> "Do not fear what you are about to suffer. Behold, the devil is about to throw some of you into prison, that you may be tested, and for ten days you will have tribulation. Be faithful unto death, and I will give you the crown of life. He who has an ear, let him hear what the Spirit says to the churches. The one who conquers will not be hurt by the second death" (Rev. 2:10-11).

There are several other things to note in those verses, each of which draws our attention to the obvious parallel in Revelation 20. First, it speaks of martyrdom as the result of steadfast faith ("be faithful unto death"). Second, the faithful are promised "the crown of life". And third, the faithful martyrs are exempt from the second death ("he who overcomes shall not be hurt by the second death"). This is precisely what we find in Revelation 20:1-6!

Also consider the promise to the overcomer in Revelation 3:21 that he will be enthroned with Christ. When a Christian dies, he/she does not fall into a state of unconsciousness. Rather the believer enters into life in the intermediate state where he/she is enthroned with Christ and rules with Christ. Since John (and Jesus) in Revelation 2 and 3 conceived of the intermediate state as "souls" living beyond death (hence a resurrection), and as an experience characterized by enthronement with Christ (hence reigning with him), we should not be surprised that in Revelation 20 he likewise describes the intermediate state as souls living and reigning with Christ!

One Thousand Years: Literal or Figurative?

Many insist that the words "one thousand years" must mean literal years, which is to say, arithmetically and chronologically precise years. But as we have seen repeatedly in our study of Revelation, in virtually every instance where a number is mentioned it is symbolic of theological truth. In other texts "one thousand" rarely if ever is meant to be taken with arithmetical precision.[4] We are told in Psalm 50:10 that God owns "the cattle on a thousand hills." Obviously, this does not mean that the cattle on the thousand and first hill belong to someone else. His point is that there are countless cattle on countless hills and he owns them all! So why the number 1,000 here? The sacred number seven is combined with the equally sacred number three, pointing to the number of holy perfection, which is ten. Ten is then cubed to equal one thousand to remind us of absolute completeness. The saints live and reign with Christ for an exalted and perfect period of time.

The Amillennialist's Millennial Kingdom

That John is talking about the intermediate state in Revelation 20:4-6 seems obvious once the parallel with Revelation 6:9-11 is noted. A careful examination of these two passages will reveal that they are describing the same experience of believers who die and enter into the life of the intermediate state.

Revelation 6:9	*Revelation 20:4*
"And ... I saw"	"And I saw...
"the souls of those who had been slain"	"the souls of those who had been beheaded"
"because of the word of God"	"because of the word of God"
"and because of the testimony they had maintained.:	"because of the testimony of Jesus"

That John is describing the same scene, namely, that of the blessedness of the intermediate state, seems beyond reasonable doubt. The key is that John, in both instances, is describing the experience of disembodied "souls" who had been martyred for their faith in Jesus Christ.

---

4. This is true whether the context is non-temporal (Ps. 50:10; Song of Solomon 4:4; Josh. 23:10; Isa. 60:22; Deut. 1:11; Job 9:3; Eccles. 7:28), in which case the usage is always figurative, indeed hyperbolical, or temporal (Deut. 7:9; 1 Chron. 16:15; Pss. 84:10; 90:4; 105:8; 2 Pet. 3:8).

John could hardly have been more explicit concerning the location, and therefore the nature, of the millennial rule of the saints when he said that he saw "thrones" (*thronous*). Where are these thrones upon which the saints sit, which is also to ask, what is the nature of their millennial rule? The word "thrones" occurs forty-seven times in Revelation. Twice (2:13; 13:2) it refers to Satan's throne (being synonymous with his authority or power) and once to the throne of the Beast (16:10). On four occasions it refers to God's throne on the new earth in consequence of its having come down from heaven (21:3, 5; 22:1, 3). In every other instance (forty times) the word refers to a throne in heaven, either that of God the Father, or of Christ, or of the twenty-four elders, etc.

Let me briefly sum up what I believe Revelation 20:1-10 is saying. John has a vision of the binding of Satan that is designed to prevent our ancient enemy from leading the unsaved nations into a premature provocation of the final battle, Armageddon. In addition, so long as Satan is restrained in this way, the gospel may spread beyond the borders of Israel to bring salvation to the Gentile world. John also sees the martyred saints: those who had refused to worship the Beast but instead remained faithful to Jesus Christ. In spite of having lost their physical lives, they are raised to life together with Christ in the intermediate state (as disembodied souls) where they rule and reign with the Lord for the duration of the present church age (2 Cor. 5:1-10; Phil. 1:19-24; Rev. 6:9-11). This is the first resurrection.

These faithful servants are truly blessed and holy, as they will never suffer the second death. Indeed, they reign as priests of God and of Christ (cf. Rev. 3:21). Near the close of the current church age, as the "thousand" years approaches its end, Satan will be released from the abyss and all restraints will be lifted. He will deceive the unbelieving nations into thinking that an assault against Christ and his church will succeed, only to suffer sudden and decisive defeat when the Lord Jesus returns from heaven with those believers who have until now shared his dominion and rule (Rev. 20:7-10).

The Final Battle

When the millennial reign reaches its climax just before the second coming of Christ, Satan will be released from his prison. That is to say, the restraint that God has placed on Satan during this present church age will be removed. Satan will immediately take steps to gather the unbelieving nations of the earth to make war on the people of God. This war is identical with the war of Armageddon that we read about earlier in Revelation 16 and again in Revelation 19. These are different descriptions of the final battle between the kingdom of Satan and the kingdom of Christ.

There is an important theological lesson for us here. This scenario reminds us that the tendencies of the human heart do not improve or evolve upwardly over time. No sooner does God release Satan to deceive the nations once again, that the nations quickly fall in line and follow his wicked deception. Satan's success in leading all the nations of the earth into rebellion "makes it plain that the ultimate root of sin is not poverty or inadequate social conditions or an unfortunate environment; it is the rebelliousness of the human heart."[5]

These unbelieving nations are symbolically referred to as "Gog and Magog" and "their number is like the sand of the sea," a standard way of describing an innumerable multitude. In other words, from a strictly human point of view, this final assault against the church will appear to be an easy win for the forces of Satan and evil. The number of those who gather to destroy the church is beyond calculation. But such is no problem for the risen Lord Jesus Christ. Even though the enemies of Christ's kingdom surround "the camp of the saints and the beloved city," they have no hope of defeating the King of kings and Lord of lords.

And contrary to what many of you have been taught, there is no biblical basis whatsoever for trying to identify Gog and Magog with Russia or Iran or any other single nation of the earth. Notice that Gog and Magog are constituted by "the nations that are at the

---

5. George E. Ladd, *A Commentary on the Revelation of John* (Grand Rapids: Eerdmans, 1972), 269.

four corners of the earth" (v. 8). In other words, *Gog and Magog are all the nations of the earth aligned in opposition to the church of Jesus Christ.*

Here the church is portrayed in terms taken from the Old Testament. Just like ancient Israel, "the church on earth is a wilderness community, camping but not at home in the earth."[6] We, the church, are a pilgrim people passing through life on this earth toward the promised land of the new earth yet to come. In spite of the fact that the church is an alien community in a world that is not their home, our identity is clear: we are "the beloved city." Remember, all through Revelation the people of God are portrayed as the New Jerusalem (Rev. 3:12; 11:2).

Satan's defeat and the destruction of the unbelieving nations is swift and final. We don't know if this "fire" that comes down from heaven is literal, like unto what consumed the people in Sodom and Gomorrah, but it is in any case a consummate victory for God's people and a total defeat for Satan and his forces. Paul spoke of this in 2 Thessalonians 1:7-8 and said that when Jesus returns, he will be "revealed from heaven with his mighty angels in flaming fire, inflicting vengeance on those who do not know God and on those who do not obey the gospel of our Lord Jesus."

Satan and the Beast and the False Prophet will be cast into the lake of fire. Remember, Satan is a spiritual being. Literal fire cannot harm him. And the Beast and False Prophet in Revelation are primarily symbolic images of corporate or institutional opposition to Christ, be it political, religious, educational, or military. So the "lake of fire and sulfur" is designed to evoke an image of pain and suffering, even if it is not physical in nature. It is a vivid and graphic way of portraying the endless suffering of all who stand in unrepentant opposition to God and the Lord Jesus Christ.

The Final Judgment

What we have in verses 11-15 is a more detailed and graphic portrayal of the judgment that was first mentioned back in Revelation 11:18:

---

6. Dennis Johnson, *Triumph of the Lamb,* 295.

The Millennium, the Final Battle, and the Final Judgment

"The nations raged, but your wrath came, and the time for the dead to be judged, and for rewarding your servants, the prophets and saints, and those who fear your name, both small and great, and for destroying the destroyers of the earth." Simply put, the time of God's patience and longsuffering and mercy is over. The time for judgment has come. Paul warned the philosophers of Athens in Acts 17, declaring unequivocally that God "has fixed a day on which he will judge the world in righteousness" (Acts 17:31).

You've probably heard people speak of the final judgment as the *Great White Throne* judgment. That language comes from verse 11. We earlier saw in Revelation 4 and 5 John's description of the throne of God and the majesty and beauty that surrounds it. But the throne is also the place from which God will bring judgment upon an unbelieving world. The whiteness of the throne symbolizes God's own purity and the righteousness with which he judges.

God's presence on the throne of judgment is so overwhelmingly powerful that "earth and sky fled away." This is a way of describing the cosmic upheaval of God's judgments and the trauma brought to bear on the material or created realm. Remember the many times in Revelation that John spoke of great earthquakes, of mountains and islands being ripped out of place and cast aside, of the darkening of sun and moon, and of stars falling to the earth. The point of all this is that the first creation, the creation that was subjected to a curse because of man's sin, is now fleeing away, never to be seen again, and soon to be replaced by the second and final creation, the new heavens and the new earth (Rev. 21–22).

John then speaks of seeing "the dead, great and small" (v. 12). This undoubtedly is a reference to all of mankind from every age, both unbelievers and believers. The fact that they are "standing before the throne" indicates that a universal resurrection has taken place: all are now standing before God in their resurrected bodies. This is confirmed in verse 13 (see also John 5:28). That both believers and unbelievers are standing before the throne of judgment is evident also from the fact that two sets of books are opened: "the books" and "the book of life."

The "books" that are opened contain the record of everything that every unbeliever has ever done or said. God will bring justice to bear upon them in perfect harmony with the deeds they have committed. But those who are by faith in Christ will not be judged based on their works but solely on whether or not their names are written in the book of life. This "book" appeared earlier in Revelation in 3:5; 13:8; and 17:8. There we were told that the names in it were written down "from the foundation of the world". This is the Lamb's book of life. "It is the registry of those from every nation whom he 'purchased for God' with his blood (5:9), and it is the one book in all the universe that spells the difference between eternal life and unending death."[7] Only those whose names were written down in the Lamb's book of life before the foundation of the world will escape the judgment of the lake of fire (v. 15). Of course, all who are believers in Jesus Christ will be judged, but it is a judgment not to determine who enters God's kingdom and who is excluded, but a judgment to determine the rewards that God will bestow on all of them for the works they have performed for the glory of Christ (see 2 Cor. 5:8-10).

Here, though, the focus is on the judgment of all the unbelieving from every age of human history. And you can rest assured that no one will be exonerated or found innocent. The evil, selfish, sensual, godless lifestyle of unbelieving mankind will stand as witnesses against them. The only hope for acquittal is the blood of Jesus Christ which they have spurned and rejected throughout their lives on earth.

How do I know that believers in Jesus Christ will not be judged based on their evil and sinful deeds? I know it because God has declared that he will not "remember" their sins ever again (Heb. 8:12). He has "cast" all their sins "behind his back" (Isa. 38:17). And as David declared in Psalm 103, "he does not deal with us according to our sins, nor repay us according to our iniquities" (v. 10), but rather "as far as the east is from the west, so far does he remove our transgressions from us" (v. 12).

---

7. Ibid., 299.

John also speaks of Death and Hades being cast into the lake of fire. This is again a symbolic way of describing the defeat of death. Paul spoke of this in 1 Corinthians 15:26 where he said, "The last enemy to be destroyed is death." Don't press the language of Revelation as if John is to be interpreted in some literal or wooden way. Death and Hades are thrown into the lake of fire just as the Beast and False Prophet were. This is John's way of describing the final defeat of God's enemies and his eternal victory over every force or person that has opposed him. God wins!

John describes this final judgment as the "second death." The first death is physical death. The "second death" is spiritual death, eternal and everlasting separation from the presence of God. Believers need never fear facing the "second death" for Jesus himself says in Revelation 2:11, "He who has an ear, let him hear what the Spirit says to the churches. The one who conquers will not be hurt by the second death." This echoes what John says in Revelation 20:6, namely, that "the second death has no power" over believers who experience the first resurrection.

Conclusion

There is only one conclusion: God wins!

Chapter Thirty-Five

The New Heaven and New Earth
(Revelation 21:1-8)

Not everyone thinks it helpful to focus on the future. They've bought into the old saying that people who do are "so heavenly minded they're of no earthly good." On the contrary, I'm persuaded that we will never be of much use in this life until we've developed a healthy obsession with the next. Therefore, we must take steps to cultivate and intensify in our souls an ache for the beauty of the age to come. And that is precisely my aim as we turn our attention to Revelation 21 and 22.

Why Think About Heaven?

A contemplative focus on the beauty of heaven frees us from excessive dependence upon earthly wealth and comfort. If there awaits us an eternal inheritance of immeasurable glory, it is senseless to expend effort and energy here, sacrificing so much time and money, to obtain for so brief a time in corruptible form what we will enjoy forever in consummate perfection. "Our citizenship," says Paul, "is in heaven." Knowing this enables the soul to escape the grip of "earthly things" (Phil. 3:19) and to "stand firm" (Phil. 4:1). Paul in no way denies or minimizes the reality of our earthly obligations. He reminds the Philippians that their bodies were in Philippi. Their names were enrolled as Roman citizens. They had voting rights. They owed their taxes to an earthly king.

They were protected by the laws of a this-worldly state. The same goes for those of us who live in Oklahoma City. We cannot ignore the obligations that fall upon us as citizens of this state and country.

But our fundamental identity, and thus the affection of our hearts and the focus of our minds must be in heaven! Paul appeals to our patriotic pride, not in Philippi in the first century or in Oklahoma City in the twenty-first, but in the New Jerusalem, our real residence! Therefore, be governed by its rules, its principles, its values. Paul is careful to insist that our citizenship "is" (present tense) in heaven, not "will be". We are already citizens of a new state. We are resident aliens here on earth.

Peter contends that the ultimate purpose of the new birth (1 Pet. 1:3-4) is our experience of a heavenly hope, an inheritance that is "imperishable," by which he means incorruptible, not subject to decay or rust or mold or dissolution or disintegration. It is "reserved in heaven" for us, kept safe, under guard, protected and insulated against all intrusion or violation. This hope is the ground for our joy that sustains us in trial and suffering (v. 6).

A few verses later he exhorts his readers to "set your hope fully on the grace that will be brought to you at the revelation of Jesus Christ" (1 Pet. 1:13). This is a commanded obsession. Fixate fully! Rivet your soul on the grace that you will receive when Christ returns. Tolerate no distractions. Entertain no diversions. Don't let your mind be swayed. Devote every ounce of mental and spiritual and emotional energy to concentrating and contemplating on the grace that is to come. What grace is that? It is the grace of the heavenly inheritance described in 1 Peter 1:3-6!

The expectation of a "city that has foundations" energized Abraham's heart to persevere in a foreign land. All the patriarchs are described as "seeking a [heavenly] homeland" (Heb. 11:14). Their determination in the face of trial was fueled by their desire for a "better country, that is, a heavenly one" (Heb. 11:16). As pleasant as it may be now, what we see and sense and savor in this life is an ephemeral shadow compared with the substance of God himself. Earthly joys are fragmented beams, but God is the sun.

Earthly refreshment is at best a sipping from intermittent springs, but God is the ocean!

A concentrated focus on heaven and the age to come enables us to respond appropriately to the injustices of this life. Essential to heavenly joy is witnessing the vindication of righteousness and the judgment of evil. Only from our anticipation of the new perspective of heaven, from which we, one day, will look back and evaluate what now seems senseless, can we be empowered to endure this world in all its ugliness, injustice, and moral deformity.

Setting our hearts and minds on heaven produces the fruit of perseverance now. The strength to endure present suffering is the fruit of meditating on future satisfaction! This is the clear message of several texts such as Matthew 5:11-12; Romans 8:17-18, 23, 25b; Hebrews 13:13-14; and 1 Peter 1:3-8. Let's consider one of these many passages.

Romans 8:18 is Paul's declaration that "the sufferings of this present time are not worth comparing with the glory that is to be revealed to us." We do not lose heart because we contemplate the unseen things of the future and nourish our souls with the truth that whatever we endure on this earth is producing a glory far beyond all comparison! Christians are not asked to treat pain as though it were pleasure, or grief as though it were joy, but to bring all earthly adversity into comparison with heavenly glory and thereby be strengthened to endure. The exhortation in Hebrews 13:13-14 to willingly bear the reproach of Christ is grounded in the expectation of a "city which is to come," namely, the heavenly New Jerusalem.

Nowhere is this principle better seen than in 2 Corinthians 4:16-18. Gazing at the grandeur of heavenly glory transforms our value system. In the light of what is "eternal", what we face now is only "momentary". Suffering appears "prolonged" only in the absence of an eternal perspective. The "affliction" of this life is regarded as "light" when compared with the "weight" of that "glory" yet to come. It is "burdensome" only when we lose sight of our heavenly future. The key to success in suffering, as odd as that may sound, is in taking the long view. Only when juxtaposed with the endless ages of eternal bliss does suffering in this life become tolerable.

There is yet another contrast to be noted. In verse 18 Paul juxtaposes "transient" things "that are seen" with "eternal" things "that are unseen." Note especially the connection between verse 18 and verse 16. Our "inner nature" is being renewed as we look or while we look at the unseen, eternal things of the age to come. If you don't "look" you won't change! The process of renewal only occurs as the believer looks to things as yet unseen. As we fix the gaze of our hearts on the glorious hope of the age to come, God progressively renews our inner being, notwithstanding the simultaneous decay of our outer frame! Inner renewal does not happen automatically or mechanically. Transformation happens only as we "look not to the things that are seen, but to the things that are unseen" (v. 18).

Nothing exerts such purifying power on the heart as does a contemplative focus on heaven. Meditation on the unseen glories of heaven energizes the heart to say no to fleshly desires. This is the clear witness of Colossians 3:1-4; 1 John 3:2-3; and 2 Peter 3:11-13.

Unpacking the Glory of Eternal Life in the New Heaven and New Earth

Here's how I propose to work our way through this remarkable portrayal of the age to come. We'll look at it in terms of what is present and what is absent, or again, what we will see and feel and experience and what we won't.

But first we need to look at verse 1. This present earth and the heavens above will "pass away" when Jesus Christ returns to destroy his enemies and consummate his kingdom. But observe closely that this present earth does not give way to a purely spiritual existence somewhere in the clouds above. The "first heaven and the first earth" give way to a new heaven and a new earth. The relationship between the former and the latter is ambiguous. Will the new heaven and earth replace the old or simply be a renewal of what we now experience? Certainly there are elements of continuity, even as there are between our present, corruptible bodies and our future, incorruptible and glorified bodies. In heaven we will be the same, though transformed, people that we are now. Yet, the heaven and earth to come are also said to be "new" or *kainos*, a word which typically indicates newness of quality, not time.

One element of discontinuity is the absence of the "sea" in the new creation. Those of you who love to fish and sail and water ski and ponder the expanse and beauty of the ocean need not worry. John does not mean that there won't be bodies of water in the new earth for us to enjoy. Let me explain what he does mean. The "sea" was typically regarded as symbolic of evil, chaos, and anti-kingdom powers with whom Yahweh must contend.[1] And we must not forget that in Revelation 13:1 (see also 17:2, 15) the "sea" is the origin of the Beast as well as the pagan and rebellious nations that oppose the kingdom of God. It is also the place of the dead (Rev. 20:13) and the location of the world's idolatrous trade activity (18:10-19). As Ladd has noted, in ancient times the sea "represented the realm of the dark, the mysterious, and the treacherous."[2] Thus, this is John's way of saying that in the new creation all such evil and corruption and unbelief and darkness will be banished. When Jesus stilled the storm on the Sea of Galilee, he was giving us a foretaste of heaven. It was his way of saying that one day he will rid the heavens and the earth of all opposition and rebellion and disturbances.

What we will See, Sense, and Enjoy in the New Heaven and New Earth

There are several things that call for our close attention.

(1) The New Jerusalem (v. 2). I've lived in nine cities in my life, some small and some exceedingly large. They all had their strengths and weaknesses. But none could ever be compared to the New Jerusalem. We'll look more closely at the New Jerusalem in the next chapter. But rest assured today that in the New Jerusalem there will be no pollution or traffic jams or property taxes or crime or ghettoes or smog or overcrowded streets.

---

1. See especially Isaiah 17:12-13; 27:1; 51:9-10; 57:20; Jeremiah 46:7-8; and Job 26:7-13.

2. Ladd, *Revelation,* 276; cf. Psalm 107:25-28; Ezekiel 28:8; and Daniel 7:3ff.

But the New Jerusalem is more than a place. The New Jerusalem is also a people: you and me! Here we see that the descent of the New Jerusalem from heaven to earth is compared to a bride coming to her husband. It would appear that John is equating the New Jerusalem with the bride of Christ, hence the church = the New Jerusalem (see Rev. 3:12; 19:7-8). This identification is explicitly reinforced by Revelation 21:9-10 where John is told, "'Come, I will show you the bride, the wife of the Lamb.' And he carried me away in the Spirit to a great, high mountain, and showed me the holy city, Jerusalem, coming down out of heaven from God." In other words, whereas in one sense the people of God shall dwell in the New Jerusalem, in another sense the people of God are the New Jerusalem (see also Heb. 11:8-10, 13-16).

(2) Intimate Fellowship with God (v. 3). The point of verse 3 is to interpret the significance of both the city and the marriage metaphor in verse 2. In other words, the imagery of verse 2 is designed to portray intimacy and spiritual communion between God and his people (in fulfillment of such Old Testament texts as Leviticus 26:11-12 and Ezekiel 37:27; cf. 2 Corinthians 6:16). This is what makes heaven so heavenly! What makes heaven to be heaven isn't the absence of the things that we dislike now on earth. What makes heaven to be heaven is the presence of God! Heaven will be glorious not primarily because there will be no sin or death or pain or tears but because of the presence of God.

No longer will there be any sense of distance between us and God. Never again will you feel that God is absent or remote. Loneliness is banished from the new heaven and new earth. Our constant companion, our closest and most intimate friend, will be God himself! Yes, God is omnipresent. He fills the galaxies with his glory. But his primary place of residence is with you and me! If today you don't sense God's nearness, you should comfort and reassure yourself with the promise that in eternity future you will always and forever be with God, and God will always and forever be with you.

This isn't to suggest that we must live now bereft of a sense of God's presence. The Holy Spirit lives in each of God's children.

Jesus promised in the Great Commission that he would be with us even unto the end of the age (Matt. 28:20). But Paul also said that "while we are at home in the body we are away from the Lord" (2 Cor. 5:6). But when the new heaven and new earth arrive, we will be "with the Lord" in every conceivable sense: spiritually and physically.

(3) Tears of sorrow and pain will be banished from the new heaven and new earth (v. 4). How could we possibly weep in sorrow and sadness and anguish if we are with God and God is with us? There are, of course, multiple reasons why we cry. Tears of joy and gratitude and amazement will certainly be present on the new earth. But gone forever are the tears caused by grief and pain and sin. The tears that we shed now because of persecution and slander will nowhere be found in the age to come.

But look closely at what is said in verse 4. It isn't the case that you and I will wipe away our own tears. God will wipe away every tear from your eyes. Many of you are weeping today. Some of you hold back tears of sorrow and suffering for fear that if you ever yielded to the tendency to weep you wouldn't be able to stop the flow. But in the new earth God will personally wipe away every tear! He will personally banish from your thoughts and your experience everything and anything that in this life led you to cry.

I'm a hopeless romantic and I love movies that portray it well. There's a particular scene in the film "You've Got Mail" that illustrates what we read here in verse 4. Tom Hanks and Meg Ryan have been corresponding anonymously by email. Hanks knows who she is, but she has no idea that he is the man behind the flow of correspondence. In the film's final scene, she discovers that it was Hanks all along. She begins to weep. He pulls out a handkerchief and begins gently and lovingly to wipe away her tears. "Don't cry, Shop Girl," he says. "Don't cry." Of course, I cry every time I watch that scene. One day God will pull out a handkerchief and wipe every tear from your eyes. "Don't cry, Susan. Don't cry, Max. Don't cry, Sam." Your sorrow today may feel overwhelming and endless, but it isn't. God will make certain of that when he wipes away every tear from your eyes. And he will do it because he will have banished from your experience every cause of pain and sorrow. Here we find the fulfillment of what is prophesied by Isaiah: "And the ransomed of the Lord shall return and come to Zion with singing; everlasting joy shall be upon their heads; and they shall obtain gladness and joy, and sorrow and sighing shall flee away" (Isa. 35:10).

(4) Death shall be no more! (v. 4). No more death. Not of husbands, wives, aunts, uncles, children, brothers, sisters, grandfathers, grandmothers, cousins, friends, neighbors. Funeral homes will be put out of business. Cemeteries will be empty, for all will have been raised in glorified bodies that are no longer susceptible to disease and decay. Never again the long meetings at the funeral home deciding on caskets and vaults and limos and flowers. No graveside services. No obituaries to be read, no video tributes of a person's life. No eulogies. No flowers to be sent or cards of condolence to be written. Never again a long caravan of cars with their headlights on. No police escorts to the cemetery. No headstones or awkward moments when you don't know what to say.

(5) Neither shall there be any more pain (v. 4). There will be no physical pain because our bodies will have been glorified and made like unto the body of Jesus. Paul spoke of this in Romans 8 and called it "the redemption of our bodies" (Rom. 8:23). Earlier in Romans 8 he made this remarkable promise: "If the Spirit of him who raised Jesus from the dead dwells in you, he who raised Jesus Christ from the dead will also give life to your mortal bodies through his Spirit who dwells in you" (Rom. 8:11).

In 1 Corinthians 15 Paul declares that "this perishable body," that is to say, this body that is subject to germs and bacteria and cancer and old age and decay, "this perishable body must put on the imperishable, and this mortal body must put on immortality... [and] then shall come to pass the saying that is written: 'Death is swallowed up in victory.' O death, where is your victory? O death, where is your sting?'" (1 Cor. 15:53-56).

This is what Paul had in mind when he assures us that Jesus "will transform our lowly body to be like his glorious body, by the power that enables him even to subject all things to himself"

(Phil. 3:21). That is why there will no longer be kidney failure or heart disease or diabetes or cancer. No more asking why me or how long? No decay or dissolution.

Those of you who live with constant, chronic pain and disability should be especially encouraged and empowered to persevere. The day is coming, and when it comes it will come forever, never to be reversed, when all pain will be gone! And not just physical pain, but emotional pain, marital pain, relational pain, the pain of a wayward child or an unfaithful spouse, the pain of disappointment and loss, indeed, the pain of every sort and from every cause, all will be gone!

You who suffer from depression or anxiety or relentless fear will forever and finally be set free! The joy and happiness and elation that will be yours will immeasurably, indeed infinitely, exceed anything you have ever experienced in this life or hope to have experienced. This is because "the former things have passed away" (v. 4). The "former things" refers to whatever may have been the cause of your pain. It will have disappeared, never to re-emerge. Indeed, as God himself declares in verse 5, he is "making all things new."

What will God Make New?

Does "all things" really mean everything? Yes! We will be made spiritually and morally new in the sense that our battle with sin and temptation and lust and greed and envy will be forever over. Your frustration with not being able to do what you know is right and your guilt for having failed will be gone. The struggle to resist wicked and perverse thoughts will give way to constant victory. As I have already stated, we will be made physically and bodily new. There will be enough continuity between what we look like now and what we'll look like then that we will undoubtedly recognize one another. But gone will be all defects and disabilities. You who are frustrated with your bodies now and live in constant envy of those you regard as more attractive or more athletic than you will never experience that on the new earth. If you hate your body now, you will love it then. Paralysis will be gone. Blemishes will be eliminated. Deafness and blindness and every deformity will be banished.

Let's be clear about this once again. You will not spend eternity as a disembodied soul or spirit. You will live forever in a new, transformed, glorified physical body that is perfectly suited and adaptable to life in the new heaven and new earth.

Reassurance from Him who Cannot Lie

"Sam, you say all this with such energy and confidence. How can you be so certain? How do you know it isn't all a pipe dream? How can I be sure that if I put my hope in this promise it won't come crashing down on me and leave me disappointed as has happened in so many other instances?" Good question. The answer is given in verse 5 – "Write this down, for these words are trustworthy and true."

How do we know they are trustworthy and true? We know because they are the words of him who is "the Alpha and the Omega, the beginning and the end" (v. 6). God has staked his reputation on it. His honor and fidelity hang in the balance. He said it, therefore it will come to pass. In fact, God speaks as if it has already come to pass. "It is done" (v. 6) is literally, "it has happened" (perfect tense). But even more to the point, the verb is plural, hence: "everything has happened"! In speaking this way God assures us as only he can that everything he promised will most assuredly come to pass.

What does it mean when God declares that he is "the Alpha and the Omega"?

As you know, "Alpha" is the first letter in the Greek alphabet and "Omega" is the last letter. But God doesn't intend for you to think about letters but about ultimate reality. He wants you to think about him! God is the first and only source and cause of all things and he is the final and only goal and end of all things. Everything originates from him, and everything finds its meaning and value in relation to how it glorifies and honors him.

This means that there was nothing before him. Nothing explains him. Nothing has caused him. He simply and eternally IS! There never was a time when God was not. There never was a time when he began to be. And there will never be a time when he isn't. He never at any time chose to be what he is. He has always been what he always is and always will be. God did not emerge out of a variety of possibilities. Rather, everything emerged out of him when he called the universe into existence. He is the Alpha!

But he is also the Omega. The goal of all things is the glory of God. The aim of all things is the praise and honor of God. Nothing has any intrinsic value aside from its capacity to enjoy God and to make him known. If history appears aimless to you, I assure you that it is not. Even the most random and seemingly senseless events in some mysterious way are serving to point to God and to shine a light on his wisdom and justice and power and love and holiness.

Two Blessings that God Supplies to those who Thirst and Conquer

In verses 6b-7 John describes both the blessings that God provides in the new heaven and new earth and the conditions that must be met to receive them. To those who "thirst", God gives freely from the spring of the water of life (v. 6b). Why doesn't he simply say, "to the one who believes"? Why "thirst"? In fact, this isn't the only time this imagery is used. In Revelation 22:17 we read this: "The Spirit and the Bride say, 'Come.' And let the one who desires take the water of life without price."

So here we have two words used: "thirsts" and "desires." His point is that saving faith or belief is more than a merely intellectual agreement with the truth of the gospel. Saving faith, the belief that leads to eternal life, is the thirsting of the soul and the desiring of the soul for the satisfaction that only Christ can bring. If you prefer the "beverages" of the world to the life-giving water of God himself, you will never know eternal life.

No one in their right mind prefers hell to heaven. But many prefer anything to God. Everyone is thirsty in the sense that all people long for and desire for their souls the deepest satisfaction possible. But unbelief is the preference of the soul for worldly pleasures and carnal joys in the place of God himself. God gives eternal life and soul-satisfying joy to those who long for and yearn for and deeply desire him above all else. When we read that God will give to the thirsty soul the water of life he means far more than simply prolonged existence. It isn't so much the length of life but the quality of life that is in view. It is life characterized by joy and delight and satisfaction and fascination and exultation in the beauty of God and all he is for us in Jesus.

But tragically the darkened mind of the unbeliever is at enmity with God. The unregenerate heart desires replacements for God rather than the refreshment that God himself provides. To the unregenerate, God doesn't taste good. He is at best bland, and at worst bitter. They see him as a threat to their joy rather than as its fulfillment. And so they eat and drink from everything the world has to offer, insanely thinking that it will bring them the happiness their hearts desire.

And would you notice how much it costs: it is "without payment"! You can't pay God for the water of life. You only have to thirst for it. You can't bargain with God. You can't trade for this water. It isn't up for sale or auction. It's a gift to those who thirst for it. Your thirst doesn't purchase the water. Your thirst doesn't merit the water. Thirst is not a work but simply another way of referring to faith. To be thirsty in the sense meant here is to be desperate and empty and persuaded that no one can satisfy except God alone. The water of life is free to those who thirst for it, for those who come empty handed and say, "God, fill me with yourself. Satisfy me with your beauty. Enthrall me with your glory. In your presence is the fullness of joy and at your right hand are pleasures forevermore" (Ps. 16:11).

But wait a minute! If we have to fulfill a condition before we can drink of this water, that is to say, if we must thirst in order to drink, how can it be said that it is given to us "without payment"? In other words, how does one fulfill a condition for receiving grace without earning grace? Part of the answer is that "when God's grace is promised based on a condition, that condition is also a work of God's grace."[3] Or to say the same thing in other terms, God lovingly and mercifully enables the conditions that he requires. The water of life is given "without cost" because it is God himself who graciously provokes and elicits the "thirst" as the condition on which the water is bestowed.

To those who conquer God grants the heritage of being God's son or daughter (v. 7). The one who "conquers" or "overcomes" is the one whose life is characterized by persevering faith in spite of persecution. For example, in Revelation 2:10–11, Jesus says to the church at Smyrna, "Be faithful unto death, and I will give you the crown of life.... The one who conquers will not be hurt by the second death" (Rev. 2:10-11). Conquering means experiencing victory over the forces of Satan and the world that tempt us to abandon faith in Christ (see Rev. 2:26; 12:11).

Look more closely at verse 7. Precisely what is the "heritage" or inheritance of those who conquer? It is the incomparable joy of being a son or daughter of the Most High God. There is no blessing greater than this: to be a child of God! That means you get God and all that God has. It means that just like the father of the prodigal son who cast aside all thoughts of personal dignity and ran down that road to embrace his repentant child, God comes to you with a ring and a robe and a never-ending feast of every spiritual blessing.

The Tragic End for those who Slake their Thirst Elsewhere

Those whose thirst for the things of this world was stronger than any thirst they might have for God will find their end in the lake of fire, which is the second death (v. 8). They were "cowardly" in the sense that they preferred the safety of blending in with the ways of the world instead of standing out by faith in Christ and happily embracing the persecution it would bring. They were "faithless" insofar as they put their trust, not in God, not in the beauty and joy of Christ, but in the satisfaction that comes with vengeance and sexual immorality and all manner of detestable things and idolatry.

---

3. John Piper, *Future Grace* (Sisters, OR: Multnomah Books, 1995), 79.

This catalog of sins concludes with "all liars" (*pseudēs*; see also the list in 22:15). In Revelation 2:2 this word was used of those who "called themselves apostles" when in fact they were not. The related verb form was used in Revelation 3:9 of ethnic Jews who "lie" by claiming to be God's people even though they reject Jesus. The word is also used in 1 John 2:4, 22; 4:20; and 5:10 of those professing church members whose doctrine and behavior reveals that they are in fact unregenerate. Thus, the emphasis isn't so much on telling lies in general as it is on professing to be a Christian when in fact one is not.

The End

All people, of every age, gender, and ethnicity will face God in the end. He is, after all, not only the Alpha but the Omega. But all will not find in him the same thing. Those who preferred the passing pleasures of sin offered by the world will meet God as the One who punishes in the lake of fire, while those whose thirst was for God and the blessings of forgiveness and fellowship that only he can provide will meet him as their Father, as the One who freely gives the water of eternal life and joy.

Chapter Thirty-Six

The Holy City: New Jerusalem
(Revelation 21:9-27; Isaiah 60:1-5,11)

Several years ago Ann and I, together with our two daughters, were driving back home from a short vacation in Estes Park, Colorado. I can't recall precisely where we were, but I think it was somewhere near the Colorado/Kansas border. We could see ahead of us that storm clouds were forming and sure enough it began to rain quite heavily. After the rain ended, we could see directly in front of us the most beautiful and majestic rainbow that we had ever seen. I've seen a lot of rainbows, but I had never seen anything quite like this one.

Now, it's important for you to understand that scientists assure us that it is impossible to reach the end of a rainbow. There is no such thing as a pot of gold to be found there, not only because there is no pot of gold but because there is no "end" point of a rainbow. I read several articles on why it is impossible to stand under or drive through the base point of a rainbow, but I'm not sufficiently educated in such meteorological phenomena that I could explain it to you, or even to myself. Nevertheless, we were captivated by the beauty and size and brilliance of this particular rainbow.

What are you supposed to do when you are blessed with an experience like that? We didn't know what to do. So we simply held our breath and tried our best to enjoy the moment before it passed. I can tell you honestly what we didn't do. We didn't pause to break down the many colors of the rainbow into their constituent parts. We didn't scientifically analyze the rainbow or try to decipher its size or shape or anything else about its meteorological properties. To have done so would have been to rob us of the overall impact of the rainbow's existence. We simply drank it all in.

It was somewhat similar to what people mean when they speak of missing the forest for the trees. In other words, it's possible to focus so intently on the individual trees that one loses sight of the majesty and beauty of the forest itself. Or again, it would be like standing at the base of Niagara Falls and trying to calculate the quantity of water that is ceaselessly crashing down all around you. Or again, it would be like standing at the edge of the Grand Canyon and failing to appreciate its breath-taking grandeur because you are too busy trying to figure out how deep and wide it is and how it was actually formed.

I mention these things as a way of preparing you for your encounter with the holy city, the New Jerusalem. Now, make no mistake about it. I'm going to try to make sense of the many constituent parts of the New Jerusalem and of the glorious gemstones that comprise it. But I will do so in order that it might enhance the overall visceral impact that gazing upon this city is designed to evoke. I don't want you to lose sight of the majesty of this city because you are overly obsessed with making sense of or interpreting its many individual parts.

I think perhaps the best way to experience the reality of the New Jerusalem is simply to stand back a bit and take it all in as a composite whole. When you do this, you realize that the reason John is shown this vision and the reason why he recorded it for us is to overwhelm our senses with the creativity of God himself. The purpose behind this portrayal of the city is not so that you might decipher the specific dimensions or overly analyze what each constituent part might mean. Rather I want you to feel the collective force of its beauty and the dazzling brilliance of what God has created. I want you to emerge from our study of the New Jerusalem with the same sort of feeling that I had as we gazed on that rainbow on our journey home from Colorado.

So, once again, my point is this: don't let your infatuation with the many trees blind you to the singular beauty and majesty and splendor of the forest itself. My prayer is that the Holy Spirit will captivate your attention and mesmerize your imagination with the glory of who God is and his immeasurable creative power that is revealed in preparing for you and me this city that will be our home for eternity.

Some Introductory Observations

First, the description of the city in Revelation 21:9–22:5 is largely based on the vision of the temple and city in Ezekiel 40–48. What will become clear is that the fulfillment of Ezekiel's vision of the latter-day Temple is found in the New Jerusalem in the new heaven and new earth. Many believe that Ezekiel's vision of the temple is to be literally fulfilled in an actual, physical structure to be constructed either during the so-called tribulation period or during the alleged millennial kingdom of Christ following his second coming. I think both of these notions are misguided. The vision given to Ezekiel is fulfilled in the new heaven and new earth and in particular in the New Jerusalem that comes down out of heaven to earth at the time of Christ's second coming.

Second, there is an obvious contrast between the vision of the harlot or the "great prostitute" in Revelation 17 and that of the bride here in Revelation 21. Note the similarity by which the two visions are introduced:

> "Then one of the seven angels who had the seven bowls came and said to me, 'Come, I will show you the judgment of the great prostitute who is seated on many waters'.... And he carried me away in the Spirit into a wilderness" (17:1, 3).

> "Then came one of the seven angels who had the seven bowls full of the seven last plagues and spoke to me, saying, 'Come, I will show you the Bride, the wife of the Lamb.' And he carried me away in the Spirit to a great, high mountain..." (Rev. 21:9-10).

Clearly John is being shown that the people of God are like a faithful bride, a holy and pure wife in relationship to God in obvious contrast with the unholy and idolatrous community of the unbelieving world. In other words, John is being shown how the entire world, in every age, is divisible into two contrasting parts. One is a harlot, a prostitute, an idolatrous and unfaithful woman who rebels against God. The other is a beautiful bride, a faithful wife who adores her husband and lives in perfect and unbroken intimacy with her bridegroom. It's also fascinating to observe that each of the two cities (Babylon and New Jerusalem) is pictured as adorned with much the same attire ("gold," "precious stones," "pearls,"; see 17:4; 18:12, 16; 21:18-21).

I should also mention the interpretation that these two contrasting pictures are actually of the same woman. The great prostitute of Revelation 17 is what the people of God were before they came to faith in Christ and were cleansed and beautified by the saving grace of God. The bride in Revelation 21 is the people of God now that they are redeemed and purified and cleansed of all stain of sin. It's an interesting thought, but I don't think that is what we are to understand.

Third, the question is often asked: Is this a literal city or a symbolic one? I take it to be symbolic, but symbolic of something very real. Note that the community of the redeemed, that is, the Bride of the Lamb (21:2, 10) is equated with the detailed layout of the city in 21:11–22:5. When John is told that the angel will show him "the Bride, the wife of the Lamb," he is immediately shown the "holy city Jerusalem." It should also be pointed out that just as John was "shown" the great prostitute so he is "shown" the beautiful Bride. We know the great prostitute was symbolic, so it makes sense for us to interpret the New Jerusalem as symbolic as well. Also, as we'll see in a moment, the dimensions of the city in 21:16-17 point to a symbolic interpretation.

I once had lunch with a man who insisted that the New Jerusalem is physically literal. He actually constructed a picture of what it will look like and how much territory it will cover when superimposed on the land of Israel. As much as I respect his love for God's Word, that is not what John intended when he recorded for us this magnificent vision.

The Vision

John's prophetic experience "in the Spirit" is a clear allusion to Ezekiel's experience (see Ezek. 2:2; 3:12, 14, 24; 11:1; 43:5). This verbal connection between their respective experiences may also confirm the earlier suggestion that John's vision of the New Jerusalem is the prophetic fulfillment of Ezekiel's vision of the future temple in Chapters 40–48 of his book.

Most important of all is that John is clearly told that the holy city, the new Jerusalem, is in fact a beautiful picture of the people of God. Back in Revelation 21:2 John saw the new Jerusalem coming down out of heaven from God, "prepared as a bride adorned for her husband" (v. 2). Then again, here in verses 9-10, when John is told that he will be shown "the Bride, the wife of the Lamb," he is carried away by the Holy Spirit and shown "the holy city, Jerusalem coming down out of heaven from God" (v. 10)! In other words, the city symbolizes the saints, the people of God. We don't simply live in the new Jerusalem. We *are* the new Jerusalem. This city *is* the church, the Bride of Christ, adorned in the beauty and loveliness that she has received by grace from God.

This may seem to stretch the limits of what you can believe, so bear with me. Think of the church today, with all its warts and splits and flaws and controversies. Yet here in Revelation 21 and 22 we are shown the church in its eschatological beauty as the Bride of the Lamb, adorned with every imaginable precious jewel and bathed in the glory of God! It's a good reminder to us all that as often as we may be tempted to bail out on church, thinking it beyond hope and repair, God has a plan for it that exceeds our wildest imagination, a plan to glorify and redeem and clothe this rag-tag gathering of believing men and women in heavenly splendor.

The Architecture (vv. 11-21)

We will examine each element in turn. But remember that the purpose here is not to stir up a focus on the individual pieces of the city but to construct an overall vision that stirs the imagination and awakens our emotions.

The city or Bride of the Lamb is said to have "the glory of God" (v. 11). In the Old Testament the physical temple was the place where God's glory resided and was manifest. But in the new creation God's presence (i.e., his glory) will abide in and with his people: they (we) are the holy city in which he dwells. Of course, this "glory" already lives inside every Christian in the person of the Holy Spirit. Jesus himself made this clear in John 17:22 when he said, "The glory that you [the Father] have given me [the Son] I have given to them" (see also 2 Corinthians 3:18). That glory will reach its consummate expression in the new earth and in the New Jerusalem.

On the "jasper" stone, see Revelation 4:3, where it is used to describe the appearance of God's being. Jasper "is an opaque quartz mineral and occurs in various colors, commonly red, brown, green, and yellow, rarely blue and black, and seldom white."[1]

The city had "a great, high wall," a reference most likely to the inviolable and secure nature of that fellowship with God which characterizes those within the city (cf. Isa. 26:1; Ezek. 40:5-6). No enemy can ever hope to breach that wall or assault God's people ever again. Of course, by this time all God's enemies have been defeated and judged. But John's point is simply to make use of the most vivid image in the ancient world for safety and security, namely, that of a high wall surrounding a city. No intruders. No unwelcome guests. Eternal life that is free from any and all threats.

The wall had twelve gates with an angel stationed at or on each one (vv. 12-13). On the gates were written the names of the twelve tribes of Israel. The wall also has "twelve foundation" stones on which were written the names of the twelve apostles (v. 14). The number twenty-four, the sum of the twelve tribes and twelve apostles, has already occurred in Revelation 4:4. Some point to David's organization of the temple servants into twenty-four orders

---

1. Alan Johnson, *Revelation*, 199.

of priests (1 Chron. 24:3-19), twenty-four Levitical gatekeepers (26:17-19), and twenty-four orders of Levites (25:6-31).

I agree with Beale that "the integration of the apostles together with the tribes of Israel as part of the city-temple's structure prophesied in Ezekiel 40–48 confirms further... that the multiracial Christian church will be the redeemed group who, together with Christ, will fulfill Ezekiel's prophecy of the future temple and city."[2] Thus, here again we see an emphasis on the one people of God, comprised of believing Jews and believing Gentiles, who together equally inherit the promises. Again, the New Jerusalem symbolizes the unity of God's people from every age: both believing Israel and the church together as one covenant people!

The image of an angel measuring the city-temple is drawn from Ezekiel 40:3-5. The measuring itself portrays the security of the inhabitants. "This cordoning off of the city guarantees protection for God's end-time community and especially guarantees that its walls will provide eternal protection, in contrast to old Jerusalem's walls, which were broken through by God's enemies."[3] See also Revelation 11:2, although there the protection was only spiritual as God's prophetic witnesses were subjected to physical persecution. Now, in the consummated temple, God's people are protected in every way, spiritually as well as physically.

Although the city is initially said to be laid out as a square with its length and width being equal, John indicates that it is also a cube ("its length and width and height are equal," v. 16). Each side is said to be twelve thousand stadia. A stadion was about six hundred and seven feet. Hence, twelve thousand stadia were about fifteen hundred miles. "A city this size would occupy the entire Mediterranean world from Jerusalem to Spain."[4] You may recall that the Holy of Holies inside the tabernacle was a perfect cube as well (1 Kgs. 6:20). I believe John is telling us that the New Jerusalem is itself the Holy of Holies of God's abiding presence for

---

2. Beale, *Revelation,* 1070.
3. Ibid., 1072.
4. Phillips, *Revelation,* 644.

eternity! Ultimately, then, the eternal Holy of Holies isn't a place but a people in whom God dwells and manifests his glory!

The wall of the city (v. 17) is one hundred and forty-four cubits (cf. 7:4-9; 14:1,3), i.e., seventy-two yards (two hundred and sixteen feet). There is obvious symbolism in this number, as the twelve tribes of Israel are multiplied by the twelve apostles of the church, pointing to the fundamental unity of all God's people. This fact points again to the symbolic nature of the city, for a wall of only two hundred and sixteen feet would be very out of proportion for a city that is fifteen hundred miles high. Some have argued that the two hundred and sixteen feet is the wall's thickness not its height. But again, two hundred and sixteen feet is only a fraction of the width needed for the base of a wall that surrounds a city nearly eight million feet in height!

Anyone who would try to envision the literal appearance of the city according to the human measurements given by John would be understandably confused. That is why John immediately adds that this vision is to be understood more deeply according to its angelic, which is to say its symbolic or heavenly meaning (v. 17).

We are told in Revelation 13:18 that the number of the beast, 666, "is the number of a man." Here in 21:17 we are told that the angel who showed John the new Jerusalem measured its wall: "144 cubits by human measurement, which is also an angel's measurement" (v. 17b). Thus we see a contrast between 666, the number of the beast, and 144, the number/measure of an angel. Interestingly, just as 666 is the numerical value of the Greek word "beast" (*thērion*) written in Hebrew letters, so 144 is the numerical value of the Greek word "angel" (*angelos*) written in Hebrew letters!

The material of the wall was "jasper" (cf. 4:3) and the city itself was "pure gold, like clear glass" (v. 18). If literal, how could gold be like glass? No matter how devoid of alloy and impurities, gold is still opaque, unlike glass which is transparent. But the problem only exists if one insists on a literal city. John is deliberately straining the limits of human imagination in his portrayal of the beauty and majesty of the city.

The foundation stones of the city wall are now enumerated. The list of twelve jewels is very similar to and probably based on the list in Exodus 28:17-20 and 39:8-14 of the stones on the high priest's breastplate. Note well that the jewels which in the Old Testament represented the tribes of Israel are now applied not to the gates of the city, i.e., the twelve tribes, but to the foundation stones, i.e., the apostles of the church! And we must never forget that in 1 Peter 2:5 the church of Jesus Christ is described as "living stones" that "are being built up as a spiritual house." The jewels and gems that comprise the material of the city are not designed to evoke thoughts of wealth, as if to suggest that money will be in endless supply in heaven. Rather, they point to the transcendent beauty and splendor and holiness of God's character as now revealed in his people.

That we are dealing with prophetic symbolism (and hyperbole) here is evident from verse 21 where each gate is said to be "a single pearl". How could there be a single pearl big enough that it would constitute a gate proportional to a wall that is two hundred and sixteen feet high? And how big must the oyster have been from which such pearls were derived? If one should respond by saying that God is certainly capable of creating an oyster that could produce such pearls, then one must acknowledge that he/she has departed significantly from what would legitimately be called "literal" hermeneutics.

Finally, the words "the street of the city", found here in verse 21, occur elsewhere in Revelation only in 11:8 where it is said that the bodies of God's prophetic witnesses were laid while the world looked on in contempt and derision. The phrase is repeated here to underscore that the street on which their shame was displayed has now been replaced by the street of their eternal glory.

The Temple: The Lord God and the Lamb

When verse 22 says that John saw no temple it means no physical temple, no literal building such as existed during the time of the Old Testament. There is a temple in the new heavens and new earth: God and the Lamb are themselves the temple! If this imagery is odd, recall that we have already seen the identification of the New Jerusalem with the bride of Christ. It is actually quite stunning, and instructive, to consider that John applies the prophecy of Ezekiel 40–48, in which the physical temple figures prominently, to the eschatological New Jerusalem in which there is no physical temple!

The Luminaries: the Glory of God

Does verse 23 mean that there will literally be no sun or moon in the new cosmos? Perhaps. But it may also simply mean "that God's glory is incomparable in relation to any source of light of either the old or the new creation."[5] If you were to light a candle in a dark room it would shine brightly. But if you were then to take that candle outside on a cloudless day, the brilliance of the sun would be so much greater that the light of the candle would be reduced to virtually nothing. So John's point may be that even if there were sun and moon in the new heaven and new earth, in comparison with the blinding brilliance of God's glory these luminaries would hardly even be noticed!

The presence of "light" in the New Jerusalem is just as likely a reference to enlightenment; that is to say, it points to the illumination of our minds and hearts to see and enjoy the splendor of God and his glory. We will understand then in a way that now we can only partially grasp. We will no longer struggle in darkness, wondering about what it all means, frustrated by our lack of insight and wisdom. No, then, in the new earth, we will see clearly and completely and never be in doubt as to the nature and truth of who God is and what Christ has done.

But how will we not be utterly consumed and vaporized by the full revelation of God's dazzling glory and brightness? You may remember that when Moses asked to see God's glory, he had to be placed in the cleft of the rock. We read of this in Exodus 33:18-23:

> "Moses said, 'Please show me your glory.' And he said, 'I will make all my goodness pass before you and will proclaim before you my name "The Lord." And I will be gracious to whom I will be

---

5. Beale, *Revelation,* 1093.

gracious, and will show mercy on whom I will show mercy. But,' he said, 'you cannot see my face, for man shall not see me and live.' And the LORD said, 'Behold, there is a place by me where you shall stand on the rock, and while my glory passes by I will put you in a cleft of the rock, and I will cover you with my hand until I have passed by. Then I will take away my hand, and you shall see my back, but my face shall not be seen.'"

Yet here in Revelation 21 we are immersed in God's glory, surrounded by it, inundated by it, beholding the fullness of it and yet we live! In fact, in Revelation 22:4 it says that we "will see his face"! How can this be? It can only be because whereas Moses was still in his unglorified and perishable body with lingering sin and corruption, such as is true of all of us now, when the New Jerusalem comes, we will be transformed into the likeness of Jesus himself. We will stand before God fully forgiven, cleansed, justified, and altogether glorified in our resurrection bodies.

This, then, is the consummate fulfillment of Isaiah 60:19-20: "The sun shall be no more your light by day, nor for brightness shall the moon give you light; but the LORD will be your everlasting light, and your God will be your glory. Your sun shall no more go down, nor your moon withdraw itself; for the LORD will be your everlasting light, and your days of mourning shall be ended."

The Residents

Verses 24-27 are a direct allusion to Isaiah 60:1-11. It would appear that John interprets the pilgrimage of the nations to latter-day Jerusalem in Isaiah's prophecy as being fulfilled in the future New Jerusalem, of the eternal state, on the new earth. There are several points to note.

The "nations" and "kings of the earth" (v. 24) probably refers to those formerly rebellious but subsequently redeemed from among the nations who will submit to God, praise him, and so become unified with the redeemed of all ages (e.g., Isa. 11:6-12; 60:11). These "nations" remind us of the promise in Revelation 5:9-10 that Christ has redeemed people from "every tribe and tongue and people and nation" (see Rev. 7:9; Mic. 4:1-2).

But what is the "glory" that the nations bring into the city? In Isaiah it appears to refer to material wealth and resources. But here in Revelation it is the praise and worship and service of the people themselves. It is interesting to note that the only other occurrences in Revelation of the phrase "glory and honor" are found in 4:9, 11 and 5:12 where it refers to the praise of God and the Lamb.

The absence of "night" (v. 25b) points to the unhindered access to God's glorious presence as well as the fact that there will be no darkness to dim the brilliance of God's glory. Indeed, as Revelation 22:5 indicates, the absence of darkness is due to the continual illumination that God himself provides: "And night will be no more. They will need no light of lamp or sun, for the Lord God will be their light, and they will reign forever and ever" (Rev. 22:5).

One final glorious truth about the New Jerusalem, God's people, is that sin will find no place there. "Nothing unclean" will enter or be present there nor anyone who does anything that is "detestable or false" (v. 26). Only those whose names "are written in the Lamb's book of life" (v. 27b) will be granted entrance and there they will live and enjoy God forever and ever!

Some are tempted to ask: "Is my name written down in the Lamb's book of life?" That is not a question that we are permitted to ask. The only relevant question is this: "Do you thirst for the living water that only Jesus Christ can supply? Do you desire him above all else? Is he the pre-eminent treasure and prize of your soul? Do you love him? Do you trust him? Have you invested your hope for eternity in his life, death, and resurrection? Do you believe that his death on the cross was for you, in your place, to endure the wrath of God that you deserved?"

If you can answer Yes to those questions, then I can assure you that your name is inscribed indelibly in the Lamb's book of life. But if you answer No to those questions, why won't you today, right now, instead answer Yes? There is nothing preventing you from doing so other than your own sin and selfishness and pride. So, repent! Embrace Jesus Christ as Lord and Savior by faith alone!

Chapter Thirty-Seven

Enjoying God Eternally: Eight Blessings of Life in the New Earth

(Revelation 22:1-5, 8-9)

So, there I was sitting at my desk, staring at Revelation 22:4 and the incredible declaration by John that in the new earth we "will see his [God's] face." It sounds beyond belief. We will see God's face! What does that mean? Later that day, during a short break, I logged on to a popular internet news site and saw the headline of an article that had just been posted. The title of the article was: What does God look like? The sub-title that followed said: "Liberals and Conservatives have different ideas." Yes, I was sufficiently curious that I read the article, written by a man named Mark Price. The study was paid for with grants from the Templeton Foundation and National Science Foundation.

A research group of psychologists at the University of North Carolina at Chapel Hill surveyed five hundred and eleven professing American Christians, asking them each: What does God look like? They actually put together what they referred to as a "composite mugshot" of God. The portrait that emerged shows that God is white, young, and clean cut, "not unlike someone from an 80s' boy band." As for the expression on his face, "Mona Lisa's vague smile comes to mind."

They also discovered that those who are politically liberal have a different picture of God in their mind from what is in the mind of those who are politically conservative. Liberals imagined God as "more feminine, younger, and more loving," while conservatives have a white male in mind who was "more powerful." According to this study, "Past research shows that conservatives are more motivated than liberals to live in a well-ordered society, one that would be best regulated by a powerful God. On the other hand, liberals are more motivated to live in a tolerant society, which would be better regulated by a loving God." The study also found that demographics often came into play with our image of God: Caucasians tended to see a white God; African Americans imagined a black God; younger people saw a younger God; and attractive people imagined a more attractive God.

A process called reverse correlation was used to create the final image, said the report. The five hundred and eleven test subjects were shown hundreds of randomly varying pairs of faces and asked which of the two looked more like "the face of God." Psychology Professor Kurt Gray, the study's senior author, said the study revealed people tend to believe in a God that looks like them. In other words, it isn't so much that humans are created in the image of God, but that God has now been created in the image of humans!

I hope I don't have to remind you, but I will anyway, that God is spirit. Yes, the second person of the Trinity became human in Jesus Christ, and Jesus certainly has a face, but I'm fairly certain that he doesn't look anything like this image! So let's turn our attention from the ridiculous to the sublime. And it is truly sublime to think that in the new earth, forever and ever, we will behold and gaze upon the face of God. Does that mean the face of Jesus Christ? After all, neither God the Father nor the Holy Spirit have faces. Or does seeing God's face mean something other than your seeing my face and my seeing your face?

Seeing the face of God is but one of eight glorious blessings that will be ours in the new heaven and new earth. Each of the eight is described in Revelation 22:1-5, 8-9. So let's turn our attention to them. But before we do so, I need to point out something that is very important. It doesn't take a genius or a biblical scholar to recognize that the new earth is patterned after the Garden of Eden. But it isn't merely Eden brought forward into the future. The new earth is a garden of such great glory and majesty that Eden pales in comparison with it. But there is no getting around the fact that in the consummation, that is to say, in the new earth, there are features that harken back to what God had in mind when he created the Garden of Eden, before Adam sinned, and God subjected it and all of creation to the curse.

What we'll see is that circumstances in Eden were prophetic of God's ultimate purpose in human history. But the last things, in the new earth, far surpass the former things in Eden. If Genesis 3 tells the story of "Paradise Lost," Revelation 22 tells of "Paradise Regained." The new heaven and new earth are but the glorious consummation of God's original design for the Garden of Eden. What the first Adam lost by his transgression, the last Adam, Jesus, has regained by his obedience.

(1) Perpetual, unbroken access to the very life of God himself

You may recall that back in Revelation 21:6 God promised to all who desire and yearn for him that he would quench their thirst "from the spring of the water of life." The "spring" is now portrayed as a river! But why does the river of the water of life flow from God the Father and the Lamb, God the Son, but no mention is made of the Holy Spirit? Ah, but mention is made of him! The Spirit is himself the living water. But it is not just the Spirit we receive but everything the Spirit does: cleansing, refreshing, empowering, etc.

This picture is clearly drawn from the Garden of Eden as described in Genesis 2:10. There we read that "a river flowed out of Eden to water the garden, and there it divided and became four rivers." In Ezekiel's vision of the temple, he is shown a flow of water coming from beneath the threshold. It was at first only ankle deep, then knee deep, then waist deep. We then read in Ezekiel 47:5 that "it was a river that I could not pass through, for the water had risen. It was deep enough to swim in, a river that could not be passed through."

We can't be certain, but it is likely that the ever-increasing depths of the water points to the increasing power of God's grace as it advances in redemptive history. In other words, as we approach the return of Christ and the consummation of all things in the new earth, the presence of God's power will grow, and its impact will deepen until there are no limits to it. This verse is also an echo or perhaps even a fulfillment of Psalm 46:4: "There is a river whose streams make glad the city of God, the holy habitation of the Most High" (cf. Rev. 7:17).

But why do I say that his river of "water" is most likely a reference to the Holy Spirit, or better still, to all the glorious blessings that the Holy Spirit brings to us? We see this in John's Gospel. It begins in John 4 with Jesus and his encounter with the Samaritan woman at the well:

> "If you knew the gift of God, and who it is that is saying to you, 'Give me a drink, you would have asked him, and he would have given you living water.... [For] whoever drinks of the water that I will give him will never be thirsty again. The water that I will give him will become in him a spring of water welling up to eternal life" (John 4:10, 14).

Later in John's Gospel, we read this:

> On the last day of the feast, the great day, Jesus stood up and cried out, "If anyone thirsts, let him come to me and drink. Whoever believes in me, as the Scripture has said, 'Out of his heart will flow rivers of living water.'" Now this he said about the Spirit, whom those who believed in him were to receive, for as yet the Spirit had not been given, because Jesus was not yet glorified (John 7:37-39).

Notice that the water flows from the throne where the Father and the Lamb, Jesus Christ, are sitting. This "water" is the Holy Spirit who brings us into the highest possible experience not only of himself but also of the Father and the Son. That, then, is the first of eight blessings that are promised to us. We could stop there. Who needs anything more? But there is more!

(2) Perpetual, unbroken access to the tree of life

We read in verse 2 that the river of life that symbolizes the Holy Spirit flows "through the middle of the street of the city," and that "on either side of the river" is the "tree of life with its twelve kinds of fruit, yielding its fruit each month." Thus once again we hear echoes of Eden, for it was in that original garden that the tree of life was first seen. Now it appears yet again.

It is possible that the street and the river are parallel with each other with trees growing between them. More likely verse 2a goes with verse 1b, in which case the "river of the water of life" is located "in the middle of" the city's street. Likewise, the "tree of life" should be taken as a collective reference to a multitude of trees that line up on both sides of the river (as is the case in Ezekiel 47:12). In other words, the one tree of life in the first garden of Eden has now become many trees of life in the consummated state of the second garden.

It's also possible that the "tree" of life is a reference to the cross! In Acts the cross is often referred to as a "tree" (Acts 5:30; 10:39; 13:29). See especially 1 Peter 2:24. In any case, we will have free and unhindered access to the tree of life and its many fruits. This points to the unending pleasure and satisfaction that is granted to God's people in this consummated Garden of Eden.

(3) Sustained health and happiness

The healing effects of the tree(s) of life extend to all peoples ("nations") who have believed the gospel. This cannot be pressed literally, for according to 21:4 there will be no more death or pain or sorrow that require healing in the eternal state. Again, as we have seen so many times before, John uses imagery that corresponds to earthly realities with which he is familiar to describe eternal realities beyond his comprehension.

Also, if the city "has no need of the sun or the moon to shine upon it" (21:23), the monthly yielding of fruit, which would otherwise be based on solar days and lunar months, must also be figurative. Thus the "healing" leaves indicate the complete absence of physical and spiritual want. It points to the abundant provision and perpetual availability of life and power and grace to meet every imaginable need. Johnson put it this way:

> "The imagery of abundant fruit and medicinal leaves should be understood as symbolic of the far-reaching effects of the death of Christ in the redeemed community, the Holy City. So powerful is the salvation of God that the effects of sin are completely overcome. The eternal life God gives the redeemed community will be perpetually available, will sustain, and will cure eternally every former sin."[1]

You may recall that after Adam and Eve had sinned, God placed the angelic cherubim "to guard the way to the tree of life" (Gen. 3:24). But not now! There is nothing standing between us and the enjoyment of true life forever in God's loving presence.

(4) The permanent, eternal banishment of the curse

Verse 3 tells us about the reversal of the Fall. What Adam set in motion by his disobedience is now overcome and replaced by the blessing that Christ set in motion by his obedience. The reference to "anything accursed" likely points to the global effects of Adam's fall. Everything that was subjected to the curse, material creation, humanity, our bodies, our broken relationships, etc. will be eliminated in the new earth. Richard Phillips points out that there are one thousand, one hundred and eighty-nine chapters in the Bible and all but four of them describe what takes place under the curse. The first two chapters of Genesis and the final two chapters of Revelation show life as God intended it to be and life as God will ultimately make it to be: free from every last vestige of the curse!

(5) Unending enjoyment of God / worship

The fifth of the eight blessings is unhindered, endless enjoyment of God in praise and adoration. We read in verse 3b: "and his servants will worship him!" Let's skip down to vv. 8-9. There we see how

---

1. Alan Johnson, *Revelation*, 203.

critically important it is for us to worship God and only God. Hear the warning of the angel who speaks to all of us who are tempted to worship and love and cherish anything but God: "You must not do that!"

"You must not do that!" (v. 9). You are tempted to worship sex. Don't do that! You are tempted to worship success. Don't do that! You, like John, are tempted to worship angels. Don't do that! You are tempted to worship money and possessions. Don't do that! You are tempted to worship some athletic hero or Hollywood star. Don't do that! You are tempted to worship yourself. Don't do that! You are tempted to worship peace and comfort and the security of life in the western world. Don't do that! You are tempted to worship the earth or the sky or the oceans. Don't do that! Worship God!

Worship in the new heaven and new earth will be endlessly fresh. It will never grow old or boring because God is infinitely appealing and infinitely fascinating. Think with me briefly about the infinity of God. When we say that God is infinite, we mean that there is no end to what is true of him. He never runs out of characteristics or features or fascinating facts about his personality and power. When you and I worship on a Sunday, many of you struggle to endure for thirty minutes. You sing a few songs and focus on a handful of truths about God, and then you're done. You're ready to move on to something else. Not in the new earth! Every moment of every day we will discover new and exciting things about God. Every moment of our life throughout eternity some fresh and previously unknown thing about God will captivate us and overwhelm us.

Let me give you just one example of what I mean. Consider what Paul says in Ephesians 2:7. God made us alive together with Christ and raised us up with him "so that in the coming ages he might show the immeasurable riches of his grace in kindness toward us in Christ Jesus." Making us alive in Christ and setting us free from the guilt and bondage of spiritual death was only the penultimate purpose of God. The ultimate motivation in God's heart for saving lost souls was so that we might become, throughout all eternity, trophies on display for all to see the magnificence and the surpassing riches of God's grace in kindness in Christ!

Paul's language is carefully chosen. He employs the plural "ages" to accentuate the stunning reality that redeemed sinners will bear ceaseless witness to the mercy of God, both now and hereafter. Like waves incessantly crashing on the shore, one upon another, so the ages of eternity future will, in endless succession, echo the celebration of sinners saved by grace, all to the glory of God. There will not be in heaven a one-time momentary display of God's goodness, but an everlasting, ever-increasing infusion and impartation of divine kindness that intensifies with every passing moment.

To emphasize both the extravagance and inexhaustible plenitude of God's display of grace, Paul makes four points. First, God is going to put on a continuing and perpetual public display of his "grace" toward us! Heaven is not one grand, momentary flash of excitement followed by an eternity of boredom. Heaven is not going to be an endless series of earthly re-runs! There will be a new episode of divine grace every day! A new revelation every moment of some heretofore unseen aspect of the unfathomable complexity of divine compassion. A new and fresh disclosure of an implication or consequence of God's mercy, every day. A novel and stunning explanation of the meaning of what God has done for us, without end.

Second, it isn't merely his grace, but the "wealth" or "riches" of his grace. God isn't simply gracious: his grace is deep, wide, high, wealthy, plentiful, abounding, infinitely replenishing. Third, as if mere grace weren't enough, Paul refers to the "immeasurable" or "surpassing" riches of his grace! His grace cannot be quantified. His mercy exceeds calculation.

Finally, one particular aspect of God's grace is going to be uniquely highlighted and experienced: his kindness! There is a deeply passionate and emotional dynamic in God's gracious affection for us that entails tenderness and gentleness and longsuffering and joy and heartfelt compassion.

Will there ever be an end to this grace? Does it suffer from entropy? Will it ultimately evaporate? Is there a specified quantity to God's kindness that will slowly diminish and someday run dry?

The point of Paul's effusive language is to emphasize that the grace of God in Christ is endlessly infinite, endlessly complex, endlessly deep, endlessly new, endlessly fresh, endlessly profound. God is infinite. Therefore, so too are his attributes. Throughout the ages to come, forever and ever, we will be the recipients each instant of an ever increasing and more stunning, more fascinating, and thus inescapably more enjoyable display of God's grace than before.

With that unending and ever-increasing display will come an unending and ever-increasing discovery on our part of more of the depths and greatness of God's grace. We will learn and grasp and comprehend more of the height and depth and width and breadth of his saving love. We will see ever new and always fresh displays and manifestations of his kindness. The knowledge we gain when we enter heaven will forever grow and deepen and expand and intensify and multiply.

We will constantly be more amazed with God, more in love with God, and thus ever more relishing his presence and our relationship with him. Our experience of God will never reach its consummation. We will never finally arrive, as if upon reaching a mountain peak, we discover there is nothing beyond. Our experience of God will never become stale. It will deepen and develop, intensify and amplify, unfold and increase, broaden and balloon. Our relishing and rejoicing in God will sharpen and spread and extend and progress and mature and flower and blossom and widen and stretch and swell and snowball and inflate and lengthen and augment and advance and proliferate and accumulate and accelerate and multiply and heighten and reach a crescendo that will even then be only the beginning of an eternity of new and fresh insights into the majesty of who God is!

There never will come a time in heaven when we will know all that can be known or see or feel or experience or enjoy all that can be enjoyed. We will never plumb the depths of gratification in God nor reach its end. Our satisfaction and delight and joy in him are subject to incessant increase. When it comes to heavenly euphoria, words such as termination and cessation and expiration and finality are utterly inappropriate and inapplicable.

If our ideas and thoughts of God increase in heaven, then so also must the joy and delight and fascination which those ideas and thoughts generate. We enter heaven with a finite number of ideas about God, with obvious limits on what we know of him. There is no indication that everything that can be known of God will be known all at once and forever. How could a finite being ever know all there is to know of an infinite being?

With increased knowledge comes intensified love. As understanding grows, so too does affection and fascination. With each new insight comes more joy, which serves only to stoke the fires of celebration around the throne. All of this accelerates our growth in holiness. When the soul is filled with ever-increasing depths of knowledge, love, joy, and worship, the more it is conformed to the image of Christ. In other words, the more we like God the more like God we become!

New ideas, new revelation, new insights, new applications, together with new connections between one idea and another all lead to deeper appreciation for God and thus fuel the flames of worship. And just when you think you're going to explode if you learn anything more or hear anything fresh or see anything new, God expands your heart and stretches your mind and broadens your emotions and extends every faculty to take in yet more and more and more, and so it goes forever and ever.

(6) Unhindered, unparalleled intimacy with God

Ah, we've finally arrived at the vision of God's face. What does this mean? In one sense it is to be taken quite literally. We will see Jesus' face. In case you didn't know, God the Son, the second person of the Trinity, when he became a human being in Jesus Christ became a human being forever. Eternally! The incarnation will never end. It will never be reversed. There will never be a time in eternity future when God the Son isn't incarnate as Jesus the man. And we will see his face.

However, to "see his face" is more than physical sight. It is certainly that, but it also means to know him in the depths of who he is, to enjoy him in all his glory, to experience and feel his love for us and to go deeper into intimacy and affection with him than we could possibly imagine in this life. Thus to see God's face means not only that we will literally see Jesus but that we will experience ever-increasing insight and comprehension of ever-expanding truths about what God is like! The "face" of a person gives expression to who they really are. We will see and know God in ways that we could never begin to grasp in this life.

This is remarkable given the consistent testimony of Scripture that in this life, as long as we are in this fallen, perishable body and live under the lingering curse of sin and death, no one can "see" God and live:

> "But [God] said, 'you cannot see my face, for man shall not see me and live'" (Ex. 33:20).

> [Jesus declared]: "No one has ever seen God" (John 1:18a).

> "he who is the blessed and only Sovereign, the King of kings and Lord of lords, who alone has immortality, who dwells in unapproachable light, whom no one has ever seen or can see" (1 Tim. 6:15-16).

But what has been true ever since the fall of man in Eden will no longer obtain for the children of God in the new heaven and new earth! What are the characteristics of this "vision" or "sight" of God's face?

- It will be utterly transparent. Paul says that now "we see through a glass darkly." But God will one day unveil himself in all his resplendent brilliance, glory, and clarity for us to see!

- It will be altogether transcendent. It will in every conceivable respect transcend the glory and majesty of anything we have ever seen on this earth. It will transcend any and all joy we have experienced here. We will never grow weary of seeing him!

- It will be totally transforming. By his grace we become wholly pure in heart.

We are told in 2 Corinthians 3:18 that "we all, with unveiled face, beholding the glory of the Lord, are being transformed into the same image, from one degree of glory to another." In the new earth the final stage of this transformation will be attained. We will, by God's grace, reach the final degree of glory. Just as the vision of Christ in the present (in Scripture) sanctifies us progressively, the vision of Christ in the future will sanctify us wholly. It is our experience of Christ that sanctifies. If progressive assimilation to the likeness of Christ results from our present beholding of him through a glass darkly, to behold him face to face, i.e., "to see him as he is," will result in instantaneous perfection or glorification.

John spoke of this in 1 John 3:1-3, where he said: "Beloved, we are God's children now, and what we will be has not yet appeared; but we know that when he appears we shall be like him, because we shall see him as he is. And everyone who thus hopes in him purifies himself as he is pure."

What is the precise causal relationship between this vision of Christ and final glorification? Two views are possible. On the one hand, it may be that we shall see Christ because we are like him; likeness, then, is the condition of seeing him (cf. Matt. 5:8; Heb. 12:14). Thus, this view says that holiness is a prerequisite to the vision of Christ and thus must precede it (the holiness, of course, is God-given, not earned by man). More likely, however, is that he shall appear, we will see him, and as a result of seeing him we shall be made like him, i.e., in his presence sin will be eradicated from us and we will reflect his glory and through the majesty of that moment we will be made like him.

(7) The joy of always and forever belonging to God

We have already come across this truth in the form of a promise. Now in the new earth we enter into its fulfillment. Jesus promised in Revelation 3:12 that on the one who conquers he "will write on him the name of my God." This is the same truth that we encountered in Revelation 7:2-3 where God's people are "sealed ... on their foreheads." This is God's way of saying: "You belong to me! You are mine! I will never, ever let you go! Nothing will harm you.

No one can snatch you out of my hand. I've branded you with my own name." Just as the "mark" of the Beast signified loyalty to him, the mark of God on our foreheads reminds us that he purchased us and that we belong to him.

[We've already considered the meaning and blessing of living in the "light" of God himself (see Rev. 21:23, 25), so we move to the eighth and final blessing.]

(8) Eternal co-regency with Christ / ruling and reigning forever

Over whom or what shall we reign (v. 5)? John doesn't tell us. It's possible that we will reign over (a) holy angels, (b) fallen angels (in hell), and (c) the created realm (animals in eternity?). Could it be that God has purposes and plans for new worlds over which we will reign? I don't know. Although we may struggle to identify the precise manner in which we will reign with Christ and although we struggle to understand over whom or over what, rest assured that God has plenty in store for us.

Conclusion

We saw from 1 John 3:3 that "everyone who thus hopes in him purifies himself as he is pure." This means that the most practical and purifying thing you can do in this life, on this earth, is to set your hearts and minds and affections on the promise of seeing Christ in the next life, on the new earth! The possession of such hope is the strongest imaginable incentive to purity of life. It is no passing fancy; it is a hope securely fixed upon him.

Chapter Thirty-Eight

The Spirit and the Bride say, "Come!"
(Revelation 22:6-21)

I trust that you have seen and heard and learned much from this study of Revelation, but here are the ten primary themes or points of emphasis that have most greatly impacted me.

(1) Christians in this present age can expect to suffer intense persecution at the hands of an unbelieving and idolatrous world. No one is exempt. To suffer is not an indication of God's disappointment with us but of our identification with Jesus and when embraced with humility and courage can be a tremendous way to make known the sufficiency and beauty of all that God is for us in Jesus.

(2) God is absolutely and comprehensively sovereign over all the affairs of all mankind. I say "all mankind" because not even the most wicked are outside of God's providential power. It often appears that the entire world reels with one blow after another. In Egypt dozens of Christians are killed when ISIS detonates a bomb on Palm Sunday. Bloody civil wars continually erupt all around the globe. Racial strife plagues our own country. Threats against Israel by Iran and other Muslim countries is a daily fixture. And drug cartels continue to supply a seemingly endless flow of illegal narcotics into various countries. The world, by all external appearances, appears horribly unstable and chaotic and out of

control. But the book of Revelation is God's word to us that he is in complete control.

(3) Jesus Christ is preeminent above all earthly powers and persons. At the heart of human sin is idolatry: the tendency to exalt as god anything or anyone above or in preference to Jesus Christ. But he is the King over all kings and the Lord over all lords. Jesus Christ is alive from the dead and seated at the right hand of the Majesty on high, reigning and ruling and exercising absolute sovereignty over all the kings of the earth, all the events in the Middle East and throughout Central and South America, and even in the lunatic plans of North Korea and China and Russia.

As "the ruler of the kings on earth" he mysteriously governs and regulates what all earthly kings and presidents do, sometimes restraining them from doing evil, sometimes frustrating their plans, sometimes ordering events so that they might serve his purposes. We can't figure out how he does it, but do it, he does! Thus, Paul declares in 1 Corinthians 15:25 that "he must reign until he has put all his enemies under his feet." So don't just read the newspaper or scour the internet. Read and reflect with the eyes of faith and confidence in the supremacy of Jesus Christ over all things.

(4) We have the assurance that God will accomplish his purposes and bring all things to their consummation in Christ Jesus. No matter how bad circumstances may become, no matter how oppressed the church may be, no matter how successful and powerful the world and its wicked ways appear, nothing can derail or disrupt God's purpose in history to bring a Bride to the Bridegroom at the wedding feast of the Lamb.

(5) As the global oppression of the church increases and intensifies, there will come a time when it will seem that the church has been destroyed. For a time, its voice will have been silenced and its presence barely noticeable. But this is only in appearance, as the church will rise up in power and be the catalyst for a global harvest of souls.

(6) Satan hates God and hates you and hates the church and will do all within his power, under God's sovereignty, to undermine

your confidence in God's goodness and lead you to abandon your faith. But we are assured complete and final victory as we overcome him by the blood of the Lamb and by the word of our testimony.

(7) Although the wrath of God against sin and idolatry will intensify and expand as we approach the second coming of Christ, no Christian will be the object of it, but will be preserved eternally safe and secure. God has sealed his servants, all of them, with the Holy Spirit and no amount of suffering or hardship can separate us from the love of God in Christ.

(8) Neither eye has seen nor ear has heard the marvelous blessings that God has in store for his people in the new heavens and new earth. Or to use the words of Paul in Romans 8:18, "For I consider that the sufferings of this present time are not worth comparing with the glory that is to be revealed to us."

(9) Judgment is certain. The one thing that will guard your heart from becoming cynical and pessimistic is the repeated assurance in Revelation that a time of reckoning is coming when God will bring justice to bear on the earth. Truth will be vindicated. Evil will receive its rightful recompense.

(10) Christ is coming soon. This is the very theme not only of Revelation 19 but also of Revelation 22. This is our only hope. This is our blessed hope!

A Miscellany of Observations

There is no clear structure in Revelation 22. What we find here is a series of statements, declarations, warnings, and promises, most of which have already appeared in one form or another earlier in the book. I will focus on a dozen of them.

First, once again I'm greatly encouraged by what the angel said to John in verse 6. After reading Revelation one is left in a whirlwind of amazement, perhaps a little fear, and especially with a question in mind: Is this all true? Or is it science fiction? Is this the real world or a fantasy land? Jesus knows that we all struggle with the bizarre images and graphically symbolic pictures in the book. It leaves us wondering if we can really trust and believe what we read here. Will the wicked of the earth really be judged? Will Jesus win out in the final day? Is life on the new earth as glorious and splendid as it is portrayed in the final two chapters? The answer is an unequivocal Yes! Earlier in Revelation 21:5 John was told by God himself to "write this down, for these words are trustworthy and true." Now again in 22:6 Jesus commissions the angel to tell John who in turn tells us, "these words are trustworthy and true."

Second, as a way of confirming even further that what God has revealed through John is trustworthy and true, notice how he is described in verse 6. He is "the God of the spirits of the prophets." The idea in this phrase can be paraphrased: "God over the spirits of the prophets" or "God ruling or inspiring the spirits of the prophets." In any case, God is clearly portrayed as sovereign over what prophets prophesy. God, as it were, owns, operates, and oversees the ministry of true prophets. This confirms what we see elsewhere, especially in 1 Corinthians 14, that the prophetic is entirely dependent on God, always awaiting his anointing and activity. Prophets may prophesy at will, but they only receive revelation by the initiative of God. Thus, more so than with the gift of teaching, prophets are somewhat passive, being instruments or conduits for the revelatory word of God, whereas teachers are more active, drawing directly from the Scriptures and expounding what they interpret. This is, in fact, the primary distinction between the prophetic gift and the teaching gift: the former is dependent on a spontaneous revelation while the latter is dependent on an inscripturated text. However, this should not be taken to mean that the Spirit is not also active in the exercise of other spiritual gifts, such as teaching.

Is the word "spirits" a reference to the human spirit of each prophet or is it a reference to the Holy Spirit? I think the answer is Yes. Let me explain. Some find it problematic to suggest that the Holy Spirit would be mentioned in the plural. But remember: (1) the plural is used for the Holy Spirit in Revelation 1:4; 4:5; 5:6; and (2) when the human spirit is energized by a charismatic manifestation of the Holy Spirit (i.e., when a spiritual gift is in operation), Paul seems to have in mind both. In 1 Corinthians 14 it is difficult to know when one should translate pneuma as "Spirit" and when as "spirit". Gordon Fee simply renders it S/spirit. Paul uses the same terminology in 1 Corinthians 14:32 ("the spirits of prophets are subject to prophets"; the only difference is that in Revelation the definite article appears: "the spirits of the prophets"). There Paul has in mind the control by the prophet of the manifestation of the Spirit. In other words, Paul is saying that, contrary to those who think prophecy is an ecstatic and uncontrollable phenomenon that overwhelms and overrides the will of the prophet, each individual is capable of consciously refraining from prophetic utterance in accordance with the rules and decorum for prophetic ministry in the church.

Third, several times in this concluding chapter we are told that the events in Revelation and the coming of Christ are "near" and will happen "soon" (vv. 6, 7, 10, 12, 20). I discussed the meaning of those terms earlier in this book, but let me remind you of what I think is being said. Some say that the words "near", "shortly," and "soon" mean that once the appointed time arrives the events will unfold suddenly or will occur rapidly. In other words, the emphasis is on the speedy manner of fulfillment. Still others contend that all that is meant is that the events are certain to occur. Some point to 2 Peter 3:8 ("With the Lord a day is like a thousand years") and argue that John is writing from the divine perspective. What may seem like incessant delay to us is "soon" and "near" for the Lord who views time from a heavenly perspective. Robert Mounce argues that behind these words is the prophetic principle of imminence: i.e., John's point is that the events could transpire at any time, even soon (although there is no way for anyone to know that with certainty; therefore, we must always be ready).

G. K. Beale contends that John's words "quickly" (or "soon") and "near" are a substitute for Daniel's phrase "in the latter days" (e.g., Dan. 2:28). In other words, Daniel, in the sixth century B.C., referred to events that would occur in some distant future, in a time that he called "the latter days." John, in the book of Revelation, understands Daniel's words as applying to his own time. "What Daniel expected to occur in the distant 'latter days' – the defeat of cosmic evil and the ushering in of the divine kingdom – John expects to begin 'quickly,' in his own generation, if it has not already begun to happen."[1] John is declaring that prophetic fulfillment has already been inaugurated in his own lifetime, in the first century. But the consummation, however, is yet to come.

We know from numerous texts in the New Testament that the "last days" began with the resurrection and exaltation of Jesus Christ to the right hand of the Father and will extend all the way until the second coming of Christ at the close of history. That is why John substitutes the words "soon" and "near" for "the last days" as found in Daniel. His point is that what was future to Daniel is now being fulfilled in John's day and will continue to unfold and occur until the time of Christ's return. It seems as if John's intent is to bring events which were once in the distant future into the immediate present. In that sense, then, "the time is near." Thus we may translate this phrase, "things which must soon begin to happen." Again, "as soon as his letter reaches its destination in the churches of Asia, they will be able to say, 'These things are happening now.'"[2]

Fourth, there is hardly a more important statement in this final chapter than the blessing pronounced by the angel in verse 7: "Blessed is the one who keeps the words of the prophecy of this book." This is a healthy reminder to those who are inclined to dismiss Revelation as too bizarre or obscure to be of any practical benefit.

Compare this with Revelation 1:3 where a similar blessing is announced: "Blessed is the one who reads aloud the words of this prophecy, and blessed are those who hear, and who keep what is written in it." To "keep" the words of the prophecy of Revelation is not simply to believe them to be true but to respond with obedience to their commands. Note the emphasis on the "words" of the book. We believe in verbal, plenary inspiration of the Bible. Don't ever think that Revelation is beyond your ability to understand or that

---

1. Beale, *Revelation*, 153.
2. Wilcock, *The Message of Revelation*, 33.

its commands and exhortations are irrelevant to people living in the twenty-first century. God's "blessing," his favor and grace and power, rests especially on those who take this book seriously and commit themselves in the power of the Spirit to follow its dictates and to believe its teaching.

Fifth, you may remember that at the conclusion of his prophecy, Daniel was told to "shut up the words and seal the book, until the time of the end" (Dan. 12:4). John, on the other hand, is told to do precisely the opposite with what has been shown to him. What Daniel was commanded to seal up for a future season, John is told to declare to all openly, for the time of fulfillment of such prophetic truth is at hand. The sealing of Daniel's prophecy was due to the fact that the time of fulfillment was still in the distant future, in a different age of God's redemptive plan for his people. What has been revealed to John, on the other hand, concerns the time in which he lived and the age or epoch of the church, spanning the years between the two comings of Jesus.

Sixth, perhaps the strangest statement in Revelation 22 is what we read in verse 11: "Let the evildoer still do evil, and the filthy still be filthy, and the righteous still do right, and the holy still be holy." Something similar to this is also found at the close of Daniel's prophecy. We read in Daniel 12:10: "Many shall purify themselves and make themselves white and be refined, but the wicked shall act wickedly. And none of the wicked shall understand, but those who are wise shall understand."

If this were merely a statement of fact, no problem would exist. But it is an exhortation. How is it that an angel exhorts unbelievers to be unholy? One commentator suggests that since the end is near "there is no longer time to alter the character and habits of men."[3] But we now know that for John and his readers the time of the end has extended for some nineteen hundred years. Perhaps the angel's point is that "the bent of one's choices forms an unchangeable

---

3. Mounce, *The Book of Revelation,* 392-93.

character, so that the imperatives have the sense of 'be what you always have been as you face judgment.'"[4]

Others argue that the meaning is to be found in Isaiah 6:9-10 and its use by Jesus in Matthew 13:9-17, 43. In both these passages unbelievers are exhorted not to hear because of their insensitive response to the prophetic word. "To such communities," explains Beale, "God sent prophets whose words increased the blindness of the apostate but served to shock the elect remnant out of the spiritual torpor characteristic of the majority. The impious were even exhorted not to understand, as a punishment for their apostasy and idol worship."[5] The exhortation of Revelation 22:11 would thus be a judgment in which those who have rebelled and resisted the word of God are, in a sense, consigned and given over to a deeper aggravation of their chosen behavior.

Perhaps the point is that the end time events will make a sharp distinction and division between those who are committed to godliness and those who are equally devoted to ungodliness. The intensity of God's wrath and the judgments to come will harden the unbelieving. You may recall these words that were part of the sixth trumpet judgment:

> "The rest of mankind, who were not killed by these plagues, did not repent of the works of their hands nor give up worshiping demons and idols of gold and silver and bronze and stone and wood, which cannot see or hear or walk, nor did they repent of their murders or their sorceries or their sexual immorality or their thefts" (Rev. 9:20-21).

This may then be a command for people to act according to their nature. It establishes human responsibility. Do what you want to do on the basis of who you are. But know that you will be held accountable. Or it may also be that this passage is designed to awaken sinners into the reality of what they are choosing to do and to realize that they will be judged.

---

4. Beale, *Revelation*, 1132.
5. Ibid.

Perhaps an illustration will help. Imagine that you are visiting the Grand Canyon. Your tour guide leads you to the precipice. You look over the edge into the canyon below, and he says to you: "Let the self-assertive fool who wants to destroy himself disregard caution, ignore my instructions, and jump over the edge into the canyon below and certain death." Is that what the guide wants you to do? No. he wants you to be careful and obey his instructions and stay back from what will certainly result in your gruesome death. Thus this "command" is God's way of saying: "Do you realize who you are, what you are like, and how you have chosen to live? Do you realize this brings judgment?" So stop and turn.[6]

Seventh, I mentioned earlier that one of the primary themes of Revelation is that God will bring judgment on those who have lived in willful disobedience and idolatry. When we look around in our world and see murderers and thieves and abusers and ruthless dictators seemingly getting away with their crimes with no repercussions, we can reassure ourselves that this will not last: "I am coming soon," said Jesus, "bringing my recompense with me, to repay each one for what he has done" (v. 12).

Eighth, we look next to the glorious promise of verse 14. What does it mean to "wash" your robes in the blood of Christ? It means you acknowledge your robes are dirty, filthy, stained with sin. You can't get saved until you know you are lost! It means you know you can't wash them in anything else: not water, not the soap of good deeds, not in the detergent of promises you kept. It means there is only one solution to the guilt and stain of our idolatry and rebellion: the blood of Jesus. And what does the blood of Jesus refer to? It refers to his substitutionary death in which his blood was shed as he endured the judgment and wrath reserved for us.

Ninth, we have already seen in Revelation 21:8 and 27 what we encounter yet again here in 22:15. Here John adds one element: "dogs", which in Scripture are generally regarded as unclean and despised and often refer symbolically to unbelievers (see Phil. 3:2-3; 2 Pet. 2:22). The unbeliever and the rebellious are like a dog because

---

6. I owe this illustration to James Hamilton.

he wallows in filth. Others choose not to submit to God but try to control the world through demonic sorcery. Rather than rejoice in the pleasures of marital intimacy they are sexually immoral. Rather than love and serve others, they kill them. Rather than worship God alone, they are idolaters. Rather than believe and live by the truth, they love and practice lies and falsehoods.

Tenth, Jesus has been described in many different ways in Revelation. Here in verse 16 he speaks of himself as "the root and descendant of David, the bright morning star" (see Isa. 11:1; Num. 24:17). Jesus is both the root, or source, of David as well as his descendant. He is thus the fulfillment of all the promises given to David. He is both David's Lord and his physical descendant!

Eleventh, there are no fewer than three invitations in verse 17. In the first one, the Holy Spirit speaks through the Bride, the people of God, issuing an invitation to Jesus to "Come!" Does that request fill your prayers each day? It does mine! "Oh, Lord Jesus, don't delay. Come now!" The second invitation is issued by the "one who hears," again a reference to those of us who are listening to the reading of this book. It is also directed towards Jesus for the same purpose. The final invitation is really an exhortation issued to people in general to believe and treasure and embrace Jesus as the only one who can quench their spiritual thirst (see 21:6).

Here is the solution to the problem of divine sovereignty and human responsibility. Do you want to come to Jesus? Then come. He will never cast you out. Do you prefer not to come to Jesus? Then you have what you want and you have no one to blame but yourself. Do you desire the water of life that Jesus offers? If so, then drink! He gives it freely. If you don't desire it but prefer to slake your thirst at the well of this world and what it offers, then you can't complain. Again, you get precisely what you desire.

Twelfth, these verses are clearly built on Deuteronomy 4:1-2 (cf. 12:32) and 29:19-20. Moses commanded Israel, "You shall not add to the word that I command you, nor take from it." What does it mean to "add" to or "take away" from the words of the prophecy of Revelation? In Deuteronomy it refers to those who taught, contrary to what God had said, that compromise with idolatry was not inconsistent with faith in Yahweh. To "add" or "take away" from the words of Revelation is to distort or twist its teaching to conform to what we want and believe rather than submitting to what God has said. He is talking about deliberate distortions and perversions of the truth of this book, often done in order to justify one's personal sins.

What are the consequences for disobedience to this exhortation? Some suggest that forfeiting one's "share in the tree of life and in the holy city" refers to something other and less than the loss of salvation. Perhaps it means heavenly reward or position. Some contend that true believers can and, in fact, do violate this command and thus forfeit or lose their salvation. Others contend that whereas loss of salvation is theoretically possible, it will not in fact occur. The threat of loss is the means by which God stimulates his people to obey the command. In other words, if a believer were to "add" or "take away" he/she would lose their spiritual life. But a believer, in point of fact, will not. The threatened consequence is what the Spirit uses to energize and motivate the believer to obey the command. Others contend that those who "add" or "take away" are not true believers in the first place. A true believer is, by definition in Revelation, one who refuses to compromise with paganism. These are people who by their profession and outward behavior appeared for a time to belong to the church, but whose unregenerate condition is subsequently revealed by their disobedience to John's command (cf. 1 John 2:19).

Conclusion

I close with a word of counsel to each of you regarding the urgent expectation of Christian men and women for the second coming of Christ. When we read in verse 20 the declaration of Jesus, "Surely I am coming soon," do you respond with unbridled enthusiasm and declare: "Amen! Come, Lord Jesus"? I hope and pray you do.

How seriously and sincerely do you look forward to the second coming of Christ? Does it occupy your thinking on a regular basis? I'm not asking whether or not you enjoy engaging in speculative debates with friends about the identity of the Antichrist or whether or not Russia will conspire with other nations to invade Israel. I'm not asking you about your opinion on whether or not there will be a so-called Great Tribulation and where you stand on the timing of the Rapture in relation to it.

I'm asking you: Does your heart pulsate in anxious expectation of seeing your Savior, Jesus Christ, face to face? Do you awaken each day with the hope that this day might be THE day of his return? And if your answer to that question is anywhere from "Sort of" to "Absolutely" to "Well, every so often I do," what is it that you expect him to do? What do you envision the purpose of his second coming to be? What is it about the return of Jesus Christ that makes the thought of it so exciting and fascinating?

Do you think about the coming of Jesus primarily as a remedy to the global war with Islamic terrorism? Do you think about the coming of Jesus as the solution to our planet's problems, whether it be sexual immorality or economic chaos or the on-going reality of abortion or some such other problem? Why do you want Jesus to come back? What is the predominant motive in your heart? What is it that you not only expect him to do when he comes but want him to do when he comes?

The second coming of Christ is not about the Antichrist or 666 or rebuilt temples or events in Israel. Stop thinking about or arguing and dividing over such stuff and start preparing your hearts to marvel at him! The second coming is all about Jesus Christ and our great privilege of glorifying God by marveling at his Son! Paul tells us that Jesus is coming back "to be marveled at among all who have believed" (2 Thess. 1:10).

Do you know that this is why you exist, this is why you were created, this is why God continues to sustain and uphold you in being? He made you and redeemed you so that you might marvel. Yes, to marvel is primarily a spiritual experience. Even quadriplegics can marvel. But for those with full use of their bodies, to marvel is to behold Jesus Christ with gaping mouths, bulging eyes, flowing tears, endless goose bumps, rapid heartbeat, deep joy, unending gratitude, dancing feet, and unending meditation on truths and ideas and images about Jesus that are so glorious and great that you will live in constant fear that your mind and heart are on the verge of exploding!

We will marvel at Jesus Christ:

- For his limitless power in subduing and defeating all enemies of God.
- For his impeccable justice in rendering punishment to those who rejected and mocked him.
- For his measureless love in caring so deeply about you and me.
- For his unimpeachable authority.
- For his incomparable beauty in dazzling our senses and far exceeding our expectations.
- For his integrity in having fulfilled all his promises to us.
- For his blinding radiance that infinitely surpasses all beauty and brightness in this universe.
- For bringing our salvation to its final consummation.
- For transforming our bodies to be like his own (Phil. 3:20-21).
- For being a perfect Savior, never failing to provide and supply what we need most.
- For eradicating from your mind and will and heart and soul every last vestige/impulse of sin!
- For pouring out his saving grace on us in such a way that we are not numbered among those who do not know God and who do not obey the gospel.
- For loving us into his kingdom so that we will not suffer the punishment of eternal destruction.
- For making it possible that we might experience his intimate presence rather than being cast away from him and the glory of his might.

Even so, come Lord Jesus!

Scripture Index

Genesis
1 284
2:10 513
3 .... 51, 340
3:8 243
3:15 336
3:24 516
5:24 325
10:1–11:9 381
13:16 270
15:5 270
16:10 .... 270, 310
17:4-6, 16 270
19:24 383
19:24, 28 .... 295, 296
20:6 309
22:11-18 310
22:17-18 270
24:7 310
24:60 295
26:4 270
28:14 270
31:11-13 31
32:12 270
32:28 170
48:19 270
49:8 258
49:10 258
49:17 258

Exodus
3:2-12 ....
3:14 .... 35, 195
4:31 273
6:3 .... 463n
7:11 365
7:14-24 326
7:17ff 409
7:17-21 409
7:20 283

8:1-15 413
8:10 .... 360n
9:9-11 408
9:22-25 282
10: 288
10:12-15 286
10:15 286
10:21ff 411
10:21-23 284
13:9, 16 .... 257, 369
13:21 311
14:19 310
15 .... 400, 401, 464n
15:11 .... 360n
15:12 347
15:16 331
16:32-34 94
16:34 402
19:6 39
19:9-16 403
19:10, 14 273
19:16-18 193
20:3 357
20:3-5 366
20:18-20 193
25:21 402
28:4 .... 51, 273
28:17-20 507
28:36-38 .... 168, 169
30:1-10 230
31:18 402
32:13 270
32:15 402
32:31-33 139
33:18 188
33:18-23 508
33:20 521
33:23 46
34:6 151
39:8-14 507

39:29 51
40:34-35 .... 403n

Leviticus
4:7 230
10:6 288
13:45 288
17:7 .... 422n
20:5-6 .... 422n
21:10 288
23:24 280
26 402
26:8 295
26:11-12 490
26:18-28 218
26:26 220

Numbers
1:3, 18, 20 269
2:3 267
5:18 300
6:27 174
7:12 267
10:14 267
10:35-36 308
12:8 47
14:33 .... 439n
15:39 .... 439n
16:12-14 361
22–24 94
22 .... 22, 32 354n
23:19 156
24:17 561
26 .... 2, 4
33:5ff 337
34:19 267
35:30 .... 339n

Deuteronomy
1:10 281

1:11 .... 500n	18:30 268	16:15 .... 500n
2:30 .... 323n		24:3-19 .... 199, 530
3:24 .... 375n	**1 Samuel**	27:23 269
4:1-2 561	2:6 321	28:9a 62
4:28 311	2:9 426	
6:8 .... 266, 384	4:8 338	**2 Chronicles**
7:9 .... 156, 500n	14:6, 15, 20 .... 323n	5:13 .... 418n
10:22 281	15:2-3 457	6:28 .... 297n
11:5-6 361	17:44, 46 .... 342, 487n	7:13 .... 297n
11:18 .... 266, 384	17:46-47 488	13:14-16 .... 323n
17:6 .... 339n	21:5 273	21:11 .... 439n
19:15 .... 339n	29:1 430	35:22-24 .... 430n
21:7-9 457	29:4 .... 353, 354n	
23:9-10 273	31:1-7 430	**Ezra**
28:10 174		1:1 .... 37, 322
28:26 .... 487n	**2 Samuel**	6:22 322
28:27, 35 424	5:10 41	7:27 322
28:38 .... 297n	8: 2b	9:6 457
28:49 296	11:8-11 273	
28:62 281	17:11 281	**Nehemiah**
29:17-18 295	17:14 .... 323n	9:23 281
29:23 309	19:22 .... 354n	
29:29 326	22:5 .... 360n	**Job**
31:16 .... 439n	22:9 309	4:10 300
32:4 416	24:1-9 269	4:16 255
32:17 311		6:10 155
32:30 308	**1 Kings**	9:3 500
32:39 321	5:4 .... 354n	9:5-10 320
32:40 327	7:13-22 169	18:15 398
32:42 229	8:10-11 .... 418n	23:10 187
33 .... 485n	8:37 .... 297n	26:7-13 .... 365, 511n
33:2, 17 308	11:14 353	26:7-14 320
	11:14, 23, 25 .... 354n	37:2-24 320
Joshua	12:11, 14 298	38:8-41 321
11:20 .... 323n	12:15 .... 323n	42:2 321
21:4 267	14:1 .... 487n	
23:10 .... 500n	16:4 .... 487n	**Psalms**
	16:31 104	2 122
Judges	17:18 337	2:2 315
1:2 267	20:28-29 .... 323n	2:6 598
2:1 323	21:24 .... 487n	2:7-9 351
2:17 .... 439n		2:9 485
4:6-16 .... 430n	**2 Kings**	8:6 325
5:5 .... 250, 432n	9:7 471	11:6 398
5:19 .... 430n	9:10 .... 342, 487n	16:11 468
5:31 54	9:36-37 104	18:4, 16 .... 360n
6:22 323	23:29-30 .... 430n	18:7 .... 250, 432n
7 .... 430n		30:7 .... 442n
7:2-3, 22 .... 323n	**1 Chronicles**	31:17 .... 255n
8:27 .... 439n	5:1-2 267	35:10 .... 375n
13:20-22 323	5:25 .... 439n	45:3-5 227
18:16-19 268	12:24 267	46:2-3 .... 250, 432n

Scripture Index

46:3 .... 360n
46:4 540
50:10 500
60:3 .... 397n
66:12 360
68:15-16 .... 442n
69:1-2, 14-15 ...... 360n
74:13-14 .... 365n
71:11 162
71:19 .... 375n
72:10 .... 432n
73:27 .... 439n
75:8 397
78:44 295
78:46 .... 298n
79:1-5 3427
9:5-6 242
86:8 .... 375n
86:8-10 417
89:8 .... 375n
89:10 .... 365n
91:5 455
97:1 .... 432n
98:2 417
103 .... 226, 506
103:10 413
104 321
105:16 321
105:34-35 298
105:38 344
106:48 471
107:25-28 .... 512n
109:6 .... 354n
109:14 457
113:5 .... 375n
115:17 .... 255n
124:4-5 360
137:8 457
141:1-2 255
144:7-8, 11 .... 360n
144:12 162

Proverbs
2:13 426
3:11-12 188
5:4 295
16:21-24 328
16:31 52
18:10 486
19:21 321
20:24 321
21:1 .... 37, 322

24:13-14 328
27:21 187

Ecclesiastes
2:14 426
7:28 .... 500n

Isaiah
2:2 .... 442n
2:10,18-21 251
4:3 144
5:25 .... 250, 432n
5:26-29 .... 307n, 428n
6 .... 200, 201
6:1 .... 418n
6:9-10 559
6:13 345
7:20 .... 307n, 428n
8:7-8 ...... 307n, 360n, 428n
10:22 281
11:1 561
11:4 .... 54, 485
11:6-12 535
11:15 .... 427n
13–14 396
13:9-10 249
13:21 .... 453, 454
14:12-15 295
14:19-20 342
14:29-31 .... 307n, 428n
14:31 .... 307, 428n
17:5 .... 408n
17:12-13 .360n, 365n, 511n
18:4-5 .... 408n
20:4 429
22:22 .... 156, 169
22:23 169
22:23-25 170
23:2 .... 255n
23:15-18 396
24:13 .... 408n
25:8 286
25:6 475
26:1 529
26:16–27:6 .... 485n
27:1 .... 365n, 511n
28:16-17 .... 334n
29:13 132
30:7 .... 365n
30:33 398
34:4-5 249
34:6 229

34:9-10 ...... 309, 398, 471
34:11 454
34:11-14 454
34:14 455
35:10 514
38:17 506
40:18, 25 .... 375n
40:25 155
41:1 .... 250, 432n
41:1-5 .... 255n
41:2-4, 25-27 427
41:15 .... 442n
42:8 185
42:10-13 212
43:2 360
43:4 161
43:7 .... 170, 173
43:15 155
44:7 .... 375n
44:24-28 .... 427n
45:14 161
45:16 .... 432n
46:11-13 427
46:5 .... 375n
47:5 255
47:7-8 457
47:7-9 453
47:9 458
47:9-10 311
47:9, 14 458
48:5 311
48:11b 185
48:19 281
49:1 250
49:1, 22 .... 432n
49:2 .... 54, 485
49:10 .... 286, 426
49:23 161
51:2 281
51:5 250
51:9 .... 365n
51:9-10 .... 365n, 511n
51:17, 21-23 397
52:11 456
53:7 210
53:9 273
54:4 458
54:10 .... 250, 432n
56:5 .... 173, 174
57:15 155
57:20 .... 365n, 511n
59:15-20 .... 485n

60:1-5, 11 .... 523, 524
60:1-11 535
60:9 250
60:11 535
60:14 161
60:19-20 524
60:22 .... 500n
61:10 473
62:1-12 272
62:2 .... 98, 173
63:1-3 484
63:1-6 .... 409, 485n
63:2-6 486
63:6 .... 397n
64:1 .... 250, 432n
65:4 273
65:15 174
65:16 182

Jeremiah
3:2 95
3:1-10 273
4:13 296
5:14 41
7:5-11 311
8:13-14 295
8:16 268
9:15 295
13:27 .... 95, 273
15:16 328
23:15 273
31:2 397
31:10 250
48:40 296
49:22 296
50-51 .... 396, 453
51:4 273
51:7 396
51:25-26 .... 250, 432
51:27 300

Lamentations
1:1 458
3:12-13 229
3:22-23 156
4:19 296

Ezekiel
1:5-25 200
1:7 280
1:24 53
1:26-28 323

1:28 196
2:2 528
2-3 328
3:3 328
3:12, 14, 24 528
4:10, 16 229
10:1-22 200
11:1 528
14:12-23 227
16:15-58 .... 95, 273
16:36 429
17:3 296
23:1-49 .... 95, 273
23:25 446
23:29 429
23:31-33 .... 397n
26-27 .... 453n, 459
26:7-11 .... 307n, 428n
26:12 462
26:18 .... 250, 251, 432n
27:7-25 459
27:28-33 461
28:8 .... 512n
29:3 .... 365n
39:5 .... 487n
32:2-3 365
32:7-8, 15 249
37:5, 10 343
37:9 263
37:26-28 285
37:27 513
38:6, 15 .... 307n, 428n
38:20 .... 251, 432n
38:22 309
39:2 .... 307n, 428n
39:4, 17-20 487
39:7 155
40-48 .... 526, 530, 533
40:1-6 .... 334n
40:3-5 530
40:5-6 529
42:20 .... 334n
43:2 53
43:5 528
43:7 .... 95, 273
47:5 540
47:12 541
48:35 174

Daniel
1:12-15 81
2:25 .... 442n

2:28 556
3 .... 116, 380
3:25 116
4 462
4:35 322
5:4, 23 311
7 .... 365, 368
7:2 263
7:3ff 512n
7:9 52
7:10 .... 144, 308
7:13 .... 40, 407
7:13-14 52
7:17 .... 378, 442n
7:25 335
8:8 263
9:18-19 174
9:27 366
10:5-11 54
11:4 263
12:4 558
12:7 327
12:10 558

Hosea
1:2 .... 439n
1:10 281
2:4 .... 439n
3:1-4:2 311
4:15 .... 439n
4:17-14:8 268
5:4 .... 95, 273
5:10 .... 360n
6:10 .... 95, 273
6:11 .... 408n
8:1 296
9:1 .... 439n
9:9 457
10:8 251
11:9 155

Joel
1-2 299
1:4 298
2:1 292
2:11 429
2:1-11, 20-25 .... 307n, 428n
2:1, 15 299
2:2 426
2:4 299
2:4-5 300
2:10, 31 297

Scripture Index

2:25 298
3:13 .... 342, 408, 408n
3:15 297
3:19 342

Amos
4:1-3 457
4:7 321
4:9 .... 298n
5:3 345
5:7 295
5:20 426
6:12 295
7:2 .... 298n
8:2-3 .... 255n

Jonah
1:2 457
1:10, ... 16
344

Micah
1:4 .... 251, 432n
7:18 .... 375n

Nahum
1:5 .... 251, 432
3:5 429
3:15 .... 298n

Habakkuk
1:6 .... 432n
2:16 .... 397n
2:20 .... 255n
3 .... 485n
3:6 .... 442n
3:8-15 .... 365n

Zephaniah
1:14 429
1:15 426
1:17 255

Zechariah
1:16 334
2:6 263
2:11 432
2:13 255
3:1-2 .... 354n
4:1-14 338
4:2-6 339
4:2, 10 .... 51, 61

4:7 .... 250, 432
5:5-11 396
6:5 263
6:1-8 227
12:2 .... 397n
12:10 40
14:1-21 .... 485n
14:4 .... 432n
14:2-14 429

Malachi
3:2-3 187

Matthew
2:11 202
2:16-18 351
4 353
4:8 313
4:9 202
5:8 549
5:11-12 .... 279, 509
7:15-23 379
7:21-23 .... 104, 109
7:22 380
8:6 350
8:19 273
9:14-15 473
10:28 .... 384, 399
10:32 .... 149, 152
10:33 152
10:34 229
10:38 273
13:9-17 .... 69, 559
13:24-30, 36-43 .... 408n
13:30, 43 .... 408n
13:40-42 .... 485n
14:24 350
15:8-9 132
15:32 204
16:16-17 484
16:18 61
16:27 .... 485n
17:2 324
17:3 338
18:8 400
18:10 59
18:16 .... 339n
18:26 202
18:34 204
20:2 229
20:28 305
22:1-14 473

23:5 .... 266, 384
23:25-28 132
24 40
24:21 282
25:1-13 473
25:31-32 .... 485n
25:46 402
27:33 409
28:19 497
28:20 513

Mark
3:5 204
4:9,23 69
4:21 69
4:29 .... 408n
5:7 350
6:48 350
8:34 273
8:38 485
9:47-48 400
13 40
13:22 38
13:23 390
15:22 409

Luke
2:25-38 350
3:11 230
3:13 .... 351n
3:29 473
4:2, 13 353
4:25 337
4:28-30 351
5:28 505
8:2 151
8:14 .... 351n
8:16 69
8:28 350
8:31 297
9:26 485
9:54 338
9:57 273
10 142
10:1 339
10:2 .... 408n
10:17-19 142
10:18 353
10:19 298
10:19-20 144
10:20 142
10:21 204

543

10:22 484	14:14 64	11:5 109
12:8 .... 149, 152	14:22 .... 164, 283	11:30-32 106
12:9 152	16 103	14 555
19:41-42 204	16:11-15 115	14:1 102
22:15 204	16:14 103	14:3 102
23:33 409	16:16-18 .... 104, 109	14:25 202
	17 504	14:32 556
John	17:11 .... 64, 112	15 515
1:18a 547	17:31 504	15:7 64
2:13-19 204	18:8, 10 60	15:24-26 124
2:17 204	18:18-22 60	15:25 .... 38, 553
3:16 .... 188, 305	19:19 60	15:26 506
4 540	20:20-27 240	15:50-55 487
4:10, 14 541	21:9 109	15:53-56 515
4:35-38 408	22:11 47	16:9 157
5:19 313	26:13 47	
5:28-29 398	26:16-18 497	**2 Corinthians**
5:31 .... 339n		1:9 77
6:35, 37b, 40 394	**Romans**	1:20 182
6:48-51 96	1:3-4 351	1:21-22 .... 264n
7:37-39 541	1:18 412	2:4 204
8:17 .... 339n	1:18ff 107	2:4, 9 181
10:17-18 413	1:24-32 412	2:11 496
12:31 313	2:28-29 75	2:12 157
13:3 .... 351n	3:21-26 413	3:18 ..... 46, 48, 49, 529, 548
14:30 313	8 515	4:3-4 .... 495n
15:9 204	8:1 356	4:3-6 47
15:11 204	8:1, 31-38 356	4:4 .... 313, 498
15:19-20 164	8 159	4:4, 6 47
15:26-27 .... 339n	8:17-18, 23, 25b 279, 509	4:7-12 164
16:5, 28 .... 351n	8:18 .... 279, 510, 554	4:16-18 .... 83, 279, 510
16:11 313	8:28 261	4:17 85
16:33 .... 164, 283	8:31 159	5:1-10 .... 124, 501
17:2 151	8:35-39 274	5:1, 8-10 238
17:13 204	10:1 75	5:6 513
17:15 164	11 160	5:8-10 505
17:22 529	11:33 38	5:10 403
20:14b-16 151	16:17-20	5:17 99,
		175, ... 357
Acts	**1 Corinthians**	6:11 204
2:17 .... 369n	1:18-25 74	6:16 .... 334, 513
2:17-18 109	2:10 121	8:16-17 .... 323n
2:23 376	3:16 169	11:2 .... 139, 273
4:27-28 323	3:16-17 334	11:14 496
5:30 .... 70, 542	4:3-5 119	11:24-25 164
5:32 339	4:11-13 164	12:4 326
5:40-41 164	5:5 .... 495n	12:19 204
5:41-42 241	5:9-11 181	13:1 339
10:25 202	6:19 169	
10:39 .... 70, 542	10:11 .... 369n	**Galatians**
12:15 59	10:14-22 95	1:6 16
13:29 .... 70, 542	10:20 311	1:19 64

Scripture Index

2:9 170
2:20 39
2:20b 413
3:13 .... 70, 85
4:25-27 272
4:26 .... 174, 335
5:13 93
5:20 311

Ephesians
1:11 321
1:13-14 265
1:15ff 358
2:1-7 356
2:2 313
2:5 133
2:7 .... 495, 544
2:10 475
2:11ff 271
2:19-22 133
2:21-22 169
2:22 172
4:1 138
5:2 39
5:5 311
5:8 356
5:26-27 139
6:10-20 495
6:12 349
6:14 390
6:16 .... 353, 496, ... 354
6:17 356

Philippians
1:8 204
1:19-24 501
1:20-23 238
2 217
2:1 204
2:8-11 417
2:9-11 395
2:10-11 161
2:12-13 .... 48, 147, 474
3:3 75
3:8 203
3:9 433
3:19 .... 277, 399, 508
3:20 272
3:20-21 ... 47, 277, 487, 564
3:21 .... 191, 246, 515
4:1 .... 204, 277, 508

4:2-3 144
4:8 299

Colossians
2:1 .... 157, 180
2:13-15 356
2:15 306
3:1-4 511
3:3b 100
3:4 47
3:5 311
4:3 157
4:16 181

1 Thessalonians
1:3 62
2:6 64
2:7-8 204
2:18 .... 495n, 496
4:13-18 .... 481, 487
4:14-17 485
4:16-17 344
5:3 399
5:19 112
5:20 109
5:21-22 112
5:23 47

2 Thessalonians
1:5-10 242
1:7-8 503
1:9 399
1:10 .... 246, 563
2:3-12 370
2:7 370
2:9 380
2:9-10 .... 104, 109

1 Timothy
1:3 60
2:1-2 59
3:15 170
3:16 .... 351n
4:1 .... 360n, 378
4:16 378
5:15 .... 360n
5:19 .... 339n
6:15-16 548

2 Timothy
1:2 204
1:13-14 378
2:13 156

2:19 108
2:23-26 360
3:1 369
3:5 132
3:12 .... 164, 241, 283
3:16 393
4:3-4 378

Titus
2:13-14 481

Philemon
12 204
20 204

Hebrews
1:2 .... 369n
1:7, 14 59
1:8 227
2:11 150
2:14-15 .... 299, 306
4:13 62
5:7 204
6:10 68
7:25 353
8:12 506
9:4 .... 96, 238
10 80
10:28 .... 339n
10:34 .... 80, 358
11:8-10 512
11:10 335
11:14 .... 278, 509
11:16 .... 278, 509
11:24-26 355
11:32-34 81
11:35-39 81
12 108
12:14 549
12:22 .... 174, 335
12:22-23 .... 272, 145
13:5-6 356
13:12-13 409
13:13-14 .... 279, 509, 510
13:14 335
13:20-21 62

James
4:7 .... 495n
5:16-17 340
5:17 337

545

2 Peter
2:15 94
3:8 .... 33, 556
3:11-13 511

1 John
1:3 17
1:7 356
2:1-2 353
2:2 353
2:4, 22 520
2:18 370
2:18, 22 371
2:19 .... 146, 370, 562
2:22 .... 369, 370
2:22-23 370
3:1-3 .... 357, 548
3:2 .... 47, 191, 246
3:2-3 .... 481, 511
3:3 550
3:5 306
3:8 306
3:11-18 67
4:1-6 379
4:3 .... 369, 370, 371
4:4b 89
4:20 520
5:10 520
5:19 .... 313, 453, 462
5:19b 91

2 John
1 105
7 369

Jude
3 378
4 93
11 94
14–15 .... 485n
24 159

Subject Index

1,260 days 319, 322–5
144,000, the 252, 256, 258–63,
.... 286, 321, 368, 393
666 .... 257, 277, 363–76, 56, 536

A

Abaddon 285
Abimelech 309
Abraham 72, 260–62, 270,
.... 271, 309, 471, 486
access to God's presence 51, 188, 510,
.... 513–14
Adams, Jay 19
addendum (Roman emperors) 425, 430–31
Ahab 101, 324
AIDS 223
Alpha and the Omega, the 40, 494–5
already/not yet 205
'Amen', the 175–6
American Civil War 222
amillennial 25, 26, 470
amillennialism 120, 121, 470–72
Ananias 104, 105
annihilationism 384–8
Antichrist 257, 291, 350, 355, 364, 372, 536
666 374
Beast, the .. 329, 349, 350, 351, 354, 373
etymology 355
identity 16, 218, 349, 351,
.... 352, 356, 535
modern candidates 375
tribe of Dan 258
antinomians 93
Antiochus Epiphanes 324
antisemitism 73
Apocalypse, the 13, 15, 17, 18,
.... 19, 21, 24, 29, 188
four horsemen of 213–25
apostolic authorship 12, 13
Aquila and Priscilla 59
Arian heresy, the 351

ark of the covenant 94, 97, 302, 303
Armageddon 405–17, 473, 475, 478, 479
Asclepios 86
Asia Minor 12, 15, 31, 57–8, 71, 86, 148,
.... 161, 182, 229, 361, 366, 439
Athene 86
Atlas 317
Augustus, Emperor 13, 15, 59, 86,
.... 370, 430–31
Aune, David 17, 312, 367, 438, 452

B

Babylon 16, 22, 36, 240, 241, 268, 283, 330,
.... 350, 366, 381–2, 412, 419–21
Babylon the great 329, 381, 416,
.... 421, 442, 447
fall of 381–2, 433–43
Balaam 91–2, 101
Balak, King of Moab 91, 92
Barna, George 133
Bauckham, Richard 210, 247, 332, 370n,
.... 371, 375, 440
Beale, Greg K 11, 14, 23–4, 33, 134, 159,
.... 165, 219, 230, 326, 413, 426,
.... 436, 450, 505, 529, 532
Beasley-Murray, G R 122
Beast, the 21–3, 142, 143, 160, 187, 219,
.... 320–25, 328–30, 349–62, 365, 382
identity of 277, 356, 387
mark of 255–7, 367–70, 373–4, 380,
.... 409, 415, 523
number of, the 375, 440, 506
scarlet 419, 421, 422, 424
sea beast 350, 352–4, 364, 380
Beeke, Joel .... R 24, 299
Bereans 64, 110
Bibi, Riaz 228
biblical eschatology 120, 122
binding of Satan 471, 472–6, 478
Black Death, the (Bubonic plague) 223, 409
book of life, the .. 70, 137, 138–44, 145, 147,

547

..................361–2, 424, 481–2, 510
bowl judgments 21, 31, 159, 210, 216,
..................241, 253–4, 277–80, 328,
.... 398–9, 402–3, 407–9, 411
brotherly love 66, 67
Brown, Dan 146
bubonic plague (Black Death, the) 223,
.... 409
Bunyan, John 234

C

Caird, G B 43, 44, 127, 300
Calvin, John 21, 121, 352
Charles of Lindos 312
Christ
  as manna 96, 97
  Bride of 452, 490, 503, 508
  commendation 62, 63–6, 71, 89,
  .... 173, 278
  commitment to 125, 131, 158, 222, 344
  co-regency with 120, 122, 184,
  .... 470, 523
  crucifixion 69, 330
  diety of 115, 118
  disciplinary visitation 132, 133
  fellowship with 178, 183
  freedom in 92
  holiness 183, 209
  lamb, the 204, 205, 207, 244
  lion, the 208–10, 211
  longsuffering 105–6
  love for 66, 67, 68
  resurrection 33, 36, 91, 146, 176,
  .... 203, 206, 260, 338, 340–41, 343,
  ....359, 406, 424, 427, 472, 530
  risen, the 43–5, 47, 49, 50–51, 55,
  .... 57, 286, 311, 314, 462
  sovereignty .... of 37, 61, 121, 176,
  ....306, 311, 407
  supremacy of 38, 132, 526
Christian living 24, 45, 46
Christmas 291–3, 303
Christo-centricity 132
Christophany 434
Classical Pre-tribulational Dispensational
  Premillennialism 22
Claudius, Emperor 59, 371, 430
Clement of Alexandria 12
Colossae 174, 177
Colossus of Rhodes 312
commendation 62, 63–6, 71, 89,
  .... 113, 127, 149, 173

common grace 224, 387
commonplaces 214, 216, 279, 407
compromise 64–5, 79, 90, 92, 99–101,
  ....104–5, 113, 114, 117–18,
  .... 133–4, 263–4, 365, 462, 534–5
conquering Satan 160, 341–6
Cook, James 223
Covid-19 223
Cyrus, King of Persia 36, 310, 412

D

da Todi, Jacopone 22
Da Vinci Code, The 146
darkness 89, 284, 286, 385, 411,
  .... 474, 475, 508, 510
Darwinism 351
David, King 61, 150, 157, 192,
  ....96, 448, 482, 534
Davidic kingdom 151
Death (fourth horseman) 221–3
Decius, Emperor 351
de-creation 284
demonic
  agents 220, 254
  army 295–7
  beings 154, 286
  hordes 281, 285, 287, 473
  spirits 138, 285, 288, 366, 413, 415
Demosthenes Philalethes 181
Devil, the 80, 118, 204, 257, 289, 303,
  ....359–60, 364, 384, 473, 475
  conquered by the church 335–48
Dionysius of Alexandria 12
Dionysus 86
disillusionment 75, 76
dispensationalists 322, 339, 346, 364
divine discipline 74, 104, 178
divine justice 39, 233, 234, 397, 398
divine wrath see also wrath of God 160,
  225, 248, 277, 278, 382, 395–9, 402, 407
Dodd, C H 395
Domitian, Emperor 13, 14, 15, 17, 30,
  ....373, 430, 431
doxology 38–40, 208, 449
dragon, the 22, 263, 295, 312, 336–9,
  ....346, 349, 353–4, 360, 364,
  ....366, 380, 400, 423, 456, 463
duration of hell 383–4

E

'eating the scroll' 315–17
Edom (Idumea) 240, 241, 435, 450

Subject Index

education, exultation, exaltation......208–10
Edwards, Jonathan............21, 54, 55, 83, 121
Egypt...................37, 160, 240–41, 282, 284,
..................286, 328–9, 342, 350, 356,
.... 400, 411, 417, 469, 525
eight blessings of life.................274, 511–23
Eliakim.. 151, 165
Elijah, prophet............ 101, 320, 324–8, 331,
.... 332, 365
Elliott, E B.. 21
encircled...................................188, 191–4
end of history, the........29–31, 161, 216–17,
...279–81, 302, 339, 360, 408, 438, 455
end of the world, the....................... 405, 406
enthroned . 121, 183, 184, 185, 188–91, 476
enthroned, encircled, extolled.......... 187–99
Ephesus...............49, 59–61, 62–4, 67, 69, 70,
....113, 162, 231
eschatological war........................ 260, 414
eternal conscious suffering.........384–8, 391
eternal punishment................81, 122, 378,
.... 379, 382–4, 391
eternal state.................... 120, 408, 509, 515
eternality.. 194, 195
Ethbaal, king of the Sidonians............... 101
ethical error.. 90
ethnic diversity.................................206–7
Euphrates, river........ 294, 296, 297, 411, 412
Eusebius.. 15, 17
explanatory interludes................... 289, 298
expulsion of Satan........................... 339, 340
extolled........................ 188, 191, 194–8, 446

F

'faithful witness', the 35, 36, 89
fall of Babylon..................... 381–2, 433–43
false apostles.. 64, 365
false Jews... 72, 155
False Prophet, the 187, 256, 264,
..................277, 295, 312, 339, 364–5,
.... 368–9, 375, 384, 413, 467–8, 480
famine................ 154, 220–22, 224, 264,
.... 282–4, 289, 296, 438
Fanning, Buist.. 25
Fee, Gordon.. 529
fifth bowl... 411
fifth seal.. 247
fifth trumpet.........................285–9, 408
final battle, the................ 428, 466, 469, 473,
....478, 479–80
final judgment............... 156, 216, 244, 247,
.... 282, 295, 302, 380, 391–4, 400,

.... 401, 410, 464, 480–83
first bowl... 408–9
first horseman 218, 219, 220
first seal 218–20
first trumpet... 282
'first-born of the dead, the'...................... 36
flu...223
forty-two months............... 319, 320, 322–5,
.... 339, 356
four beasts.. 350, 353
four horsemen of the apocalypse.....213–25
four living creatures 184, 191–3, 195,
.... 202, 205, 207, 210, 212,
.... 218, 270, 384, 448, 450
fourth bowl..410–11
fourth Gospel, the.................................. 12
fourth seal..221–3
fourth trumpet.. 284

G

Galba, Emperor........................13, 430, 431
Garden of Eden....................69, 512, 515
gematria.............................. 373, 374–6, 427
Gentiles.................156–7, 260–62, 271, 275,
.... 320, 474–5, 505
Gentry, Kenneth 20
global revival..332–3
God
   access to....................... 313–14, 520–22
   glory of........ 46, 70, 189, 206, 386, 441,
   ....455, 495, 503, 504, 508, 518
   holiness....151, 183, 189, 194, 210, 211,
   .... 219, 232, 303, 378, 386, 410, 507
   sovereignty.......... 29, 77, 155, 194, 221,
   ....225, 296, 300, 301, 307–10,
   ....314, 316, 357, 446, 526, 534
Gog and Magog 467, 473, 479, 480
golden bowls 399, 402–3
Gray, Kurt 512
Great Commission, the........................... 491
Great Dragon, the.................................. 187
Great Prostitute, the 421–4, 429, 433,
.... 447, 449, 501, 502
Great Tribulation, the.......30, 159, 213, 260,
..................272, 273, 322, 339, 346, 536
Great White Throne judgment 481

H

Hadrian, Emperor................................... 59
Hamilton, James 198
Handel, George Frederick 211
Har-Magedon.. 414

549

harvest, the 392–5
health and happiness 515–16
heaven see also New Heaven 265–70,
 .... 273–5, 335–48
heavenly reward 192, 261, 271, 535
hell 81–3, 122, 194, 377–89,
 .... 391, 400, 450, 495, 523
Hemer, Colin 69, 139, 182
Herod, King 338
Hierapolis 177
Hippolytus 12
Hitler, Adolf 222
Hoekema, Anthony 471
holiness 70, 114, 119, 155, 198, 248,
 .... 387, 395, 495, 520, 522
 God's 151, 183, 189, 194, 210, 211,
 .... 219, 232, 303, 378, 386, 410, 507
 Jesus' 183, 209
Holy Spirit, the 35, 101, 106, 193, 212,
 ..... 224, 255–7, 273, 303, 316, 528, 534
hope 459–61, 468
'hour of trial' 158, 160, 161
Hunt, Dave 352
Hus, John 351

I
identity 167, 168–72
idolatry 44, 47, 60, 64, 92, 103–4,
 .... 109, 127, 134, 238, 263, 297–8,
 ...... 365–6, 420–23, 436, 526–7, 533–4
Idumea (Edom) 240, 241, 435, 450
imminence 33, 183, 246, 529
immorality 60, 64, 78, 87, 90, 92, 108,
 .... 127, 134, 199, 382, 406, 430, 465
 sexual 91–3, 99, 102, 104–5,
 .... 109, 115, 244, 263, 288, 349,
 .... 421–3, 436, 497, 532, 536
innumerable multitude, the 258–61,
 .... 270, 479
inoffensive Christianity 127
intermediate state 120, 135, 229, 230,
 .... 464, 470–71, 475–8
Irenaeus 12, 16, 17, 258
Isaac 72, 260, 262, 270, 271, 471
Izmir 71

J
Jacob 72, 260, 262, 270, 271, 471
'jasper' stone 189, 190, 504, 506
Jeremiah 94, 302, 310, 381
Jewish War, the 14, 371
Jezebel/Jezebel Spirit 99–112, 115, 117,
 .... 118, 120, 324, 365
Joachim of Fiore 21
Johannine Epistles, the 354–6
John the apostle 11, 13, 17, 30, 57, 215
John the Baptist 452–4
John the Elder 12
John's vision 49–53, 55
Johnson, Alan 24, 356, 357, 433
Johnson, Dennis 24, 305, 306
Julius Caesar 13, 59, 430
justification 91, 135, 147, 234
Justin Martyr 12

K
Keener, Craig 24, 346, 375, 437
Kimball, William 241
kings of the earth 36, 37, 302, 413, 422,
 .... 428, 434, 439, 509, 526
Kuyper, Abraham 463

L
Ladd, George 24, 489
lamb of God 204, 208–10, 245, 291, 359,
 361, 400
Laodicea .. 15, 22, 49, 120, 126, 173–85, 438
last day(s), the 33, 141, 156, 299,
 .... 331–2, 354, 530
Late Great Planet Earth, The 327, 466
'latter days', the 33, 501, 529
licentiousness 91–3
Lilith 435, 436
Lindsey, Hal 327, 346, 466
Lion of Judah, the 55, 203, 208
locusts 281, 285, 286, 287, 288, 296, 297
luminaries 508
Luther, Martin 21, 121, 352
Lydia 100, 112, 126

M
Magdalene, Mary 121, 146
manna 94, 95, 97
Mao, Chairman 222
mariners 434, 441
mark of the Beast, the 255–7, 367–70,
 .... 373–4, 380, 409, 415, 523
Marriage Supper of the Lamb 135, 136,
 445–57
martyrdom 54, 119, 149, 192, 220, 289,
 .... 321, 330, 335–7, 358, 361, 476
 Antipas 89–90
Masih, Sharoon 227–35
Smyrna 76–7, 79, 82–3

Subject Index

martyrs' request 246, 247
Masih, Elyab 228
Masih, Sharoon 227–9, 231, 232, 235
material poverty 78, 179
material wealth 179, 510
mega-church 125, 128, 150, 152, 178
Megiddo 414, 415
Melancthon, Philip 21, 352
Melito of Sardis 12
merchants of the earth 434, 439–41
messianic kingdom 135, 151, 153, 183
messianic reign 471
Michael (angel) 339, 340, 450
mighty angel, the 202, 233, 310–14
millennial earth 120
millennial kingdom 121, 470, 477–8, 501
millennium 120, 121, 469–74
mini-church 128, 150, 151, 152
missionary activity 153
Mohler, Al 206
moral transformation 44
Morris, Leon 282, 396
Moses 46, 139, 188, 320, 325–6, 328,
.... 342, 347, 400–402, 508–9, 534
Mounce, Robert 13, 24, 166, 415, 529

N

Naboth 101
National Science Foundation 511
natural calamities 238, 252, 306, 307
nature of hell 382–3
Nebuchadnezzar 366, 442
Nero redivivus 16
Nero, Emperor 13–16, 20, 21, 358, 360,
.... 363, 370–73, 375, 430, 431
New Earth 121, 205, 266, 275, 379,
.... 388, 406, 471, 478, 481, 485–98,
.... 501, 511–23, 527–8
New Heaven 379, 388, 459, 485–98,
.... 501, 508, 512, 513, 517, 521
New Heavens 29, 97, 121, 266, 275,
.... 284, 406, 481, 527
New Jerusalem 53, 70, 141, 151, 157,
.... 166, 170, 189, 262, 301, 394,
.... 441, 480, 486–90, 499–510
'new name' 94, 96, 97, 164, 168–71, 263
Nicolaitans 16, 64, 91–4, 101, 365
nominal Christianity 125–36
non-Christians 182, 202, 225,
.... 257, 292, 369

O

obedient behaviour 66
Olivet Discourse, the 39, 272
Origen 12
orthodoxy 63–5, 67, 113, 117, 119, 130
Osborne, Grant 25

P

Packer, J I 248, 396
Page, Sydney 435
papacy, the 21, 22, 23, 351, 352
Papias 12
parenthetical pause 252, 298, 305
Parousia, the 40
patient endurance 62–3, 113, 129,
.... 158, 161, 201
Patmos 48, 71, 173, 201, 272, 447
Paul 196, 197, 363
  Laodiceans 174
  letter to the Colossians 174, 293
  letter to the Corinthians 81, 102,
    ..... 109, 119, 121, 487–8, 526, 528, 529
  letter to the Ephesians 66, 67, 231,
    .... 335, 343, 517
  letter to the Philippians 72, 237,
    .... 266, 485
  letter to the Romans 72, 73, 154,
    .... 156, 487
  letter to the Thessalonians 112,
    .... 237, 487
  letters to Timothy 363, 378
Pergamum 16, 59, 64, 85–93,
    .... 100, 101, 113, 127
Perriman, Andrew 239
pestilence 221, 222, 224, 406, 438
Philadelphia 71, 149–62, 164, 166,
    .... 167, 174, 352
Phillips, Richard D 24, 329, 516
Phrygia 174
phylacteries 257, 369
Pilgrim's Progress 234
pillars 165–7
Piper, John 142, 143, 380, 386, 448
plagues of Egypt 282–4, 286–8, 326,
    .... 328, 408, 409, 411, 413, 417
Pliny 126
Pol Pot 222
premillennialists 120, 260, 472
preterist view 19–21, 30, 32
pre-tribulation rapture 159, 160
Price, Mark 511

progressive dispensational
   premillennialism 22–3
progressive parallelism 217
progressive sanctification 47
prophetic hyperbole 238, 241, 242,
   .... 282, 416
prophetic symbolism 415, 507
Protestant Reformation, the 22, 351

R

racism 206
rapture 23, 159, 160, 213,
   .... 260, 331, 466, 536
recapitulation 215–17, 279, 280, 408, 471
Red Sea, the 347, 400, 411
remember, repent, do 69, 70
replacement theology 261
reputation versus reality 128–9
resurrection 204, 319, 330–31, 358, 372
   body 120, 135, 509
   Christ's 33, 36, 91, 146, 176, 203,
      .... 206, 260, 338, 340–41, 343,
      .... 359, 406, 424, 427, 472, 530
   first 81, 470, 476, 478, 483
   universal 481
retributive justice 397, 398, 410
Revelation
   allusions to Rome 13, 358
   Apocalypse, as an 18
   authorship 11–13, 17, 30
   Beast of see Beast, the
   date of writing 13–17, 19, 20, 21
   dragon of, the 22, 263, 295, 312,
      .... 336–9, 346, 349, 353–4, 360,
      .... 364, 366, 380, 400, 423, 456, 463
   epistle, as an 18
   futurist view 22–3, 31
   grammar 12
   historical view 21–22
   idealist view 23, 31
   interpretation 19–24, 30–32
   literary form 17–19
   observations 527–35
   preterist view 19–21, 31, 33
   prophecy, as 19, 22
   sea beast, the 350, 352–4, 364, 380
   seven beatitudes 34
   themes 525–7
   whore of 23
reverse correlation 512
Revelation 133
risen Christ, the 43–5, 47, 49, 50–51,
   .... 55, 57, 286, 311, 314, 462
Roman emperors 430–31
Roman empire, the 16, 21, 221, 294,
   .... 351, 412, 427, 434, 436, 450
Rome 15, 73, 363, 371, 372, 381, 425
   Babylon 16, 21, 329, 440
   Beast, the 358, 366, 426
   fall of 19, 433
   Roma aeterna (eternal Rome) 450
   seven hills 13, 424, 431
'ruler of the kings of the earth, the' 36–8

S

salvation 47, 70, 117, 135, 141, 153,
   .... 166, 216, 260, 271, 316, 331,
   .... 407, 452–4, 468, 478, 535, 537
sanctification 46, 47, 74–7, 452–4
Sapphira 104, 105
Sardis 12, 15, 125–48, 162, 174
scarlet beast, the 419, 421, 422, 424
scroll, the 201–3, 212, 311, 312, 315
sea beast, the 350, 352–4, 364, 380
Sea of Galilee 489
seal judgments 210, 216, 218–25, 243,
   .... 252, 254, 278, 279, 305, 399, 407
sealing of the saints 252–7
seals *see* seven seals
second bowl 409
second coming, the 22, 31, 33,
   .... 39, 120, 131, 183, 204, 213–17,
   .... 237–49, 393, 407–8, 466,
   .... 471, 527, 530, 535–6
'second death' 73, 77, 81–3, 475, 476,
   .... 478, 483
second horseman 220
second seal 220
second trumpet 282–3, 409
Seleucids of Syria 425
seraphim 192, 193
seven angels 210, 398, 501
seven bowl judgments 216, 277, 279,
   .... 398, 399, 407–17
seven bowls 245, 299, 335, 398–400, 402
seven churches 18, 21, 31, 35, 49, 50
seven facets of physical creation 243
seven golden bowls 399, 402
seven golden lampstands 50, 51, 60
seven heads 337, 350, 353, 354,
   .... 424–7, 430
seven judgments 216, 279, 402, 407
seven kings, the 13, 14, 425
seven letters 133, 141, 159

Subject Index

Ephesus 59–70
Laodicea 126, 173–85
Pergamum 85–93, 100, 103
Philadelphia 149–62
Sardis 125–48
Smyrna 71–83
Thyatira 99–123, 127
seven seals 30, 201, 202, 224, 311
seven spirits, the 35, 193
seven thunders 313, 314
seven trumpets 210, 224, 245, 246,
 ....280, 281, 398
seventh bowl......211, 241, 331, 408, 416–17
seventh trumpet............ 211, 293, 298–301,
 .... 303, 305
Severus, Emperor 59
sexual immorality 91–3, 99, 102,
 .... 104–5, 109, 115, 244, 263, 288,
 ..... 349, 382, 421–3, 436, 497, 532, 536
Sibyl Sambathe 100
Sibylline Oracles 372
silence (seventh seal)............245, 246, 247
Sinai, Mt. 94, 193, 302, 403
sixth bowl 411–15
sixth seal 238–45, 284, 331
sixth trumpet 293–8, 408, 532
slander 78, 79, 82, 83, 154, 289,
 ....340, 344, 491
Smalley, Stephen 12, 14, 15, 16
smallpox 223
Smyrna 49, 71–8, 80–82,
 .... 86, 87, 113, 127, 149, 174,
 .... 179, 254, 272, 476, 497
Sodom and Gomorrah ... 296, 383, 420, 480
Song of Moses 400–402
sovereign purpose 234, 311, 428–9
sovereignty 88, 122, 219, 294, 312,
 ....354, 409, 411, 421, 453, 526
Christ's ..37, 61, 121, 176, 306, 311, 407
God's 29, 77, 155, 194, 221, 225,
 ....296, 300, 301, 306–10, 314,
 ....316, 357, 446, 451–2, 534
Spanish flu 223
spiritual apostasy 92, 263
spiritual darkness 89, 91, 411
spiritual poverty 179
spiritual warfare 335, 341, 345
spiritual wealth 179, 180
Stalin, Joseph 222
Stott, John 57, 58, 79, 100, 127, 128, 386
substitutionary atonement 82, 398
substitutionary death 39, 206, 533

suffering and sanctity 74–7
syphilis 223

T

temple of Diana (Artemis) 69, 70
temple of God 164, 320–22, 352
temple of Solomon 165
Templeton Foundation 511
ten horns 337, 350, 353, 424, 427–8
Tertullian 12
'theological backbone' 117–19
third bowl 409–10
third horseman 220–21
third seal 220–21, 282
third trumpet 283–4, 409
Thomas, Robert 25
three and a half years 322–5
throne of God, the 191, 201, 258,
 .... 268–9, 273–4, 451, 456, 481
Thyatira 99–110, 112–14, 116–18,
 ....123, 127, 174
Tiberius, Emperor 71, 126, 430
Titus, Emperor 14, 371, 430, 43
toil 62, 63
tree of life, the 68–70, 515, 516, 535
tribulation and poverty..........77, 78, 79, 82
Tribulation, the 50, 161, 201, 260, 272
triune God, the 29, 35, 188, 212,
 ....270, 417, 447
true Jew 72, 262
true worship 196, 456
trumpet judgments 216, 244, 247,
 .... 277–301, 303, 335, 407–9, 532
trumpets see seven trumpets
tuberculosis 223
twelve apostles 193, 261, 336, 504, 506
twelve tribes 193, 261, 336, 504, 506, 507
twenty-four elders 184, 191, 195,
 .... 202–4, 207, 212, 269, 272, 274,
 .... 301–2, 448, 450, 478
two witnesses, the 320, 323, 325–8,
 .... 329, 331, 333, 364, 365
typhoid 223
Tyre 433, 434, 439, 442

U

universal resurrection 481
universalism 379, 384, 402

V

Vespasian, Emperor 14, 16, 359,
 ....371, 430, 431

Viet Nam War 222

W

Waldensian sect 21
Walvoord, John 25
war 220, 335–48, 405–17, 429,
.... 438, 462, 475, 479
warfare worship 344
white garments 136, 138, 145, 179,
.... 192, 464
white stone 94, 95, 96, 263
whore of Revelation, the 23
Wiersbe, Warren 190
Wilcock, Michael 24, 221, 297, 329
Woman', the 336–9, 339, 347,
.... 349, 364, 423
word of God 50, 161, 163, 175, 231,
.... 464, 469, 528, 532
works 61–3, 67, 87, 104–5, 113–15,
.... 129–30, 177, 401, 482
World War One (WWI) 222
World War Two (WWII) 222
Wormwood 283, 284
wrath of God *see also* divine wrath 82,
.... 160, 205, 210–11, 224–5,
.... 242, 253, 289, 393, 395–9,
.... 402, 407, 510, 527
Wycliffe, John 21, 351

Z

Zeus 85, 317

ISBN 978-1-78191-132-7

KINGDOM COME
The Amillennial Alternative
Sam Storms

There is something in here to challenge and to encourage all of us, no matter our persuasion. I pray this book will help others in the same way it has helped me.

Justin Taylor,
Executive vice president for book publishing, Crossway, Wheaton, Illinois

Storms marshals exegetical and theological arguments in defense of his view in this wide-ranging work. Even those who remain unconvinced will need to reckon with the powerful case made for an amillennial reading. The author calls us afresh to be Bereans who are summoned to search the scriptures to see if these things are so.

Thomas R. Schreiner,
James Buchanan Harrison Professor of New Testament Interpretation and Associate Dean,
The Southern Baptist Theological Seminary, Louisville, Kentucky

Sam Storms' book, *Kingdom Come: the Amillennial Alternative,* is a substantial work on the viability of the amillennial perspective on eschatology, including that of the book of Revelation ... Even those who may disagree with Storms' amillennial approach will definitely benefit from his book.

G. K. Beale,
Professor of New Testament and Biblical Theology,
Westminster Theological Seminary, Philadelphia, Pennsylvania

Imminently readable, this is the book I would recommend on amillennialism from here on out.

Jared C. Wilson,
Director of Content Strategy for Midwestern Baptist Theological Seminary and Managing Editor of For The Church, Midwestern's site for gospel-centered resources.

REVELATION
A MENTOR EXPOSITORY COMMENTARY
DOUGLAS F. KELLY

ISBN 978-1-78191-132-7

Revalation

A Mentor Expository Commentary

Douglas F. Kelly

Written from a semi-preterist point of view, Dr. Kelly provides both theological and pastoral insights of great consequence to John's apocalyptic vision that often puzzles its readers. Highly recommended.

Derek W. H. Thomas,
Teaching Fellow, Ligonier Ministries; Retired Senior Minister,
First Presbyterian Church (ARP), Columbia, South Carolina

The church, including the Western church and the global South, need to read the book of Revelation now more than ever. Let Douglas Kelly be your guide. I commend the book and I commend the publisher for such a time as this.

Michael A. Milton,
President and Senior Fellow at D. James Kennedy Institute for Christianity and Culture

"What a great blessing it is for the church to regain clarity about the message of Revelation! Kelly's commentary will prove invaluable in restoring this vital message to the pulpits of our churches and the lives of suffering believers."

Richard D. Phillips,
Senior Minister, Second Presbyterian Church, Greenville, South Carolina

Christian Focus Publications

Our mission statement –

STAYING FAITHFUL

In dependence upon God we seek to impact the world through literature faithful to His infallible Word, the Bible. Our aim is to ensure that the Lord Jesus Christ is presented as the only hope to obtain forgiveness of sin, live a useful life and look forward to heaven with Him.

Our books are published in four imprints:

CHRISTIAN FOCUS

Popular works including biographies, commentaries, basic doctrine and Christian living.

CHRISTIAN HERITAGE

Books representing some of the best material from the rich heritage of the church.

MENTOR

Books written at a level suitable for Bible College and seminary students, pastors, and other serious readers. The imprint includes commentaries, doctrinal studies, examination of current issues and church history.

CF4•K

Children's books for quality Bible teaching and for all age groups: Sunday school curriculum, puzzle and activity books; personal and family devotional titles, biographies and inspirational stories – because you are never too young to know Jesus!

Christian Focus Publications Ltd,
Geanies House, Fearn, Ross-shire,
IV20 1TW, Scotland, United Kingdom.
www.christianfocus.com